T0381527

Foundations

A Discipleship Textbook and Tool

Dr. James Ross

WestBow
PRESS

WestBow Press books may be ordered through booksellers or by contacting:

WestBow Press
A Division of Thomas Nelson
1663 Liberty Drive
Bloomington, IN 47403
www.westbowpress.com
1-(866) 928-1240

Because of the dynamic nature of the Internet, any web addresses or links contained in this book may have changed since publication and may no longer be valid. The views expressed in this work are solely those of the author and do not necessarily reflect the views of the publisher, and the publisher hereby disclaims any responsibility for them.

Any people depicted in stock imagery provided by Thinkstock are models, and such images are being used for illustrative purposes only.

Certain stock imagery © Thinkstock.

ISBN: 978-1-4497-0311-0 (sc)
ISBN: 978-1-4497-0310-3 (e)

Library of Congress Control Number: 2010931010

For More Information Write:
dimensionalmen@yahoo.com
or
Dr. James A. Ross
www.dimensionalministry.org

Printed in the United States of America

WestBow Press rev. date: 03/21/2011

Acknowledgments

All things are the Lord's.
A special thanks to my wife for all
the countless hours you have helped me.

To Phyllis Estill for her wonderful editing.

All Scripture references are from the King James Version, unless otherwise stated.

I want to thank Thomas Nelson Publishing
for allowing me to use the Strong's Concordance
as a reference in this book.

Strong's numbers and definitions used by permission from Thomas Nelson Publishing.

Contents

Foundations Discovered

Section 1

"Thus saith the Lord of hosts; Let your hands be strong, ye that hear in these days these words by the mouth of the prophets, which were in the day that the foundation of the house of the Lord of hosts was laid, that the temple might be built. For before these days there was no hire for man, nor any hire for beast; neither was there any peace to him that went out or came in because of the affliction: for I set all men every one against his neighbor."
(Zechariah 8:9-10)

Preface

"In this hour of all-but-universal darkness one cheering gleam appears: within the fold of conservative Christianity there are to be found increasing numbers of persons whose religious lives are marked by a growing hunger after God Himself. They are eager for spiritual realities and will not be put off with words nor will they be content with correct interpretations of truth. They are athirst for God, and they will not be satisfied till they have drunk deep at the Fountain of Living Water. This is the only real harbinger of revival which I have been able to detect anywhere on the religious horizon. It may be the cloud the size of a man's hand for which a few saints here and there have been looking. It can result in a resurrection of life for many souls and a recapture of that radiant wonder which should accompany faith in Christ, that wonder which has all but fled the Church of God in our day. But this hunger must be recognized by our religious leaders."
A.W. Tozer – Preface from The Pursuit of God

"Foundations" is a book written for church leaders and students of the Bible. It is designed for those who want to comprehend the fullness of the Spirit, the validity of the Scriptures, and the Bible's power to deliver the faithful believer. It is for the leader who wants to know Jehovah God and His son, Jesus Christ intimately and personally. It is for those disciples who wish to express their relationship with Christ without apology. If you have not repeatedly and diligently read the New Testament several times, I challenge you to take a journey of faith - a journey many church leaders and Christians fail to take. To those of you who only read a few verses here and there in your daily study of the Bible, you will find that you will not completely understand the purpose of the biblical mandate "to make disciples". We must become students of the Bible if we are to comprehend the fullness of the Scriptures. As an aid to the reader, I have included the Strong's Concordance numbers to many of the words we will be studying.

There is a very important statement that is found throughout the Bible: it is "the way of God." As we make an effort to apply God's ways to each topic in this study, we will also look into why God does things the way He does. If we do not first understand the "way of God" as we review each topic, we will find that it is difficult to discern the purpose of God's revelation. When Jesus said: "I am the way, the truth, and the life" it is more than a cliché. This may sound overly simplistic, but

I have discovered that there are vast numbers of Christians, Pastors, and Church leaders who do not understand the Gospel the way God intended it to be understood. One of the many reasons for this oversight are the extremities of traditions one can find in congregational life. The Church has not handled the massive growth it has experienced in the past forty years very well. This has caused the maturation process, spiritual growth, and discipleship to be hindered throughout Christendom. God wants us to learn more than His acts; He wants us to understand "why" He does things the way He does them so that we can know Him in a more meaningful way (see Psalms 103:7). Because so many Christians seek His acts and not His ways, many remain spiritually immature and unable to overcome the onslaught of attacks they experience. Hebrews 5:13 says it this way:

> "For everyone who uses milk
> is unskillful in the word of
> righteousness, for he is a babe."

It is within the facets of the Christian "church-life" that discipleship must occur, and many believers suffer defeat and discouragement because of their inability to grow spiritually and come to a greater attainment of spiritual discernment. One such tradition is that Solomon asked God for "wisdom," yet we see in 1 Kings 3:9 that he actually asked for an "understanding heart."

> "Give therefore thy servant an understanding heart
> to judge thy people, that I may discern between good and bad:
> for who is able to judge this thy so great a people?"

Solomon wanted to "hear God" so that he could be "inclined" toward wisdom. There is a difference between asking for wisdom and asking God to let you hear Him. When you can hear God, wisdom will not elude you, but if you cannot hear God you will find yourself guessing about His will and purpose for your life. To understand spiritual things is one of the keys to the Kingdom of God. We must learn to hear the voice of the Spirit if we are to distinguish between the deception of the enemy and the truth of God's Word.

In order for anyone to gain a fundamental and basic understanding of discipleship, you must take time to read the New Testament thoroughly and to read it several times. As you read and meditate on the word of God, "rhema" comes from the Spirit and gives revelation to the humble and hungry ones. Rhema is "the voice of God in the heart of man". Rhema occurs as we read the Bible, pray, and listen to the voice of the Spirit being revealed to our heart. This is how you can know the mind of the Spirit as it is expressed through the Bible's authors, when the Spirit of God inspired them to write what Jesus had trained them in. Through a technique of reading the Bible a book at a time, the Word and the Spirit unite in the heart and mind of the reader, and you will gain revelation and understanding as you learn to hear God. Wisdom is gained as the Scripture is applied to your life and expressed in your lifestyle. We learn what is in the heart of God through the Spirit and the

Scriptures; He discloses His purpose to us as His plans are expressed in each book of the Bible. The Bible calls this kind of learning "discipleship." When we are disciples, learning Christian doctrines and their application in our lives, the Spirit molds and forms our hearts in virtue and obedience. Being disciplined in Christian doctrine is the application of any teaching that is ministered into the life and heart of an individual. It is through the discipleship process that fathering, prayer, and doctrine have the ability to produce maturity in individuals. You cannot leave any of these out and expect to increase in spiritual discernment and virtuous maturity. In other words, without application the discipleship process is futile.

We should make a special note that the Bible states that there are six foundational principles of the doctrines of Christ found in the teachings of Jesus (see Hebrews 6:1-2). This is not to say that there are only six doctrines; the Scriptures state that these are the six "foundational principles" of the doctrines of Christ. These are the beginning or origin of doctrines about Christ and from these all other Christian doctrine must proceed. It is from these six principles that all doctrines must be built upon and expressed in the Christian life. These are the first doctrines that should be implemented into the life of a new believer and these principles build a foundation from which the child of God can add to. "For other foundation can no man lay than that is laid, which is Jesus Christ" (see 1 Corinthians 3:11). When you do not apply God's first principles to your life your foundation will be weak and brittle and you simply become someone who "knows to do good, and does it not" (see James 4:17).

Every Christian leader should have goals that exceed evangelism. The elevation of spiritual maturity has always been at the core of the biblical mandate; to make disciples. Evangelism must have discipleship added to it for it to be complete. Building the foundation of Jesus Christ into every Church is a necessity. The church or ministry that is not founded will be oriented toward the "acts of God" (miracles, signs, etc.) and will not pursue His ways. God is moving all over this earth and moving for His people, but it was Jesus who said, "an evil and adulterous generation seeks a sign" (see Matthew 12:39). It is vitally important that the Body of Christ changes its spiritual focus to the "quality" of the believer, rather than on the "quantity" of church members.

> "For though ye have ten thousand
> instructors in Christ, yet have ye not
> many fathers: for in Christ Jesus I
> have begotten you through the gospel."
> (1 Corinthians 4:15)

The Lord understands the nature of man and He looks upon our hearts. The Lord measures our heart and there is no one that is not "naked and opened" to Him (see Hebrews 4:13). He sees and knows everything about us and we must learn that a part of discipleship is the "admonishing" of the spiritual babe and the "dealing" with the soul of the untrained believer. When we join this with an honest look at what the Bible teaches us about "making disciples", this in itself builds spiritual maturity and helps us to overcome the wicked one. The process of building a spiritual house is not a short-term task. Discipleship is established through the word of truth, grace, and the work of spiritual warfare (see 2 Timothy 2:4-5).

Spiritual fathers must be men of strong character and integrity, demonstrating grace and truth that cannot be left out of the process. It is the Lord's desire to build a kingdom of people that have been established in love, and who reproduce love. Discipleship is not complete until the Christian can reproduce what they have received. Most believers never reproduce anything outside of themselves. When you do not recognize this, you will not fulfill the Gospel or your purpose. The processes of admonition and "dealings" are how disciples become mature Christian beings (see 1 Corinthians 4:14 and 'warn' in Strong's 3560). The anointing comes upon us to preach good tidings to those that are meek. The Spirit gives the anointing to bind up the broken hearted, that they may be healed and delivered. The Spirit anoints us to proclaim liberty to the captives, that they may be free from oppression. When the Spirit of God is in someone, these are the evidences of His presence. By the way, the Scripture states that the Spirit anoints us to also appoint, build, raise up, and repair the Body of Christ. Jesus says and the Bible declares that we are to love one another and we show our love and devotion to God by distributing honor and by the process of fulfilling our purpose, while we mature in our faith. Love is fulfilled as we encourage one another, minister to one another, admonish one other, and honor one another. When the Spirit of the Lord is on, or rather in someone, there is more to that experience than tongues and evangelism. This is not to say that the manifestations of the Spirit or evangelism are not important, I am saying that they are not enough to complete the process of discipleship. We forget this, it seems, and all too often because the world has closed us in. We are surrounded by anti-Christian and anti-Christ influences. The world imposes upon us their concept of what a Christian should be, and then persecutes us for not living the way they expect us to live.

Genesis 4:20-22 shows us the beginnings of these world systems. The Church must battle these worldly concepts in itself. We must arise and declare that Jesus is the only Savior and you must be born again. We must also declare that you must grow up in your faith and be converted (see Luke 22:32) lest you continue in your sin and worldliness. Only Jesus can save us and only the Holy Spirit can change people. People are changed by the word and the work of the Holy Spirit. By the word of the Spirit as we evangelize the lost, and by the work of the Spirit as we train the saved. Again, what is discipleship? It is biblical training in doing what the Bible says, and that we can become what it says we are. A changed man has a renewed mind toward the things of God. Not my ways, but His ways. "Not my will, but His will be done, on earth as it is in heaven". I have heard people say, "I'm not Jesus." It is true that we are not Jesus, but we are His representatives. The question is not, "What would Jesus do?" But rather, what are we going to do in His name (i.e., in His place)? Especially since He told us to be stewards here in His place, to be ambassadors here in His place, to be salt here in His place, to be light here in His place, to be sons and daughters here in His place, and to be a witness of Who He is. How are we going to explain all the carnal division and strife that is found in the Body of Christ when we see our Lord face to face? If we are not part of the solution, we may be the problem. The Lord commands us to be one Body, and He also commands us to be united in our faith, and there is a difference between the unity of the faith and the oneness of the Body. Unity is the fact that we come together in Jesus' name, whereas oneness is when we are unified (developed in the same purpose as a Body). Oneness is not multifaceted courses of ministry; it is the singleness of vision a local church has. It seems that everyone in today's Church has his own interpretation of the Bible. Paul asks, "Nevertheless, what saith the Scriptures," (see Galatians 4:30) and we are admonished to "study to show ourselves approved" so we will not be ashamed (see 2 Timothy 2:15). The shame and lack of power many in the Church are experiencing comes because of our division. The division in the Church has made us weak. The world will not recognize the truth of Jesus Christ until we love one another, and we will not mature until we are one.

> "And the glory which thou gavest me I
> have given them; that they may be one,
> even as we are one: I in them, and thou in me,
> that they may be made perfect (mature) in one;
> and that the world may know that thou hast sent me,
> and hast loved them, as thou hast loved me."
> (John 17:22-23)

What will make us one? Only the implementation of the principles of the doctrine of Christ into our lives will set the course and prepare a foundation for the faithful to grow on. These six principles, when applied to one's life, create a foundation of truth that can be built and stood upon. This is the substructure we can add to that will be solid and stable, grounding faithful Christians and making them spiritually and emotionally secure. This is Jesus, the Rock on which I stand. These are the foundations the early church fathers used to disciple the people that changed the world. These principles of the doctrines of Christ are the only foundation that can be built upon with any lasting value. No other foundation can support us as we go through the trials of life.

In closing, there is an important thing to note. We must recognize that there are two types of knowledge discussed in the Bible. They are "information" and "application". With this in mind we should review two verses in the Scripture. The first being:

> "Knowledge puffs up..."
> (1 Corinthians 8:1)

The question is which kind of knowledge puffs up? It is the information one receives that has no application to their life, not knowledge in general, but religious teachings. People with lots of information seem to be "knowledgeable", but just "knowing" Scriptures does not produce a virtuous life. True doctrinal training should be the application of information that produces an overcoming faith. This is why the Scripture also says:

"My people are destroyed for lack of knowledge."
(Hosea 4:6)

The kind of "knowledge" Hosea is writing about is the knowledge that comes through the "experience" discernment, understanding, and wisdom produces through the discipleship process. This is why "Foundations" has been written. It is not a book to read and set aside. It is something to study, it is lessons in spiritual life, and it is a journey of faith.

Chapter 1 – Introduction

> "It is the glory of God to conceal a thing:
> but the honour of kings is to search out a matter."
> (Proverbs 25:2)

One of the most important aspects of Christianity is to determine our source of truth. Why is this first step in the discipleship process so paramount? Without a biblical source of truth a believer's point of origin will be slanted, and the end result will be a worldly foundation of wood, hay, and stubble, rather than a foundation of gold, silver, and precious stones. The only source of truth that is viable for the Christian is the Bible. Some Christians use history as their source of truth, but the problem with history is that it can be rewritten and has been. It has been observed throughout time that those who are in control write history to their liking and slant the historical point of view to meet their subjective needs. Some people use church doctrine as their source of truth. Experience shows us that God's revelation is progressive, and He reveals His will to us at His appointed times (see Daniel 2:20-22, Acts 1:7, 1 Peter 1:11-12, 2 Peter 1:12), so each of us must have clarity in understanding God's ways and His present purpose in the Body of Christ. Fifty years ago the Church had very little understanding, as a whole, about the power of God's Kingdom and the operation of the Holy Spirit. God's master plan has determined the revealing of His secrets according to His timetable and not ours. It is inevitable that the Church will focus and remain entrenched in the revelation they have received, as denominationalism has already proven. Each denomination has a tendency to "get stuck" in their founding doctrines, and it is difficult for them to see beyond their specific biblical perspective. They have a tendency to create dogmas based on their founder's vision and revelation, and refuse to move on with God as He leads us to the promised land of His Kingdom.

Some people use their pastor as their source of truth. Our experience in ministry proves that you can hear fifty variations of truth if you listen to fifty different preachers. There is therefore only one verifiable and unchanging source of truth, and the Christian can only have one foundation, that being Jesus Christ, the Word of God (see John 1:1). Anything else is not only unreliable; it is outside the parameters of faith.

When the Bible is not our source of truth, our worldview will also be out of focus. What is a biblical worldview? It is the biblically declared foundation of truth that is expressed in the Scriptures, which begins with God's purpose in creation, then continues with God's redemption of mankind, and ends with the second coming of Jesus. A Bible based worldview begins with an understanding of who created the heavens and the earth, how He created the heavens and the earth, and why He created the heavens and the earth. The Bible declares God created the heavens and the earth and all that is in them in six days (see Colossians 1:16-17; Genesis 1-2), and it is the power of God that holds it all together. Now we know that God is a God of laws and He set in order the natural laws of physics, as well as the spiritual laws of life. Being a Christian does not mean that our faith is weakened because we believe God has set natural laws in motion, we trust in those laws as they are revealed to us. In fact, our faith should be strengthened believing the heavens and the earth and all that is in them were created for our benefit and enjoyment and so God built natural laws into the fabric of His creation. There is ever increasing evidence (outside of faith) of a Divine Creation; punching many holes in the theory of evolution. The evidence of a young universe is continually mounting. The evolutionists are scrambling to hide and/or hinder the release of this information to the general public, knowing it points to divine or Intelligent design.

(Some of the evidence for creationism can be found at these websites: www.creationevidences.org, www.allaboutcreation.org, and www.nwcreation.net.)

A Biblical Worldview

The simple aspects of a biblical worldview are as follows: We believe that God the Father is the Originator of the Divine plan, and that it was Jesus Christ Who formed the heavens and the earth. We believe that Jesus Christ is the first-born of all Creation, and that He is the Son of God. We believe Jesus was born of a virgin, lived a perfect and sinless life, that His blood was shed for the remission of our sins, and that His blood cleans us and covers our sin: past, present, and future. We believe that Jesus' sacrifice on the cross has restored us back to God, and that we are also righteousness by His gift (see Romans 5:17) allowing us access to God even in our present state of being. We believe that Jesus rose from the dead, that Jesus is the only way to God the Father, and that He will return one day. We believe in the priesthood of the believer and that the Church (the Body of Christ) was established to manifest the Kingdom of God in the earth, and that every believer is anointed and gifted with a specific purpose in God's Eternal Design. We believe in the fellowship and communion of the Body of Christ and in the fellowship and communion of the Holy Spirit, and the Spirit's work in the lives of every believer. We believe the Bible is the infallible and inerrant word of God and that it expresses the total revelation necessary for the Body of Christ to complete its purpose in the course of history. These are the basic tenants of the Christian worldview.

The Bible declares that mankind was created in the image of God (see Genesis 1:26) and for fellowship and communion with Him. God created the universe for man's pleasure, and in its origin, all things worked for man's benefit. Man was also created to be a speaking being and was instructed to speak by God. In Genesis chapter two, God gave Adam a commandment and the first law for man to live by. That law was simple: do not eat from the tree of the knowledge of good and evil. Later when Adam was instructed to "name" (8034) the animals, this is understood to be the beginning of language. This primitive Hebrew word means "to call out their character, as a mark of memorial of their individuality." How long did it take for Adam to name all the animals is an important question because it reveals that Adam walked with God for some time before Eve was brought to him? Some believe that as fast as Adam saw the animals he would name them immediately. An exegesis of the Scripture will reveal this to not be true. In order for Adam to name the animals by their nature, he would have to study them as they lived. This would not be a simple task because animals function differently in nature. This process may have taken Adam several years. Somewhere during this process Adam saw that every animal had a mate (an aid, or a companion) except for him. It was at this time God brought Eve to Adam, and he named her and declared her purpose. Why is this important? It shows that Adam spent quite a long time with God, both personally and individually. God instructed Adam (who had neither natural father nor mother) in the nature of the family. We do not know the number of years Adam and Eve were in the garden before the fall, but it may have been quite a long time. Sometime after Eve was brought to Adam, they broke God's commandment and paradise was lost. Cain and Abel were thus born out of paradise, and the sin nature of man revealed itself in Cain as he murdered his brother. Cain was thus cursed and fled to the land of Nod which is a Hebrew word that simply means "in exile" and is translated as the word "vagabond" in Genesis 4:14 (both coming from the same root). Cain met his wife there, married her, and had children. Many have wondered where this woman of Nod came from. Adam and Eve had many children who are not listed in the canon as Genesis 5:4 states. It was common for only the blood line of the Messiah to be listed and it was through the linage of Seth that Messiah came. As evidence, let me pose a question, how many children did Abraham have? Many would say just two, Ishmael and Isaac. A review of Genesis 25:1-6 will find that he had six other sons, and possibly daughters as well (due to the tradition of not listing the daughters in the linage). We know Adam and Eve had daughters, though they are not listed. One of the theories concerning this is that Adam and Eve lived for many years in paradise before the fall, and over the process of time, had many sons and daughters. Cain and Abel were listed aside from these because they were the first two children born after the fall. Seth is also listed because his linage is necessary for us to understand the line from where Jesus came from. Seth is also listed in the canon because he was born after the fall and it is through the fallen linage the redemption of mankind was planned (See the chart below that reveals that Seth was born in Adam's 130th year). Along with this, the earth was being populated by the descendants of Adam, and Cain found his wife from the descendants of Adam in Nod. An interesting note to this subject can be found in Genesis 6:2,

"That the sons of God saw the daughters of men that they were fair;
and they took them wives of all which they chose."

Who were these sons of God? Many foolish notions have been propagated that these were demons of some sort. That idea is laughable. This notion has been propagated because of the Hebrew word nephiyl (giants-5303) found in Genesis 6:4. This word means "tyrants" or "mighty men" and is also used in Numbers 13:33 of the men that the spies saw when they entered the Promised Land. In the thirteenth chapter of Numbers the spies said "and we were in our own sight as grasshoppers, and so we were in their sight." There is no discounting that there were some very large men in those days (the sons of Anak) of whom Goliath was one. There is no evidence, however, that these were demons; that is a false traditional concept. These sons of God were the sons, or more likely, the grandsons, great-grandsons, and others from the linage of Adam, who served the Lord. Recognizing that Genesis 6:5 tells us how wickedness, evil, and violence covered the earth during this time, it is more likely that these were tyrants who took advantage of others. Some use the passage in Job 1:6 and Job 2:1 which talks of the sons of God and believe that Satan came with them as evidence that somehow a demon can have sex with a woman. Job said, "Satan came also among them," not that he was one of them. Make a note that Satan came "among" them; for the Scripture does not declare that he was one of them. Satan's purpose was to bring accusation. He is not a son of God and that philosophy is a false doctrine. Hosea 1:10 states,

> "Yet the number of the children of Israel shall
> be as the sand of the sea, which cannot be
> measured nor numbered; and it shall come to
> pass, that in the place where it was said unto them,
> Ye are not my people, there it shall be said unto them,
> Ye are the sons of the living God."

We also find in the New Testament,

> "But as many as received him,
> to them gave he power to become the sons of God,
> even to them that believe on his name."
> (John 1:12)

> "For as many as are led by the Spirit of God,
> they are the sons of God."
> (Romans 8:14)

> "That ye may be blameless and harmless,
> the sons of God, without rebuke, in the midst
> of a crooked and perverse nation, among whom
> ye shine as lights in the world."
> (Philippians 2:15)

These passages show us who the sons of God are and no demon is a son of the Living God.

The Bible affirms that after the fall of man and before the flood, mankind's life expectancy was much greater than it is today. The pristine world gave man a long life and the ability to develop the necessary skills he would need to secure his future, populate the earth, and spread out from the Garden of Eden. The following chart demonstrates the long life of Adam and his children, up to the Flood and how life expectancy diminished greatly after the Flood. Also make a note that Adam died in the year 930, which was but a few years before the Flood. See Genesis 11 for this listing.

Name	Biblical year of Birth	Had a child at this age	Years lived afterwards	Total years lived	Died in this year
Adam	1	130 (Seth)	800	930	930
Seth	130	105	807	912	1042
Enos	235	90	815	905	1140
Cainan	325	70	840	910	1235
Mahalaleel	395	65	830	895	1290
Jared	460	162	800	962	1422
Enoch	622	65	300	365	927
Methuselah	687	187	782	969	1656
Lamech	874	182	595	777	1651
Noah	1056	500	450	950	2006
Shem	1556	100	500	600	2156
Arphaxad	1656	35	403	438	2094
Salah	1691	30	403	433	2124
Eber	1721	34	430	464	2185
Peleg	1755	30	209	239	1994
Rue	1785	32	207	239	2024
Serug	1817	30	200	230	2047
Nahor	1847	29	119	148	1995
Terah	1876	70	135	205	2011
Abraham	1946	86	89	175	2121
Ishmael	2032	?	?	137	2169
Isaac	2046	60	120	180	2226
Jacob	2106	?	?		

As you can see by the chart, life expectancy was greatly diminished after the Flood. Apparently the Flood had destroyed the earlier eco-system, and thus life expectancy declined.

What actually happened during the Flood? Genesis chapter six reveals that three things transpired during the Flood event. First, "the fountains of the great deep" were broken up. What were these fountains? According to many biblical scholars these fountains or "tehom" (8415) were the massive water table God had created when He spoke the earth into existence. The earth must have cracked like an egg at the time of the Flood event, and the water spewed out under tremendous pressure. Several articles have been written concerning this (see the web sites given to read more extensively about this subject), and some scholars believe the water spayed as high as thirty miles up into space. As gravity pulled on the water, the earth's magnetic field drew it mainly to the two poles, covering them with ice and forming what is generally called the Ice Age (remember it is cold in space). The water broke though the upper atmosphere and caused the second flood effect, that being "the windows of heaven were opened". In Genesis 1:6, on the second day of creation, God created a "firmament" (7549) to separate the waters above from the waters beneath. The Hebrew words translated as "divide" (914 and 996) mean to "separate and make a distinction." This could mean one of two things. It could mean that during the creation of the earth in its pristine state, there was water above the atmosphere that protected the world from ultraviolet rays and other destructive forces, or this firmament is thought by some scholars to be a thin layer of hydrogen that acted like a bubble perfectly suspended above the surface of the earth and covered the whole world. Another recently discovered phenomenon is that there is a thin layer of ice in some areas of the upper atmosphere. This could also be what is to be understood by the statement found in Genesis about the firmament. The third flood effect was that as the firmament melted and degenerated and it "rained for forty days and forty nights". The water massed and covered the entire world. One of the things that puzzled me is how the evolutionists find evidence of water covering the highest mountains, yet they cannot understand, nor do they believe in the biblical Flood. The flood waters covered the whole earth for 150 days (see Genesis 7:24) or five months. The months in those times consisted of twelve months, each containing thirty days. The ancient Egyptian calendar consisted of twelve months, each being thirty days long and beginning in August. The Babylonian year was much the same as the Egyptian year except it started at the end of our February. The following chart outlines the Egyptian year.

Month's Name	Number of Days in the Month	Beginning about
1-Thyoth	30	August 29
2-Paophi	30	September 28
3-Athyr	30	October 28
4-Choiac	30	November 27
5-Tubi	30	December 27
6-Mecheir	30	January 26
7-Phamenoth	30	February 25
8-Pharmuthi	30	March 27
9-Pachon	30	April 26
10-Pauni	30	May 26
11-Epiphi	30	June 25
12-Mesori	30	July 25
The Egyptian's year was not corrected until about 1000 years after the Flood.	Assis added five days to their year and inserted them at the end of the twelfth month.	The Greeks were the first to discover that the year was 365 days as well as the addition of one day every four years.

The Hebrews calendar was much like the Egyptian calendar, having twelve months, but had a different beginning. The Hebrew calendar is as follows.

1-Abib or Nisan = Exo. 12:2-37
2-Iyar or Zif = 1Ki 6:1
3-Sivan = Est 8:9
4-Tammuz = Eze 8:14
5-Ab
6-Elul = Neh 6:15
7-Ethanim or Tishri = 1Ki 8:2
8-Marchesvan or Bul = 1Ki 6:38
9-Chisleu = Zec 7:1
10-Tebeth = Est 2:16
11-Sebat = Zec 1:7
12-Adar = Est 3:7

The Flood began, according to the Bible, in November of our calendar year, and the Ark came ashore on Mt. Ararat in April of the next year. After forty days, Noah sent out a bird which found no place to rest and so returned to the Ark. Noah and his family stayed in the Ark until November of the following year and at that time they came out of the Ark to sacrifice to the Lord. At this time God gave Noah some new rules to follow, (see Genesis 9:3-7) and Noah and his sons began to repopulate the earth. Genesis 10:25 tells us that in the days of Peleg, the earth was divided. In other words the Continental plates broke apart. One of the unusual things about the Bible is it does not tell us where Noah went to live. The sons of Noah began settling in and around the Plain of Babylon, which is where Nimrod's kingdom began. We are told that the grandsons and great grandsons of Noah began to spread all across the land, but the order and progression of these events are not stated.

In ancient days, historians believed that ancient Persia is where mankind came from, because after the flood it was believed that Noah traveled eastwardly to modern day Iran shortly after the Flood. It was from this area that mankind first began to repopulate and then travel westward to Mesopotamia or the ancient land of Shinar.

One thing the Scripture states is that the whole of mankind was of one language. Methuselah was born and lived with Adam for about 243 years. Methuselah didn't die until the year of the Flood (approx. 1656 years after the fall of man). It seems likely that Noah, who lived for 600 years before the flood, and was born only fourteen years after Seth's death, spoke the same language as Adam. He would therefore teach his sons that same language and they would teach their sons and grandsons the same. Thus the whole earth had one language in the beginning and that one language prevailed until the time of the Tower of Babel. The Bible says they made bricks to build the tower and used "slime" (2564) for mortar. The mortar they used is thought to be some form of tar. The Hebrew word translated as "slime" means "to bubble or boil up," which shows it may have been tar or some form of oil. When the Lord commanded Noah to put "pitch" on the Ark inside and out, He was commanding him to use "butimen", the same substance. It was during the building of the tower of Babel that the Lord "confounded" (1101) man's language. The word translated as "confound" means "to mix". This is thought by some scholars to have been accomplished at once, but the biblical evidence shows that this was consummated over a period of time. We see that during Abraham's day, as he traveled from Ur of the Chaldees (see Genesis 11:28) to Haran, (in present day Syria and on down to Egypt) he could speak intelligently to the people in these lands (see Genesis 12:15-20). We do understand that around a hundred years later, Joseph spoke through a translator to his brothers as he deceived them, not wanting to reveal his identity. The language of man at this point in time changed, sufficiently enough at first to confuse mankind, but as man began to separate and settle over the earth, diverse pronunciations of the same thing would have become common. As people discovered new things, they would develop new words, new descriptions, and new ways of saying them until time itself would cause their dialects to evolve into different languages. Their environment would also cause variations in their pronunciations, and thus over the process of 200 years, some languages would develop totally different from others. Philologists have determined that there were three or four great types or families of languages. The Semitic or Hebrew family is one of them.

God called Abraham to be the originator of the Hebrew nation. It was through Abraham's linage that the Messiah was to come. Through Isaac, Jacob was born, and through Jacob's twelve sons, came the twelve tribes of the Jews. Remember God changed Jacob's name to Israel and this was the beginning of the nation of Israel. Through one man the nation was born. Jacob and his sons were set apart and moved into Egypt during the great famine that occurred, while Joseph was Pharaoh's Administrator. Then after 450 years of slavery, the Hebrews returned to the land of Canaan and established the nation of Israel. At this time God set up Judges to form a government. These judges were tasked to help men in their newly found freedom. Over time, some of the judges sinned and God judged the nation. Israel faltered and became weakened by disobedience, and was overrun by its enemies several times. God gave Israel a king as a ruler over them (because they wanted to be like other nations), but Saul was found to be disobedient and unfaithful to the Lord's word. David honored Saul as God's anointed, and David was crowned only after Saul's death. We know Solomon increased the nation's glory and wealth, but after Solomon's death there was a civil war and the nation was divided into Judah (Judah and Benjamin), and the northern ten tribes. This again weakened the nation and it was eventually defeated and taken into captivity by the Babylonians for seventy years. God was faithful, and after the appointed time, re-established the nation and rebuilt Jerusalem and the Temple. Idolatry crept back into the people and the nation was again occupied by foreign powers, such as the Greeks and the Romans.

Sometime after the Babylonian Captivity the religious mandates changed in the nation. As we read through the Old Testament we find no mention of the Sadducees or the Pharisees, yet once you open the New Testament we find that they are in control of the Temple, and the religious order found within the Synagogue system.

'Jesus was also the originator of a Nation. We are the seed of Christ in the earth. We are the ones who are commanded to continue His mandate. If we sin, as those in the past, we will undoubtedly repeat history's lessons. We are now waiting on Jesus' return and the Church must stand firm in faith, as we expect that the last days are here.

> "Moreover, brethren, I would not that ye should be ignorant,
> how that all our fathers were under the cloud, and all passed through the sea;
> And were all baptized unto Moses in the cloud and in the sea;
> And did all eat the same spiritual meat;
> And did all drink the same spiritual drink:
> for they drank of that spiritual Rock that followed them:
> and that Rock was Christ.

But with many of them God was not well pleased:
for they were overthrown in the wilderness.
Now these things were our examples, to the intent
we should not lust after evil things, as they also lusted.
Neither be ye idolaters, as were some of them; as it is written, The people sat
down to eat and drink, and rose up to play.
Neither let us commit fornication, as some
of them committed, and fell in one day
three and twenty thousand. Neither let us tempt Christ,
as some of them also tempted, and were destroyed of serpents.
Neither murmur ye, as some of them also murmured,
and were destroyed of the destroyer. Now all these
things happened unto them for ensamples:
and they are written for our admonition, upon whom
the ends of the world are come. Wherefore let him
that thinketh he standeth take heed lest he fall."
(1 Corinthians 10:1-12)

I want to remind you that the Church has a purpose in Christ. Without a biblical worldview we will find that our foundation of faith will be greatly diminished. God has declared in His Word what His plan is, and how the Church can successfully complete it. The Church cannot effectively accomplish its purpose until believers have been founded and grounded in their spiritual walk. "Foundations" is designed to aid Christians in the completion of the maturity process. The Principles of spiritual maturity are clearly established in the Bible, and we should anchor our hearts to the purpose God has commanded us to fulfill.

Chapter 2—The Remnant People

"Except the Lord of Hosts had left unto us a very small remnant,
we should have been as Sodom,
and we should have been like unto Gomorrah."
(Isaiah 1:9)

"And it shall come to pass in that day, that the remnant
of Israel, and such as are escaped of the house of Jacob,
shall no more again stay upon him that smote them; but they shall stay
upon the Lord, the Holy One of Israel, in truth."
(Isaiah 10:20)

"Set up the standard toward Zion…
Behold, therein shall be left a remnant that shall be
brought forth…And they shall comfort you,
when you see their ways and their doings:
and you shall know that I have not done without cause
all that I have done in it, saith the Lord God."
(Ezekiel 14:22-23)

"Even so then at this present time also there
is a remnant according to the election of grace."
(Romans 11:5)

"And the dragon was wroth with the woman, and went to make war
with the remnant of her seed, which keep the commandments of
God, and have the testimony of Jesus Christ."
(Revelation 12:17)

What translation of the Bible do you use? Let me begin this chapter by giving you some basic facts about some of the translations that are in use today, other than the King James Version. The New International version has removed 695 of the original verses, and has also removed more than 64,000 words from the Bible as a whole (compared with the King James Bible). 650 of these words are the words of Jesus, that's the red letter words you would recognize. In some instances, parts of whole chapters have been removed (See Matthew 18:12; Matthew 21:29-30; Hosea 11:12; Luke 24:51; 1 Corinthians 11:24, 29 [9 words missing] these remissions cause the Scriptural meaning/emphasis to change at times). The New American Standard version eliminates more than 900 verses, while the Revised Standard Version removes 788 verses. The Amplified version also has removed some 484 verses. Some of these translations systematically remove the name of Jesus, the term Christ, the term Lord, the word God, as well as the phrase "the kingdom of God" from many of their verses. Most believers do not take time to read their Bible cover to cover or to compare one Bible against the next. You will not find these flaws in the translations without help or diligence in study, so it is important to know what you are reading. It is true that you would have to be a genius to retain all the information found in the Scriptures, and I'm not trying to advocate that you throw away your Bible if it is not the King James. I personally read more than fifteen translations, but I have learned that my exegetical and doctrinal studies should come from the King James Bible, because it is the more complete translation. Why? The King James translators were trying to bring fort "a more perfect translation". They were not trying to intentionally impose a predetermined religious philosophy on their readers, even though they had a predisposition about aspects of theology, but their desire was to produce the purest translation that could be used by the English speaking world. They wanted to produce an English translation from the manuscripts that was easy to read and easy to be understood by the common people of their day. That is not to say that they did not have a specific doctrinal frame of thought, they most definitely did, but their desire was to generate a Bible translation that was pure, free from the Catholic influence, and would get the Biblical message out to their society. You may find the "thy," "thee," "thou," and such the like harder to work through, but after a few readings it is easy to mentally change them to you or me.

Many people would say that they are Christian, but do not study or agree with the Bible. While others rely on the Bible as their source of truth, yet they read the Bible from a religious frame of mind, never realizing that the Bible teaches us to implement its various truths into our lives. The Bible declares itself to be a living book, the Word of God. It is the written "logos" (the Greek word for "word") and becomes "rhema" to those who implement it into their life. Rhema is the Greek word that also means "an utterance". We receive rhema as we read the Bible, and as it becomes alive and personal to us. Jesus said that it is possible to go to the Scriptures and never find who He really is (see John 5:38-40 and Luke 6:46-49). Have you heard the statement, "Well my Bible says...," and when you ask them where to find it all you get is, "I don't know where it is at..., but I know it is in there!" Many who love the Lord do their best to live faithfully and pursue godliness with great effort. One of my deepest concerns is that there are so many different doctrinal positions in Christendom that many sincere Christians are confused about the truth. When believers do not study the Bible for themselves, then deception is easy for the devil to accomplish. If a Scriptural half-truth is preached many people are none the wiser. They have not studied enough to know the difference. They accept the half-truth as the whole and live for years with that deception undermining their faith. This causes a spiritual confusion in the person, weakening their spiritual foundation and is the downfall of many. Some people believe that they are saved, but do not have a personal relationship with Jesus Christ, causing them to fall into various failures, fall short of a joyful Christian experience, or live outside the biblical mandate. Since their understanding of the Lord and salvation has been obtained by second hand information; their knowledge of God is second hand and their salvation is based on various doctrinal beliefs, rather than on a personal relationship with the Lord. They have a pseudo-salvation based on an assumption, which consequently adds another tare to some church role, instead of a saint to the Lambs book of Life. These people are generally confused, living for years as a good church member, but never get truly born again. I had an evangelist come to a church I had been pastoring and two-thirds of the congregation walked the aisle and were born again. The point is, they had believed they were saved, yet lived as a church member without a full assurance of their salvation for years. When God quickened them, there was a marked difference in the reality of their salvation. When Jesus brings true salvation, there is no confusion about it. Listen to me pastors and church leaders, you cannot disciple lost people! The problem is not your teaching style or the congregations I.Q., we are not saved in the mind, but it is from the heart we believe unto salvation. The truth is that many people are not saved, even when the Gospel is preached, because it was not mixed with faith (see Hebrews 4:1-2). A pseudo-gospel, namely, "make a decision so you can go to heaven" was proclaimed and accepted, but Jesus Christ often times is not received as the Lord of their lives. The evidence manifested in a false salvation is that there was no death in the person. Remember no death, no resurrection. One part of repentance is the acceptance of death to self will and a turning away from sin. It is a change of mind that leads us into a change of life. It is the recognition of our lostness, and an acceptance of God's gift of righteousness. Repentance is the first step in Salvation.

> "For God is not the author of confusion,
> but of peace, as in all churches of the saints."
> (1 Corinthians 14:33)

A person who is living with a confused state of salvation must recognize that confusion is often times the evidence of lostness. The reality of being born again is a change in the person's nature. If there is no change in your nature over an initial period of time, there is no salvation. We have been given a new nature in Christ. Too many people water down salvation in order to get another church member. This was not the way Jesus handled people. This is not spiritually wise, nor is this prudent in saving today's society. This is demonic wisdom and gross error.

> "This wisdom descendeth not from above, but is earthly, sensual, devilish.
> For where envying and strife is, there is confusion and every evil work."
> (James 3:15-16)

21

I guess I am on a bit of a soapbox, but I have a point in my madness. Much of ministry in today's churches seems to have left the basic framework of faith in developing the maturity of the modern disciple. The thought and need for money has taken over the rational thinking in many congregations. As a pastor, I realize that it takes money to run a ministry and the tithe is part of the Scriptural mandate, but many pastors are being defeated because of mammon, and they dumb down true salvation with concepts of rededication and the like, as well as a whole host of unbiblical theological positions and dogmas. You will find the ideology of "success" at the heart of carnal ministry, rather than the ideology of "service". There is simply no apostolic oversight in these types of ministries, and I use the term "ministry" loosely. One of the main focus' of this book is to emphasis that "quality" should always have a priority over "quantity" in the ministry. Ministers are an emissary of the Lord Jesus, and are ambassadors of the Kingdom of God. When an ambassador fails to represent the kingdom and king who sent him, he is no longer a valid representative and should be dismissed. But that is generally not the way it works in many modern congregations. Nowadays people just start another church with those who agree with them when they are confronted with truth. The biblical mandate to make disciples should be the overriding factor in the Church today. Jeremiah understood this very well and wrote,

> "See, I have this day set thee over the nations and over the
> kingdoms, to root out, and to pull down, and to destroy,
> and to throw down, to build, and to plant."
> (Jeremiah 1:10)

Jeremiah knew that there is twice as much demolition in the process of maturing disciples than building them up and re-planting the truth in them. We have to undo much of what is been done in the lives of God's people. Most of God's people do not know how much they are loved by their Father in heaven. Many do not understand that righteousness in a gift and that dead works hinders them from having a renewed mind in Christ. As ambassadors of Jesus Christ and His Kingdom, we are held accountable for our stewardship of the Gospel of the Kingdom. Jesus warned us that an enemy would be sowing tares in His field (see Matthew 13:25-40). We have been looking for tares in the wrong place. Many of us have been looking for them in the audience; as though that is the only place they can be found, when one should consider that the pulpit may have a few of them as well. One thing that is not often recognized is that there is something worse than a wolf in sheep's clothing, that being a wolf in shepherd's clothing. I am not talking about men and women who are called, but are immature. I am speaking of those who have a self-centered ministry, and they do what they do for personal gain and promotion. We should become conscious of the fact that while some believers are growing in grace and truth, the "pseudadelphos" (the Greek word for false brethren-5569) are coming into our congregations in mass and by stealth, both in the congregation as participators, and in the pulpit as teachers. Mass media has produced a lopsided church and a watered down truth. With our ability to reproduce literature, CD's, DVD's, and broadcast to the nations, we should be making disciples by the billions, but we seem to be focusing on individual ministry and personal success, not on the ministry of Jesus.

> "And that because of false brethren unawares brought in,
> who came in privily to spy out our liberty which we have in Christ Jesus,
> that they might bring us into bondage: To whom we gave place by subjection,
> no, not for an hour; that the truth of the gospel might continue with you.
> But of these who seemed to be somewhat, (whatsoever they were,
> it maketh no matter to me: God accepteth no man's person:)
> for they who seemed to be somewhat in conference added nothing to me."
> (Galatians 2:4-6)

The Rise of the Remnant

The Bible (the Old and New Testaments) reveals that Father God has brought a remnant through history for the purpose of continuing a foundation of grace and truth in the earth (make a note of the introductory Scriptures at the front of this chapter). As the remnant is being prepared and purified, Satan is upgrading his attacks against them, focusing on the weak, and generating many problems among the faithful. This is why Revelation 12:4-5 states,

> "And his tail drew the third part of the stars of heaven
> and did cast them to the earth: and the dragon
> stood before the woman which was ready to be delivered,
> for to devour her child as soon as it was born.
> And she brought forth a man child, who was to
> rule all nations with a rod of iron: and her child was
> caught up unto God, and to his throne."
> (See Revelation 1:20 to clarify what "stars are.")

Satan is largely accomplishing this goal through variations of watered down interpretations of the Bible and through political correctness in the Church. Who is this" man-child" the book of Revelation speaks of? It is the remnant people being birthed into God's Kingdom, which are being brought into prominence in the earth. It is the remnant Church that God is calling us to be, a people who have excellence of spirit, and who walk honorable before the Lord and in the strength of His Kingdom's power. This end time birthing and the maturation of the remnant Church is the reason we find Satan pulling out all the stops. The spirit of anti-Christ is erupting in the world through terrorism (the propagation of a false religion), apathy, moral decay, and false doctrines. We must discover that the remnant people are designed to be the by-product of God's moving in the last days, and we must move with Him during this time in history.

"Hear the word of the Lord, ye that tremble at his word;
Your brethren that hated you,
that cast you out for my name's sake, said, Let the Lord be glorified:
but he shall appear to your joy, and they shall be ashamed.
A voice of noise from the city, a voice from the temple,
a voice of the Lord that rendereth recompense to his enemies.
Before she travailed, she brought forth; before her pain came,
she was delivered of a man child.
Who hath heard such a thing? who hath seen such things?
Shall the earth be made to bring forth in one day?
or shall a nation be born at once?
for as soon as Zion travailed, she brought forth her children.
Shall I bring to the birth, and not cause to bring forth? saith the Lord:
shall I cause to bring forth, and shut the womb?
saith thy God. Rejoice ye with Jerusalem, and be glad with her,
all ye that love her: rejoice for joy with her, all ye that mourn for her:
That ye may suck, and be satisfied with the breasts of her consolations;
that ye may milk out, and be delighted with the abundance of her glory.
For thus saith the Lord, Behold, I will extend peace to
her like a river, and the glory of the Gentiles like a flowing stream:
then shall ye suck, ye shall be borne upon her sides,
and be dandled upon her knees.
As one whom his mother comforteth, so will I comfort you;
and ye shall be comforted in Jerusalem."
(Isaiah 66:5-13)

Isaiah saw this man-child for who he was. Notice a few things about this prophesy. First, there was no hard delivery. The child was delivered by God. Second, this remnant child was of the Gentiles. Yet God Himself was the Comforter. This sounds like John 14:26, speaking of the Holy Spirit. Jeremiah 6:9 also gives us a picture of who this remnant is and how God is calling and selecting them,

"Thus saith the Lord of Host, They shall thoroughly
glean the remnant of Israel as a vine: turn back thine
hand as a grape gatherer into the baskets."

Jeremiah is saying that God is going through His basket and re-inspecting the grapes that have already been picked. The statement, "turn back thine hand as a grape gatherer into the basket" is declaring how the Father is selecting the remnant from the cluster. God is inspecting the root and the fruit of every believer in this season. I also know that every church and every congregation has a remnant people in them. The remnant churches are those who love the Lord and are seeking Him with all their heart, mind, soul, and strength. The Lord is opening the eyes of the remnant to see the foolishness of the doctrines and the tradition many people are propagating. The remnant people are coming out of bastard churches and are resisting the status quo. When studying about the remnant we must consider that 1 Peter 4:17 states,

> "For the time is come that judgment must begin
> at the house of God: and if it first begin at us,
> what shall the end be of them that obey not the gospel of God."

There are various theological approaches to the end times in today's Church. Some Christians do not understand eschatology, or are confused about these things because of the variations of the theological interpretation relating to the rapture of the Church. With all the doctrinal variations about the end of days being taught in the Church today, someone has to be wrong. The Bible teaches that judgment begins in the Church, and judgment has begun. God is judging his sheep and Jesus said, "My sheep hear my voice" (see John 10:27). The Bible also states that God will separate the sheep from the goats (see Matthew 25). The remnant will hear God while the others will not. I am not speaking of the remnant church in a cultic sense. The remnant people I am speaking of serve the Lord because of love and have a passion for obedience. They are not high minded, but humble. It is from the depth of their humility that honor is distributed as they hold the standard of Christian living in an uncompromising purity. They are iconoclasts, a people who cannot accept the political correctness of our modern society when it supersedes God's Word. And again I say, God is drawing out this people. He is demanding that the Church matures and this is the season when God is separating the prophets from the preachers, the preachers from the preachers, and the prophets from the prophets. There was a time in recent history when people would ask, "Are you a preacher?" Then the question of the next season became, "What kind of preacher are you?" Now it is not are you a Preacher, or what kind of preacher are you; in God's mind it is, "What kind of person are you?" We are in a time when virtue and honor carry the highest value. Virtue and honor are now overflowing into the Church.

> "And as for you, O my flock, thus saith the Lord God;
> Behold, I judge between cattle and cattle,
> between the rams and the he goats…
> And ye my flock, the flock of my pasture, are men,
> and I am your God, saith the Lord God."
> (Ezekiel 34:17 and 31)

This is the time when God is making a clear distinction between Christian and Christian (i.e., the separation of the sheep and the goats). Jesus is bringing to pass the fulfillment of the parables found in Matthew 24:36-51 and Matthew 25. Pray and ask the Holy Spirit to give you clarity of mind, and then take the time to read the New Testament completely. Start at Matthew 1:1 and read at least nine chapters a day and you will complete the New Testament in less than one month. It only takes an average of forty-five minutes a day to accomplish this task. After you finish, ask yourself a simple question. Why do we have church the way we have it, and since many of our present concepts of church structure are not found in the New Testament, why do we focus so much time on entertaining the congregation and so little time training them? You will have to ask this question because you will learn that our present day system of church order, church government, and the Church's focus are not biblically accurate. The five-fold ministry is not the government of God; they are the governors of God. The Kingdom of God is the Government of God and that is the order of God's government. Please do not become a proof-text reader; one who reads just a few verses here and a few verses there, never getting a concentric understanding of the plan of God as the Bible reveals it. Some read one verse and then build whole doctrinal structures from it. You know I am telling you the truth! We are just afraid to speak out about it because the Church has become so religiously traditional in a bad sense. Many people have an American concept of Christianity, and they persecute anyone who disagrees with their theology or points out these subjects that I am touching on here. These are hard sayings, "who can hear them" (see John 6:60-66). We have to be shocked into reality the way Jesus hit His followers with the statement, "You must eat my flesh and drink my blood." (see John 6:53). Jesus stunned them with piercing words of truth. He then asked, "Does this offend you?" Truth is always offensive to those who are not seeking it.

Take the rapture theology being propagated by many preachers today. They have their charts and graphs, but they do not line up with the whole Scripture. There are some verses we must ask Christians to consider when discussing the rapture. The first is 1 Corinthians 15:51-52:

> "Behold, I shew you a mystery; We shall not all sleep,
> but we shall all be changed, In a moment, in the twinkling
> of an eye, at the last trump: for the trumpet shall sound,
> and the dead shall be raised incorruptible, and we shall be changed."

When shall we be changed or raised from the dead? It is at the "last trumpet" not at the first trumpet. The last trumpet does not occur until Revelation 11:15. This trumpet is after the second woe and the church cannot be raptured before this trumpet or the Scripture is untrue. Jesus said in Matthew 24:29-32 that we will not be gathered to Him until "immediately after the tribulation." These coupled with Revelation 20, which says that the first resurrection occurs after the Great Tribulation, are all evidences of the timing of the rapture. Most of the "rapture" theology never touches on the "when;" they address only the "what" of the tribulation. Take a look at Matthew 24:3:

> "And as he sat upon the mount of Olives, the disciples
> came unto him privately, saying, Tell us, when shall
> these things be? and what *shall be* the sign of thy
> coming, and of the end of the world?"

Notice the two questions the disciples ask Jesus. "Tell us, *when* shall these things be?" And "*what* shall be the sign of thy coming?" Jesus answered the "what" first in verses 4-28 and the "when" in verses 29-42. If you take an honest look at Matthew 24 you find several evidences that the Church will go through the tribulation. The first and most obvious is that Jesus says: "Immediately after the tribulation." The second evidence is that Jesus says that it will be like the days of Noah. Who were destroyed in that event? The righteous or the wicked? It was the wicked who were destroyed and righteous Noah and his family were saved in the Ark. What will be the Ark of the end times? You will find that the Kingdom of God is our Ark and the Body of Christ's salvation during the tribulation. An honest study of the Scripture reveals many things about this time and season. It is ALWAYS the wicked that are taken away in the New Testament. Matthew 13:40-43 states:

> "As therefore the tares are gathered and burned in the fire;
> so shall it be in the end of this world. The Son of man shall
> send forth his angels, and they shall gather out of his kingdom
> all things that offend, and them which do iniquity; And shall cast
> them into a furnace of fire: there shall be wailing and gnashing of teeth.
> Then shall the righteous shine forth as the sun in the kingdom
> of their Father. Who hath ears to hear, let him hear."

During Noah's time on the earth the Bible says, "And God saw that the wickedness of man *was* great in the earth, and *that* every imagination of the thoughts of his heart *was* only evil continually." We are experiencing the very same thing today. Notice that Jesus said, "Then shall the righteous shine forth as the sun in the kingdom of their Father." Churches and ministries that are functioning in Kingdom reality will go through the tribulation unscathed as Noah and his family was saved from the flood. The Kingdom is our salvation during the tribulation. There are too many pastors and congregations that do not understand how the Kingdom functions and "church as usual" goes on week in and week out. The tribulation will catch them as a thief in the night. The remnant sons and daughters of God function in the "Issachar" realm and know what to do and how to prepare the Body of Christ for the end times and the tribulation (see chapter twenty for a more in-depth study of this subject).

This is just some of the evidence touching one of the doctrines found in the Church today. There are many more doctrines that must be scrutinized and measured by the truth.

The New Buzz Word: Ministry

Ministries in today's environment consist of everything from those who make you laugh in the Lord to puppet ministries. We have Christian fortune-tellers roaming through the Church as Prophets and have sold out to love offerings. We have everything the world has with the name "Christian" attached to it; compromise is found everywhere in the Body of Christ. The Church is in moral decay and no one has the courage to stand up and declare it from the mountain tops. No, we have preachers now propagating that if you are suffering as a Christian, it is because you are not living by faith or that you are living in sin. These are truly serious matters. Are God's ministers developing a system of religion where they entertain the congregations because if they do not, they cannot pay the bills? These types of things are done and justified in the name of evangelism, single's ministry, children's ministry, youth ministry, or whatever other type of ministry the parishioners demand.

Let us ask ourselves another question, do we study the Bible because we want to know our Savior and His truth, or do we read the Bible to prove our own personal doctrine and theological stance? Many individuals use the Bible to prove their present flavor of doctrine rather than study the Scriptures as they are and receive the truth that they declare. You will notice that there is a distinctive irrationality connected to many doctrines being preached in some ministries. There are central truths in the Scriptures that cannot be devalued or misrepresented without severe consequences to the Church's framework. American church meetings have become very predictable in recent years. People come to churches looking for the various forms of entertainment, and they want to feel the good fluff, rather than looking for truth and biblical accuracy. I have had people tell me, "We're shopping for a church home." The Church is not a Mall! We are not commanded in the Scriptures to pick and choose ministries for individuals to shop around for. I have come to understand that not very many believers actually know what the Church is. Many think the Church is the building, the steeple when the true Church is the people. What did Jesus mean when He said, "upon this rock I will build my church; and the gates of hell shall not prevail against it" (see Matthew 16:18). Where is the church that is free from strife, full of peace, with its members maturing, and turning their communities upside down? Where is the impact of the Church in the community today? Are you or is your church turning your community, city, or location away from pornography, crime, and general worldliness? Or are those things growing while you have good services? It may seem that I am church bashing, but this is not my intent. I love the people of God, but we must deal with these issues in a straightforward and concise way. As stated, the Church is the people, the Body of Christ. It is the "ekklesia" (1577), "the *twice* called out people." It is not sectarian, independent local fellowships, nor is it denominational sects as a whole. The Church is the combined people of faith and has a local manifestation in every city, town, and community where the Body of Christ resides. We are the Church, to put it bluntly. It is not this church here or that church there with this name or that name; it is we the people of God in every place that names the name of Jesus Christ as his or her personal Lord and Savior. Everything else is just churchanity. I use the term "churchanity" to describe a mindset found in many congregations and Church leaders. Churchanity describes the attitude among many Christians who only consider church as being their own local church, and leave out the rest of the Body of Christ. These people rarely think of God in living terms. Church to them is the week in and week out filled with religious liturgy, the idea of "going" to church, and listening to a new teaching or proposition; never considering that has God desired to be active in their life. In churchanity everyone has an idea, and it seems every idea becomes a particular kind of church. Churchanity has its very foundation in denominational pride and piety. People who are involved in churchanity disregard other Pastors and believers in their communities and think of themselves as though they are holier or better Christians than other believers. They think it is godly to speak evil of others Pastors or believers in their communities; believing that they hold higher esteem in God's eyes by doing so.

The most used statement in the Church today is, "I believe." Remember when people said, "We've never done it that way before." Now it is expected and hip to be different and unique. Now the norm is to offer a different style of service or worship. This is good and bad. Good because people are recognizing that there is a need to move on with God out of the traditional norm, and bad because change is being done for the sake of user friendly concepts that detract from the true nature and purpose of the Gospel. Why are there so many different formats of service and worship? Why have congregations developed a ministry-minded consciousness, to the degree that "ministry" is more important than truth? It is because a spirit of competition permeates the Christian ministry. Immaturity has caused people in the Church to need to be entertained. People now say that going to church is boring, because they have to be pumped up, rather than living the fullness of the Christian experience. The fact is the Church has to minister to fleshly minded people constantly, because they are not training them up to walk in greater levels of maturity.

Being blunt again, weak Christians come from weak leaders. The leaders may be good speakers, but the anointing to mature people in the faith is not found in their administrative ability or anointing. We should realize that the spiritually weak believers have long-lasting problems.

> "Why is my pain perpetual, and my wound incurable,
> which refuseth to be healed? wilt thou be altogether unto
> me as a liar, and as waters that fail? Therefore thus saith the Lord,
> If thou return, then will I bring thee again, and thou shalt stand before me:
> and if thou take forth the precious from the vile, thou shalt be as my mouth:
> let them return unto thee; but return not thou unto them."
> (Jeremiah 15:18-19)

Jeremiah was told by the Lord to "separate the precious from the vile". This simply means to take an inventory of your life and recognize that each of us have internal areas that cause us external problems. In order to train the weak, we must first be discipled and weaned from the things that keep us weak. When we study the Scripture, we do not find Jesus leading groups of people in a singing ministry. They may have sung a song as an expression of worship, but Jesus' emphasis was always on the Father. Jesus always led the people in righteousness; He didn't have a music ministry. Music ministries are part of the Temple worship and there have always been psalmists in the order of the Temple, and music has its place. Ephesians 5:19 says, "Speaking to yourselves in psalms and hymns and spiritual songs, singing and making melody in your heart to the Lord". This means we have joy in our hearts and a song in our mouth, but we are not commanded to create entire music ministries for the sake of entertainment.

I love Christian music, it has its place in the Church, but we have taken it way out of the place it is purposed to be. Even though I am taking a hard stance on this issue, I am not trying to say it is some kind of sin to sing or to have music in the Church; just the opposite. If people propagate that, it is because they are not hearing the voice of the Lord on this aspect of ministry. Singing is good for the soul, but biblical worship and praise are more than singing songs. One of the main issues here is that we should allow the music to arise from our hearts toward God and not have to wait on someone else to stir our hearts to praise God. It is a song in the heart that God desires. Songs are acceptable to the Lord only when the one singing is singing out of his personal love and adoration. Religious singing is just that, religious singing. Again, I am not trying to denigrate praise and worship as a whole, but it is necessary to address the order of worship many congregations have, because praise and worship has become a god to many people. I am speaking negatively about an order of worship that is religious in nature, and one that does not build up the Body, nor does it give glory to God: the kind of thing that happens when the musicians get the glory. The same can be said of the preaching. Who gets the glory? Jesus Christ or the preacher? These are the issues of spiritual life, the spiritual life in each and every congregation that finds itself in the presence of God.

> "Let the word of Christ dwell in you richly in all wisdom;
> teaching and admonishing one another in psalms and
> hymns and spiritual songs, singing with grace in your hearts to the Lord."
> (Colossians 3:16)

> "Speaking to yourselves in psalms and hymns and spiritual songs,
> singing and making melody in your heart to the Lord."
> (Ephesians 5:19)

Make a note of three statements found in these Scriptures. First, "singing with grace in your hearts," second, "speaking to yourselves," and thirdly, "making melody in your heart". This instruction from Paul is simple enough and is self explanatory. Paul is teaching how the believer should maintain an attitude of gratitude. When you love the Lord and when you are grateful for all He has done, this is the manifested disposition of the heart. Joy rises up and the overflow can be expressed through singing and having a melodious heart. In the Old Testament, David stated it this way:

> "My heart is inditing a good matter: I speak of the things which
> I have made touching the king: my tongue is the pen of a ready writer."
> (Psalm 45:1b)

The Hebrew word translated as "inditing" (7370) means "to gush". When your spirit is full of God, it gushes with songs of praise and we worship through its overflow. Christians must also realize that praise is more than singing,

"I will praise thee with uprightness of heart,
when I shall have learned thy righteous judgments."
(Psalm 119:7)

"Give unto the LORD the glory due unto his name;
worship the LORD in the beauty of holiness."
(Psalm 29:2)

Again, these are serious matters. The people of God must praise God from a pure and upright heart, not just because it is the religious thing to do. I cannot say that enough about this subject. Praise and worship are wonderful when coming from the heart, but it is lying by song when it is just religious jargon.

I do not want to beat a dead horse, but how can we read the Scriptures and justify the present state of the modern Church? There are hundreds of different denominations who all claim to have the revelation of the truth. It takes an exceptional amount of carnality to justify the different theological approaches and the spiritual division individual interpretation has produced. How has this happened? It is due to the fact that we ordain leadership that is the most popular, rather than the most anointed, or we ordain business men rather than those signified by God to lead the Church. We search for the best preacher, rather than search for the person God has called and ordained for our particular city. We ordain people with gifts, rather than those anointed by God who operate in governments. Nowhere in the Bible does God ordain a person because of their gift, not once! God sets a person in a place of authority because of the individual's Kingdom government authority, not because of their gift. Each of us has spiritual gifts and we are fore-ordained for a purpose, but there is always the promise within the call before the preparation for the call, and preparation always comes before the performance of the calling. Men and women of God are called from the womb, and serve until the tomb. We are called to be with Jesus (see Mark 3:14), and to fulfill the Great Commission. We are commanded to make disciples, not to grow bigger churches (see Matthew 28:19). Remember, quality has a higher priority than quantity in God's mind. God gives some of us five talents to work with, some of us three to work with, and gives some of us only one to work with. Making disciples has always been the Lord's directive, not growing large churches with immature congregations. Many churches are immature because there are many pastors that are immature. They may have been to college or seminary but they have not matured in the ways of God. You may be trained to preach, but are you mature enough to handle the circumstances you will face as a Pastor? Most Pastors learn by trial and error. This is part of the growth process in the modern Church structure, but it only occurs because there are not many fathers in the faith to raise them up before they are sent out to lead a congregation. They have no spiritual father to guide them and to teach them, and thus, many Pastors wind up wounded, or worse. A Pastor asked me once, "Are any of us mature enough to Pastor?" The statement sounds like the question asked of Jesus in Mark 10:26, "And they were astonished out of measure, saying among themselves, Who then can be saved?" If you, as a Pastor, have not matured even one person's talents, you should reconsider your ministry priorities. The Greek word translated as "talents" means "a fixed weight or sum of money," but it originally was defined as "to weigh in a balance." Pastors and disciples are to be weighed in the balance of life. Large congregations are not an automatic sign of a dynamic church. You will discover that the larger churches have the greater level of immaturity due to the fact that it is easier for people hide. Our goal as Pastors should be to mature men and women in the Lord so they can assist us in the discipleship process. Our purpose is to be one in the faith, not splinter groups promoting our favorite doctrines and ministry approaches.

There are many different types of churches in America; nevertheless they all have the same problem. Since no one discipled them in the truth nor led them to maturity, they do not understand truth or maturity. In not understanding truth or maturity, they choose their own truth and define spiritual maturity (if they define it at all) in a non-biblical way. When there is no standard of truth for them to follow, then a law is formed within each individual's inner man. Whatever he wants, desires, or lusts for becomes his law. If he wants money, power, and place he will justify his ways, and if you are in his way, you become expendable. What is sad is these types of things are happening in the Church. Revelation 2:14 calls this the doctrine of Balaam and Jude 11 states that they, "ran greedily after the error of Balaam for reward." It's amazing what people will do for money in the name of ministry!

I have long held to the fact that there is only one truth. Truth is not a thing, it is a Person. Jesus is truth. He is the Word of God personified as the express image of God. The words "express image" (5481), found in Hebrews 1:3, are defined from the Greek word "charakter" (not misspelled). This word is where we get the English word for "character". If you have ever wondered what character means, just look at the life of Jesus. He is Character in material form. The word is also defined as "agency." The word "character" contains the idea of an engraving, or a "stamped impression", but the original idea of the word holds the notion that character is "that which cannot be moved or undone by circumstances". You are what you are and that is your character. People spiritually and morally fall because of a lack of character. Christians are not readily respected anymore. There are so many fruit loops in the Church calling their actions and attitudes spiritual, when in reality they are just flakey. The plain fact of the matter is that there are many people in the Church who have no character at all. In particular, have you ever had a brother or sister borrow something from you and find that they never return it or they bring it back to you broken? Biblical character has a different manifestation than that. Character returns borrowed items as soon as possible, or fix what they break. As one man said, "If you cannot afford to fix it, you cannot afford to borrow it!"

People in the general population of America are falling out of faith and into false religions by the hundreds of thousands. Why, because pseudo-men and women of God have compromised the message, changed the message, and corrupted the message of the Gospel. The good news was the Gospel of the Kingdom of God, is the Gospel of the Kingdom of God, and always will be the

Gospel of the Kingdom of God. It is the Gospel Jesus proclaimed, though religious piety and rebellion have never adhered to, nor accepted it. Jesus' Gospel is about the dominion of God that is found in the heart of the believer (see Luke 17:21). This Kingdom of God's dominion is supposed to be in all of us who believe in Jesus Christ as Savior. Who rules your life and consciousness? If God does, integrity and character will be found and manifested from the inside out. If it is not, we have a problem, don't we. It is not hard to see the Kingdom when you are truly born again. An easier way to understand the Kingdom is by studying the Greek word "basileia" (932). It comes from the Greek root word that means the "foundation of power." The Kingdom of God is the dominion of God (i.e., the foundation of His power within us). Who rules you? Do you accept the Word of God as your final authority, or do you have another source of truth?

Again, history has become many individuals source of truth. They view the Christian experience as a part of truth that is manifested in the social norm. As the social norm changes, so does their religion. They believe whatever was Christian a hundred years ago has no relevance to us now. Others view denominational interpretation as their source of truth. Whatever their denomination declares as true and relevant is all they care to teach. The Bible is the basis of our Christian faith and the only source of truth for the Christian. The Bible is truth that has endured for more than four thousand years. Many have tried to prove that the Bible has errors, yet time and time again they have found that the Bible was right after all.

The failures of immaturity are twofold. First, our spiritual fathers did not teach us foundational truths, and since we did not know them, we did not incorporate them into our spiritual administration. This has caused many Pastors to overlook these basic foundations in the people they pastor. Since they do not understand what Church leadership was created for, they are not maturity minded; they are ministry minded. Most people in the ministry say that they were called to preach, as though preaching is all you are supposed to do. Ephesians 4:11-32 gives you a good over view of the ministry's responsibility. Second, the cycle of faith that matures believers has been broken. Since maturity is not handed down by osmosis, each untrained generation spiritually declines into a lesser mature state of being than the previous. Satan has duped us by working immorality into our culture in twenty to thirty year cycles. If we do not apprentice our children in the ways of God, they will not know the ways of God, they will not train their children in the ways of God, and their children will not understand God, nor will they know God, or the things of Gospel. The standard has been removed in America. When laws took the Ten Commandments off the walls of our public schools, and when God was not allowed in the classroom (whether it be through prayer or influence), and laws removed correction and discipline from the family and transferred it to the State, it is no wonder that children are being murdered in our schools today. When they removed God, they removed every moral governor. The schools became places where rebellion could brood, and everyone does what is right in their own eyes. This rebellion is expanding and decadence is increasing with every passing decade. Drugs and sexual misconduct are out of control, and the best the world has to offer is condoms. There have been more killings on public campuses in recent years, and they are growing in intensity and in number. Ninety percent of Christians have been educated in the public school system. They are trained in the world, by the world, and it is no wonder Christians have incorporated worldly concepts into their ministries and church programs. These worldly attitudes and beliefs are brought into the Church and mingled with perceived Christian doctrine. Over the past fifty years the Church has been overpowered by this lawlessness. Where there is no law, there can be no liberty. Jesus has given us eternal life, but there can be no eternal life in us without His truth. The remnant people see and understand this reality. It is time to rise up and declare "enough!"

> "Men are qualified for civil liberty in exact proportion
> to their disposition to put moral chains on their own appetites.
> Society cannot exist unless a controlling power upon
> the will and appetite be placed somewhere, and the less of it
> there is within, the more there is without. It is ordained in the
> eternal constitution of things that men of intemperate minds
> cannot be free. Their passions forge their fetters."
> (Edmund Burke)

The modern progressive thought is that you cannot legislate morality. We must govern our passions and control ourselves. Edmond Burke said it well, "the less of it there is within, the more there is without." When people are being taught self-control, this equates into the less control our society will need to legislate. Christians must mature and deal with doctrinal differences if we are to overcome this onslaught. Remember, what does it profit a man if he gains the whole world, but loses his own soul? It is time for Christians to get off their complacency and deal with these issues. The Body of Christ has become so fickle that every time some terrorist event takes place on the world scene, Christians run, duck, and operate in fear. Y2K had Christians hoarding and making a mockery of faith in God. It is time for the Church to arise and cast off this form of worldliness. The remnant will know the difference between the true necessity for preparation in life and the hype the world makes. In the last few years I have seen the media in America propagate every kind of fear on the American public for political gain. But "wisdom is justified of her children" (see Matthew 11:19b). The remnant people have faith, vision, and understand how to prepare for the future because they are overcomers who flow in the clarity of the Holy Spirit.

The Spirit of Christ and Epichoregeo

> "God, who at sundry times and in divers
> manners spake in time past unto the fathers
> by the prophets hath in these
> last days spoken unto us by his Son,
> whom he hath appointed heir of all things,
> by whom also he made the worlds."
> (Hebrews 1:1-2)

"For the prophecy came not in old time by the will of man: but
holy men of God spake as they were moved by the Holy Ghost."
(2 Peter 1:21)

"Searching what, or what manner of time the Spirit of Christ
which was in them did signify, when it testified beforehand the
sufferings of Christ, and the glory that should follow."
(1 Peter 1:11)

One of the most basic doctrines in Christianity can be found in the statement "the Spirit of Christ". As stated before, the remnant Church knows how to hear God. It is the Spirit of Christ within us that teaches us and leads us. Believers have the Holy Spirit in them and Peter says the Holy Spirit "searches" (2045) out two things in every situation. The Spirit of Christ not only searches (investigates) "the what" (5101) in a matter, but also "the what manner of time" (4169/2440) that something will/should occur. The word "what" and the statement "what manner of time" are describing the Spirit's direction within us that declares Who He is, what He wants to accomplish in us, and the appointed time of His work in us. The word translated as "time" in the above passage is the Greek word "kairos". There are two basic words for time found in the original language of the New Testament; they are "kairos" (2540) and "chromos" (5550). Kairos time is a fixed time or special occasion, an appointed time, while chronos time is the chronology or space of time needed to accomplish a task. The manner of time found here is the kairos time (i.e., appointed time) the Spirit of Christ has determined for something to occur. Men of old (i.e., men of God) were "moved" (5342) by the Spirit of Christ to understand the times and the seasons (see 1 Chronicles 12:32 and Hebrews 1:1-2). The Bible states that these men "commanded all their brethren" because they knew what to do and when to do it in every situation. These types of men were called the "sons of Issachar" and in Genesis 49:14-15, Israel (Jacob) prophesied over them declaring that they have two burdens to bear. These burdens are rest and service. These types of prophets understand many kinds of events that the Church is experiencing. People are to be led into rest and they should rest in Christ as they serve one another. The Spirit of Christ is in these prophets revealing the "what" the Church should do as well as the "what manner of time" the Church should do it in. The Spirit of Christ is continuously moving the Church in specific directions and purposes even when overshadowing events cloud the Body's vision. This divine guidance is called "epichoregeo" in the original language of the New Testament. This Greek word "epichoregeo" (2023) gives us some wonderful insight into the heart and ways of God, especially when trying to figure out what to do in certain situations. The word is used in various applications and is translated in the New Testament as the word "add" in 2 Peter 1:5, "ministereth" in 2 Corinthians 9:10 and Galatians 3:5, "ministered unto" in 2 Peter 1:11, and also as the word "nourishment" in Colossians 2:19. The word is derived from the preposition "epi" (1909) and the word "choregeo" (5524). Epi is kin to the English word epic and accomplishes the thought of an overriding or overshadowing purpose, like an epic event. It is defined in the Strong's Concordance and has the meaning of a "superimposition (of time, place, order, etc.), as a relation of distribution". This distribution carries the design of being over or upon someone or something. It is also defined as "the act of dividing (something) among a number (of people); dealing in parts or portions". Therefore the word "epi" is relaying the thought that "the Spirit has an overriding presence that distributes a predetermined purpose upon us". The word "choregeo" is where we get the English word choreographing. It means "to supply or furnish abundantly", and also carries the notion "to procure and supply all things necessary to fit out a chorus" (i.e., to supply in abundance). The word "epichoregeo" therefore can be defined as "to supply a preplanned choreographed event in abundance". It can be literally defined "to completely supply, to totally furnish with, or to fully present to someone, the distribution of a predetermined plan and purpose". In other words, the Spirit of Christ has a prearranged plan that He is accomplishing every day in a believer's life, and will without fail give the revelation of what He is presently doing in the Church and how long it will take Him to do it. He is affecting the local Body and the individual believer's life in order to produce His predetermined ordained purpose, so we can be like Christ. That is why we call ourselves Christians, because we want to be like Christ. When you find resistance to this God formed goal and action, you have just touched the spirit of anti-Christ (see chapter 6 – "The spirit of anti-Christ" for more info on this spiritual influence). All of the Holy Spirit's efforts to complete His purpose in us have a determined short term goal. Moreover, each of us has a specific status in His purpose. This may seem simple enough to recognize, but when we view epichoregeo in the context of the Scriptures, it gives us an understanding of God's inner working that is revolutionary. One of God's primary goals is to produce a qualified people who walk in and by the Spirit and who will accomplish His purpose in the last days, this is the remnant Church. These people are also called "the sons of God" in Romans 8:14. When the Spirit's working is seen in light of the parables of the Kingdom (see Matthew 13, Mark 4:1-32, and Luke 8:4-18), we should be aware that He is working in the good ground of our lives, even without our knowledge at times, and is orchestrating results that produce a harvest of 30, 60, and even 100 fold.

> "Now he that ministereth seed to the sower both minister
> bread for your food, and multiply your seed sown,
> an increase the fruits of your righteousness."
> (2 Corinthians 9:1)

In our review of the Scriptures where epichoregeo is used, we will discover how the Spirit of Christ is working in us. The common interpretation of 2 Corinthians 9:1 focuses on the aspect of money. Most of my Christian life I have heard this passage preached in relation to giving money to the Church and ministries. Many ministers and ministries use this verse preaching if you give a "seed faith offering" then God will bless you for it. If we would take the time to read 2 Corinthians, chapters eight and nine, we would discover the offering is an offering of righteousness, not money. Righteousness is defined as "a right standing with God", but can be better understood as "having access to God", and is our ability to stand before God's presence (see Romans 5:17). Many define righteousness as a right standing (i.e., I have a right to stand before God the Father) because Jesus has given me access to the throne room by His sacrifice. The New Testament teaches that we have access to God by the redemptive sacrifice of Jesus on the cross. It is by grace that we are allowed into the throne room of the Father, therefore the remnant should be viewed in light of this. The word "grace" is most often interpreted as being God's unmerited and unearned favor, but the translation of the Greek word "charis" (5485) is defined in the Greek language as "graciousness (as gratifying), of manner or act, especially the divine influence upon the heart, and its reflection in the life". This is what grace is, the influence of God on our lives. We would normally call this the anointing in many Christian circles. The word "anointing/unction" (5545-1 John 2:20 and 27) is defined in the Hebrews language "to smear," but in the New Testament means "a special endowment". When we see that grace is an expression of the anointing our Lord bestows upon the believer, we can better understand the power of the Spirit of Christ in our lives. If we would, for the sake of simplicity, use the word anointing, in place of the word grace in 2 Corinthians 8-9, one would understand what epichoregeo (God's prearranged plan) the Lord has determined for us. In 2 Corinthians 8:1 the word "wit" should be understood as "to make known." Paul is stating he wants you to know about the anointing the Lord has given to the churches. In verse four, he uses the Greek word "charis" (grace), but it is translated as the word "gift" in the King James Bible. This anointing is the gift that brings "the fellowship of the ministering to the saints" (verse four). Paul later expresses in verses six and seven that this anointing needs to be finished in us in order for us to abound in faith, utterance, knowledge, and diligence. His purpose is for "equality" in the Body of Christ (verse fourteen). This "equality" is not financial, but spiritual (verse twelve). The Lord deals with us according to the anointing that we have, not according to what we do not have. The Lord wants us all to grow up equally, and this declaration continues as Paul explains why certain men were chosen to travel with him to the churches. The "impartation" (i.e., the distribution) from these leaders was necessary in the preparation of the believer's maturity (see 2 Corinthians 8:16--9:7). The bounty Paul is talking about is the bountiful anointing we are to have for our "sufficiency for every good work." The sower has sown the seed of righteousness (i.e., the Word of God), not dollars. This is why Paul explains that the fruit of righteousness is increased (see 2 Corinthians 9:10), because he knows every "seed produces after its own kind" (see Genesis 1). This impartation is called a distribution in 2 Corinthians 9:13. The Greek word translated as "distribution" is "koinonia" (2842), the same Greek word translated as communion and fellowship throughout the New Testament. These men had come to have communion with the churches. Not the traditional ordinance of bread and wine but the sharing which one has in anything (it can be better understood to mean "joint participation"). The context of the passage stands firm in this interpretation. When Paul, in 2 Corinthians 10, deals with the notion of the "measure of rule", he wanted the Corinthians to know that he would not boast in another man's line of things; since the apostolic leaders had established true communion in the Church. Again, this communion was more than the ordinance; it was the predetermined fellowship Christ had purposed for us to live in. In view of the fact that the apostles fathered the churches in this simple truth, there could be no mistake in understanding the purpose the Lord. Epichoregeo then, having been predetermined by the Spirit of Christ in each community, was established to produce a unified Body. The Greek word translated as "messengers" in 2 Corinthians 8:23 is the word "apostolos" (652), of which Titus was one. God, the Father, uses apostolic ministry to produce this oneness. The Spirit of Christ is continuously building the remnant in these last days with this in mind. The mind of Christ must be imparted into us so we think in common (i.e., in communion with Jesus' purpose). Paul told them to show the proof of their love. The ministering of the "seed" (4690) spoken of in 2 Corinthians 9:10 is the epichoregeo of the seed of God's predetermined plan for believers and is to bring an increase in the anointing, so the communion and unity of being one in Christ could be fulfilled (see John 17). Again, I am not speaking of the ordinance of communion, but the fellowship of communion.

Let me ask a question. Why are we commanded to develop the fruit of the Spirit? Is it just to have the fruit or would you consider that we need the fruit of the Spirit in order for the people of God to be one in faith? Without the fruit of the Spirit it is virtually impossible for different people to relate to each other, to become one in faith, and to have a singleness of heart and mind. We must develop the fruit of the Spirit in order for us to tolerate each other, if I may. At times, it takes a lot of grace to have unifying fellowship in the local church. Carnal believers are called babes in the Scriptures because they are unskilled in the word of righteousness (see Hebrews 5:13). These babes are inexperienced with righteousness, so the fruit of the Spirit does not manifest in their lives. They find it difficult to be united with other people who "get on their nerves". We all get on each others last nerve every once in a while, but we should be mature enough to handle it and remain one in Spirit. When we look at the Greek word translated as "fruits" (1081), we should know that it comes from a root word that can be translated by the English word "choice". The Holy Spirit gives us the choice to love, the choice to have joy, the choice to be at peace, the choice to be longsuffering, good, gentle, temperate, meek, and the choice to be full of faith. Babes do not make the right choices. Why? Babes do not have their soul (their mind, will, and temperament) under control (see Foundations chapter 15), and they do not have the spiritual experience to manage controversy. They are like the ones Jesus spoke of in the parable of the sower. These have no root of the Kingdom deep enough to govern their emotions, so by and by they are offended (see Matthew 13:21). 2 Corinthians 9:10 also reveals that God's epic plan is for the believers to increase in their experience of adding the fruits of righteousness to their lives. This fruit of righteousness is called "quietness and assurance" in Isaiah 32:17, and is shown to create "sincerity" (1506), and is said to be "inoffensive" (677) in Philippians 1:10-11. Another aspect about fruit can be found in John 15:4-5. One will never produce fruit if they do not abide in the vine. James 3:18, also states,

"And the fruit of righteousness is sown in peace of them that make peace."

Peace thus becomes the principle factor and is the evidence of spiritual growth and maturity. Peter, in Galatians 2, was confronted by Paul, because Peter separated himself from the Gentile believers when a prominent Jew came into the fellowship that was sent from James. Peter's ego or his insecurity caused him to separate himself and leave the assembling of the Body. This is why Paul said, "I do not frustrate the grace (anointing) of God," in verse twenty-one. The anointing is the tie that binds. Since the epichoregeo of the Spirit of Christ is to bring the Body together as one, anything that hinders that union is sin and part of the spirit of anti-Christ. Peter was to be blamed because his example of communion was not godly. He failed in the purpose of God's epichoregeo at this point in his maturity. His position caused many of the believers to err from the truth concerning the communion of all Christians, even in the relationship between the Jews and the Gentiles. In Paul's understanding, the epichoregeo had been breached.

"He therefore that ministers to you the Spirit,
and works miracles among you."
(Galatians 3:5)

"And not holding the Head, from which all the
body by joints and bands having nourishment
ministered, and knit together, increaseth
with the increase of God."
(Colossians 2:19)

These verses were also written with the knowledge of God's Epic Plan. The superimposition of the Spirit of Christ will outweigh any decision that was contrary to it. In Galatians 3:5, we see the epichoregeo of the Spirit as it pertains to "ministering in the Spirit". It is the ministering to you in the Spirit that is necessary. This is why I say it is the ministers who are at fault when parishioners are continuously weak in their congregations. No minister can be responsible for the babes in his congregation, especially when the babes are rebellious and refuse to grow up. But babes are a part of God's Divine Plan (see 1 Corinthians 12:23-26) and are to be cared for. If they remain as immature children for years while attending the same local church, then their attendance under that spiritual administration has to be judged. There are a few things that cause babes to remain stagnant. First, the minister is not anointed, second, that so called babe has never been saved, or third that babe is a spoiled brat. As we minister the Gospel and minister the Spirit of God to the congregation, we must also minister the spiritual move of God as well. The book of Galatians tells us that the epichoregeo of God's design is ministered by faith and not by the law. You cannot force the Spirit on people, they must respond to Him or He will never affect them. If you try to produce maturity by the law, your work will be in vain. Many pastors try to control people through Scriptural manipulation. Doctrines are created to impose specific denominational norms on people, forcing them to comply with the denominational tradition, or be expelled from the local church. This is how denominationalism has taken control in many people's lives. The Scripture teaches us that maturity or spiritual completion cannot come by the law. This is why Colossians 2:19 uncovers the simple wisdom and reality of the epichoregeo of God by showing that the Body of Christ, by joints and bands (i.e., by the fellowship of relationships) have the "nourishment" (epichoregeo) to be knit together and to increase with the increase of God. Just because a congregation increases in size does not mean that it has grown and matured. Many churches are full of spiritual babes because the purpose of God's design is not being fulfilled. Our unity is more important to God than our church programs. Churches have ministry after ministry, activity after activity, and program after program, but the Body is not being joined together and connected, it is just being added to. Many Christians get involved in gossip, backbiting, and being busy bodies so strife does not cease in the Church. Paul says in Colossians 2:20-23 that many are still involved in "touch not, taste not, and handle not" concepts. This is due to so many individuals who believe sin is touching the wrong things, tasting the wrong things, and handling the wrong things. This is a law mentality; trying to make people submit, rather than leading them in the way they should go and the work that they must do. Sin is separation from God and separation from the Body of Christ. Jesus defined the greatest commandment as to love God and to love God's people. Satan, in the beginning, separated himself from God, and then he separated himself from his place in God. Many separate from the Body of Christ because they do not like what another touches, tastes, or handles. Sin is present when you allow your meat (lifestyle) to divide (see Romans 14:20). It is not the meat that is sin, but it is the one who sins with the meat that God has a problem with. Jesus said it is what comes out of you that defiles you, because of the meat, that is sin (see Matthew 15:11). When I was a teenager, it was common for many individuals to smoke outside the Church before and after a service. Smoking wasn't thought of as sin in that congregation, but as a bad example, that is, if it was thought of at all in a negative way. Today smoking is not politically correct so we call it sin. The question is simple, why wasn't smoking dealt with as a sin in the 1960's? People accepted it and did not think of smoking as a sin back then. In the same line of thinking, many churches thought it was a sin for women to wear pants back then, yet today it is as common as water for women to wear pants in most of today's Churches. Back then, you would not dare wear a pair of shorts to church on Sunday morning, yet today many of us are casual and no one thinks it is a big deal. The real issue is that Satan will use anything to bring division and separation to the Body of Christ. He intends to destroy our koinonia (fellowship), so he propagates various traditions in order to manipulate and divide. Satanic influence can remain in our lives for years, even after we have been born again and Spirit filled. When we do not recognize that Satan's influence is sometimes both direct and indirect, he gains an advantage over us in his attack. God named him Lucifer (pride), Satan (the accuser of the brethren), the Devil (a deceiver), and the Dragon (a devourer) for a reason. He manifests all of those characteristics. One other thing to consider is that the Greek word translated as the English word "name" (3686) in the New Testament means to be in the "authority, character, likeness, and representation" of the one whose name you are using. When Jesus is our Lord we are commanded to live in and under His authority, character, likeness, and we are to represent Him. When you are full of pride, accuse people, deceive people, or devour people, guess who you are representing then? That is what is meant by the phrase "in His name." When satanic forces operate, they function in the spirit of the anti-Christ, and we find people who operate in their name in every place and town in America and all over the world. This is the opposite of the Spirit of Christ. Demonic influence does not operate singularly, and we must realize that it is a strategic attack when Satan manipulates our unity. These demonic forces know you are aware and able to sense them so they work in the shadows of light. I have witnessed the systematic exploitation demons produce through the spirit of the anti-Christ in individuals and in groups of people. I have watched Christians speak very hatefully about each other. The nature they reflect is the nature of our enemy and is the spirit of error (see 1 John 4:1-6). It is also the abomination of desolation when the people of God allow Satan to sit on the throne of their heart. I have witnessed Spirit filled, tongue talkers spew the most hateful things you have ever heard out of their mouths. Many see the personified anti-Christ as a person in our future, but we must realize he is a right now enemy! John said the spirit of anti-Christ had already started to work 2000 years ago. Satan's influence is two-fold, first, his effect is on the soul and on the body, and second, he is working his deception so that we will defile our spirit. In other words, Satan is able to affect our spirit through the corruption of the soul, and he will use the symptoms of the body to affect our state of being. When Satan attacks the soul and body, his purpose is to degrade or defile the spirit of the person. This is why he uses sickness in his plan. Sickness weakens our resistance physically and spiritually. That is why it is easier to fall into sin when you are tired or not feeling good. Whatever you focus on enhances or hinders your emotional state.

> "And Jesus said, Are ye also yet without understanding?
> Do not ye yet understand, that whatsoever
> entereth in at the mouth goeth into the belly,
> and it is cast unto the draught?
> But those things which proceed out of the mouth,
> come forth from thy heart; and they defile the man.
> For out of the heart proceeds
> evil thoughts, murders, adulteries, fornications,
> thefts, false witnesses, blasphemies: These are the things
> which defile a man: but to eat with unwashen hands defile not a man."
> (Matthew 15:16-20)

Jesus made the point clearly. There is to be no doubt in the matter. It is not what goes into the man that defiles him, but that which comes out of him that is sin. Satan uses ideas of piety and self righteousness to produce pride within an individual. When pride is introduced, Satan can then affect a person's heart so that they become haughty. Pride produces a fall, and a haughty spirit, destruction. As stated before, Satan's influence can directly or indirectly affect you. Someone can tell you a lie when you are a child and because you do not realize the lie was demonically influenced, you still believe the lie when you are forty or fifty. If a demonic spirit is manipulating and lying to you and you are too busy to study the Word of God on the subject, you will be anchored in the lie. Direct influence occurs when demonic manipulation directly affects you. Indirect demonic influence occurs when demons influence someone who influences you, like peer pressure. When Paul wrote to the Colossians he made the point, do not let any man be spoiled through philosophy and vain deceit. If you are being demonically influenced, you will not hold the Head (Jesus) correctly (see Colossians 2:19). His name may be on your lips, but His character will not be in your heart. Satan can then hinder God's plan for you and the epichoregeo of God is thus hindered as well.

> "And beside this, giving all diligence, add to your faith virtue;
> and to virtue knowledge; And to knowledge temperance;
> and to temperance patience; and to patience godliness;

> And to godliness brotherly kindness; and to brotherly kindness charity.
> For if these things be in you, and abound,
> they make you that ye shall neither be barren nor unfruitful
> in the knowledge of our Lord Jesus Christ."
> (2 Peter 1:5-8)

In 1 Peter 1:5 the word epichoregeo is used to describe part of the process of maturation. Peter uses the statement, "add to your faith". The word epichoregeo is translated as the word "add" and is establishing the fact that we are to have virtue added to our faith before we focus on knowledge. Virtue has priority over knowledge in God's divine plan. It is first in order and place after faith. God wants us to prosper. Even the apostle John says in 3 John 2

> "Beloved, I wish above all things that thou
> mayest prosper and be in health, even as thy soul prospers."

Virtue in the first century Church was understood to have a three-fold manifestation in someone's life. It manifested spiritually, it manifested in one's temperament, and it could be seen physically. Virtue is defined as "excellence or manliness" in the Strong's Concordance. One can compare virtue in terms such as the difference between a husbandman, as compared to a keeper of the vineyard, or a horseman as compared to a rider, or even in the difference between clean and unclean dietary animals. The virtuous husbandman is an owner who has a vested interest in his garden's production and health. He knows about the garden and has concern for its care. The keeper of the vineyard who lacks virtue is one who just works for the husbandman. He is one who has no interest in the garden, per se, but is most concerned with his pay. The garden is how he makes a living, nothing more, and nothing less. Job 7:2 reveals that the hirelings look for the "shadow and the reward of his work" (i.e., the shade and the wage). God's epichoregeo has determined that His divine nature is to manifest in us, or the knowledge we are taught will be perverted. When there is no virtue, there are no lasting changes in us. In reading John 15, we get a wonderful explanation of spiritual virtue. John 15:8 teaches us that a virtuous vine will glorify God by bearing much fruit. Virtue is also viewed as levels of skill. A horseman is a skilled equestrian, whereas a rider is someone who just gets on a horse for fun. Virtue is also like the clean animal that chews the cud and has a split hoof. These represent that virtue is like one who meditates on the nourishment of God and relates it to his life repeatedly, rightly dividing the word of truth. When an animal has a split hoof it represents the ability to rightly divide the word. Therefore, if you chew the cud, but do not split the hoof, you frustrate the grace of God because you will not properly apply the truth you are commanded to walk in. If one properly discerns the truth but does not ruminate on its application, it becomes dead works. Again, virtue is the first thing we are commanded to add to our faith. The virtue of the soul is seen in the personal increase within the communion of faith. The koinonia or fellowship throughout the Body of Christ is our Romans 12:1-2 fulfillment (i.e., our becoming a living sacrifice). As we complete the task of adding virtue to the lives of believers, our churches are strengthened. When the virtue within the believer bears fruit and glorifies God, it is only then that knowledge can be added rightly, having an impact on the person, while affecting the necessary changes he needs. When knowledge is not superseded by virtue, it puffs the new believer up, and that knowledge is then channeled through the old man. It is just information without application when virtue is lacking. Virtue is our ability to do what we know, and to do what we say we will do. We must walk out our faith with fear and trembling (see Philippians 2:12).Temperance can then be added to one's knowledge and bring control to the old man as he remembers his old ways. We receive a new nature when we are saved, but our problem is that we can still remember the pleasures of the flesh. Our transformation does not happen in the blink of an eye, it is progressive and related to the degree of fruitfulness we aspire to attain. One hundred percent fruitfulness comes after the sixty, and the sixty only comes after the thirty (see Matthew 13:23). Patience is then choreographed in at this point because you will need it. Some go through great personal anguish when they do not come to the maturity that they desire. Their failures will pile up and the spirit of anti-Christ will continue his operations to divide and subdue, when one does not add patience to their walk. Godliness comes to solidify the believer as they increase in their fellowship with God and man. God stabilizes our spirit as we grow in the Body of Christ, the Church stabilizes our soul by correction and through our personal interaction, and it is the believer's responsibility to stabilize his body (see 1 Corinthians 9:27). We are responsible for our own physical being. This is why we must learn to fast, take up our cross, and follow Him. Brotherly kindness is significant at this stage because without mercy and forgiveness, the anointing will not abide, and help will not be received. The strength of love cannot be manifested without the courage to forgive all of the shortcomings we see in the lives of those around us, and the shortcoming we carry, as we walk through this life. True love is added when we are able to understand and look beyond each other's failures to become a family of God, a family of believers who have one purpose, that being to love one another and pursue unity. 2 Peter 1:11 states,

> "For so an entrance shall be ministered (epichoregeo)
> unto you abundantly into the everlasting kingdom
> of our Lord and Savior Jesus Christ."

An entrance shall be choreographed unto you for your journey of faith. And not only is the entrance ministered, it is orchestrated by the Lord every day as well. To be one in the faith is the true test of character. Anyone can be a loner, but not everyone can walk as a brother or sister in Christ's Body, the Remnant Church.

Epichoregeo is the overall operation of God the Father in the world. His plan is to bring sons and daughters into his Kingdom, to grow them up, and to send them out into the world to be salt and light. From our beginnings with Him, He trains us, strengthens our walk, and anoints us with a specific purpose. God's plan is to make us one in heart and mind, to make us a remnant people.

Chapter 3 – Foundations Discovered

Some of my terms and definitions in "Foundations" may be new to you because I use concepts and principles that I find in the original language. As you have already discovered, I use an extensive amount of the original languages in this study. I do this, because in my view, many biblical principles and terms have been so traditionalized, they have become redundant. As an example let us consider the word "discipleship". Many Christians will tell you that their church is full of disciples, thinking they can train the folks in their church from the pulpit or in a small group setting. Small groups are where Bible training is most often adequate and formal discipleship should take place, but discipleship without fathering cannot be accomplished (see 1 Corinthians 4:14-16 and Chapter 19). This study is designed to bring you back to the mind of the writer, as he was lead by the Spirit, and by defining these principles in their Scriptural context. As we dig as deeply as we can we should consider each principle and discern the original idea and purpose of the Word. We should also draw out of the well the implications and origins of each principle, which will enable the reader to discern the mind of Christ in the passages we will use throughout this course. As we continue this study of God's Word, and as we take a journey away from worldly ideology, we will also be acquainted with a central theme found in the Scriptures. Peter said for us to be established in the "present truth" (see 2 Peter 1:12). Present truth is the revelation of what God is doing at this time in history in the Church. Present truth is the truth that is at hand, and that is readily available for each of us to implement into our lives at this present time. The Scripture teaches us that we should dig out of the Word principles and doctrines that are both old and new. This is why the Holy Spirit uses two different Greeks words to describe the concept of "time" in the New Testament. As we have seen before these two words are "kairos" (2540) and "chronos" (5550). We previously learned that kairos means "the occasion or proper time of an event that God has arranged", while chronos is "the chronology of an event" (i.e., the periods or intervals of an event); generally speaking. The two show a distinction in the way God deals with us individually and with the Church as a whole. The Lord says He is waiting on the Father to fulfill all things and none of us know the time of God's completeness. The Lord has times that He is working in us for a specific purpose and He also uses periods of our life to accomplish the fullness of things. This is called "epichoregeo" in the original language of the New Testament. Remember, God doesn't live in time, we do! He is omniscient and omnipresent and from God's perspective He is with Abraham and with you at the same time.

Take time to read the New Testament through and discover what Jesus' message is. He had one goal, one purpose, and one message, the Kingdom of God. We fit into His plan, and our salvation is part of the process. The purpose (epichoregeo-2023) of God is the establishment of His Kingdom, the maturation of the Body of Christ, and the defeat of Satan in the lives of His children. We can be a part of it, or if we choose, we can pass. He is a Father that leaves the choice up to us. He is waiting for His enemies to be put under His feet. Ministry in today's Church must prepare the Body of Christ to make wise choices. The Scripture teaches us to choose life (Deuteronomy 30:19).

The Message of Jesus Christ

"To whom also he showed himself alive after
his passion by many infallible proofs,
being seen of them forty days, and
speaking of the things pertaining
to the kingdom of God."
(Acts 1:3)

"And he (Paul) went into the synagogue,
and spake boldly for the space of three months,
disputing and persuading the things
concerning the kingdom of God."
(Acts 19:8)

"From that time Jesus began to preach, and to say,
Repent: for the kingdom of heaven is at hand."
(Matthew 4:17)

"And he sent them to preach
the kingdom of God,
and to heal the sick."
(Luke 9:2)

The ministry of the Lord Jesus is seen clearly when you discover His message concerning the Kingdom of God. From his opening statements in the Gospels (see Matthew 4:17) to Revelation 11:15, Jesus founded and presented the revelation of God's Kingdom. From the Old Testament and Abraham, through the New Testament and Paul, God showed Himself to be a faithful Creator and stressed a pattern of living that would make us victorious in life. The Kingdom of God, the salvation of our soul, fathering disciples, and the six foundations are not a new theology, nor are they new interpretation of the Bible; they have just been over-looked by most of the modern Church. They are as Scriptural as the Church and as old as Adam, yet they must be revealed to us through the Spirit. Our dilemma occurs due to the extreme doctrinal division within the Body of Christ that in itself has produced a level of division only Satan could have orchestrated. We are trained and taught from so many vantage points and perspectives of spiritual doctrines that Christians have developed a carnal mindset toward one another. Worldly influences have clouded our vision of oneness, and the towers of denominational pride have been erected and fortified within the people of God. People speak of the first century Church as though they had a greater anointing than we do today and they use their denominational evidences to try to prove their own personal point of view. The weaknesses of the modern Church have transpired from disunity, not from a lack of anointing. Being anointed is the abiding power of the Holy Spirit in and on our lives. It is the presence of God within that leads and guides us. We have the same anointing available to us as the first century Church had. Ours has been hindered and weakened because of disunity, division, and strife. We have allowed denominational prejudice, selfishness, individually preferred doctrines and pride to come between us. We seek God's acts rather than his ways (see Psalm 103:7), and this continues because many believers are simply selfish. The first century Church was unified in one purpose: to spread God's Kingdom. The Body had received training from the Lord and the first apostles, and demonstrated their obedience with their lives. Their hearts were full of faith and there was no fear of death, so their boldness made the difference (see Revelation 12:11). The resurrection of Jesus was fresh and real to them. When doctrinal questions arose, (as in Acts 15), they took them to the leadership and did not allow personal interpretation or independence to cloud the issue. Although the spirit of Diotrephes was in the Church (see 3 John 9), the Apostles and the Elders knew how to handle the problems. The divided Church in today's world cannot solve the simplest issues because of these divisions. Satan has diminished our light by using our own divided heart against us. The Church cannot allow our vision to be impaired. We should know that "where there is no vision the people will perish" (see Proverbs 29:18). When the Church is without a vision, the Church's maturity will be hindered, and we will become preoccupied with the cares of this world. Personal power is stressed in so many congregations and the doctrine of personal gain has been substituted for the Gospel of the Kingdom. We have given ourselves to worldly passions and struggle in our faith because of them. We struggle not with flesh and blood, but with principalities and powers, yet we fight one another as though we have a right to! It is written that we are heavenly citizens, a city of believers within a city, the nation of God within the Nation, but many in the Church do not live as if they truly believe it. We had better be careful. Satan is orchestrating a dangerous game in our midst. Some of us have fallen into his snare already. Some of us are closer to the trap than we think, and we are so often oblivious to demonic tactics and Satanic strategy altogether. Christians know Jesus is the only way to true salvation. The modern Church has forgotten that the Kingdom of God is established with dialog and not monolog. The Church should communicate about doctrines and various interpretations of doctrines, but the problem we face is that we will not take the time to search out the Scriptures for truth that is outside our denominational influence. There are many Pastors who have never been trained in spirituals, so they are forced to learn by trial and error. Seminaries train students in various ways, but do not have a "fathering spirit" as they guide the new generations of Pastors and Church leaders. If you struggle with these tenants, study some of the subjects of controversy in the Scriptures and try to have an open discussion in your Sunday school or Bible classroom. See how far you get before you are told to "stifle it!" So often in today's Church, faith is not allowed to think. You either believe the denominational line of doctrine or get removed from that church by various means. Our journey of faith is not secular; it is a spiritual walk. These are the issues with which we must contend for and champion. Saints are distinguished in the Kingdom of God by our obedience to His will and the effectiveness their witness has on those around them, not by religiosity, carnal piety, or adherence to a pet doctrine. Ministers will be judged by the quality of God's people under their hand, not the quantity of people in their church. We must discover our foundation and return to it.

Returning to our Roots

Many ministries seem to have the discipleship process backwards. You do not establish a church and then venture into the Kingdom. Remember the Church is the people, not the building with the steeple. The Kingdom is in you (see Luke 17:21). God's rule in your life must be established first. One must establish the Kingdom in the lives of people in order to have the Church. Again, the Church is the "called out" people of God; those who live in, but are not of this world. Swallow deeply before you amen that statement. Jesus knew how to establish the Kingdom. He said, "I am the way." Jesus sought to draw men to the Father and to have them recognize the truth He proclaimed. Today people are drawn to church and not to Christ, in many instances. The Pharisees and the Sadducees were just the liberals of Jesus' day and the Romans remind me of government politicians. The liberals cry for blood and the Romans give it to them, in spite of the fact that they find no fault in the accused. Jesus continuously battled with the Pharisees and Sadducees about biblical truth and interpretation. He contended with the religious leaders about the basics of salvation, about God's plan, and about God's government, as did the prophets. The priests viewed salvation as ritualistic sacrifice while the prophets preached, "the just shall live by faith" (see Habakkuk 2:4). God is not pleased with sacrifice (see Habakkuk 2:6, Micah 6:7-8, and 1 Samuel 15:22). We shall realize that this is the same war occurring today between the "priests" and the prophets. Today the modern prophets are found in many backwoods churches, in the post-Congregationalist movement, and on talk radio. That is why so many people attend home churches. This internal Christian war is occurring just as it has in the past, but this is a different age (chronos) of contention. The Kingdom of God is still at the heart of this issue, and today conservative values are the life of the Nation. When conservative values fall, so does the Nation. As the Church gives in to liberal values, those values are spread in the Nation as well. The people of God should realize that the Church is the porter to the Nation. As goes the Church, so goes the Nation. When the Church votes for liberalism it porters degradation into the Nation which then leads to the downfall of that society. Personal property rights diminish, and personal freedom declines when the Church moves away from conservative values. We find in today's world those who want instant gratification, and it is they who will destroy in a few years what has taken over 200 years for the Nation to accomplish. This is exactly how Rome fell. People learned to vote for the one who promised the most. Those who will not work for bread, expect those who do work to give to them bread, cars, houses, or whatever their soul desires. Charity is a good thing, but charity to those who refuse to improve their state is a waste of effort. Jesus teaches us to give to the poor, but He also tells us that if you do not work you will not eat. You cannot eradicate poverty by giving to the poor. Poverty is a state of mind. In Christ's Kingdom, we renew the mind of the person in order for him or her to see themselves as blessed. Satisfaction is also a state of mind. You will never be satisfied if you are looking at how much others have compared to how much you have. The Bible says it is not wise to compare ourselves among ourselves. I live in a part of Texas where some ranches are as large as 100,000 acres. I do not see those ranchers as greedy because they have a large ranch. I see an opportunity for my family to increase through hard work and smart investing. Buy something small, fix it up and sell it for a profit. If I want more acreage all I have to do is sell what I have and start over again. "I can do all things through Christ who strengthens me." Envy is not acceptable in the Christian life. We must put all that behind us as faithful and satisfied believers. It is God's Kingdom that we pursue, and we should be grateful for everything He blesses us with. I am blessed with my place in life. We must be satisfied with what we have attained in our few years on this earth, although we press on to better our families and ourselves. When Christians work together for the increase of each other, they help themselves. That is the Kingdom way; that is God's Way for us to live.

Discovering God's Kingdom and its Purpose

The word "kingdom(s)" is used 163 times in the Gospels and in conjunction with this, the word "disciple(s)" is used 272 times in the Gospels, while the word "church" is only used on two occasions in the four Gospels. This shows Jesus' emphasis. When we consider the plan and purpose of God, we must recognize the difference between the goal of building a church and the commission of building God's Kingdom. Jesus set out to establish God's Kingdom. How did He go about this plan? He worked in the lives of people through discipleship. It was with disciples that the Church came forth. It was with disciples, who had God's Kingdom established within them that changed that ancient world. The Kingdom process always begins with making disciples, and something to know is that disciples are made, while converts are birthed. A lesson for all of us is you must develop what you birth. People who do not develop their children throughout their childhood and youth only produce under-developed adults, or immature adults. Ministers must strive to develop this area of their ministry. Many ministers do not know how to handle the spiritually immature, because no one trained them in these issues. When I was in Bible College I was told by my professors to refer the "hard cases" to a psychologist. Liberalism has destroyed the higher educational system in this country, especially the Christian higher educational system. Students are not taught the foundations of history, and they therefore do not know how to see the future of their decisions. In the Church, this is a deathblow. When people are taught that when you are good, God blesses you; this undermines many of the basic tenants of Christian faith. Jesus taught us that we would suffer persecution, and persecution comes in many forms. Jesus was hated and despised and taught us to expect the same. If you do not want to be persecuted, you should rethink your Christianity. You will be persecuted if you follow the ways of God unless you compromise your Christian core values. There are too many compromisers who wear the title 'Christian'. So many compromisers that true Christian living is becoming a thing of the past. Disciples have the character to overcome any obstacle. Disciples are what the modern Church is in great need of.

> "Go ye therefore, and make disciples of all peoples...Teaching them
> to observe all things whatsoever I have commanded you."
> (Matthew 28:19)

Matthew said "go", with the purpose and vision of making disciples and to teach them to "observe" (5083) all of the things Jesus commanded. (To observe means "to watch and guard from loss or injury"). The idea is to keep something protected like a fortress keeps the enemy at bay. Jesus said "we are to love God with all our heart and to love one another". These two commandments are one in the same and must be kept. We are to be one in Him and one with each other in the faith. All teachings and doctrines must be sifted through these commandments. Consider this question: "what is your witness?" The question is not what do you believe, but what does your life say about your faith in God? What you actually believe is how you will live. The issue is "what witness do you declare by your life and your way of living?" Each of us will either represent the Lord by walking in His ways, or we will substitute another way in its place. There is a way that seems right to a man, but the end does not produce the fruit of the Spirit. Every way of a man seems right in his own eyes, but the Lord ponders the heart.

> "And why call ye me, Lord, Lord,
> and do not the things which I say?"
> (Luke 6:46)

We must discover the foundation of God, and apply God's principles to our life. These principles of the doctrines of Christ are the stabilizing factors of the Christian experience. We do not need a Baptist, Methodist, Pentecostal, or charismatic doctrine. We only need Jesus' doctrine. These foundational doctrines of Christ, along with an understanding of the salvation of the soul of man, the Kingdom of God, and the process of making disciples must be reintroduced into the Church. It is only with these foundational truths in place that a believer will be able to have his spiritual house built and in order. All instruction must come from these roots. The writer of the book of Hebrews understood this fact. This is why he wrote that those who did not apply this truth had to be "re-trained" (see Hebrews 5:12). He was aware that spiritual babes are "unskillful (i.e., inexperienced) in righteous living". The beginning of wisdom is the fear of the Lord (see Proverbs 9:10). The beginning of maturity is discovering these foundations and applying them to our life. Some believe these foundations are talking about some ancient Jewish doctrine. If that theology is true, why are they called the "principles of the doctrines of Christ?" Hebrews 6:1 says that one must complete these principles before they can go on to perfection (maturity or completeness). These are the milk of Christ's doctrine. These principles are "baby food."

Without a foundation of righteousness you will never be able to live securely in Christ! Without a foundation of faith toward God, one cannot accomplish the task of living in this world free from fear, insecurity, and rejection. Faith toward God is the right kind of faith. It is not faith in the Church, faith in the minister, or faith in oneself; it is faith "toward" God. God is the object of this kind of faith, and God is the receiver of this kind of faith. People have faith in many things, but their faith has no value or manifestation because God is not the focus or aim of their faith. Many have faith to receive from God, but their faith is focused on what they receive, rather than on the Giver. Many in today's world expect the blessings of God regardless of how they live. We have faith for the blessing, many times more than faith toward the One who blesses.

Understanding the Foundation

"Whosoever comes to me, and hears my sayings, and does them,
I will show you to whom he is like: He is like a man which built a house,
And digged deep, and laid the foundation on a rock:
And when the flood arose, the stream beat vehemently upon the house,
and could not shake it: for it was founded upon a rock."
(Luke 6:47-48)

Jesus originated the process of founding someone. Luke used the Greek word "bathuno" (900), translated as the word "deep" in the above passage to describe the procedure of establishing a believer on the Rock of Jesus Christ. The Greek word means "to deepen," but comes from the root meaning to "profound" (i.e., to have a basis or a foundation). The word carries the idea of having a depth of purity by un-layering the sedimentary strata that is produced in our lives as we live in this fallen world. These environmental strata of insecurity, rejection, religious notion, worldliness, and demonic influence produce layers of weakness that must be removed before the believer can stand secure on the Rock. Hence, digging deep is like taking a bath (bathuno); one washes the dirt of the world away. The end result is an unfettered basis of pure Christian stability.

"Therefore leaving the principles of the doctrine of Christ, let us go on
unto perfection; not laying again the foundation of
repentance from dead works,
and of faith toward God,
of the doctrine of baptisms,
and the laying on of hands,
and of the resurrection of the dead,
and of eternal judgment."
(Hebrews 6:1-2)

The main thrust of the Church over the past few centuries has been evangelism. This revival has been ongoing for over 600 years and has produced a diverse Church Body throughout the world. The Reformation and evangelism are part of God's plan and design, but we have been narrow-minded in believing that evangelism is all encompassing in the complete restoration of man to God. Evangelism is but a phase (chronos) in the restoration of spiritual things. As this chronology and the focus of the modern Church in ministry continue, many congregations have failed in their ability to develop a more mature Church from these masses. The correction necessary in this present move of God is simply to rearrange our spiritual emphasis. We should continue to evangelize, but also disciple those that are birthed. If we do not train the Body of Christ, it will continue to divide. As stated, the purpose of the foundational principles listed in Hebrews 6:1-2 is to mold believers so that they will become increasingly able to overcome the modern idealism of the world, and for them to mature as witnesses of Jesus Christ. These witnesses are those who not only have experienced salvation, but have also grown unto perfection. Paul spoke of this matter in 1 Corinthians 15:34 when he said,

> "Awake to righteousness, and sin not;
> for some have not the knowledge of God:
> I speak this to your shame."

Paul is discussing the lack of understanding in God's people toward the resurrection, one of the foundational principles. He uses the Greek word "agnosia" (56) which is translated as the phrase "have not the knowledge". Much of today's phraseology uses the concept of agnostics to represent those who are not born again, yet Paul uses the term for the Corinthians who do not understand the God they serve. The true meaning of the word is that they were lacking the experience of God. They were ever learning, but not able to come to the knowledge of the truth. This produced a form of godliness that was carnal in its nature (see 2 Timothy 3:5 & 7), and was not the nature Paul expected them to have. Today, there seems to be a repeat of this problem. With the ever-increasing Church population, there is less time devoted to discipleship and more emphasis is placed on the quantity of church membership, rather than the quality of the church member. Quality takes time, spiritual fathering, and effort. Preaching and Sunday school alone will not accomplish the quality of Christian life that is so desperately needed in our present world. Carnal people can only reproduce carnal people. Because the modern emphasis is on quantity, the modern Church has been diminished in its glory. We have been tempered with the worldly concept of mass production. Ichabod is a word that describes the production of a carnal ministry. The name "Ichabod" (1 Samuel 4:21) does not mean someone has lost his glory; it means someone is without glory. Ichabod never had any glory, and neither does carnal ministry. Ezekiel 16 contains a prophecy relating to the Church of the last days. Ezekiel prophesied that there would be a degenerative fall that would occur in the Church just as Paul describes a "falling away" in 2 Thessalonians. He said the Church would become worse than a whore because its emphasis was on building buildings (eminent places) "at the head of every way," and on every prominent street.

Strong words from Ezekiel who saw that this fall would cause the Church to look to its own glory, rather than seek after the glory God gives. He stated,

> "That thou hast also built unto thee an eminent place, and hast made
> thee a high place in every street. Thou hast built thy high place
> at every head of the way, and hast made thy beauty to be abhorred,
> and hast opened thy feet to every one that passed by,
> and multiplied thy whoredoms."
> (Ezekiel 16:24-26)

The Church has a responsibility to her Husband just as a wife in a natural realm is has responsibility to her husband. To whom much is given, much is also required. God has called us to maturity. The Greek word translated as "perfection" in Hebrews 6:1 is "teleiotes" (5047). Its definition is "to be in the state of completeness." It is derived from "teleios" (5046) which means "to be complete in various applications of labor, growth, and mental and moral character." The primitive root form of the word, "telos" (5056), means "to set out for a definite point or goal; the point aimed at as a limit (i.e., by implication, the conclusion of an act or state of being)." This is the issue the writer of Hebrews is addressing in chapter five. What is the individual's state of being when a ministry is finished working on them? The modern ideology is that none of us will be finished until we get to heaven. This is a cop-out. There is a conclusion to the process of becoming a Christian. When individuals have not progressed in their faith toward a definite goal of maturity, they have a need to be retrained and re-discipled. Peter said to receive "the end of your faith, even the salvation of our souls" (see 1 Peter 1:9). The Bible declares that we can get to the end of our faith. The end of our faith is when we can walk the walk, being totally confident in Christ, no matter what the circumstances. Christian maturity, by the way, is not a state of sinlessness. Only Jesus is or ever will be sinless. Christian maturity is a state of completeness in Christ. It occurs when I can walk with God in spiritual rest, understanding the forgiveness I have received, with a committed determination to be faithful, able to make it through this life in spite of hindrance. When you do not mature, it is because these basic doctrines have not been laid or they have not been properly laid in your life. Hebrews 5:12-14 is a revelation of how the immature state of being occurs. It is time for these believers to teach others, but they have been unable to live the Christian life due to their inexperience in the word of righteousness. They have to be "taught" (i.e., the milk) because they cannot "live the life" (i.e., the meat). The strong meat (i.e., faithful lifestyle) comes only to those who are "teleios"; mature. The mature Christian is one who lives in righteousness and can discern both good and evil. Notice they are discerning good and evil. Do you recall which tree in the Garden of Eden these come from? They are obviously not part of the tree of Life. If we cannot recognize which tree is at the core of our motives we have lost the battle at the outset. Evil is easy to recognize. The hard part for most Christians to see is that often something may be good, but that does not automatically mean it comes from God. People create ministries and church programs that wear you out. Why? Even though it is a good thing to do, there is no "life" in it. It is either religious churchianity, or dead works. Self-rule came when mankind ate of the wrong tree. This is the reason churches contain division in their congregations. They are unable to see themselves through God's perspective. They are more concerned with the concept of right and wrong than whether it produces life. Mature Christians should despise religious rhetoric or liturgy, and yet they are manipulated and coerced to do them. Inside they feel that something is wrong, but they just cannot put it into words. It is the Spirit of Christ motivating them to leave that peculiar thing alone. Do not apologize for recognizing the life of the Spirit, it is either on something or someone, or it is not. Because of the work the cross, we can come to God freely in Christ. God also responds to us by showing us His will in these circumstances. We should respond to Him, not under condemnation, but humbly through grace. If we are serving God and we find that our effort was ineffective, do not get into despair. Go to the Father in prayer and tell Him your intention. Move forward knowing God understands the thought and the intent of your heart. Babes in Christ do not understand this basic dependability of the believer. A babe judges others by their actions and themselves by their intentions. This is called judgment without mercy (see James 2:13). These kinds of individuals do not progress in the things of God. They remain in a carnal state of Christian existence and the press for the high calling of God has not been developed in them. They remain the same because they will not say "no" even when God says "no" first. I call this the principle of measuring. We learn to measure the Spirit of God and determine His response to any situation. When He says, "Go!" I go. When He says, "Stay!" I stay. (look at David's attitude in 1 Samuel 23). This is a part of the aspect of maturity. My ability to hear God is vital (see John 10:1-4). When the congregation is full of immaturity, the standard of God thus declines in the Church to the degree that the sub-standard becomes the norm. If the babe has not been discipled to hear God, how can they ever grow up? After a generation of people not hearing God, the degradation becomes so intense people will preach that you cannot hear God, so many quit trying.

> "I press toward the mark for the prize of the high calling
> of God in Christ Jesus. Let us therefore, as many as be
> perfect, be thus minded: and if in any thing you be
> otherwise minded, God shall reveal even this unto you."
> (Philippians 3:14-15)

What will be revealed and how can it be revealed if you do not hear God?

> (For many walk, of whom I have told you often, and now tell you
> even weeping, that they are the enemies of the cross of Christ:
> Whose end is destruction, whose God is their belly,
> and whose glory is in their shame, who mind earthly things.)
> Philippians 3:18-19

The Lord has called us to obedience. To obey is better than sacrifice (see 1 Samuel 15:22). Maturity cannot be found when there is no effort to obey. God is moving us to a level of maturity far beyond our casual comprehension. Without the establishment of the foundational principles, we will never be able to reach this spiritual goal. Again, these foundational principles are the enabling factors in the Christian experience. They are the application of God's Word into our life and state of being. No one will be able to remove the sin that so easily besets him (see Hebrews 12) unless he has these six foundational principles engrafted into his life. Before we can apply the foundational principles, we must first understand the place of perfection established by God's Word. Again, maturity and perfection are not sinlessness. And also there is only one who is sinless and He is our Lord. We are commanded to be perfect and holy (i.e., mature and distinguishable) as a people of faith. When there is no noticeable difference between the Christian and the heathen, truly our salt has lost its savor.

There must be a re-establishment of the underlying doctrines found in the New Testament. These doctrines are the things the first century Church understood that we do not recognize completely, or that have been handed down with an improper interpretation. Only now in these last days have these foundations been reestablished by the Holy Spirit so that the Bride of Christ can be made ready for the wedding. The Bible says Jesus is coming back for a Bride without spot or wrinkle. We must ask the questions, "Is there enough oil in my lamp for the wedding?" (see Matthew 25) as well as the question, "Where do I, as an individual stand in my spiritual growth?" Surely because we are Christ's we will turn our hearts to the Father and search the Spirit for the answers. Learn to hear God. Prayer is the beginning of this process, and you must pray often and approach God with humility, and listen to the Holy Spirit before you will learn to hear.

Chapter 4 — The Promise of Power

There are many differences of opinion with the issue of how and when Christians receive the baptism of the Holy Spirit. Along with this, there is also terminology that is not biblically sound when expressing the idea of the baptism of the Holy Spirit. When do we receive the Holy Spirit? What is the evidence of this reception? And how one gets baptized in the Holy Spirit are some of the questions that will be addressed in this chapter. There are also some characterizations that should be made in the beginning of this study for the sake of clarity. First of all, one cannot be saved unless the Father draws them (see John 6:44, 65). Secondly, the Holy Spirit has not come to glorify Himself, He has come to glorify Jesus (see John 16:14). And third, we received the Holy Spirit and are sealed by Him at the time of salvation (see Ephesians 1:13). God is a Spirit, and it is the Spirit of God the Father, and the Spirit of Christ that inhabits our lives. Remember, God is not three different gods, He is one God who has three distinct manifestations of Himself. He is God the Father, the Originator of the plan of creation. He is Jesus Christ, the Incarnate God, manifested in this dimension and who is the Creator of all things (see Colossians 1:16-17). He is the Holy Spirit, God's own person in Spirit form who dwells with us and is in us.

It is not the Holy Spirit's intention to accentuate His coming over the ministry of Jesus. Neither is it the Holy Spirit's intention to accentuate His manifestations over the work of God the Father. The Holy Spirit's role is defined in John 14:26 and John 15:8-11. As He enters our heart, our spirit is quickened (i.e., made alive) and His presence in our lives makes us one with Him so that He can do a work in our hearts. These issues should not be in question. When one is asked "when do you receive the Holy Spirit?" one should answer, "when you receive Jesus". Now the question remains, do we get all of the Holy Spirit at one time or are there subsequent and additional fillings that come later? This is the real issue that many misrepresent. As a Pastor I asked the congregation "has anyone ever told you to be filled with the Holy Spirit?" They all answered, "Yes!" I then asked, "Has anyone ever told you how to be filled with the Holy Spirit?" They all answered "No!" I read Luke 11:13 and many people were amazed that the Bible says you ask for Him.

Believers who have not been trained in spirituals struggle with this subject. Paul said on several occasions, "I would not have you to be ignorant" (without the knowledge of a subject). This was his initial and opening statement before he began his instructions to the believers in 1 Corinthians 12.

A Study in the Word

The Bible is clear that the administration of the Holy Spirit occurs more than just at the salvation experience. As we review the Bible on this subject, we should guard our heart from traditional thinking. Traditional thinking has caused many believers to err from the truth, and causes many to get involved in division, which gives place to the spirit of anti-Christ.

> "Then said Jesus to them again, Peace be unto you:
> as my Father hath sent me, even so send I you.
> And when he had said this, he
> breathed on them, and said unto them,
> Receive ye the Holy Ghost."
> (John 20:21-22)

> "And, behold, I send (present tense) the promise
> of my Father upon you:
> but, tarry ye in the city of Jerusalem,
> until ye be endued with power from on high."
> (Luke 24:49)

These two passages are speaking about the first time the disciples received the Holy Spirit. It was on the first day of Jesus' Resurrection. Forty-seven days before the Holy Spirit manifested Himself again on the day of Pentecost. Jesus was in the grave the two nights before, then appears in the upper room on Sunday, gives the Holy Spirit to the disciples, and then tells them to wait until Pentecost for the empowering which was to come on that day. Luke separated the "of the promise of the Father" event from the "empowering of the Holy Spirit" that occurred in Acts 2:1-6. Luke is saying that he researched the coming of the Holy Spirit, and he found that an additional distribution of power came upon the disciples during Pentecost that was different from the Upper Room experience. This clothing of power is what is commonly termed as the baptism of the Holy Ghost. The King James Bible uses the English word "endued" (1746) to express the idea of this filling. The Greek word "enduo", from where endued was translated, means "to sink into a garment," or "to invest with clothing." The word carries the idea of putting something on. In Matthew 6:25 and Mark 6:9, "enduo" is translated as "to put on," and in 2 Corinthians 5:3, "enduo" is translated as "being clothed." This idea of being clothed is revealing how we put on our spiritual house that is from heaven. The idea of being clothed with the "power from on high" simply means to be invested with heavenly power. This is the reality of putting the new man on. This is allowing our Father to enter His house and to set up residence and is why Acts 1:8 states:

> "But ye shall receive power, after that the Holy Ghost is
> come upon you: and ye shall be witnesses unto me."

These verses tell us that we will receive this power after the Holy Spirit is present in our life. It is not that you get all of the Holy Spirit you are going to get at your salvation experience. Luke states that you have the presence of the Holy Spirit, and then there is an additional promise of power that will come at your feast of Pentecost. Luke's understanding of the baptism was that we receive the power from on high as an expression of becoming witnesses to the fact that Christ is alive and lives within us. Luke's proximity to the first Pentecostal experience and his understanding of the baptism is proof enough that "tongues" were not viewed in the first century church to be the *primary* evidence of the reception. The baptism was not signified in itself by the power to speak in tongues (even though tongues were manifested); it was a baptism that manifested in the power to be a witness (i.e., a martyr, or one who bears record of the Lord). This premise is also stated in Acts 5:32,

> "And we are his witnesses of these things;
> and so is also the Holy Ghost,
> whom God has given them that obey him."

The Greek word "martus" (3144) in the first century was a word that is defined as "a legal witness at a trial." A "martus" (martyr) was one who could testify for, collaborated the testimony of the one tried, or who could verify the testimony of another. When Alexander the Great had the Old Testament translated into the Greek language, the word "martus" was used in Isaiah 43:10 and 12, and in 44:8 and was used as the word "witnesses." Make a note of how Isaiah used the term 'witnesses' and what kind of witnesses these were,

> "Ye are my witnesses, saith the Lord, and my servant
> whom I have chosen; that ye may know and believe
> me, and understand that I am he: before me there
> was no God formed, neither shall there be after me...
> I have declared, and have saved, and I have showed, when
> there was no strange god among you: therefore ye are my
> witnesses, saith the Lord, that I am God. Fear ye not, neither
> be afraid: have not I told thee from that
> time, and have declared it? Ye are my witnesses.
> Is there a God beside me? Yea, there is
> no God; I know not any."

Each of these verses gives evidence that these witnesses were to give testimony that God is the "alive" God, and there is no other God but Him. In the time when men believed in gods, gods, and more gods, the pagans needed to understand that there is only one true God. God has made Himself known, and we are to declare the fact that we witnessed His manifestation. The promise of the Holy Spirit's coming was and is the evidence of Jesus' victory. Acts 2 is a continuation of Jesus' promise stated in John 14:7 that He was going to send the Comforter; he was speaking of the Pentecostal event. In John 7:39, it is stated that the Holy Spirit was not yet given because Jesus had not yet been glorified. The act of Jesus returning to the Father was the final step in His glorification, and thus the Holy Spirit could then come upon us.

When the Holy Spirit came on Pentecost He demonstrated all nine manifestations found in 1 Corinthians 12:7-11 and each of these can be found in the first five chapters of the Acts. Even though tongues manifested first, it does not signify that it is the evidence of the baptism. In fact, the first miracle was that the disciples were in one accord! Luke's purpose was not to glorify tongues. His purpose was to bear witness that the Holy Spirit was establishing the Kingdom of God (Acts 1:2-3). The chart below is but a brief look at how Luke bore witness to all nine of these manifestations in the book of Acts.

- Acts 2:3—tongues
- Acts 2:8-11—interpretation of tongues
- Acts 3:6-9—healing
- Acts 3:10—faith
- Acts 3:17—word of knowledge
- Acts 4:8-10—word of wisdom
- Acts 4:24-30—prophecy
- Acts 5:1-4—discernment
- Acts 5:12—miracles (Acts 4:22)

Luke also testifies that during the forty days that Jesus remained on the earth after His resurrection, He gave commandments to the apostles. One of these commandments (see Acts 1:4-5) was for them to wait in Jerusalem for the promise of the Father, which He then identified as the baptism of the Holy Spirit. They had already received the Holy Spirit (see John 20:22 and Luke 24:49), but they had not yet been enabled with the power from on high. Again, this power is the power to become a witness. For the sake of definition and clarity, to be a witness is not only defined as the ability to tell people about Jesus; that is your testimony. A witness is someone who has experienced salvation and the presence of the living God and who confirms that He is God in their life as well as with their tongue. It is with our tongue that we bear witness that He is our Lord. It is the tongue that shows who rules our life. It is with the tongue that everyone around me will know whether I am godly or whether I have a filthy mouth. It is with the tongue that many bless and with the same tongue that they curse. Anyone can speak of God and not know Him, but one cannot be a witness without the experience of Him.

There are several times in the book of Acts where people received the baptism of the Holy Spirit. Each of these receptions is unique. Similarly, Jesus never healed people the same way twice. There may be some commonality in these events, but that is not to be construed as a systematic formula in the baptism of the Holy Spirit. One is filled with the Holy Spirit when they have the faith to receive and ask for His presence in their life, and anyone can be filled when they long for more of God.

For example:

- Acts 2:1-6: The disciples received the baptism; no hands were laid on them; evidence: tongues and interpretation

- Acts 4:31: The second filling of the Apostles; no hands were laid on them; evidence: boldness

- Acts 8:17: The Samaritans were filled; hands were laid on them; evidence: none given

- Acts 9:17: Paul was filled; hands laid on him; evidence: scales fell off his eyes

- Acts 10:44: Cornelius and first Gentiles filled; no hands were laid on them; evidence: tongues and faith

- Acts 13:52: Gentiles filled; no hands mentioned; evidence: joy

- Acts 19:6: Apollos and his company filled; hands were laid on them; evidence: tongues & prophecy

The real issue here is we can be filled with God's Spirit and the manifestations of His presence are at His choosing. It is a matter of capacity. The baptism of the Holy Spirit is clearly defined in the New Testament as occurring after the disciples and others received an initial filling, so to speak. The issue is, then, how much have you opened up your heart to the Lord? Think of the baptism this way: what is your spiritual capacity? You can either be a pint, a quart, or a gallon. When you fill a pint it is nonetheless full, but does not have the same capacity as a quart. The same holds true with the gallon. You may be full as a quart, but the gallon has a greater capacity than the quart and is available as you open your heart to God. It is all about allowing God to expand your heart. To whom much is given, much is also required. If you want to be expanded in spiritual matters, you must open your heart to what God has for you. The truth is if you do not open the door when Jesus is knocking you will not receive anything from Him.

The Manifestations of the Spirit

When trying to understand the manifestations of the Holy Spirit, a simple viewing of the Scriptures is the best approach. There are some Christian groups who tend to pull certain concepts about these matters out of the air; such as the list of spirituals found in 1 Corinthians 12:8-10 are not called "gifts" by Paul, they are termed as the "manifestations" and there is a difference between manifestations and gifts. These are called manifestations because they belong to the Holy Spirit, whereas gifts belong to us. These are listed as the "exhibitions" or "expressions" of the Spirit of God. These "phanerosis" (5321-translated as 'manifestations'), are defined as "a rendering apparent" of the Holy Spirit's presence. This Greek word "phanerosis" is only used twice in the New Testament. In 2 Corinthians 4:2 it is used in the context of rendering apparent the truth.

> "But have renounced the hidden things of dishonesty,
> not walking in craftiness,
> nor handling the word of God deceitfully;
> but by manifestation of the truth
> commending ourselves to every man's
> conscience in the sight of God."

These manifestations of the Spirit are a part of the Christian experience for personal profit or benefit. Satan has used our lack of understanding, (where these manifestations are concerned), to hinder the clarity of God's Word in this matter and to produce division. The Greek word translated as "profit" is "sumphero" (4851). This word means "to bear together" i.e., to bring together, and to collect or contribute in order to help. These manifestations profit or help us in what way? They help us to contribute to the union and maturity within the Body of Christ. Christ came to save us and to make us one. This is why Paul declares that we are One Body in 1 Corinthians 12:12-30. These manifestations are given to bring us together, not to divide us. Satan always comes to steal, kill, and destroy the work of God. This is why pride has continued to separate the Body of Christ into sectarianistic denominations. Pride is the *phanerosis* of Satan, and separation is the evidence of its work. Now to the question, how many manifestations can I have? 1 Corinthians 12:11 states,

> "But all these worketh that one and selfsame Spirit,
> dividing to every man severally as he will."

How are they divided (i.e., distributed)? They are divided as the man wills. Some believe these are divided as the Holy Spirit wills. The Holy Spirit is the worker of these manifestations. These are the manifestations of Who He Is, but it is the man's will that releases or hinders the functioning of these manifestations. If you want to speak in tongues you will; if you refuse to speak in tongues, you will not. The Lord intended for these manifestations to be utilized. They are available for our profit and benefit, yet one group will emphasize tongues, the next will emphasize faith, and still the next will emphasize prophecy. Each group has their favorite manifestation, and each group has the same problem, they all exalt one manifestation over the other. These manifestations have the same purpose. They are to profit the individual and to bring the group into unity. By example, some exalt one "doma" which is commonly called the five-fold gift (see Ephesians 4:8 and 11). These gifts (the English word "gift" is translated from the Greek word "doma") are the Apostle, the Prophet, the Evangelist, and the Teaching Pastor). The Greek word "doma" is also defined as "a covering;" like an umbrella (i.e., a dome). Each "doma" office has its purpose and place. A saint cannot be completely equipped unless he experiences the anointing of each of the "doma" functions because they each minister to a specific area of our spirit. (see Ephesians 4:12). These "doma" gifts function specifically in the Body of Christ for very practical reasons. Apostolic and prophetic ministries are foundational, while the evangelist and the teaching shepherd have maintenance ministries. Apostolic and prophetic ministries build stability into our life, while the evangelists and the teaching shepherds maintain the integrity and function that was established by the foundational ministries. Evangelists are designed by God to teach the babes in the faith. Apostles and prophets teach foundational doctrines and deal with carnality and maturity issues. Pastors teach the flock and are guides for God's sons and daughters throughout our life. Pastors are like shepherds of old; they live with and lead God's people throughout their journey of faith. Pastors are guides and counselors, giving advice and feeding the flocks, while Apostles and Prophets are fathers who train our souls, correcting us, and setting the course as the Holy Spirit leads. Evangelists aid in the birthing and growth of the babes, passing them under the hand to the other gifts God has established in the Church.

Now to the question, does everybody speak with tongues? The answer is clear. If you do not want the release of tongues in your life, you will not speak in tongues. The same holds true for the other eight manifestations. If you do not want to prophesy, you will not speak prophetically. Each of these manifestations has purpose. For example, tongues are for those who lack faith in an area of their life. Tongues are faith builders. This is why Jude 20 states,

> "But ye, beloved, building up yourselves
> on your most holy faith, praying <u>in</u> the Holy Ghost."

This is why tongues are a sign to the faithless ("who believe not") and not to the faithful (see 1 Corinthians 14:22). Jude gives us a bit of clarity about tongues when he says "praying 'in' the Holy Ghost". Paul, in his instruction found in 1 Corinthians 14:15, uses the term "praying with" the Holy Spirit and declares,

> "What is it then? I will pray with the spirit,
> And I will pray with the understanding also."

Praying "with" or "in" the Holy Spirit is a key to understanding this manifestation. The Corinthians did not comprehend the manifestations of the Spirit or their purposes. We are much the same. There is a difference between praying with or in the Spirit, and being in the Spirit when we pray.

We should all make sure we are in the Spirit when we pray, whether we are praying in tongues or with our understanding. We should heed the admonition to the Church to change our ways and change our attitudes about these wonderful blessings the Spirit of God has graced us with. We should no longer exalt one manifestation over the other just as we should not forbid them. If we can make this transition, the Kingdom of God will draw one step closer to becoming a living reality in our lives. Paul's counsel is simple:

"Wherefore, Brethren, covet to prophesy, and forbid not
to speak with tongues. Let all things be done decently and in order."
(1 Corinthians 14:39-40)

You may not speak in tongues, but it is still the admonition of the Bible that teaches us to not "forbid" their manifestation. Why are so many people ignorant of spirituals? Mostly because groups have promoted false concepts about these manifestations which in turn has produced fear in the other groups who do not understand their purpose or who have not experienced their proper operation. One group promotes their belief about the manifestations, while yet another group promotes their interpretation. They war over who is right, but the end result is disunity in the Church and misunderstanding of these manifestations and their function in the Body of Christ. God's people should be trained in spirituals and read their Bibles. That way we will all understand the reality and function of the manifestations and their purpose in us individually.

Chapter 5 – Poieo: Being Built into a Spiritual House

The definition of 'poieo':

To make, form, produce, bring about, or to cause (spoken of any external act as manifested in the production of something tangible, corporeal, obvious to the senses, completed action). To make or endow a person or thing with a certain quality that produces and brings forth something which, when produced, has an independent existence of its own.

"I have glorified thee on the earth: I have finished the
work which you gave me to do (poieo)."
(John 17:4)

"For it is God which worketh in you both to will and to do
of his good pleasure. Do (poieo) all things without murmurings
and disputings. That you may be blameless and harmless, the sons of God,
without rebuke, in the midst of a crooked and perverse [people]…"
(Philippians 2:13-15)

Now the God of peace…make you perfect in every
good work to do (poieo) his will, working in you that which is
well pleasing in his sight, through Jesus Christ…"
(Hebrews 13:20a & 21)

"Having made known unto us the mystery of his will,
according to his good pleasure which he has purposed in himself:
That in the dispensation of the fullness of times he might
gather together in one all things in Christ…"
(Ephesians 1:9-10)

Over the years I have heard many Christians talk about fulfilling God's will in their lives, but in my experience most Christians are actually more concerned about what God's will is for them and how can they find their purpose in life. "What does God want me to do?" This is usually the question asked. The will of the Lord seems to be a mystery for believers at times. Some people act as if they have to guess about the Lord's will, when in fact Ephesians 1:9-10 tells us what the Lord's will is. His will is to gather us together into one.

The Lord's will for us has many applications. First, it is His will that I, as an individual, have a personal relationship with Him. If this first part is not implemented then none of the other applications will be in order. His will then develops in our domestic home. The husband, wife, and children all have their order and the family must be led by the "head of the household." As I serve the Lord in my personal life, I then have the ability to lead in my domestic life. When my personal life and domestic life are in order, then I will be able to function in the corporate Church. When my personal or domestic house is dysfunctional, all I will bring to the corporate house is my inability to help others who are in the same state. In Christ we are to be gathered together into one Body of believers. This is His will. Our part and God's general will for us is to be involved in this process. The work of Christ through the Holy Spirit is called "poieo" in the original Greek language. "Poieo" is the purpose of discipleship. It is the work which God the Father gives us to do. It is the God ordained purpose of ministry and the function of the Church to build a unified Body. Now we can ask the question pertaining to our personal role in the implementation of God's Kingdom and our personal work in the Church.

The Work That I must Do

There are two different occurrences in the New Testament when Jesus said He was finished with something. In John 17:4, Jesus said He was finished with the work the Father gave Him to do (poieo), and in John 19:30 He said, "It is finished." The Greek word translated as 'it' is "teleo" (5055). The word 'it' is defined in the Greek language as "to end something" (i.e., to complete, to finish, or to discharge [a debt]). In essence, the thing Jesus finished on the cross was His redemptive strategy which contains at least two parts. He defeated Satan by stealthily completing our redemption, following God's salvation plan. Satan did not know God's plan, and did exactly what was ordained for him to do. God was not caught off-guard or surprised by Jesus' crucifixion; it was part of the redemptive process. When we understand that Jesus completed two distinctly different purposes, we will be able to more completely understand and do the work of ministry. We should not get snared by the over-simplistic notion that ministry in the Church is limited to praying for the sick and preaching. True ministry contains those two aspects, but goes much further. As stated, Jesus' first completion was the work of God (the 'poieo'); His final completion was His redemptive sacrifice so we could accomplish that work. If Jesus had not redeemed us, we could not do His work. These two spiritual vocations cannot be separated, yet the Word of God makes a distinction between them for clarity. Unless we do the 'poieo' (building disciples in completion and redemption), we will not be in the center of His will, and the purpose of this chapter is to explain and establish an understanding of what Jesus' success on earth actually did; He made us one. In spite of sin and in the face of the fall, Jesus built us into a spiritual house. Jesus' goal and strategy was to cause us to unite under the banner of His Kingdom and to become a spiritual army, battling God's enemies until they are made a footstool for the Almighty. Through evangelistic ministry, Christ's redemptive sacrifice has been well covered in the Church today. Although some in the world may not have heard the Gospel of the Kingdom the majority of those who are ministry-minded preach about Jesus' redemptive sacrifice and continue preaching the salvation message; but the building aspect of 'poieo' is most often left out of the message. Preaching the good news of the Kingdom is the central theme in the work of God, but the problem that is now being seen in the modern Church is the lack of discipleship. To restate the problem, the trouble is not that we fail to preach the Gospel, almost every evangelical preacher is teaching and/or preaching from the Bible; the problem is that the Church is not maturing because the 'poieo' is not being done. We may be growing older as we attend our local church, but are we doing what Jesus commanded us to do? Just because we tell people about Jesus' sacrifice does not mean we are His witnesses. This may be a surprise to some, but our Lord said that the world will know the truth about Him when we love each other (see John 13:35), not because we declare Him. All the preaching in the world does not compare to the witness of love the Church should be expressing.

In John 17:4, Jesus stated that He finished His ministry work as commanded by the Father. His ministry work was to edify people of diverse backgrounds and cultures and to make (poieo) them one. In John 17:6 Jesus restates the work as being "manifested" (i.e., made public or revealed) in the disciples. This revelation holds one of the keys to understanding what maturity is in the life of a believer. Many ministers and ministries try to disciple babes in Christ by adding knowledge to their faith (i.e., we expect them to attend church and Sunday school), but do not emphasis the building of relationships within the congregation. In order to reach the goal of love within the Church, the establishing of relationship-focused ministry is essential. As stated before, 2 Peter 1:5 teaches us to "add to our faith," but knowledge is to be added only after virtue and not before. Of course virtue is in the believer's nature (it was given to us when we were born again) and of course, one should train people in the Word of God, but virtue should be the priority for the new convert to develop and manifest. This virtue is described as the manifestation of the name of Jesus (see John 17:6) into the life of the believer. If the focus of a church's discipleship training is to teach biblical knowledge and information and at the same time casually overlooking many of the virtuous aspects of the Gospel (see 1 Corinthians 8), the new believer will fall short of the glory God has for them. The new believer will become filled with pride and being a novice he will fall into the condemnation of the devil (see 1 Timothy 3:6). Again, the definition of virtue is the "excellence of a person," or, "the manliness of the man." Virtue is a quality of Christian thought and of moral character in the life of a believer that produces the ability to lock into the Body of Christ, and to make intimacy a primary goal within his Christian relationships. Virtue can also be defined as the "attitude in the life of a person which primarily influences his behavior in the aspect of his personal attachment and relationship with God." In simple language, virtue is the ability to live God's way (as a family in the local church) and to do God's work (building a cohesive and lasting maturity in the local church). Do you have what it takes to live as Jesus commands? If not, why? When Jesus said He had manifested the Father's "name" (3686) in the disciples, he was stating that he had manifested God's authority, likeness, character, and that He produced a reflection of God's nature into these diverse men. If virtue is not added to the new believer, then the outward demonstration of God's nature will be powerless in the believer. Notice again that I did not say that they were sinless! I must continuously communicate that we are not commanded to be sinless; we are commanded to be perfect (mature) and holy. To be mature is to walk in holiness and perfection of spirit. This is the definition of these words as they are used in the Scriptures. The struggle comes when condemnation affects the life of the new Christian. Condemnation occurs when the new believer is lifted up with pride and falls into the same judgment as the devil. When he is lifted up with pride he will think of himself more highly than he ought to think (see Romans 12:3). As this occurs the novice tries to disciple himself into a virtuous life, or he tries to defeat the internal force of sin by his knowledge.

Sin is defeated by the power of the "engrafted" word (see James 1:21), not by one's mental ability to quote verses. When the Word of God is engrafted, it is being implanted onto something else or deeply into something else by the process of attachment. That word can then grow in the good soil of the faithful Christian and produce the fruit God intended to be developed within. If the Word of God has not become flesh in you, it is because it has not been engrafted into you. Flesh can only be overcome by the spirit, not by knowledge. We must submit to the Holy Spirit as He lubricates within us the process of maturity which He does through discipleship and inner dealings. It is not the Church, nor the preacher, nor the ministry of a denomination that completes the process, and it is the work of the Word that produces maturity. We are saved by grace and this is the work of the Lord. He uses Apostles, Prophets, Evangelists, and Training Pastors in the process, but without submission and humility in the heart of the individual believer, maturity will not be accomplished. We may plant or we may water as ministers, but God gives the increase (see 1 Corinthians 3:6). When a minister thinks his anointing is the maturing factor, he is puffed up. This is a hard word but must be said. Ministers are tools in God's hands, nothing more. Colossians 2:18-19 states the premise this way:

> "Let no man beguile you of your reward in a voluntary humility
> and worshipping of angels, intruding into those things
> which he has not seen, vainly puffed up by his fleshly mind, and not holding the
> head, from which all the body by joints and bands having nourishment
> ministereth, and knit together, increases with the increase of God."

In Matthew 11:10, Mark 1:2, Luke 7:24 and 27, Luke 9:52, and in James 2:25, the Greek word 'aggelos' is translated as 'messenger(s)' or 'preacher(s)'. In Colossians 2:18 the word 'angels' (aggelos) simply means ministers. The angels mentioned here are the kinds without wings. They were men, and not heavenly hosts. Paul is speaking of the worshipping of preachers, not the worshipping of angelic beings. In the context of the passage, Paul was dealing with the idea of maturity and was relating how these ministers didn't have a clue about certain issues they were preaching about. They were intruding into areas of teaching that they have not 'seen'. The Greek word translated as 'seen' (3708) means "to discern clearly or to experience." These ministers have not clearly seen nor experienced the process of maturity, so they will spoil you through philosophy and vain deceit, after the tradition of men and not after Christ (see Colossians 2:8). These ministers, who are not holding the head of the Church in honor, have a pseudo (fake) increase. The Greek word translated as 'holding' is 'krateo' (2902) and means "to retain strength from or to have dominion from." These preachers do not maintain strength or dominion over the enemy and they get their power or authority from somewhere else. The word 'increase' in this passage simply means the process of spiritual growth. In essence, you can learn church doctrine from these ministers, but it does not have an active and positive effect in the character or integrity of the one hearing if virtue is not a part of their spiritual diet. These novices must then be controlled, and this control usually manifests through the local church's or minister's doctrinal stance or through shepherding (when ministers take a position of dominion over a believer as though they were the executors of God's wrath and judgment). These preachers teach, but do not bring an increase to spiritual maturity. The increase of this kind is ministered as only a little more knowledge in the head, not love or soundness of character from the heart. When this occurs, these people are normally learning, but do not experientially understand the truth about the Christian life while virtue only comes through responsible and directed admonition in the truth of God's Kingdom.

> "And I myself also am persuaded of you, my brethren, that you
> also are full of goodness, filled with all knowledge, able
> also to admonish one another. Nevertheless, brethren, I have written
> the more boldly unto you in some sort, as putting you in
> mind, because of the grace that is given to me of God,
> That I should be the minister of Jesus Christ to the Gentiles,
> ministering the gospel of God, that the offering up of the Gentiles
> might be acceptable, being sanctified by the Holy Ghost."
> (Romans 15:14-16)

The Bible lays down a simple pattern of discipleship. The Lord did not make the discipleship process hard or complicated. Some ministers make the discipleship process seem to be difficult, due to their own misinterpretation of the process (i.e., their lack of insight into the ways of God), or they are just inexperienced in the process of discipleship. They follow a path of discipleship that is not biblically sound. This most often is the case when ministers who are Pastoring have never been fathered in the faith. They were just sent without ever being discipled themselves. When virtue is not being added as the primary ingredient to faith, the foundation of the new believer lacks the strength to become solid. Everything that is added ends up being wood, hay, and stubble because it is built on sand and not on the foundation of virtue. Jesus is virtue. Get Jesus: get virtue.

One of the things generally misunderstood in the Body of Christ is what the Bible calls "being founded." In the Old Testament the term "founded" means "to establish, to fix, or to set," but carries the notion of "setting down together, that is, to settle or consult." In the New Testament the term "founded" means "something put down (i.e., a substructure)." Before our house of God can be built, a foundation must be laid. Isaiah 28:16 prophesies about a *sure* foundation that when translated from the original Hebrew language means a "founded foundation."

There are many types of foundations, but the only foundation for the believer is the foundation of Jesus (see 1 Corinthians 3:11). Ezekiel 13:14 and Habakkuk 3:13 speak of God discovering the foundation "up to the neck," and the un-tempered mortar we use to build the unstable soul. Discovering the "foundation up to the neck" is expressly dealing with the Body of Christ, because Jesus is the head and governs the Church (see Ephesians 4:15), while the four-fold ministry is the "neck", symbolically. Paul said in Romans 15:20 that he was apprehensive about building on another man's foundation. This is due to not knowing what kind of foundation the other has laid. You cannot disciple lost people, no matter how hard you try, and maturing the novice is a task in itself. If you try to build on another's foundation, when that foundation is based on tradition, you will find it is impossible to succeed. You have to do the work of undoing what has been set before you can do the work of building (see Jeremiah 1:10). Paul states in 1 Corinthians 3:10-12 that we are to build a foundation, but it must be accomplished wisely, and can only be completed when Jesus is the foundation you are building on. Ephesians 2:20 tells us the purpose of our foundation and that this foundation is built through apostolic and prophetic administration. This foundation with Jesus as its chief component is built so we can be "fitly framed together" and maturing into a habitation for God.

When we are founded, we are given a seal according to 2 Timothy 2:19. This seal is the recognition of our righteousness in Jesus Christ (the Lord knows them who are His) and "let everyone that names the name of Christ depart from iniquity." Remembering the definition of being founded will help us to discover its application. When I am *set, established, fixed,* or in other words, when I am *founded,* I have a basis or structural foundation to build upon. I am founded through the process of being settled down and forming my life around God. Luke 6:48 reveals that I must dig deep down through the layers of my life while I walk with God in order to remove the layers of worldliness in my life; only then can I can be properly founded. Through this uncovering process, I receive the wisdom of Lord and God's forgiveness settles me down onto the foundation of Jesus. Thayer defines the Greek word "deep" as "things hidden and above man's scrutiny, especially divine counsels." Living in worldliness adds layers of fear, insecurity, rejection, sensuality, emotional pain, and trauma, as well as many other fleshly attributes. We are commanded to be wise enough to recognize these areas of our lives and to confess them to God (i.e., confessing our sin) and building a foundation that has no flaws. These flawed layers hinder our growth and maturity. When we remove them, we remove the wood, hay, and stubble from our foundation.

The Example from Christ

How did Jesus train his disciples? He admonished (corrected) them! 1 Corinthians 10:9 tells us that we should not tempt Christ, which the children of Israel did in times past. The Scriptures are the perfect means of admonition (3559). The Greek word 'nouthesia' is translated here as 'admonition' and means "to call attention to" (by implication to mildly rebuke or warn). Biblical exhortation is accomplished as we walk others through the process of spiritual growth. To 'exhort', or the 'ministry of exhortation', is defined as "to walk together with a person" or "to call that person near to one's side." The Gospel of Mark gives us the simplest explanation of this process. Mark shows us Jesus' method and ways of discipleship throughout His ministry. Jesus' ministry and the discipleship of the twelve began when He took them away to a mountain and established a personal relationship with them (see Mark 3:13-14).

Jesus had a process that is called 'poieo'. The Scripture says in Mark 3:14 that Jesus 'ordained' the twelve to be with him. The Greek word "poieo" is translated as 'ordained' in this text and can be further defined "to produce, to construct, to form, and to fashion a quality into a person." 'Poieo', in secular Greek literature common to Jesus' day, was used to describe the process of building a house. It also had the meaning and carried the thought of bringing peace to someone by spending time with them, helping them build their house, and helping them to feel secure. We are the house of Christ (see Hebrews 3:6). This is why Paul said he was a wise master-builder. From the foundation to the roof, Paul understood this temple of God we call the Body of Christ. 'Poieo' is the process of maturing/building our spiritual house and is also defined as "the execution of a purpose and the bringing forth of the cause of the project." 'Poieo' is to build someone into a completed man or woman of God. We are built in spirit, soul, and body because there is a purpose in the final production. This is where admonition has an affect. In John 8:38-44 Jesus told the Pharisees that their father was the devil. 'Poieo' is also seen as the product of one's father, and is the evidence of the type of father you are being constructed by and is seen in your actions. When this spiritual house is being built by the wrong father, it is not constructed out of the fruits of the spirit; it is being built by using the works of the flesh. This is how wood, hay, and stubble finds its way into the foundation of many people, and eventually becomes false 'poieo'. False 'poieo' in the life of someone is seen as the proof that a corrupt foundation process has taken place in the life of a person (see John 15:5-6 and 9). Whichever vine one remains in is the source of one's results. If we gather from a corrupt source, we are gathering that which is to be burned. We can work very hard to complete the house and yet find the fruit of the flesh dominating the architecture. The source of the vine is the root of the vine and the life of the root is the soil. When we are tapped into bad soil, we will produce bad fruit. This is the basic understanding of the parable of the soils found in Matthew 13. It is rare when Jesus describes his purpose in the Scripture, but in John 14:22-23 and 31 we find one of the few times Jesus directly states what He is doing:

> "Judas said unto him, not Iscariot, Lord, how is it that thou wilt
> manifest thyself unto us, and not unto the world?
> Jesus answered and said unto him, If a man love me, he will keep
> my words: and my Father will love him, and we will come unto him,

and will make (poieo) our abode with him.
But that the world may know that I love the Father;
and as the Father gave me commandment, even so I do (poieo)."

Jesus is clearly stating how He will be manifested and how He serves the Father. He will come and build His house with us. To define 'poieo' in relation to the believer we should see it as "permanently producing a level of maturity in the life of a person so upon completion of the process, that individual has a self-perpetuating and self-existing relationship with the Lord, and a unity within the Body of Christ that goes beyond human ability." In Revelation 1:6 we are told that Jesus is "making" (poieo) us kings and priests. Revelation 3:12 says He will "make" (poieo) us a pillar in the temple, and again in 5:10 we are being "made" (poieo) to reign on the earth. Paul said it this way:

"Not as though I had already attained, either were already perfect:
but I follow after, if that I may apprehend that for
which I also am apprehended of Christ Jesus."
(Philippians 3:12)

When we realize that the word 'poieo' is used over 500 times in the New Testament, and when we see it in the context of the Scriptural mandate to make disciples (see Matthew 28:19), the discipleship mandate becomes much easier and clearer to comprehend. Ministers are to actively work on every believer's spiritual house. If you do not, one thing is for certain; Satan is working on them at all times tearing down the work that has been previously accomplished. Satan's work is anti-'poieo'. His interest is in the destruction of the fruits of the Spirit and the production of the works of the flesh. This anti-'poieo' is the work of the anti-Christ, and the spirit of anti-Christ works to divide the Church while the Holy Spirit works to unite it. We fulfill God's purpose when we are individually built and added onto, and grow into the spiritual/corporate house of God. Jesus said, "In my Father's house are many mansions." (see John 14:2). Satan uses doctrine, concepts of holiness, and many other ideologies of religion to create sectarian attitudes and divisions in the Church. The work of the Holy Spirit is the 'poieo' that creates the oneness of the Body. This 'work' (poieo) is the fulfillment of the great commission, which is to teach all nations to observe whatsoever Jesus has commanded us to do. We are not to 'poieo' people into harlotry (see 1 Corinthians 6:15-17; poieo is translated as the word "make" in this passage); we are to produce a unity in the universal Body of Christ. This was the Lord's purpose and ministry.

"For this is that message that you heard from
the beginning, that we should love one another.
Not as Cain, who was of the wicked one,
and slew his brother...Because his own
works were evil, and his brother's righteous."
(1 John 3:11-12)

What were the righteous works of Abel? They are found in the mystery of God's will. Ephesians 1:9-10 explains the purpose of Christ's work in the Church:

> "Having made known unto us the mystery of his will, according
> to his good pleasure which he has purposed in himself:
> That in the dispensation of the fullness of times
> he might gather together in one all things in Christ."

I am astonished that so many Christians struggle with this simple truth. Too many people are more concerned with ecumenicalism than the biblical mandate to become *one*. They operate in fear, rather than pursue the purpose of God. As stated before there is an anti-'poieo' (the destructive or demonic effect found in the world that produces division and separation). Separation is the ultimate purpose of sin. Separation from God, from the Kingdom of God, and our separation from one another in the Church is the work and strategy of Satan. The spirit of anti-Christ can be seen in the workings of disunity. This is why sin is so destructive in the Church. Sin is anything that separates man from God, or man from man. A man of God once said to me, "I choose to call brothers all that God calls sons." This is the heart of Christianity. Jesus banded the twelve together as a company of Apostles for the purpose of bringing about the one new man (see Ephesians 2:14-15). His goal was to make these diverse individuals self-existent in God by uniting them together as one in their faith toward God. Every time we see them in one accord the Holy Spirit came upon them. I truly believe that when we come together as a unified Body in the local church, the Holy Spirit will fall on us as well. The Holy Spirit will not honor division, strife, and contention. We, in essence, produce the conduit of power when we join together. We cannot build this spiritual house in our own strength, but have been given grace to accomplish the task. What is impossible for man is possible with God. I can do all things through Christ who strengthens me (see Philippians 4:13). By example, if I have a 5,000-pound block of stone and I command you to move it; you will easily understand that you are totally unable to complete the task by yourself. If I have mercy and grace for you, I will provide a crane for your use, train you how to operate it, and help you to move the block so you can fulfill my will. This is 'poieo'. Christ gives us the tools we need to accomplish His purpose. Psalm 127 says:

> "Except the Lord build the house, they labor in vain that build it:
> except the Lord keep the city, the watchman waketh in vain."

We are matured by a unified effort, not by individual effort. But if we do not individually mature we will never unify. This seems to be a paradox and a contradiction, but it is the way of God. This work of the Holy Spirit (creating the oneness in the family of God by personally providing gifts and manifestations to individuals in the Body of Christ) is the work of 'poieo' (see 1 Corinthians 12:4 & 7 and Romans 12:4-8). Anything that causes a division or a hindrance to this process is anti-'poieo' and anti-Christ. The word 'poieo' is also found in Galatians 6:9 and is translated thus; "And let us not be weary in well-doing (poieo)." Do not get weary, because the work of building this spiritual house is tiring and difficult, and you can expect constant attacks from the enemy. This is why we must have a multiplicity of administration (i.e., the gifts of the Apostles, the Prophets, the Evangelists and the Training Shepherds) ministering in our churches. We have the same problems as Nehemiah faced when he was rebuilding the walls around Jerusalem. His enemies caused them to work with a shovel in one hand, and a sword in the other. If Satan cannot stop your progress, he'll try to wear you out or slow you down. This is what Galatians 5:17 is speaking of:

> "The flesh lusts against the Spirit, and the Spirit against the flesh...
> so that you cannot do (poieo) the things that you would."

A look at a few passages in the New Testament will help us gain a more complete understanding about how 'poieo' and anti-'poieo' are operating in the Body of Christ:

> "In this the children of God are manifest, and the children of the devil:
> whosoever doeth (poieo) not righteousness is not of God,
> neither he that loveth not his brother."
> (1 John 3:10)

> "From whom the whole body fitly joined together and compacted by that
> which every joint supplieth, according to the effectual working
> in the measure of every part, maketh (poieo) increase of the
> body unto the edifying of itself in love."
> (Ephesians 4:16)

> "But as touching brotherly love you need not that I write unto you:
> for you yourselves are taught of God to love one another.
> And indeed you do (poieo) it toward all the brethren."
> (1 Thessalonians 4:9-10)

> "Do (poieo) all things without murmurings and disputings."
> (Philippians 2:14)

The Ministry of Jesus

The gospel of Mark from a disciplining standpoint is a shortened form of the gospel of Matthew. The lessons found in the gospel of Mark are orderly and concise. It seems that the Holy Spirit desired that the Gospel of Mark be used in this way. One of the first lessons Jesus taught the disciples was about a divided house (see Mark 3:23-29). This lesson transpired when Jesus began to train them in unity. This can be seen as Jesus related the principle of the family of God to them (i.e., the Body of Christ to the disciples). Who is in the family? Mark 3:35 says it is anyone who does (poieo) God's will. His will is to gather together in one all things (i.e., to build the Body of Christ). Jesus' kinsman came to get him because they believed he was "beside himself" (see Mark 3:21). Jesus admonished the disciples that if a kingdom is divided it will not stand. In modern terms, it is not a matter of whether you are a Baptist or a Charismatic, do you name the name of Jesus and do His will? If you bring division into the Body it is because Satan is using you. The great commandment to love one another is still in effect today. Nothing has changed. John wrote in 1 John about this matter of love some sixty years after Jesus' resurrection. Satan was trying to pervert the Gospel, to hinder the 'poieo', and Paul also addressed the same issue in 1 Corinthians 3. The Corinthians had allowed Satan to divide them into sects. Jesus did not want the disciples to be ignorant of what the enemy was trying to do. Satan was trying to divide the group by discrediting Jesus in Mark 3. He was using Jesus' friends and family to try to accomplish this task in Mark 3:21-35. This is why Luke 14:26 states that if you do not love Jesus more than you love your family, you cannot be His disciple. Mark 4:1-34 is the section of Scripture that explains how Jesus began to train and apprentice the disciples in an understanding of how God's Kingdom operates. The Kingdom of God is in us and not far off (see Luke 17:21). In Mark 4:33 we see that Jesus regulated His training. He did not give the disciples more than they were able to receive. But during His private time with them, he expounded all things to his disciples so they could understand His goal (see Mark 4:34). It was during this time that Jesus began a series of practical instructions and applications about Kingdom power. The lessons included examples of the power of the Kingdom over nature (see Mark 4:35-41), over demonic possession and oppression (see Mark 5:1-20), over death and sickness (see Mark 5:21-43), and how unbelief hinders the operation of the Kingdom's power (see Mark 6:1-6). After these lessons, Jesus then gave them the opportunity to experience the Kingdom's supremacy. He sent them out with a mission (see Mark 6:7-13). The lesson was actually for them to discover themselves. "Do not take anything with you", was the directive, because Jesus wanted to find out how much Word they had in their heart. He did not want them to minister from their notes; He wanted to see how much of His Word had become flesh in them! Spiritual fathers should train in much the same way. They should give spiritual sons the opportunity to travel and minister with them. If you give someone the opportunity to speak without prior notice, you can see the Spirit's influence on his heart. You get to see what he has been focusing on. On one particular occasion my spiritual father took me with him to a church in California. He was praying for a woman that had a clubfoot and a short leg. As I watched her foot and leg being healed, I became so excited about the miracle that I wanted to pray for the sick myself. My father in the faith gave me the liberty to pray for others even though he understood that I was acting out of zeal and not faith. As you can imagine, I did not have much success on that day. Later that evening I asked him why I was unsuccessful. He showed me how I had been presumptuous and had been lifted up with pride, thinking more highly of myself than I should have. I had assumed something. I assumed the power to heal had come upon me, not understanding the Kingdom's rule and order. We should be obedient to Mark 16 and pray for the sick, but again, presumption is not faith. My place was a place of learning at that time, and not doing. I had to realize it is the power of God that heals and that spiritual order, as well as faith holds the key. I have never forgotten that lesson! Jesus taught the disciples in this way. In Mark 6:8 he sent them out with nothing except a staff. (By the way, the Greek word used for 'staff' (4464) is defined as "a baton of royalty.") They only needed to know one thing; they were the sons of the highest God and administrators in His Kingdom. The only instruction given to them was when they came to someone's house and were received, they were to stay there and bless that house. If they were not received, the dust on their feet would be a testimony to the lack of love, oneness, and hospitality found in that place (see Mark 6:7-13). When the disciples returned to Jesus they reported what they had done (see Mark 6:30). Jesus then took them away to a quiet place so they could have some leisure time and rest from their journey (see Mark 6:31). This was sort of a debriefing. Afterward Jesus gave them a quick lesson on laying down their lives for the love of the people by feeding the five thousand. He put them in a ship and sent them away and also went to a quiet place alone. When Jesus became aware of the disciples' struggle in the midst of the sea He walked on the water to them. This was another admonition about faith. After he calmed the winds, Jesus knew that they were still hard-hearted (see Mark 6:52), so the training continued. The lesson would now continue by "reproving" (1650) them about the Kingdom's power. Mark 6:53-56 re-established the training of the twelve on healing the sick, and beginning in Mark 7 Jesus showed his disciples how tradition and religion had made God's word non-effective. *Churchianity* is a term I use to describe the attitude of a person who uses religion to further their personal goals. These have laid aside the 'poieo' for the tradition of men (see Mark 7:8). Jesus opened their understanding to the Word of God when he said in Mark 7:13:

> "Making the word of God of none effect through your tradition,
> which you have delivered: and many such like things do (poieo) you."

The lesson Jesus was giving was that disciples could not be matured by tradition. In today's churches there are doctrines and concepts of discipleship that are very traditional in their approach. These are generally personal interpretations and attitudes of ministry that have been handed down through a denominational tradition. Tradition usually comes about when someone had a revelation in the past about some Christian issue that has now become a traditional pillar. These traditions become so anchored that people believe it is heresy to take an honest look at those subjects anymore. A united Church can win the world. What can a divided Church accomplish? Well, look around. The world and the things of the world are forcing Christians into a corner. When the world took prayer and the Ten Commandments out of schools, the divided Church barely murmured and then only complained about it. The Church did not rise up to confront the politicians in that day; it simply rolled over and accepted what had been handed down. While the world promotes sex and violence on television every hour of the day, and then ridicules anyone who stands against it, the divided Church grumbles, but continues to watch the programs. The world promotes evolution and demonic philosophies of life and then restricts biblical perspectives and all the divided Church does is to wait on the rapture. Jesus prophesied that we would face these obstacles. He knew how to overcome and gave the disciples the keys to the Kingdom. These keys allow us to bring forth or "bare" (poieo) twelve manner (species or types) of fruits (see Revelation 22:2). Revelation 22:14-15 states:

> "Blessed are they that do (poieo) his commandments, that they
> may have right to the tree of life, and may enter in through
> the gates into the city. For without are dogs, and
> sorcerers, and whoremongers, and murders, and idolaters,
> and whosoever loveth and maketh (poieo) a lie.

The Work of Jesus

"I have glorified you on the earth: I have finished the
work which you gave me to do (poieo)."
(John 17:4)

The work of Jesus is fulfilling the directives given to Him by the Father. It was and is the building of the Body of Christ into one new man that was God's goal. The Father set His plan in motion to bring mankind back to his original place of dominion. This begins with our salvation, and is consummated in our maturity. The maturity process must be seen in this light. Jesus started the pattern with the disciples, and we are to follow His ways. We should also realize that even Jesus had a son of perdition: Judas Iscariot. Consider why Judas failed; He tried to divide the King from His purpose.

'Poieo' is translated into many different English words throughout the New Testament, such as make, bear (fruit), do, practicing, give, acts on, treated, produces, appointed, ordained, committed, redeemed, and divided, just to name a few. As one reads through the New Testament the work of unifying becomes increasingly clear. The Father from the beginning purposed to create one family in Christ. We originated from Adam and Eve and after the flood we find our roots in Noah's linage. Power was given to the first century Church because the Body was of one heart and one mind (see Acts 2). There is a false power in the world today and it is manifesting in the Church as a great lie. The lie is that you can be divided and anointed too! Division and strife are signs of carnality (see 1 Corinthians 3:1-3). Paul teaches that when people divide they are immature and they lack the foundation of Jesus. That foundation is the single Cornerstone. When another builds onto that Cornerstone they must take heed how and what they build onto it. Everyone's work will be tried by fire. God will discover what sort it is. He will discover whether we are His Temple or not. When ministers do not add the right materials to our foundation we suffer loss because the spirit of anti-Christ constantly works to hinder our growth.

"For such are false apostles, deceitful workers, transforming
themselves into the apostles of Christ. And no marvel; for Satan
himself is transformed into an angel of light. Therefore
it is no great thing if his ministers also be transformed as the ministers
of righteousness; whose end shall be according to their works."
(2 Corinthians 11:13-15)

In the book of Romans, Paul discusses the godly 'poieo' and the ungodly 'poieo'. Anti-'poieo' is seen in the light of those who know God's judgment yet they continue in contention, disobedience, indignation, and wrath (see Romans 2:8). There is no respect of persons with God (see Romans 2:11) so the hearers are not justified before God, but the doers of the law - the Royal Law - will be justified (see Romans 2: 13). This is the reality of God's purpose being manifested in the hearts and lives of the believers. When the Gentiles, who have not the law, do (poieo) by nature the things contained in the law they show the work of the law written in their hearts (see Romans 2:14-15).

When we see Romans 3:13-22 in the framework of unity we will then understand how the spirit of anti-Christ operates. Satan uses our mouth (verses 13-14), our feet (verses 15-16), our pride and our arrogance (verses 17-18) to hinder God's work. He uses everything found in these verses to hinder the building of spiritual unity. Unity in the Body of Christ scares the hell out of the devil. As Paul explains redemption in Romans 3:21 through 4:20, he finalizes the thought with these verses:

> "And being fully persuaded that, what he had promised, he was able also to
> perform (poieo). And therefore it was imputed to him for righteousness."
> (Romans 4:21-22)

Understanding how 'poieo' works also causes us to clearly know Paul's meaning in Romans 7:15-22. When we recognize the nature of sin, we know assuredly that sin is always in us. If I allow Satan to use me as an instrument of sin, it is proof that I am still in need of strength and maturity in that area of my life. You may wonder if anyone will ever be able to overcome the enemy. You will find that when you are walking with others in faith you have greater power and ability to defeat the devil than when you walk alone. This is seen in Romans 7:20-21,

> "Now if I do (poieo) that I would not, it is no more I that do it,
> but sin that dwells in me. I find then a law, that, when
> I would do (poieo) good, evil is present with me."

Paul is saying, when I build that which has virtue (i.e., the good thing) evil is there too! The persecution the first century Church faced came from the divisions and doctrines of the Jews, the idolatry and Gnosticism of the Gentiles, and the idolatrous mad men of the Roman Empire. The religious Jews refused to agree with the 'poieo' God had established through the Messiah. They could not accept the Gentiles without the Gentiles submitting to their doctrines. John (in Revelation 2) explained the three damaging doctrines that affected the Church: the doctrine of the Nicolaitanes, the doctrine of Balaam, and the doctrine of Jezebel. Remember the Greek word translated as the English word "doctrine" is defined as "the application of the teaching or the function of the teaching." So the doctrines that came from the Nicolaitanes, from Balaam, and from Jezebel are the applications or functions that these demonic forces use to hinder the edification of the Body of Christ. Even back then, the Church suffered with these demonic extremes. Most of the Jews could not allow the Gentiles to become part of God's people in their thinking, because it would constitute a change in their tradition and doctrine. Certain Jews taught that you had to follow the Law of Moses in order to be a Christian. Paul attacks these traditions and reveals the application of 'poieo' in the Church in Romans 9:20-21, 28; 10:5; 12:20; 13:3-4, 14; and 15:26. He then concludes the book as he writes of the Jews in Romans 16:17-18:

"Now I beseech you, brethren, mark them which
cause (poieo) divisions and offenses contrary
to the doctrine which you have learned;
and avoid them. For they that are such serve
not our Lord Jesus Christ,
but their belly; and by good words and fair speeches
deceive the hearts of the simple."

In conclusion let us remember that 'poieo' is the process of building something. One can either build something for God or you will build something against Him. We are admonished to judge ourselves in all matters of service and sacrifice. When we are fleshly, we should always be aware of Satan's ability to seduce. Any attack of the enemy no matter how subtle should be withstood. It is obvious from the testimony of the Scriptures that many in the last days will 'poieo' (build) by the wrong spirit. Their motives may be innocent, but their work is still not pure nor godly. Take heed therefore to continue your work in the Spirit, but weigh all things by grace and truth. Remember, the Word is truth.

Chapter 6 – Understanding Demonic Attacks

The primary thing about demonism and demonology is that they both generally look at demonic activity in a direct way. The Church has been trained over many years to view demonology in this way. The thing to know about Satan and his dominions is that they work on us indirectly 99.99% of the time.

Not every situation or problem in life has a demonic root, but many believers are under constant attack. The first place to start in understanding demonic attacks is to know what a demonic spirit is. Many view these beings in light of pagan philosophy, rather than from an exegetical and biblical standpoint. Early European pagan religions and some forms of Greek philosophy breed the ideas of ghosts and goblins, which is not in line with Scriptural truth. The apostles viewed demons as "beings that had knowledge" or "were experienced in a thing." This is why the Greek word 'diamon' (demon) was used to describe them. The root meaning of the Greek word translated as *demon* comes from a word that means "to assign," hence the concept of satanic assignment or appointment is derived. From the outset of this study we must recognize a simple truth concerning demons. There are only two ways an individual can experience demonic oppression on a constant basis. The first is a lack of Christian maturity, and the other is to not know Christ Jesus as Savior. This is not to say that if you experience demonic attacks you are immature. I am simply stating that when an individual cannot defeat these demonic advancements it is due to immaturity. He that is in you is greater than he that is in the world (see 1 John 4:4).

The Biblical Revelation of Spirit

The word "spirit" in the New Testament (4151-'pneuma') is defined in Strong's Concordance as "a current of air (i.e. breath, a blast, or a breeze)." The word can be literally defined from Greek exegesis as "to give life to" something. We should be aware that the word 'pneuma', as defined in the context of the human soul, is described as "the vital principle of life, or a mental disposition, and 'pneuma' has been interpreted as the spirit of a man, or as the Spirit of God, and paradoxically as a demon or an angel (also a spiritual being)." There are only two Greek words in the New Testament translated as the English word "spirit(s)"; they are 'pneuma' and the word 'phantasma' (5326). *Phantasma* is only used twice in the New Testament, in Matthew 14:26 and Mark 6:49. The word reflects the idea of a being that is spiritual by nature, whether a demon or a being of another sort. The writers of the New Testament used the word 'phantasma' to describe their attitudes when they saw Jesus walking on the water; they thought He was a "spirit." I will define and explain 'pneuma' throughout this chapter.

To better understand the influence of demonic beings in our lives we must first know how they affect us. There are several ways that Satan attacks the believer. The Scripture prepares us to combat these attacks and gives us the wisdom to see their encroachment. We need to be aware of several phases involved in Satan's approach. These phases are described in the Greek language by the Greek words: 'topos', 'methodia', 'pagis', 'noema', 'phobos', 'pathos', and 'oneidismos'. When these Greek words are translated they reveal how Satan takes an overview of our life. He then devises a method of attack by using a snare that is triggered by a demonic device which produces fear in an area of our soul, which then results in a pattern of thought or *phobia*, which in turn, creates a path or way of life (lifestyle) that results in reproach.

The Satanic Attack

> "Neither give place to the devil."
> (Ephesians 4:27)

The Greek word 'topos' (5117), translated as "place" in the above passage, means "to give a condition, an opportunity, or license" to the devil. The Bible teaches us to not give Satan an opportunity or an occasion that he can use to his advantage. *Topos* is where the English word "top" comes from. To be on top is to have the advantage by position. Webster's dictionary defines the word *top* as "the highest part of anything; the highest rank, or it is also described as a platform with the most prominent view." Militarily speaking, whosoever holds the high ground has the advantage. Satan's plan is to gain a position over us that gives him the most strategic perspective of our life. *Topographein* is another Greek word that means "to describe a place" and is a derivative of 'topos'. This is where the word 'topography' originates. To take a topographical survey is the art or practice of graphing the "delineation of a land's natural features." It is most commonly understood to be a picture of the ground taken from above. This picture from above shows the lay out of that property with its boundaries, as well as its natural features. Satan wants to gain the advantage in order to view us in this way. He surveys us from birth to discover our natural vulnerabilities and weaknesses (Satan uses 'familiar' or family spirits to accomplish this goal). These delineations or diagrams of our tendencies can then be utilized for our demise. Think about the way you are in a natural sense. Do you anger quickly? Your children will too. Are you fearful? You will see the transference of these natural tendencies into your family. We are commanded in the Scriptures to be aware of our natural tendencies that give Satan and his forces place or opportunity (i.e., 'topos'). We should not give him license or set up the right condition for him to attack us. For example, if we open the door to lust, Satan sees the opportunity and can take advantage of us with this knowledge. If we have natural tendencies, that is, if we have a common disposition or an inclination toward something, Satan will send someone or something to fulfill that desire in us. Eve gave Satan the opportunity to deceive her when she gave him 'place'. How did it happen? She gave him place simply by listening to him. When Eve listened she gave Satan access into her thoughts and her reasoning. We can remove this 'topos' from Satan through the authority of Jesus Christ and by being obedient to the Word of God. Satan does not have the right to trespass because of the work of the cross removed his power over us. We have been redeemed by the Lord and purchased by His blood, so Satan has no right to manipulate us. But remember, Satan is a thief and a robber and robbers break the law. See Deuteronomy 18:10-13 for a limited list of demonic spirits and manifestations.

Satan and his fallen angels have been cast down. When Satan wants to violate you and create vulnerability in you, he sends a demonic spirit to affect a certain thing that he sees in you. When you realize that a demonic spirit is a being that "gives life" to something in you, it will renew your mind and give you revelation and you will be able to connect the dots, so to speak. For example, it is the Spirit of God who gives life to our spirit and when our spirit is "quickened" (i.e., made alive); it becomes the source of strength for the inner, hidden man of the heart. We then have access to God because we have given place to Jesus Christ, who is the door (see John 10:9 and Revelation 3:8). When a demonic spirit comes from Satan, it gives life to something that produces the fruit of the flesh or promotes the wisdom that is from below (see James 3:15). Satan establishes a doorway through the soul to "earthliness" (1919) or worldliness. The doorway or principality is part of Satan's method. This earthliness (worldliness) is Satan's ability to create a connection between your soul (your mind, your will, and/or your temperament) and a worldly life viewpoint. Through this doorway Satan then builds a stronger demonic merger by combining sensuality and worldliness, thus reinforcing his position of control. This sensuality is called 'psuchikos' (5591) in the Greek language. When 'psuchikos' (i.e., selfishness or self-amplification) is utilized, it produces a self-motivated and self-centered person that Satan can then fabricate into a "devilish individual" ('diamonizomai'-1139). A point of interest for everyone to consider is when 'diamonizomai' is discovered you should realize that your Christian foundation is not complete.

Diamonizomai is the Greek word that means "to be demonized." It is the oppression that occurs in the life of an individual who has been under attack for long periods of time. Oppression is defined as "the depression of mind or spirit." The Greek word gives us a picture of one who is "vexed" or is "under the power of a demon." 'Diamonizomai' (i.e., oppression) can cause afflictions in the body and/or the mind. The Scripture attributes paralysis, blindness, and deafness as well as loss of speech, epilepsy, melancholy, and insanity to 'diamonizomai'. The concept of possession should not be associated with this. Demons do not possess; that is pagan ideology, not Christian theology. They control by manipulation and deception. Demons cannot possess the freewill of a person. That would give us an excuse for our actions and "the devil made me do it" ideology would be a reality. This is not so. Demons control by taking the advantage 'topos' gives them. If you want to give them total control, you can, if you choose to. Demons express themselves in the consciousness of a person by two means: direct and indirect manifestation. Direct demonic influence (manifestation) occurs when spirits are openly manifesting their influence in a person by manipulating the individual's temperament, and by perverting a person's disposition. The level of this manifestation is directly proportional to the amount of "place" a person gives the spirit. The degree of 'topos' given to demons by an individual can reflect in the intensity of the manipulation it uses. It can reach the level of oppression the Gadarene demonic walked in, as seen in Mark 5. Matthew 4:24 reveals that when someone is "demonized" it can make them sick. The Greek words translated as "sick" people in this passage describe people who are held in a condition of oppression. Direct contact with demon spirits creates an inner pathway whereby they have opened the way for this type of manipulation. Again, we all have free will and no demon can control the will, but an individual can give such place to a devil that the devil freely utilizes the person's faculties, and this is evidenced in the Scriptures.

In Mark 5 the Gadarene demoniac had several characteristics that should be noted. These characteristics are common among individuals who have direct demonic influence in their lives. First, he had an unnatural association with death (he was a man of the tombs). The Greek word translated as "tombs" (3419) has the root meaning of "remembering" or "to remember something that was traumatic." The word "tomb" is defined in Strong's Concordance as a 'cenotaph' (i.e., a monument for someone not buried at that place). We see them all the time as we travel down major highways. Little crosses on the side of the road signifying that someone has died there in a car accident, which is a 'cenotaph'. The Gadarene was obsessed with death and dying, and is described as having such demonic influence in his life that he hurt himself. Self-mutilation is a common characteristic of demonically manipulated people. Most often it is a cry for attention, but when someone cuts himself it is also evidence of a much deeper and sinister situation. The Gadarene was also out of control. He was defiant and could not be restrained. Satanic influence manifests in people as unruliness, defiance, rebelliousness, and disobedience. People who are under direct demonic influence most often reflect and manifest Satan's personality. They are pride-filled and arrogant, hostile to authority, abusive, cruel, and violent.

In Mark 5 the devils named themselves as "legion" and described themselves as 'polus' (4183) (i.e., many). The common interpretation of "legion" is that it represents a certain number of devils, but the word means much more than a number. It means "great or strong", and carries the idea of something that is prolific. The passage could have easily been translated with the phrase, "we are legion, for we rule this man like an army occupies the land". The level of demonic control also relates directly to salvation. When salvation is present the level of control is generally less than when one is not saved. The demons begged the Lord not to send them out of the 'chora' (5561- country). The root meaning of this word is "an empty place" or "a chasm." These devils had found some unoccupied territory in the man's life. Though demonic influence is a biblical reality, demonic rule should not be found in the lives of those who know God as Savior. The Gadarene had given place to a large number of unclean spirits. 'Topos' was given to the devils in such a degree that they ruled him (see Mark 5:8).

When demonic spirits come to us, they come with a purpose. An unclean spirit (169) comes to give life to impurity or lewdness within the individual. The unclean spirit is associated with idolatry throughout the Bible. The Old Testament, in its practical approach to the salvation, deals with demonic influence from their origin. Of course Satan is ultimately the originator, but he uses anything as a "producer." Rejection gives place to unclean spirits and unclean spirits thrive on these emotions.

One common cause of rejection is incest. When a person has experienced incest, self-rejection manifests through shame and an impure disposition, which directly relates to his self worth. When we look at Tamar (see 2 Samuel 13) we can see the progression of this problem in her personality. Incest produces shame, then rejection, and finally a bi-polar state of insanity (see 2 Samuel 13: 16, 19, 20). Demonic forces promote promiscuity to increase incest. Fornication ('porneia'-4202) gives place to incest, homosexual tendencies, sexual experimentation, and sexual perversion. We also find that a person who is under direct demonic influence is also without restraint. Their moral point of view is an attitude of lust where anything and everything is acceptable to them. Extreme rebelliousness is often the evidence of demonic manipulation. Submission to authority is not in the devil's nature. Every restraint will be tried and tested by demonized individuals. They will use every logical concept and thought to justify their insurgence, and they usually view all outside authority as oppressive. The person under direct demonic influence will have tendencies to scream, raise his voice inappropriately, shriek, and throw tantrums. Remember, these individuals are also involved in self-mutilation. I know of a four-year old child who was not allowed to get his way so he cut his own arm to get back at the parent. It is highly unlikely a four-year old would do this type of behavior without some form of outside influence. Parents should look at their ways if their children are manifesting extreme or out of control behavior. After the event the child confessed that he cut himself because he "wanted his mommy to give him the candy." This is not to say that out of control children are demonized, but there should be a cause for alarm when extreme behavior has moved into severe and outlandish behavior. The demonized are continuously involved in self-destructive behavior. Another manifestation of direct demonic influence is a perverted attitude toward Jesus Christ. Demonically influenced people view God as one who torments. Their concept of faith is distorted and they tend to get involved in doctrinal extremes.

Indirect demonic influence, on the other hand, is often hidden in the subtleties of one's own personality. Indirect influence is most commonly seen in people who believe a lie and refuse to believe that it is a lie. No matter what evidence is presented they have a belief that they refuse to change. Indirect influence is usually something from one's past which taps into a path of a previous root of pain or trauma, allowing the influence to remain hidden until re-ignited by a present experience. This path of the root is our ability to feel an emotion of the past as though it originated in the present. This is how a demonic spirit can affect our present disposition and suddenly bring on a state of depression, anxiety, or panic attack that seem to occur from out of nowhere in particular. (We will more fully develop The Path of the Root in a later chapter in this book.) These demonic spirits give life to something by tapping into the path that the old root has taken. For example, if you had a bad relationship in the past and meet someone new, Satan can tap into the root and cause you bring up those old feelings. It's like someone went through a bad marriage and their emotion flares up at their new mate without a cause or in an extreme. The new mate may be unaware of the trigger (i.e., some simple action) that causes a path of the root in their new husband or wife to open. I was counseling a couple where the wife had been abused by her former husband and lived in fear of abuse by her new husband. Her new husband was unaware of her fears and would say things that would trigger her emotional state and release unwarranted fear. The problem in their marriage would manifest with little or no reason. The husband would disagree with something the wife said, and she would react very inappropriately and in extremes. We should recognize that a spirit of fear breathes or gives life to fear in you or taps the path of an old fear to its source. Each time certain incidents would occur, her emotion would tap into the root of her fear and it would regenerate all the pain she had bottled up inside. Through counseling and love she was able to overcome her past and accept her husband for whom he is, not what she feared him to be. If you listen to the devil and give place to fear then the fear begins to grow. The longer you give place to it, the longer it has the time to sprout roots or return to its old path.

When you do not give Satan entrance, Satan then deceives and manipulates the individual to obtain the best condition for that entrance. Satan is constantly trying to gain access to our heart and mind. If Satan has the "topography" of your life he is able to send these demonic forces to survey and/or attack the weak area he discovers. By definition a spirit of fear is a disposition of timidity, faithlessness, dread, fearfulness, or cowardice. By example, a disciple was given the instruction to read nine chapters a day in the New Testament as he attended a discipleship class. He made excuses for two months how he was unable to follow the instruction. I read the book of Malachi to him in about ten minutes. I was reading very slow and methodically. I showed him that reading at a fifth grade level took only forty minutes to read nine chapters, give or take a few minutes. Satan had intimidated him into this attitude and had created a disposition of inability in him. He had lived with a degraded view of himself for years and this path had to be broken. He believed the task was too great and he was overwhelmed with the homework. The spirit of fear was defeated by the truth. (A spirit of fear is also defined as "to wax feeble" or "to be weak" due to pride and arrogance.)

A spirit of perversion is a spirit that introduces a distorted or twisted perspective to an individual. In the Bible this demonic influence is described as "to be a crook, to do amiss, to commit error, to do wrong, and to feel alone" . One of the purposes of a spirit of perversion is to cause you to be weighted down with feelings of guilt. This is perversion because Jesus took our sin on Himself. The Bible says that God has cast our sin as far as the east is from the west. Isaiah 19:14 says that a perverted spirit is "mingled" and that this mingling affects every work of God in our lives. A spirit of perversion affects our activities and the operation of our soul. A manifestation of insecurity is one of the things that will become mingled in our activities if a spirit of perversion is working on you. These levels of insecurity also have an effect on our worldview. When a spirit of perversion and a spirit of fear work in tandem they greatly increase their individual effect. They work to affect the "origin" of our soul's reference point. Demons influence our worldview so that it no longer originates from God centeredness, but stems from self-centeredness. This is one of the things that cause us to do wrong things or commit error. Our thought processes, our will, and our emotions become distorted due to the perversion of perceived self-ability. Satan is then able to introduce error, because from his vantage point he is able to see the shift in our paradigm (pattern). An unclean spirit works in close proximity to a perverted spirit and strengthens one's self-centeredness into idolatry. Once Satan has introduced the perversion, he can then mingle demonic, impure, and lewd concepts into the life and thought processes because of his 'topos'. When the uncleanness of the demonic spirit begins to take root, self-righteousness is used to shore-up the demonic objectives. The believer becomes uncorrectable because they justify themselves or view others as the problem. They are no longer flexible and adaptable in their responses to the Holy Spirit and thus become rigid and hard-hearted. Satan can now use other demonic forces to complete his invasion and the occupation of their land. When Satan has the 'topos' he can view an individual's weaknesses and plan his attacks accordingly. Consider the Pharisees and Sadducees in Jesus' day. Satan had blinded them by pride and self-worth. Satan used their place and stature to the degree that they murdered Jesus.

'Familiar' spirits are a unique class of demonic forces. There are fifteen different familiar spirits listed in the Bible. They operate in stealth by hiding in custom and tradition. The word "familiar" in the original language means "to talk or chatter in a meaningless or simple-minded way." It is to babble on without purpose. The etymology of the word comes from the Hebrew word that is translated as "father" or "patriarchal." To have a familiar spirit is to have an area in your life that is incomplete (usually due to improper or ungodly training), especially when the father in the household does not take an active role in the child's upbringing or does not live up to his responsibility as a dad. When fathers are critical or ignore their children, this in itself increases insecurity and produces a weakened countenance in the child. A 'familiar' spirit is a family characteristic that is passed down through the generations, creating a commonality or family distinction. The Bible lists these characteristics as necromancy, an observer of times, an enchanter, a witch, and a wizard. These are very serious and hidden demonic tendencies.

The characteristic within an individual that causes them to be preoccupied with death and dying is the necromancing spirit. This demonic force works commonly with the spirit of fear and influences morbid behavior such as hypochondria and it produces a pathological fear of ill health or unexpected death that will porter (open the door) to sickness. The degree of entrance a necromancing spirit has will dictate the degree of manifestation or affixation in the life of the person. This spirit, when accompanied by a spirit of perversion, also guides individuals into sexual distortions of the grossest kind. Also, let it be understood that necromancing spirits have the ability to produce physical symptoms.

An observer of times is one who ritualistically (almost psychotic at times) acts covertly. This spirit is a major source of paranoia. The Hebrew word is also translated as 'sorcerer' and carries the concept of "one who covers in a demonic way." This covering is the state of mind one gets through horoscopes or through the practicing of spiritualism. It also means "to gather or collect" by using soothsaying. The sorcerer is one who looks for 'place' with you so they can control you. In essence they want to be your friend because you have something they want. Once they get it they are finished with you. Individuals with the manifestation of this demonic influence manipulate friendships, coerce opportunities, and use every tactic possible to gain the advantage in relationships. When an individual is unaware of this demonic influence in their life, they tend to feel hostility within personal relationships. These people are usually control freaks. They most often are unaware that their tactics can be seen and the possessiveness they express is repulsive. This demonic spirit has influenced many of America's youth; boyfriend or girl friend control (which grows stronger in marriage) is one of the obvious manifestations.

An enchanter is one who learns by the experience of omens. An "omen" is a sign or indication of some future event or is an occurrence or phenomenon believed to portend a future event. This is common in many false prophets today. They use their knowledge of an individual or upcoming event to prophesy a course and direction that is not of God. These types of prophecies are usually general in nature and open to interpretation. In Genesis 44:5 and 15, Joseph used his cup as a "tool of divining" to get information about his father and brother. Joseph used his cup as a tool to control his brothers' actions in order to get a designed outcome. Joseph's purpose was for the restoration and deliverance of his family. Enchanters do this for profit. I am not saying Joseph was demonized; I just want you to get the framework of this devilish influence into perspective. The profit an enchanter is looking for does not have to be money. It can be power, position, honor, glory, or recognition. The idea of a "nosy person" is also expressed here. They want information about you so they can use it to their advantage. They can tell another what they know to gain stature with them. They put others down in order to make themselves look better.

The wizard and the witch are basically the male and the female manifestations of the same 'familiar' spirit, with a few idiosyncrasies particular to each one. The witch works to cut off and destroy people by evil speaking. Gossip and backbiting are the two most common manifestations of this demonic influence. Witches have the characteristics that work toward the elimination of a person's authority and effectiveness. They speak curses onto people. Curses do not have to be incantations or spells; they are more commonly misrepresentations of the truth about an individual's character. These words curse individuals by creating a biased image of their character and personage. The Hebrew word for "curses" means "to cut down" or "to cause one to be dismissed." The witch uses these demonic forces to assist her in the exclusion, destabilizing, and removal of authorities and dignities. Lies and falsities produce a hardship of service, which in turn, discourages the person from serving God, but that is the purpose of the curse: to destroy their effectiveness. The wizard operates as does the witch, but goes further in his attacks. His level of deception and manipulation is much more severe than the witch. The wizard uses his insight of a person or situation to affect and control it. The Bible teaches us that wizards are lawless and full of iniquities. They use relationships, family problems, dispositions, and attitudes to manipulate their preferred outcome. Their ability to affect someone is also increased by their position. Familiar spirits use their influence to control an individual in order that their control of one individual will affect others. Notice that these are *familiar* spirits, which means they are most commonly associated with indirect demonic influence, and are commonly propagated in the home.

The Wiles of the Devil

> "Put on the whole armor of God, that you may be
> able to stand against the wiles of the devil.
> For we wrestle not against flesh and blood, but against
> principalities, against powers, against the rulers of the darkness
> of this world, against spiritual wickedness in high places."
> (Ephesians 6:11-12)

One of the major errors in Christian circles is that we under-estimate Satan's abilities. The degree of cleverness Satan can muster to disguise his real purpose is often extreme and insightful. Our enemy will go to great lengths to out-maneuver us in his attack. One thing of interest is Paul's choice of words in describing the controlling process. The Greek word translated as "wiles" (3180) in Ephesians 6:11 is the Greek word 'methodia.' It is where the English word "method" originates. The word means "to travel over, that is, to go systematically to work, to do or pursue something methodically, and according to a set standard of procedure." Satan orderly and meticulously follows a technical procedure in the handling of an individual. The same Greek word is also used in Ephesians 4:14 and is translated as to "lie in wait to deceive." What is he lying in wait for? He is waiting for the principalities (746), powers (1849), the rulers of the darkness of this world (2888/4655/165), and the wicked spirits in the heavenly places (4152/4189/2032) to do their thing! These are progressive influences.

The Greek word 'arche' that is translated as the English word "principality" is defined as "a commencement (i.e., a beginning or doorway)." It is where the English word "archway" is derived. What are 'principalities'? They are demonic spirits that specialize in opening a door of influence to gain entrance into your life. They are the forces that initiate Satan's process. They are able beings. They know how to commence an operation and open the way for other demonic forces to gain entrance. They are Satan's Special Forces. These 'arche' (principalities) open the door for the demonic 'exousia' (authorities). These demonic powers are the spirits that control access once the entrance has been gained. They manipulate and deceive so the 'kosmokrators' (rulers of this world) can do their work of destruction and manipulation. A *kosmokrater* is a demonic spirit used to establish and promote worldliness. 'Kosmos' (2889) is the decoration or the adorning of the world. Cosmetology is the art of adorning, or making us look better. New hair-do, new nails, and new make-up are all staged to attract someone into our influence or for us to have a better impression of ourselves. These spirits influence a state of mind that diminishes spirituality and promotes fleshliness. I do not see in the Scriptures that it is a sin to put on make up or to fix your hair; but Satan uses these to gain entrance. These demonic spiritual powers also give entrance to wicked spirits in the heavenly realm. These spirits produce "plots of malice," and by their definition these spirits are hurtful, degenerative, calamitous, and derelict. This is Satan's method of operation. Satan waits for these forces to fashion an opportunity to create 'phobos' (fear-5401) in us.

Phobos, Pagis, Noema, Pathos, and Oneidismos

The psychological concept of "phobia" comes from the word 'phobos'. *Phobeo* (5399), a derivative of 'phobos', is described as the type of fear used to control any given situation. Satan uses phobias to generate unreasonable or persistent fear of things in order to eliminate an individual's effectiveness or to weaken a person causing them to become vulnerable to satanic suggestion. This is where the 'pagis' (3803) comes in. 'Pagis' is translated as the "snare" of the devil. When Satan sets a 'pagis', a trick or a stratagem (i.e., a temptation), he is trying to catch someone.

> "And that they may recover themselves
> out of the snare ('pagis') of the devil, who are
> taken captive by him at his will."
> (2 Timothy 2:26)

Satan sets these snares through his 'noema' (3540). A 'noema' is a device that is utilized as bait. *Noema* is also translated as "mind" (mindset) and "thoughts" in the New Testament. *Noema* also means *to perceive*. Satan uses his perceptions (i.e., his knowledge of us) to bait the snare he has set for us. He utilizes our weaknesses to draw us into the temptation. If one has a problem in an area of the flesh it is Satan's common approach to use it against him. This is why the Bible says "there hath been no temptation taken you but such as is common to man" and the Lord wants you to understand this truth (see 1 Corinthians 10:13). Here are some passages where 'noema' is used:

> "For we are not ignorant of his devices ('noema')."
> (2 Corinthians 2:11)

> "In whom the god of this world
> has blinded the minds ('noema') of them which believe not."
> (2 Corinthians 4:4)

"But their minds ('noema') were blinded."
(2 Corinthians 3:14)

"Casting down imaginations, and every high thing that exalts itself
against the knowledge of God, and bringing into
captivity every thought ('noema') to the obedience of Christ."
(2 Corinthians 10:5)

In 1 John 4:18, notice that fear ('phobos') has "torment" (2851/1161) attached to it. This "torment" is defined as self-imposed infliction. This self-imposed punishment will not allow the believer to mature in the faith, and is why Satan uses fear in the first place.

"For you have not received the spirit of bondage again
to fear ('phobos'); but you have received the Spirit
of adoption, whereby we cry, Abba, Father."
(Romans 8:15)

Phobos is utilized to create bondage. This bondage is designed to make the believer subject to the controls of Satan.

"And deliver them who through fear ('phobos') of death
were in all their lifetime subject to bondage."
(Hebrews 2:15)

When Satan can achieve fear in us, he can then create 'pathos' (3806). *Pathos* comes from the root word that means "a hurt, a wound, or a suffering". Pathos is defined as "the soul's diseased condition from which the various lusts spring." Pathos is the path one's mental condition takes because of the state of their inner man. The "*pathos* of a root" is a problem that produces a longing for sin. If it is not dealt with, one cannot possess his vessel in sanctification and honor (see 1 Thessalonians 4:4).

Oneidismos is the reproach the devil causes in someone. It is the internal taunting which produces a sense of disgrace. This usually causes the person to have the desire to stop fighting against what they perceive as unfixable and this is Satan's ultimate goal in the warfare.

As believers begin to recognize Satan's schemes and his attempts to weaken them they should be able to counter his attacks. Recognition is truly one of the major keys to victory. When a believer grows in the admonition of the Lord and develops soldiering skills they will ultimately mature in the resistance process and be able to hold off and counter demonic attacks. This is the purpose of Christian discipleship and spiritual training.

Chapter 7 — The Spirit of Anti-Christ

"For many deceivers are entered into the world,
who confess not that Jesus Christ is come in the flesh.
This is a deceiver and an antichrist."
(2 John 7)

"Little children, it is the last time:
and as ye have heard that antichrist shall come,
even now are there many antichrists;
whereby we know that it is the last time."
(1 John 2:18)

"Who is a liar but he that denies that Jesus is the Christ?
He is antichrist, that denies the Father and the Son."
(1 John 2:22)

"And every spirit that confesses not that Jesus
Christ is come in the flesh is not of God:
and this is that spirit of antichrist, whereof you
have heard that it should come;
and even now already is it in the earth."
(1 John 4:3)

One of the major areas of concern in Christendom is the Antichrist. Who is he? Where will he come from? What will cause his rise to power? These are all valid questions, but one cannot forget that his spirit has been in the earth and working against the Kingdom of God for two thousand years. We are closer than ever to the last of the last days and the spirit of anti-Christ is very active in today's world and in the American society as never before. The book of Revelation foretells his personal manifestation while the Apostle John makes us aware that the spiritual manifestations of the antichrist have been and are presently operating. These anti-Christ manifestations are spiritual in their origin, even though they operate through the soul and flesh of man, in and through much of our media, and in many false religions. Demonic forces are spiritual, yet they can usually be recognized as influences on the soul (i.e., influences on the mind, will, and temperament of a person), and can also be seen in anti-Christian rhetoric and anti-Christian attitudes. We should be aware that demonic forces are presently trying to influence every area of our society, pushing legislation to outlaw any aspect of God in our society. Demonic influences continuously try to affect the walk of a believer; though their influence may be more indirect than direct in many people's lives. As stated in the last chapter the Greek word "pneuma," translated as "spirit" (4151) in the New Testament can be more clearly defined as that influence which gives life to something. The breath of God or the moving of God's Spirit is God's influence on us. God's Spirit gives life to our spirit, the spirit of antichrist produces and gives life to the things that are against Christ, but the spirit of anti-Christ has been increasing in strength and intensity during the past few decades. When we can differentiate between the influences of demonic forces and how their devices affect us, we will then be able to observe how they manipulate, coerce, and hinder us and the Body of Christ. Satan is producing a false life in many Christians (i.e., the life of the flesh); a temporary thrill. Many people do not recognize the difference between the true life of God and emotionalism, which is promoted throughout the Church in our so called modern era. The Scripture states that there is nothing new under the sun and the proponents of the so called "Modern Era" are merely using this ideology to attack the Body of Christ and the Church as a whole. Much of the emotionalism propagated in today's churches is a form of spiritual life that is based on temporal things, it only satisfies the impatience of a person's soul, but has no God power to enable Christians to become overcomers. It consummates in the "I want it now and will do anything to get it" mentality. It is not just people in the world that are being affected by these demonic schemes, the Church is experiencing open manifestations of false spiritual power that is turning people away from Jesus' original plan and purpose. Paul spoke if this in 2 Timothy 3:5.

> "Having a form of godliness,
> but denying the power thereof:
> from such turn away."

Three things to notice in this passage: first, the word "form" means "an appearance, a formula, or the semblance of the real;" second, the word "denying" means "to contradict;" and third, Paul commands us to turn away and reject such things. Similarly, it is the Greek word "noema" (3450) that is translated in 2 Corinthians 2:11 as the word "devices." The Scripture says we are "not ignorant of his devices," but what are his devices? A noema (device) is a perception "i.e., a purpose in one's point of view or, by implication the intellect and disposition one uses to create a perception." As we have seen before, Satan's devices are his thoughts, and the mindset he creates in us through our perceptions, attitudes, moods, and dispositions. He deceives us into believing that his thoughts and attitudes are our thoughts and attitudes, or that those thoughts and attitudes are the general attitudes and dispositions of the Church and its leaders, thus creating in us an open door of agreement that he can use to gain entrance. The only time Satan has power to manipulate us is when we get into agreement with him. Our agreement with God is called confession, while our agreement with the spirit of anti-Christ is called deception (see Luke 21:8). As we discussed in the previous chapter, Satan and his demons use a strategy of direct and indirect influences that turn and lead us into their predetermined course. The word "noema" is also used in 2 Corinthians 3:14, when the Scripture states that "their minds (noema) were blinded." Satan used his scheme against their thinking. The Greek word "poroo" (4456) translated as blinded, gives us a clue as to how Satan worked to accomplish his goal. Poroo is defined as "to petrify or harden," but is also where our word "porous" comes from. The Greek root of this word is "poros" and is a kind of stone, a porous stone; one that has the ability to absorb. Part of Satan's strategy is to harden our heart against the spiritual leadings of the Holy Spirit so he can manipulate the truth and bring deception to the "hearer." If I am unable to distinguish between the spiritual influences of Satan and the Holy Spirit, I have lost the battle already. Satan attacks us by using the weaknesses of our natural being. It is natural for us to want to see miracles and it is natural for us to want to feel spiritual vitality, but the true course of God is to give Jesus the glory and not the miracle itself. When Satan can utilize familiar or family spirits, it gives him a greater advantage because he utilizes the familiarity of our circumstances to trick and ambush us. This is why custom and tradition are so often Satan's strongest weapons. Think about how Satan used the Pharisees and the Sadducees to work his wickedness against Jesus? The one area they had grown accustomed to, the Law (i.e., God's Word), became his tool. He used the same tactic on Jesus when He was led of the Holy Spirit in the wilderness Satan used the tradition of the religious tradition to corrupt and pervert the minds of the Sadducees and the Pharisees. How did Satan attack the Gentiles? Through the area they are most familiar with; idolatry and self exaltation. The Romans used their personal status to bully and lord over people. They were arrogant. Arrogance is defined as "assuming; making or having the disposition to make exorbitant claims of rank or estimation; giving one's self an undue degree of importance." Satan uses the process of blindness as his device to cause us to sift the truth through tradition, which calluses our heart against the Spirit of God. Isaiah 29:10-14 deals this matter from an Old Testament perspective.

> "For the Lord has poured out upon you the spirit of deep
> sleep, and has closed your eyes: the prophets and your rulers,
> the seers has he covered. And the vision of all is
> become unto you as the words of a book that is sealed, which men
> deliver to one that is learned, saying, Read this, I pray thee; and
> he says, I cannot; for it is sealed: And the book is delivered to him
> that is not learned, saying, Read this, I pray thee: and he said, I am not
> learned. Wherefore the Lord said, Forasmuch as this people draw
> near me with their mouth, and with their lips do they honor me, but
> have removed their heart far from me, and their fear toward me is
> taught by the precept of men: Therefore, behold, I will proceed

to do a marvelous work among this people, even a marvelous work
and a wonder: for the wisdom of their wise men shall perish, and the
understanding of their prudent men shall be hid."

The prophet Isaiah is simply saying that when blindness comes upon a people, they cannot understand the Word of God or the moving of His Spirit. They have no personal respect for God and have to be taught reverence because it is not in them. They began to pursue things that have no godly meaning and they venture into dead works. When Jesus quoted these verses from Isaiah in Matthew 15:8-11, He added this statement,

"But in vain they do worship me, teaching for
doctrines the commandments of men."

Paul also dealt with this in Colossians 2:20-23:

"Wherefore if you be dead with Christ from the rudiments of
the world, why, as though living in the world, are you subject to
ordinances, (Touch not; taste not; handle not; Which all are to perish
with the using;) after the commandments and doctrines of men? Which things
have indeed a show in will worship, and humility, and neglecting of the
body; not in any honor to the satisfying of the flesh."

"For the terrible one is brought to nought,
and the scorner is consumed, and all that
watch for iniquity are cut off.
That make a man an offender for a word,
and lay a snare for him that reproveth in the gate,
and turn aside the just for a thing of nought."
Isaiah 29:20-21

Isaiah 29:20-21 reveals that blinded people make a man an "offender for a word" or they turn aside the just for a thing of naught. I am amazed at how Satan uses religious notions and concepts of holiness to create division and strife in churches and with brothers and sisters in the Lord. The spirit of antichrist substitutes and changes Jesus' purpose into some hyper-spiritual concept of piety that has no value; it causes division and strife under the guise of holiness. The spirit of antichrist uses his influence to manifest a "holier than thou" mentality and manipulates both sides in any issue to support his purpose of division. The real snare occurs when both parties use the Bible to support their individual causes. As an example let me use the various doctrines related to the drinking of alcohol as an example. Deuteronomy 14:22-27 is giving commandments as how the tithe is to be used in several circumstances, but in the commandment the Holy Spirit says,

> "And thou shalt bestow that money for whatsoever
> thy soul lusteth after, for oxen, or for sheep,
> or for wine, or for strong drink, or for whatsoever thy soul desireth:
> and thou shalt eat there before the Lord thy God,
> and thou shalt rejoice, thou, and thine household."

Now if drinking alcohol is a sin, then the Holy Spirit commanded people to sin, which we know is impossible for God to do, so the only alternative is to create a series of doctrines to ban the use of it. When the passage was translated into Latin (ex ovibus vinum quoque et siceram et omne quod desiderat anima) wine and strong drink, or strong wine hold their true meaning in the translation. Another Scripture in the Gospel of John (chapter 2) gives credence to this when Jesus turned the water into wine, as well as the fact that Paul told Timothy to drink a little wine for his stomachs sake. If drinking wine or strong drink were a sin, then Paul was in sin, as well as Jesus for making the wine. Of course it is not a sin to drink wine or strong drink, as the Bible declares, but that does not stop the pious from preaching against it. These doctrines are coupled with traditional statements like, "What about all the drunks?" It is a matter of temperance and self-control. Our society does not teach either. We live in a "go for the gusto" society and over-indulgence is a common problem for hedonistic societies. The Church needs to be proactive were matters of temperance and self-control are concerned, but we do not need to teach untruths. The Bible is clear on the matter and it says:

> "He (the Lord) causeth the grass to grow for the cattle,
> and herb for the service of man: that he may
> bring forth food out of the earth;
> And wine that maketh glad the heart of man,
> and oil to make his face to shine, and bread
> which strengtheneth man's heart."
> (Psalm 104:15)

While it also says,

> "Wine is a mocker, strong drink is raging:
> and whosoever is deceived thereby is not wise."
> (Proverb 20:1)

The balance can be found when we have wisdom enough to know that wine and strong drink are not toys to play with; and again, temperance and self-control are the real issues. If you are not in control of yourself when you drink alcohol, Satan will defiantly use it to against you to make a fool out of you. Lack of self-control is rampant in our society. All the wrongs you see are caused by wicked alcohol; they are the symptoms of individuals who are out of control. Alcohol is a "soul enhancer." It can only elevate what is already in the heart. Jesus said, "It is not what goes into the man that defiles him. It is what comes out. If your heart is not pure, the alcohol will magnify what is already there. If your heart is pure, then the alcohol will magnify that. Philo says that when righteous men have too much to drink they fall down giving God their praise. Some have philosophies and doctrines contrary to the Bible and this is why they labor as they justify their "truth". They have to justify their error with dead works and platitudes of personal experiences, not bringing clarity to what the Bible actually says about various subjects. This type of preaching is why so many Christians are confused about many issues. The only right source for Christian living is the Bible; it must be our first and primary source of truth. The doctrine may be "good," but it has one too many "o". There are various doctrines that claim the wine Jesus made was actually grape juice, when the Greek word used in the passage as wine means real wine (i.e., wine that has an intoxicating effect). The Greek word for "new wine" used in the New Testament does not mean grape juice either. The Greek word "gleukos" (1098) actually means "very intoxicating wine." Strong's defines it this way: "...used of the more saccharine (and therefore highly inebriating) fermented wine." A spirit of error is thus created in the minds of people because of the attitudes toward the wrong use of alcohol or the misuse of it, and the self-idolized congregation continues to divide commanding people against drinking alcohol of any type or degree, being blinded and taken in by the Satan's scheme. It is very true that there are many people who must abstain from drinking. They cannot handle it or alcoholics. There is no shame either way. We should not allow the goodness of a doctrine to become a god to us. The situation reflects, as the Jews of old reformulated and changed the commandment, they thought the later doctrine was better than the one given by God.

Satan's skill and experience in the ways of division seems to far out-shine our individual ability to counter him. Only through the power of discernment, the Holy Spirit, and through the truth of God's Word can we ever experience victory. Though victory is guaranteed to the believer, it is guaranteed only in Jesus Christ. Being a Christian does not mean automatic victory in one's daily life. We must walk in the Spirit and obedience to experience it. That is why the Bible says if we walk in the spirit we will not give place to the flesh. Victory is given to those who do God's will and walk in God's ways. All the rest is just religion and Satan uses religion to further his cause. The spirit of error utilizes the selfish nature found in mankind to maintain deception and to promote the causes Satan has designed in his plan. This is how Satan's strategy works.

The Religious Noema

> "Beloved, believe not every spirit, but try the spirits
> whether they be of God: because many false prophets are gone
> out into the world. We are of God: he that
> knows God hears us; he that is not of God hears us not.
> Hereby know we the spirit of truth, and the spirit of error."
> (1 John 4:1, 6)

We must affirm the principle of "trying the spirits" in our lives in order for us to walk in victory. The word "try" (1381) simply means "to test, examine, or scrutinize" in order to discover the true origin and purpose of the spirit. We are to try every spirit, notion, thought, or idea that comes into our mind to discover its purpose, impact, effect, and origin. Even when Church leaders preach or promote an issue it is to be weighed against the Scriptures. Galatians 2:4 speaks about "false brethren" who bring in hidden agendas, and Jude 4 also says that these certain men crept in "unawares" (3921). Both of these statements mean that they come into the Body of Christ by stealth. These false ones, the tares, come in alongside the brethren and settle into the Church, no one noticing that they are truly snares to the work of the local church. John said there are many false prophets. John was saying that in his experience he had witnessed many individuals who hindered the work of God's anointing in the Church. John uses the term "antichristos" (500) for some of these people, because he is giving clarity to us that we may better understand the work that the spirit of antichrist performs. The word "antichrist" comes from two Greek root words. The first word "anti" (473) is defined as "opposite." It is also defined as meaning both "equivalence" and "exchange." On the positive side of the word, the Scripture states that Christ died "anti" (i.e., in our stead or place), but when the word is used of the antichrist, it shows how this spirit tries to have equivalence with Jesus by substituting his will over God's Will. The spirit of antichrist disguises itself so that our hearts and minds are deceived into believing in an alternate lord. "Anti" expresses the idea of being in contrast to, but also means to be a substitute for something, or to be in the place of someone. The spirit is "anti" when it is trying to take the place of and act as though it is the real Lord. The second word "christos" (5547) means anointed or anointing, and comes from the word "chrio" (5548), which is defined to contact or rub as to smear with oil. By implication, the combined word "antichrist" means to be opposite to Christ, due to its desire to be a substitute for, to be in the place of, and to replace the anointing of God with a deceptive anointing. In essence, Satan wants to be like the Most High (Isaiah 14:14). Satan is a counterfeiter who tries to imitate God by design. This is his "noema" (his device). Through this deception he activates his undermining forces and causes many believers to fall short of their potential. We can see this more clearly by studying the word "divination." The root word in "divination" is divine. False prophets and seducers move over into God's place in their speaking. Instead of speaking for God, they speak as God. They will give words of prophecy commanding an individual to do something that only God has the authority to command. They take God's position of authority over the believer. They try to rule over and dominate the believer by their words and position. When you look for the life of God on some of these prophesies you do not find it. We had better be careful in the Church and guard whom we let in. And it does not matter how popular they are, how many radio and television stations they are on, or how big their church is.

When Jesus defeated the devil He empowered us. How? It is through our understanding of what was actually accomplished on the cross. The only counter Satan has for the truth is a lie! Through lies Satan manipulates, deceives, and works to hide his downfall by perverting the truth. The Scripture has revealed that one of Satan's strongest tools is his ability to stealthily act as though he were God. He counters the real work of the Lord with a false religious piety. There was a time when we believed that the spirit of antichrist focused on false religions. Islam, Hinduism, Buddhism, and other false religions were and still are used to confuse and manipulate the longing for God that is in every human being. Today the spirit of antichrist is attacking the Church from within as well as from the without.

Of course Satan has always attacked the Body and individuals in the Church, but in these last days his spirit has developed some effective tactics.

"For there shall arise many false Christ's, and false prophets, and shall
show great signs and wonders; insomuch that, if it were possible, they
shall deceive the very elect. Behold, I have told you before."
(Matthew 24:24-25)

"Be sober, be vigilant; because your adversary the devil, as
a roaring lion, walks about, seeking whom he may devour:
Whom resist in the faith, knowing that the same afflictions
are accomplished in your brethren that are in the world."
(1 Peter 5:8-9)

The Greek word translated "adversary" (antidikos-476) comes from two root derivatives. Having already looked at the word "anti" (473), the second word "dike" (1349) means to "be right (as self-evident; i.e., justice; the principle, a decision, or its execution)." The word adversary therefore means in the original language that someone who is against our rightness and justification; or someone or something that tries to substitute, or take the place of our true position in Christ. We must realize that God named our enemy. The Lord called him Lucifer which means "to make a show, to boast, or to be prideful." When Lucifer manifests in the life of an individual it can be recognized as pride, as a boastful disposition, and leads to one who makes an open show of their person. This manifests through the pride of life. The Lord named him Satan, because this means "the accuser of the brethren or opponent of the brethren." Satan manifests himself through a believer's life by using an accusative and contrary attitude. We can see this manifestation in people who criticize and degrade the Body of Christ, or individuals in it. Our enemy is also called the devil. This is because he is a deceiver. He is a manipulator and a worker of evil. He works in stealth to cover his tracks and to place the blame on anything or anyone else. This is our enemy. If we let our guard down he uses his deception as a device to weaken and then destroy us. When Paul used the word "device" in 2 Corinthians 2:11 it was in the context that Satan uses unforgiveness to get an advantage of us. This is not to say that we are to overlook error, but it is to say that we are to love one another enough to help each other when we see that someone is weak or under attack and to have grace for the unstable soul.

"But if our gospel be hid, it is hid to them that are lost:
In whom the god of this world has blinded the minds of them
which believe not, lest the light of the glorious gospel
of Christ, who is the image of God, should shine unto them."
(2 Corinthians 4:3-4)

I have been researching the biblical concept of "lost-ness" and I have only heard the word lost used in the context of those who do not know Jesus as their Lord and Savior. In my research of the Bible

I have discovered that "lost-ness" has an Old Testament root. The Greek word "apollumi" (622-lost) literally means to "destroy" or "kill" in battle. Figuratively it is used in relation to the soul. The soul is an object of value in which the Lord is interested in saving. The Jewish expression for "lost-ness" was that a man could "trifle away his life" by bad personal choices. The Jewish thought was that one was lost when they suffered a loss that was attributable to their foolish will or was the fault of the one who suffers it. This does not mean that he destroys himself with suicide, but that he did not keep himself pure from the influences of the world that lead him into loss. In Luke 15, three parables are told from God's point of view; the lost sheep, the lost coin, and the lost son. It is God who sees their lost-ness. The sheep's lost-ness occurs when they leave their pasture and shepherd, not because they have no pasture or shepherd. The coin's lost-ness occurred when it was separated from the whole and was not useful to its master. The son's lost-ness occurred when he took his inheritance and used it to enter into riotous living; he squandered his inheritance. Psalm 119:176 gives us a pure definition of lost-ness as well as Isaiah 53:6, and Jeremiah 50:6.

"I have gone astray like a lost sheep;
seek thy servant; for I do not forget thy commandments."
(Psalm 119:176)

"All we like sheep have gone astray; we have turned everyone to his own way;
and the Lord has laid on him the iniquity of us all."
(Isaiah 53:6)

"My people hath been lost sheep: their shepherds
have caused them to go astray, they have turned
them away on the mountains: they have gone
from mountain to hill, they have
forgotten their resting place."
(Jeremiah 50:6)

Job 26:6 also states that destruction has "no covering." The word translated as "destruction" (11) is a part of the concept of lost-ness. In Ezekiel 34:4, God is critical of the shepherds who do not search for those who are "lost," while verse sixteen contrasts this criticism with the statement, "I will seek that which is lost." The Bible then states in Ezekiel 34:17, "I will judge between cattle and cattle, between rams and he goats." And again in Ezekiel 34:20-22 and 31 it is stated:

"Therefore thus saith the Lord God unto them;
Behold, I, even I, will judge between the fat
cattle and between the lean cattle.
Because you have thrust with the side and
with the shoulder, and pushed all the
diseased with your horns, till you have scattered

them abroad. Therefore will I save my flock,
and they shall no more be prey;
and I will judge between cattle and cattle...
And you my flock, the flock of my pasture, are men
and I am your God, saith the Lord God."

In essence, the Bible is revealing that lost-ness is not merely a term that relates to those outside the people of God, it also applies to those who know God, but have moved away from Him in their hearts due to improper leadership wounding them. Lost-ness is also seen in the context of those that have been "run off from church." The Bible reveals that there are those in the Body of Christ who are immature and have ruinous ways (i.e., they are lost). They are lost from the reality of Christian love and true communion, because they are lost from Christian fellowship and friendship. They are lost in a crowd of believers and feel alone and abandoned. They are lost from maturity, because maturity only comes through building wholesome Christian relationships. False shepherds and tares will bully God's people when the spirit of antichrist deceives them. They are like a mean ram in the field; they butt everything that gets in their way. Ministers may view their ways as promoting holiness, but their actions are not Christ-like; as Ezekiel states. These "shoulder thrusters" may think that they are preaching against sin and confronting sin, but in reality Satan has used a noema in them to embitter God's people by their preaching and haughtiness.

"Because you have had a perpetual hatred, and have shed the blood
of the children of Israel by the force of the sword in the time
of their calamity, in the time that their iniquity had an end."
(Ezekiel 35:5)

Ezekiel is warning us to be discerning in the nature of the believer. If someone is young in the Lord and fails, they should be handled respectfully. Immaturity means their iniquity has an end. In Texas terms if they are flexible, adaptable, and correctable then they are capable of change. When a young brother or a sister is struggling in an area of their life we are not to use the "force of the sword" (the Word of God) in the time of their calamity; we are to walk them through the recovery process. The "force of the sword" does not recover, heal, and change the man; the sword under these circumstances wounds and destroys. It is the goodness of God that leads us to repentance. Satan has used these religious devices to hinder the maturity and unity of the Church.

"And then shall many be offended, and shall betray one another,
and shall hate one another. And many false prophets shall
rise, and shall deceive many. And because iniquity shall
abound, the love of many shall wax cold."
(Matthew 24:10-12)

Notice that the false prophets shall "rise." The Greek word "rise" (1453) is defined as: to collect one's faculties, to awaken from obscurity or inactivity. These false ones come out of a time when offense, hatred, and betrayal are in the religious world. The Greek word "skandalizo" (4624), translated as "offended" means to trip up, to entrap, or to entice to sin. It is where the English word "scandalize" comes from and this word is a derivative of the word "skandalon" (4625) which is the "trap-stick" in a snare. Some doctrines snare you. Skandalon in the Greek language is a bent sapling that is used as a trigger to set a snare. Satan uses snares to catch us in a strategic scheme. He wants to divide us. We are weak when we are in division so his goal is to keep us divided. He has been using racism, denominationalism, and ignorance to separate us from one another throughout history. The Bible also states that the love of the Church will "wax cold." To "wax cold" (5594) is to maintain an attitude of giving up on the people of God. The spirit of antichrist utilizes and promotes this coldness of Christian love to produce strands of separation within the local church and the universal Church. Correction is necessary in the Body of Christ and a mild rebuke can go a long way in correcting these attitudes. Wisdom brings a balance between the correction that is necessary and the seriousness of a rebuke. Wisdom in these matters is the principle thing.

Christians in today's Church have been duped by false theology and doctrine so that their understanding of the antichrist has been limited. Some doctrines have the anti-Christ manifesting only in the tribulation, which perverts the reality of his presence today. The spirit of antichrist is very active and present in our world. It is operating inside and outside of the Church and he is using the political systems in the Church and in the government for his own benefit. He is continuously working to undermine Christ Jesus and the Kingdom of God by distorting the certainty of who he is in spirit. He will manifest openly someday, but in this present time we should be aware of his influence. It is time for the Church to see him and his ministry for what it is. It is time to prepare yourself for the spiritual battle that is at hand.

The Apostles Doctrine

Section 2

"And they continued steadfastly in the apostles' doctrine
and fellowship, and in breaking of bread, and in prayers."
(Acts 2:42)

"Therefore leaving the principles of the doctrine of Christ, let us go on unto perfection; not laying again the foundation of repentance from dead works, and of faith toward God, Of the doctrine of baptisms, and of laying on of hands, and of resurrection of the dead, and of eternal judgment." (Hebrews 6:1-2)

Chapter 8 – Repentance from Dead Work

"How much more shall the blood of Christ,
who through the eternal Spirit
offered himself without spot to God,
purge your conscience from dead
works to serve the living God?"
(Hebrews 9:14)

Most of us in the Body of Christ, when studying salvation, think about repentance from sin and not repenting from dead works. Yet repentance from dead works is a major issue within the doctrine of sanctification. What does the Bible mean when it says for us to repent from dead works? It is the difference between having a heartfelt love for God and a sense of religious obligation when we pray, read the Bible, or attend Church. Our walk of faith should stem from our love toward God and not from an attitude of requirement. One of the major aspects of Christian growth can be seen in Christians who love God for Who He is, rather than for what He gives. There are believers who have a religious mindset that creates a tendency to motivate them toward pious activities, but this is how dead works gets a foot hold in us at times.

As stated before, some scholars view the foundational principles in Hebrews 6:1-2 as though they are speaking of Jewish doctrines, but one should consider that the writer of Hebrews (under the Holy Spirit's anointing) called these the "doctrines of Christ." Many of the principles found in the Old Testament law are reiterated in the New Testament by Jesus and the early Apostles and that is common. But when these principles are carried over into the New Testament they are delivered to us in light of the new covenant (such as, the just shall live by faith). The words translated as "not laying again" in Hebrews 6:1 could be translated as "not throwing down anew." The Greek work translated as "again" (3825) is something that is "oscillatory;" defined as moving backward and forward like a pendulum. The notion generated is that these principles must be firmly and carefully laid down in believers, so "that we henceforth be no more children, tossed to and fro, and carried about with every wind of doctrine, by the sleight of men, and cunning craftiness, whereby they lie in wait to deceive" (see Ephesians 4:14). After people are saved we find that babes in Christ can be led astray from the basic tenants of the faith if they are not "founded" in the faith. The writer of Hebrews was making a point about this and that is why he referenced five other things about the process of growth in this section of Scripture (see Hebrews 6:4-9). When he wrote that "it is impossible for those who were once enlightened" to fall away, he was referring to the believer's foundation. These references and an exegesis of the passage declare without question that if you are not founded in the doctrines of Christ, you will be cursed and not blessed, as Hebrews 6:7-9 states.

> "For the earth which drinketh in the rain that
> cometh oft upon it, and bringeth forth herbs
> meet for them by whom it is dressed, receiveth
> blessing from God: But that which beareth thorns
> and briers is rejected, and is nigh unto cursing;
> whose end is to be burned. But, beloved, we are
> persuaded better things of you, and things that
> accompany salvation, though we thus speak."

One thing we must address is the matter of the "conscience" (4893) as it pertains to the sanctification process or the salvation of the soul. The consciousness is defined as "the internal knowing (i.e., the internal or self-knowledge, or judgment of right and wrong; or the faculty, power or principle within us, which decides on the lawfulness or unlawfulness of our own actions and affections, and instantly approves or condemns them)." Conscience is called by some writers "the moral sense," and considered as an original faculty of our nature. The conscience manifests itself in the feeling of obligation we experience, which precedes, attends and follows our actions. Conscience is first occupied in ascertaining our duty, before we proceed to action; then in judging of our actions when performed as they relate to that duty. It is also the apparatus by which we apprehend the will of God and understand right and wrong. The consciousness is breached when we know our duty to the will of God, and violate that knowledge with inappropriate activity or thought. Have you ever asked yourself in relation to another person, "How can they do what they do and not feel guilty, or not have a sense of conviction?" God designed the consciousness to help us govern our lives, and there are many aspects of the consciousness that we should be trained in. They are:

The conviction within it (John 8:7-8)
The awareness of it (Acts 5:2)
Living with a good conscience (Acts 23:1)
Having a conscience void of offence (Acts 24:16)
Conscience that bears witness (Rom 2:15; 9:1)
The necessity of not breaching ones conscience (Rom 13:5)
The union of the spirit and the consciousness (1 Cor 4:4)

Weak and defiled conscience (1 Cor 8:7)
Defiling a weak brother's conscience 1 Cor 8:10-13; 10:25-29
The testimony of the conscience (2 Cor 1:12)
Commending our conscience (2 Cor 4:1-4)
The conscience makes things manifested (2 Cor 5:11)
Being made perfect in the conscience (Heb 9:9)
Purging the conscience (Heb 9:14; 10:2)
Forgiveness is understood in the conscience (Heb 10:22)
Consciousness of suffering (1 Peter 2:19-20; 3:16)
Baptism and the consciousness of man (1 Peter 3:21)

One can see that the New Testament has much to say about the conscience.

A good place to start in understanding repentance from dead works is with the knowledge that without purging the consciousness spiritual maturity cannot be gained. In essence, the Lord has united our spirit with our consciousness, which produces awareness in us when we transgress. Our dilemma is that we have a tendency to ignore our consciousness when it speaks to us and we thus transgress ourselves and one another. When we get involved in iniquity we bring reproach to the Lord and offence to those around us. God has made us sensitive to these things and has given us the "conscience" so that we can understand offensiveness. As we mature in our faith we will give much consideration to our relationships and the personal struggles each of us face (we will be able to walk with people who have weakness and will be careful around them; we do not want to cause them to stumble). When I say "weakness" I imply each of us have particular areas of our lives that we struggle with. One may be strong in one area, while another is weak in that same area. Where one is weak, another has no problem with that area (see 1 Corinthians 12:22-26). God wants us to live a life full of forgiveness and compassion. When I was first born again the Holy Spirit visited me on this issue. He showed that I needed to wake up every day with this prayer: "Good morning Lord! I choose to not let anything offend me today. I choose to forgive any offence or transgression that I experience. I choose to bless and not speak curses on everyone I meet." This is the way to walk in a purity of heart and mind, without which we will not see God (see Matthew 5:8).

As stated earlier, the conscience of man must be "purged" (2511) from dead works. This purging process is necessary for us to live in peace with ourselves and with others. If we are aware of our iniquities and transgressions and do not live with an overcoming conviction about this matter, we are hindered in our ability to walk faithfully with other people. In other words, our conscience will be defiled. Righteousness is our state of being with God; it is a gift (see Romans 5:17). We may all agree that this is true, yet too many of us live a Christian lifestyle that makes works a part of their religious experience. The statement, "If you want to be right with God you have to...", and we then fill in the blanks with the activity religious piety demands. If we do not repent from things that cause offence, we will hold on to offences and they will hinder our communion (see 1 Corinthians

11:28-33). Christians do not want the heaviness that accompanies this kind of spiritually weighted lifestyle. Spiritual and personal liberties in Christ have often been replaced with church dogmas that are work based and oppressive. We long for the truth, but are forced to walk on eggshells around the pious. We should consider the issues stated in Romans 14:4.

> "Who art thou that judgest another man's servant?
> to his own master he standeth or falleth.
> Yea, he shall be holden up: for God is able to make him stand."

Without the ability to walk in faith we cannot please God and will open a way for our enemy to accuse and obstruct us from our Christian duty. Satan utilizes offensive things in his schemes to hinder the "common union" within the Church, thereby weakening the Body and causing ministry to become ineffective. Some local churches, at times, are in a state of offensive tension and have a weakened ability to defeat Satan's plots due to the strife and conflict they contain. Satan works his wicked plan to create and maintain schisms between Christians.

> "Which show the work of the law written in our hearts, their
> conscience also bearing witness, and their thought the mean while
> accusing or else excusing one another."
> (Romans 2:15)

Consider this statement: "Do not judge others by their actins and yourself by your intent." One of the issues we face is our ability to accuse others and to excuse ourselves when we do the same things. We have all fallen short of the glory God has called us to walk in, so we must not abuse His gift of grace. The Scripture states that we go from "glory to glory" and it also says we go from "faith to faith." Whatever your faith is in one year, it holds the potential to grow into a better faith next year. The same holds true for the glory God has called us to. Knowing this helps us to realize that each of us has a responsibility to God and to each other. Each of us mature spiritually at different rates. We should forgive others when their transgressions hurt us, and we should not forsake the fellowship of our faith. We should exhort one another with the knowledge that we will all stand before the judgment seat of Christ (see Hebrews 9:22, 25, 30).

> "But when ye sin so against the brethren, and
> wound their weak conscience, ye sin against Christ."
> (1 Corinthians 8:12)

There are three things one can find in a weak conscience: a shipwrecked faith (see 1 Tim 1:19), a seared conscience (see 1 Tim 4:2), and a defiled conscience (see 1 Corinthians 8:7 and Titus 1:15-16). There are also three things that can be found in maturity: love out of a pure heart, a good conscience, and faith unfeigned (see 1 Timothy 1:5, 19). These are the goals of a spiritually mature faith.

There are two words in the Greek text that have been translated by the same English word "repentance." Though they are both translated as repentance, they do not mean the same thing. The first word we will study is "metamellomai" (3338) and is defined as "to care afterwards or regret" (see 2 Corinthians 7:8; Hebrews 7:21; Matthew 21:29, 32 and Matthew 27:3). This should be understood as ineffective repentance. Metamellomai is the product of two root words, which when united carries the concept that an individual is not cautious in his actions until he afterwards sees the results of his behavior. This is false repentance because the true love of God is not being manifested in the life of the person. The care and concern for others that should be maturing is deficient in the life of the person who is not properly repentant. This individual does not consider the implications his behavior has until after the consequences of that behavior is realized. This is the type of repentance used when Judas betrayed Jesus (see Matthew 27:3). Even though Judas threw the money down the damage had already been completed and his actions had already caused the Lord to be put into jeopardy. As an example, when one gets involved in gossip and has not considered its destructive force, they destroy someone's character and reputation without consideration. Oftentimes people may not realize that their childish behavior has caused great damage. The reason they never recognize their error is that they are operating in "metamellomai." It is then too late to undo what has been done, much like Judas who could not undo his betrayal of the Lord. This type of repentance is also related to the Lord who said "He would not repent" (regret afterwards) the decision He made concerning Israel. Think of metamellomai as the ability to change your mind when you realize you are wrong. This is the positive aspect of the word.

The other Greek word translated as repentance is "metanoia" (3341). Metanoia is defined as "a reformation or a reversal." Its root is defined as "to think differently (i.e., to have a change of mind that leads to a change of life)." It is often spoken of as an about face, but repentance is more than just a turn; it is a change. Repentance is the first thing God commands us to do in the process of salvation and sanctification. The reason there must be a change that takes place when salvation and/ or sanctification comes is that it is impossible for us to come to God unless we turn from sin by changing the way we think about sin. If a person does not change their mind they cannot change their life. Metanoia is different from metamellomai because metamellomai can occur over and over, whereas when metanoia occurs, it is maintained. Metanoia is defined as "a compunction; a pricking of heart; poignant grief or remorse proceeding from a consciousness of guilt; the pain of sorrow or regret for having offended God, and incurred his wrath; the sting of conscience proceeding from a conviction of having violated a moral duty." This why the Scripture states: "as a man thinks in his heart, so is he." Repentance is my ability to agree with God about what He says about sin or dead works and then live according to that belief (such as changing your opinion about sin and even when you fall into a sin, you come back to God as soon as you realize it). Metanoia is a change in direction. The Christian, being born again, is re-created as a new creature and will then live in consideration of their actions and influence. Old things (i.e., old ways of thinking, living; old habits, moods, desires, dispositions, and influences) are changed. True repentance is the key to the change we desire to make. Without true repentance confession of sin becomes impossible. Remember, to confess your sin is to agree with what God has said about sin. Confession is more than mere acknowledgment of an act; it is acknowledging the fruit or result of the act (i.e., it is the effect of the act that matters most in terms of repentance).

Dead works can now be defined, with this in mind. It is dead works to cause damage to someone and then try to undo the actions by simply saying, "I'm sorry." We should consider and think before we say or do something that hurts others. It is also a form of dead works to teach and to preach about the love of God while operating in a spirit of error; not being in one accord with the Body of Christ. Some people use the bully pulpit to attack others that they are at odds with in the congregation, while some congregants use slander to attack the Pastor they are at odds with. It becomes a vicious cycle and many churches and believers are destroyed because of it. Pastors have a difficult job as it is. They are under tremendous amounts of pressure at times. Congregations are involved in dead works when they do not support and bless a man of God that is working the field with diligence and commitment (see 1 Timothy 5:17). We must have true repentance if we have sinned against someone. Not only should our repentance be as broad as our transgression (i.e., if you sin privately, you should repent privately; if you sin publicly, you should repent publicly), but our goal should be to negate the wrong done. If we think being sorry is enough when we transgress, the apology is actually dead works, being alone. When we think we have to "make amends" to God by accomplishing a religious atonement, this is also dead works. Jesus is our atonement. To be a part of the Body of Christ is to be aware that you are in the family of God. You are a child of God, a fellow citizen with the saints, and of the household of God (see Ephesians 2:19) and as such, we should realize that all of us sin at times. Living carefully and having your wits about you helps each of us to maintain a repentant lifestyle. The disciple understands that we are part of the Church and we will eventually make a mistake. That is just the way it is. Our goal is to strive for perfection in these matters, but when we fail get up and walk more cautiously the next time.

The English word "church" comes from the Greek word "ekklesia" (1577). The Church can be defined as "the twice called out people of God." Why should the Church be defined as the "twice called out" people? Because we are called out of the world and we are also called out of carnality. Just as the nation of Israel was called out of Egypt and then called out of the wilderness, we are called out in the same way. When we receive salvation we are called out of the world. When we go through the sanctification process, we are called out of the wilderness. If we do not become one with the Body of Christ we will be unable to overcome the weaknesses of human frailty. Only through the fellowship with other believers can we overcome the old man. This is the reason so many believers fail in their Christian walk. Their efforts are dead works because they stand as an individual, not as an attached part of the whole. We are stronger when around other believers. We cannot fulfill the great commandment to love God and love God's people when we are not in communion with others in the Church. The definition of true repentance (i.e., godly sorrow), is found in 2 Corinthians 7:11.

> "For behold this selfsame thing, that ye sorrowed after a godly sort,
> what carefulness it wrought in you, yea, what clearing of yourselves,
> yea, what indignation, yea what fear, yea, what vehement desire,
> yea, what zeal, yea, what revenge. In all things ye have
> approved yourselves to be clear in this matter."

Notice how the change of lifestyle occurs in the Christian when true repentance is a reality. The believer walks in carefulness. They clear or purge themselves from sin and iniquity. They have indignation at anything that diminishes their faith or causes them to fail. They fear God, and understand judgment. They are zealous to do good works, and they seek revenge against Satan and sin which causes them to fall. Paul then states, "In all things ye have approved yourselves to be clear in this matter." To "approve" (4921) yourself in a matter is defined as: to stand together with. This means you stand with the transgressed one. This is the process of repentance from dead works. Repentance from dead works is an initial part of the sanctification experience. It is the beginning principle in the six foundational doctrines of Jesus. It must be accomplished first, after the Cornerstone of Jesus is set in order so that the other principles have a foundation to build upon. Hebrews 9:14 tells us we have the potential to purge our conscience from dead works to serve (worship) the living God, and Hebrews 9:15 states, "for this cause" Christ is the mediator. Jesus, "for this cause" mediates between God and man. The law (i.e., the schoolmaster) only instructs, it does not mature; it does not change the inner man. We are commanded to grow together and Hebrews 10:25 states,

> "Not forsaking the assembling of ourselves together, as the
> manner of some is; but exhorting one another: and
> so much the more, as you see the day approaching."

The Greek word translated "assembling" (1997) means a complete collection. One cannot experience the fullness of the Spirit without first repenting from the works that are divisive and detrimental to their becoming one in Christ. My daughter was three years old and my wife and I wanted to buy her a wagon. We went to a local store and found the perfect wagon on display, but when I purchased it they gave it to me in a box. All the pieces were gathered together, in the box and not "assembled." I had to put it together. This is a similitude of the Church. The Body may be gathered together at the local church, but they must be assembled before they will function properly. Many behaviors and attitudes cause division and strife in the local and corporate Body. All the parts of the Body of Christ have a purpose. Many local congregations gather together each week, but do not function as the Lord ordained us to. It takes a wise master builder to assemble the Church. We must understand this "assembling" in light of James 3:12-16.

> "Can the fig tree, my brethren, bear olive berries? Either a
> vine, figs? so can no fountain both yield salt water and fresh.

> Who is a wise man and endued with knowledge among you?
> let him show out of a good behavior his works with
> meekness of wisdom. But if ye have bitter envying
> and strife in your hearts, glory not, and lie not
> against the truth. This wisdom descendeth
> not from above, but is earthly, sensual, devilish.
> For where envying and strife is, there is
> confusion (unquiet-ness) and every evil work."

There are several points to make in lieu of this passage. First, it must be perfectly understood that you are either bitter or sweet of spirit. James 3:12-13 clearly states this and there are many other passages that confer with this truth. People who are divisive may feel they are spiritual, but in reality they are carnal. The question asked is this, "who is really a wise man and endued with knowledge in your church (see James 3:13)?" The question is not who thinks or believes they are wise, but what is true Christian wisdom? Some in the Church have not repented from envy and strife, and they lie against the truth by their temperament and communication. We must recognize that there are tares in the Church and their nature is demonically motivated. Their wisdom is not godly, it is satanic. They operate by a type of wisdom that is "earthly" (1919), "sensual" (5591), and "devilish" (1141). Earthly wisdom means that it is worldliness and comes from the root Greek word that is defined as a "superimposition." This worldliness is superimposed over the one that believes they are a Christian. They do not live by biblical dictates they live by worldly means. They use the proper Christian rhetoric, but there is no reality of godliness in their life. They talk the talk of faith, but trust in their job as the source of their livelihood, or trust in their own fleshly ability to get their provision, rather than trust God as their source. To be a Christian is to be like Christ and Christian faith is to put one's trust in God. It is not going to church that gives a distinction to the Christian life, it is the change in our "being" that shows true Christian transformation.

The second manifestation of this false wisdom is distinguished by the word "sensual." This sensuality (i.e., soulishness or manifested lower nature) reflects in the individual's personality, ministry, and also manifests as a disposition of spiritual independence. It is through our personality that false wisdom exhibits itself and causes the person to view themselves in unrealistic terms. They usually are haughty by nature, yet they often see themselves as being bold. They are sensual in their livelihood, but they talk of God and faith. True boldness is the confidence one has in Jesus' ability as their Savior; whereas haughtiness is the expressed self-reliance one has in their own person, as compared to others. This is what the Scripture describes as "sensual." The sensual male will use his prowess as a means to gain place, while the sensual female will use her form as a means to attract. Both are manipulative and each seeks to gain an advantage through sensuality. Jude 19 says,

> "These are they who separate themselves,
> sensual, having not the Spirit."

These "separate themselves" (not having the Spirit) by their carnality and lust. They separate themselves by a mental process that allows them to think of themselves more highly than they ought to think. They have a selfish nature that can only be changed through the discipleship process or a miracle…which the Lord is indisputably capable of accomplishing. 1 Corinthians 2:14 describes "sensuality" as fleshly natured. Paul says that these fleshly natured people do not receive the things of God, because they are spiritually discerned. These fleshly or naturally natured people, do not understand spirituals (i.e., they ignore the spiritual aspects in life). The naturally natured person must have their soul trained before they can respond to spiritual truth on a conscious level. They have to be trained to recognize spiritual truth. 1 Corinthians 15:44 explains that we are sown a natural body and are to be raised (up as) a spiritual body. To be naturally minded is to manifest the things that are natural and it is natural for new Christians to be more inclined toward their flesh. In other words, it is reasonable for the new creature to be a babe. This is why babes in Christ should be trained in these matters and when so many Christians have never been trained in spirituals, it is time repent and change the way we minister. The third manifestation of false wisdom is devilishness. The Greek word "daimoniodes" (1141- devilish) comes from two words that draw the idea of one who is influenced by Satan and distributes fortunes. Webster's dictionary defines fortunes as: "properly, chance; accident; luck; the arrival of something in a sudden or unexpected manner." Hence the heathens deified "chance" and consecrated temples and altars to the goddess of fortune. From this the ideology of the word "fortune" or the idea of "being fortunate" have crept into our social mindset. Christians need to understand that chance, fortune telling, or other forms of divination take your faith and attention away from Jesus Christ. Chance then becomes an attitude in prayer, "If the Lord wills." The babe in Christ must be taught the difference between an attitude that is full of faith and an attitude that leans toward chance.

The girl who prophesied over Paul and Silas in Acts 16:16-18 had the right words, but her spirit was not right. Paul cast the demon out of her because she grieved his spirit. In today's Church setting if someone prophesied by divination many would never realize it. There are people that operate by divination today. The diviner will come to a church and tell fortunes and may say things like, "the Lord wants you to do (this or that)," "the Lord wants you to (go here or there)," and no one realizes what is occurring. Only those who have spiritual discernment will be able to determine that it was a divination manifesting. Not all traveling prophets are thus, but we must discern between those that serve God and those that serve their pocketbook; who wish to gain a better offering. James 3:16 explains how confusion encumbers many believers.

> "For where envying and strife is,
> there is confusion and every evil work."

The true wisdom of God produces fruitfulness in the life of a believer that is pure, peaceful, easily corrected, and merciful. The wise congregation will be free from argumentativeness, posturing, and hypocrisy. The individual members of the Body of Christ must take the initiative in this matter. We must correct ourselves, not waiting on the elders to correct us.

To repent from dead works is to have a change of mind that leads to a change of life in every area of your conscious thoughts. The blood of Jesus has the power to purge the consciousness of impure thoughts, attitudes, and dispositions, especially those that are contrary to God's Word. To better understand repentance from dead works we must also understand the New Testament definition of righteousness.

> "For if by one man's offense death reigned by one;
> much more they which receive abundance of grace
> and of the gift of righteousness shall reign in
> life by one Jesus Christ."
> (Romans 5:17)

"Righteousness" (1343) is simply a right standing with God and is my ability to approach the throne of God because of Jesus. I should never consciously separate myself from the Lord. As soon as I find myself at odds with God or the Scriptural evidence in the Bible I should repent. Righteousness by definition means that God has granted us equity (i.e., He has justified our right to be grafted into the vine). Jesus paid the price for our sin (separation) and through the atonement we are freed from the judgment of our sin, but not the consequences. The Greek root word which righteousness is derived is the word "deiknuo" (1166) and means "to show." The word "dike" (1343) is a derivative of "deiknuo" and means "right, as self-evident (i.e., justice; the principle, a decision, or its execution)." The Hebrew word translated as "righteousness" (6666) means "to make right" or "to cleanse" and brings out a more prominent relationship in the definition. When Abram believed God, God "accounted" it to him as righteousness. This definition is maintained in the New Testament by the fact that God has warranted (given us a guarantee) our right to be with Him by the sacrifice of Jesus. The revelation of righteousness comes to us when we recognize that righteousness is a gift from God. You are righteous because God made you righteous through Jesus Christ. You cannot earn righteousness, you cannot attain rightness, and you cannot acquire righteousness on your own. Righteousness is the gift of God (see Romans 5:17) that allows us to freely come to God anytime we want to. When you try to do something in order for God to love you more, or when you try to pay God back after you have failed in some way, you are in dead works. You cannot go to church enough to make yourself righteous, nor can you pray enough to make yourself righteous, nor can you tithe enough to make yourself righteous. Only the God the Father, through His Son Jesus Christ, can give you or make you righteous. It is a gift, the gift of God, not of works, so no one can boast. You cannot make atonement for your sin, nor is there any sin that cannot be forgiven. What sin is greater than God's grace? There are none. Are you withholding the thing God wants because you feel unworthy? We are all unworthy, but God's great love has given us this gift to set us free from guilt and shame.

"Blessed are the pure in heart:
for they shall see God."
(Matthew 5:8)

"Not that any man has seen the Father,
except he which is of God, he has seen the Father."
(John 6:46)

"Now faith is the substance of things hoped for,
the evidence of things not seen."
(Hebrews 11:1)

How do we see God? Only the pure (i.e., clean) heart can. Only those who are able to accept God's gift can see the Father. Faith is the substance of righteousness and faith is the evidence of righteousness. Faith will keep me guiltless now, and faith will continue to keep me guiltless as long as I believe. In order for me to see God I must believe that He is, and that He is a rewarder of them that diligently seek Him (see Hebrews 11:6). It is through faith that I know God has made me righteous; this helps me to remain faithful. It is the goodness of God that leads us to repentance. How can we retain the knowledge that the righteousness God has given to us is His grace gift? Consider these next passages.

"And the work of righteousness shall be peace; and the effect (fruit)
of righteousness is quietness and assurance forever."
(Isaiah 32:17)

"But the wisdom that is from above is first pure, then peaceable, gentle,
and easy to be entreated, full of mercy and good fruits, without partiality,
and without hypocrisy. And the fruit of righteousness is sown
in peace of them that make peace."
(James 3:17-18)

Consider the work of righteousness. As it works in me, it produces peace in me. When one trusts in the gift of God and believes God, one receives righteousness. Salvation comes when I recognize that God loves me and wants me to be with Him forever. God wants us to spend eternity with Him. This was why He created us in the first place. Through disobedience, sin separated us from God, but God designed a solution to the problem before the problem occurred. Trust God and He will bring you back to the fellowship mankind had before the fall. How? It is simple; He gives you the right to come to His presence anytime you want to as long as you are in Christ. You can even live in His presence if you will! When this right standing is in place it begins its work which is the production of peace. The amount of faith and belief we have can actually be gauged by the amount of trust we have in Jesus. The more I trust God, the greater my faith will be. Our trust gives us a sense of peace that allows us to be honest and open with The Holy Spirit. Confession and repentance are therefore easy for us to accomplish. The evidence of my salvation is recognizable by my "peace of mind." This peace of mind causes me to not fear death, tribulation or persecution. The peace referred to in Isaiah 32:17 is the safety one feels in their "completeness in God." It is the actual reconnection of our place with the Father. Adam lost it; Jesus gave it back. And we now have access to our heavenly Father. God will not reward disobedience, and neither should we. When my children fail I do not cast them off, but I do expect them to see the error of their ways and turn away from those things whereby they have fallen. I do everything in my power to help them recognize the truth, but the decision is theirs to make. I cannot make the decision for them. "A man convinced against his will, is of a different opinion still." It brings me great joy to see my children make the right decisions, and even greater joy when they do it on their own. The byproduct of righteousness has an effect in the life of the Christian. The effect of righteousness is the fruitfulness that produces "quietness" (8252) within us. The definition of quietness is "the ability to keep your seat in troublesome times." Quietness is a state of rest (i.e., being tranquil and at peace). Biblical quietness is the state of stability and harmony one experiences in Christ Jesus. It is the settled emotions, dispositions, and mood that allows us to walk with humility, confidence, and persistent strength as we fellowship with Him. The assurance righteousness produces is the internal place of refuge. It is safety; both the fact (i.e., the security) and the feeling (i.e., the trust) have in God. Assurance is the security I have with Jesus; the confident and bold hope that keeps me persistent. When I feel any internal pressure to make restitution for my faults and failures, I can withstand the pressure, and I can stand in righteousness because Jesus is my atonement. Self-atonement is dead works and must be repented of. You must repent from your attempts to make restitution and accept the atonement Jesus made for you. This is when righteousness will begin its work in you. This is when you will be on the road to freedom from dead works.

Chapter 9 – Faith Toward God

You cannot be persuaded it will work
until you are convinced it is true.

"But what saith it? The word is near you, even in your mouth,
and in your heart: that is, the word of faith, which we preach."
(Romans 10:8)

"For I say, through the grace given unto me,
to every man that is among you, not
to think of himself more highly than he ought to think;
but to think soberly, according as God has dealt
to every man the measure of faith."
(Romans 12:3)

Even though the subject of faith has been written on extensively I want to comment on some of the aspects of the subject. Without faith one cannot please God nor will one be able to overcome the world and its temptations. We must be determined to be faithful to the ways of God in the discipleship process. True faith can be revealed in the way we approach covenant. Husbands and wives manifest faith in the marriage through their trust of one another. The same is true in Christ. If one has faith it is manifested through the level of trust one displays toward God. Lack of trust or confidence in God is simply a lack of faith in God. One thing to note is that the word translated as "believe" in the New Testament is actually the Greek word for "faith-er." We are "faith-ers" in God so James 2:17 states,

"Even so faith, if it has no works, is dead, being alone."

Another interesting note is that the word translated as "works" can be defined as effort; so then "faith without effort is dead, being alone." The phrase being alone means "by itself." God did not design faith to be a widower. Effort must accompany faith. Faith and patience are like a husband

and a wife. They are a team. They collectively have become more than they are individually. Patience undergirds and supports faith like a wife to a husband; she helps to stabilize him. If we cannot wait patiently there may not be faith enough to strengthen us through the process. Effort is necessary in order to make the marriage work. When one says that they have faith and there is no effort in their walk, they do not understand the basics of faith. True or living faith has effort behind it. Without effort, faith is dead. We can therefore understand that faithful effort demonstrates our belief in God. We are not saved by effort, but effort is the proof of our belief. The Bible teaches that worldliness is akin to ungodliness. The hard-line approach would be to recognize that worldliness is disobedience. This form of disobedience is called "unbelief" in Hebrews 3:11. One can see that a lack of faith and disobedience to God goes hand in hand. When the Lord leads me He gives me faith to do what He has asked of me. If I cannot accomplish the task, I am either being hindered in the process or I did not hear God correctly. I know that if the mission cannot be accomplished, maybe God is not leading me to do it. God finances His undertakings by building a support base for His purpose. A remnant people who move in the Spirit and who flow in the river of life.

Another aspect of faith we must consider is that faith is "now" (i.e., in the present tense). Faith is neither past nor future it is present (hope is future). In order to understand faith we must grasp its first order. Faith understands that God created the solution to the problem, before the problem became a problem! What did God create first, the water or the fish? Which was first, the air or the birds? God created the water first so that the fish could swim. God created the atmosphere first so the birds could fly. You should be confident to know that any problem you face God has already created the solution to it before you recognized it as a problem. Identifying this basic tenant of faith helps us to believe that God is working with us (see Mark 16:20). When we see circumstances arise in our lives, we must be aware that the Lord has the solution to our situation before we ever encounter the obstacle. In Hebrews 11:6 it is stated, "For he that comes to God must believe that he is, and that he is a rewarder of them that diligently seek him." This is called the way of faith. When we do not see the end of the situation we must hope for it and be patient with God as He walks us through the process of deliverance, no matter what the circumstances. Faith and patience strengthen and stabilize our spirit, while hope and patience strengthens and stabilizes the soul. Hope stabilizes our soul and eases the pressure we feel in the midst of a trial, if we patiently trust in the Lord. If we do not consider that the only way to receive something from God is by faith, then we will become fretful and impatient, and will move into unbelief. Urgency is not an evidence of faith; persistence is. Urgency is soulish; a self-seeking and a self-determined solution. There is a difference between persistence and "pressing in" on an issue. Even though Luke 11:8 uses the word "importunity" (335), importunity does not mean to press; it means "without shame." The word expresses the idea of having no modesty when asking for something. It is the earnestness and the perseverance in prayer, not the continuous and soulish press for something to motivate God to meet your need. We are commanded to be persistent, but there is a time when we must acknowledge the "no" that God speaks.

Faith is the track the believer is to ride on. Without faith we become derailed. The Bible teaches that faith is the substance of things hoped for and the evidence of things unseen. "Hupostasis" (5287) is the Greek word translated as "substance" in Hebrews 11:1 and means "to support" or "set under." Faith is the foundation we stand on, and to have faith is to stand on proof and not supposition, because there is no such a thing as blind faith. The evidence of faith is the conviction we have that God will come through for us. It is sound belief in what God has revealed to us.

"Now faith is the substance of things hoped for,
the evidence of things not seen."
(Hebrews 11:1)

Faith in Jesus Christ is accepting His work on the cross. Faith is forgiving myself for my failures, past and present, and believing God has cast my sin as far as the east is from the west. Faith is not tempting God with excuses, but understanding that there is an internal war going inside of each of us. Faith is being free from doubt and is substantiated by a patient persistence toward the high calling of God (see Philippians 3). Trusting is faith in action. When I actively trust in the work of Jesus I have living or active faith. When my failures cloud my vision of Him doubt has crept in. The Greek word "distazo" (1365 - doubt) means "to waver" or "to duplicate." The root meaning comes from the word "two." James 1:8 says "a double minded man is unstable in all his ways." A faithless person is "unstable" (182 - i.e., not settled or placed down firmly). He is not founded in rest, nor is he living in peace. Hebrews 3 and 4 speak of God's rest and that unbelief hinders our place of rest. These chapters teach us about three different kinds of unbelief. The first kind of unbelief is found in Hebrews 3:18. The phrase "that believed not," comes from the word "apeimi" (549). Apeimi means "to go away" (i.e., to leave God's way of doing things). The English word "should" (mello - 3195) gives us the focus of their failure. Mello is a strengthened form of the Greek word "melo" and means "to be of interest." The Greek word "mello" is an interest or personal expectation. It carries the thought of duty, purpose, possibility, necessity, and hesitation. These people "should not" enter into God's rest because they have no interest in God's way or they do not believe God's way is possible. This kind of unbelief is manifested in people who go to church, but have no interest in other people or the needs in the Church. They have another way that seems to be right, and since they have left God's way they substitute another way when trying to reach their spiritual goal. They know the "promised land" awaits them, but like the Jews of old pass up their chance to enter in year after year because of their unbelief (lack of interest in the Christian life). Eventually frustration occurs and a standard is reestablished at a lower level, which is thought to be attainable by them. This "lower level" is not a faith based goal, but a substitution of their will over God's will. The second word translated as unbelief in Hebrews 3:10-12 and 19 has a different core than "apeimi." The Lord said,

"They do always err in their heart; and they have not known my ways...
having an evil heart of unbelief, in departing from the living God...
So we see they could not enter in because of unbelief."

117

The Greek word translated as unbelief here is "apistia" (570). Apistia is faithlessness and is disobedience to the will of God. When God says "do it" and we have no faith to do it, this is apistia. When we are disobedient and make excuses why we cannot fulfill His commandment, it is another evidence of unbelief. This kind of unbelief is an expression of self-justification. Jesus had to deal with the disciples who had "little faith." The Scripture says they "could not enter." They "could not" enter in to rest due to their faithlessness which affected their ability to overcome their fears. The word Greek word translated as "could" (see Hebrews 3:19) means "to be able" or "possible." It is the Greek word "dunamai" (1410 - translated as "miracle" in other passages), and is the root word for "dunamis" (1411) is translated as the word "power." Faith is power. They could not enter into rest because they have no power in them. Unbelief has drained their strength and has weakened them. They have no faith in the Lord's ability, so they could not do what He commands. The third kind of unbelief is found in Hebrews 4:11 and is translated from the Greek word "apeitheia" (543 - i.e., apathy). Apeitheia is "obstinate and rebellious disbelief" and means "to be un-persuadable." The Bible teaches us to not follow the same example as those who are stubbornly disobedient and rebellious to God by being apathetic. Apathy is to be without feeling, to have a lack of feeling, or to be passive in your concern. Living faith is manifested as concern about what God wants, whereas apathy could care less about what God wants or says, apathy wants what it wants. Living faith is active and full of effort. Passive faith is dead, because it has no belief in it!

> "So then faith comes by hearing,
> and hearing by the Word of God."
> (Romans 10:17)

If we discover that our faith is small, what can we do to increase the operation of our faith? Well, "faith comes by hearing." I must learn to hear the voice of God if I am to increase my faith. One of the ways I can learn to hear is by reading and studying the Bible. If I do not know God's Word I cannot recognize His voice or His leading. Without His Word (rhema - i.e., present utterance) faith cannot come.

Faith toward God is my ability to believe for something as well as to believe in something. I must believe "for" results, not just believe "in" them. You can believe in something and still not receive what you at striving for. Peter is a good example. His belief that Jesus wanted him to walk on the water was not sufficient for his completion of the task. He lacked something very significant: virtue. He had faith to step out of the boat, but no virtue to sustain his faith.

> "And besides this, giving all diligence, add to your faith virtue,
> and to virtue knowledge, and to knowledge temperance,
> and to temperance patience, and to patience godliness,
> and to godliness brotherly kindness; and to brotherly kindness love."
> (2 Peter 1:5-7)

As Peter learned from his experience, we must also add to our faith before our faith is finished. Faith that stands alone will not stand long.

Chapter 10 – The Doctrine of Baptisms

"Therefore leaving the principles of the doctrine of Christ,
let us go on unto perfection; not laying again the
foundation of repentance from dead works,
and of faith toward God, doctrine of baptisms…"
(Hebrews 6:1-2)

"God shall hear, and afflict them, even he that abides of old. Selah.
Because they have no changes, therefore they fear not God."
(Psalm 55:19)

I usually receive very interesting comments when I teach the doctrine of baptisms. When the doctrinal theme of baptism is taught; only one or two baptisms are generally discussed, but there are at least seven baptisms listed in the New Testament and possibly as many as ten. Why have these other baptisms been ignored? How can God's Ministers overlook so much in their Bibles? In this chapter we will discuss the baptism unto repentance (see John's baptism…Matthew 3:11; Acts 1:5; Acts 19:3-4; Mark 1:4), the water baptism (see Matthew 3:11; Acts 1:5), the baptism with the Holy Spirit (see Acts 1:5, 8, Acts 2:4; Matthew 3:12), the baptism with fire (see Matthew 3:11-12, 4:1-11; Acts 2:3), the baptism into the Body (see 1 Corinthians 12:13, Matthew 26:26-30), the baptism of His death (see Romans 6:3-4; Colossians 2:12; 1 Corinthians 15:29), and the baptism into the cloud (see 1 Corinthians 10:1-33). We can also find the "baptism of Jesus," "the baptism into the Sea," "being baptized into Christ," and the "baptism of Moses" in the Scriptures, but we should recognize that these represent what I would call combinations of the other baptisms. For example, Jesus' baptism is revealed to be the baptism with the Holy Spirit and the baptism of fire, as stated by John the Baptist. The Greek words translated as "baptism" were first used in the Jewish culture as the words used for "dying cloth" or "to dip into or under." As far back as Pluto and Hippocrates the words were also used to mean "to sink a ship." The New Testament uses the word in a literal sense "to dip into." The concept of "baptism" was used in the New Testament times to reflect "a change." Each of these baptisms represents a piece of the whole change that leads us to a more mature life in Christ Jesus. Water baptism, being the widely understood baptism, became the focus of the Reformers as they fought to counter the Catholic baptism and the doctrines that accompanied infant baptism. Philo uses the Greek words to as "to be overwhelmed" by faults, desires, and sickness; reflecting the idea that we can be "overburdened" by trouble. The concept of baptism should be understood in light of its original meaning; "to be changed" or "overwhelmed" by what you are immersed into. If your thoughts overwhelm you with anxiety, you will be overcome by anxiety. If your thoughts are overwhelmed with Christ as the center of your personality and life, then Christ will overwhelm you. Either way, what you are overwhelmed with will change your life.

Baptism

The origin of the Greek word transliterated as baptism is an idiomatic expression of the word "bapto" (911). This primitive verb translated as "baptism" means to whelm, and according to Webster's Dictionary is defined as "to turn upside down as a dish, usually to cover something: to cover or engulf completely." It is also understood to mean "to be overcome in thought or feeling, and to pass or go over something, so as to bury or submerge it." The Greek words translated as "baptism" originated from the textile industry in the ancient days. It was used as a word meaning "dying cloth." Baptism in the secular world of the first century was "to submerge cloth into a vat of dye (i.e., to baptize the cloth into the dye) and thereby changing the cloth by the dye." John the Baptist carried this definition over into his ministry and baptized "unto repentance." Those who came to John were baptized in water as a representation of their repentance. Baptism was used as a similitude by John. Again, this similitude expressed the change of life an individual should have already experienced. Each of the seven baptisms are a part of the whole baptismal conglomeration (i.e., the one total Baptism or change) that is reflective of the complete transformation a believer should make.

> "Wherefore the law was our schoolmaster to
> bring us unto Christ, that we might be justified by faith.
> But after that faith is come, we are no longer under
> a schoolmaster. For you are all children of God by
> faith in Christ Jesus. For as many of you as have
> been baptized into Christ, have put on Christ."
> (Galatians 3:24-27)

Paul said after "that faith" (that specific faith) is come we have the evidence that we have "put on Christ". What does Paul mean when he says "that faith?" He is expressing a completeness that happens to us over a process of time, which causes and helps us to develop a more complete faith. Not just any ole' faith, but that kind of faith that one finds in a completed state which results in a change in us; a kind of faith that is finished. 1 Peter 1:9 talks about "receiving the end of our faith." The Greek word translated as "receiving" is "komizo" (2865) and is defined as "to tend, that is, to take care of" by Strong's Concordance. Thayer defines the word as "to carry, bear, bring to, to carry away for one's self, to carry off what is one's own, or to bring back." The idea expressed here is that we are to be brought back to the salvation of our soul, which was originally ours and lost due to the fall of Adam. Baptism expresses this idea as well. We are to "put on" each of these baptisms because we originally walked in them. If we only view baptism as an ordinance, in the traditional sense, we miss the primary focus of its intent. Yes, we are to baptize with water, but the question regarding immersion is answered when we understand the changes baptism represents. When someone is born again they must "tend to" and "take care" of their faith; in essence, when one is to be baptized, one has to take care of that baptism in their life. The water is just a similitude of an inward happening. When there is no inward change the water baptism is meaningless. Baptism isn't some kind of magic! It is not the water that changes us; it is the Holy Spirit that makes the change in our inner man. It is the power of His presence that makes a reality out of the immersion. Again, the immersion is only a symbol. We must understand that the doctrine of baptisms can also be understood as the "doctrine of changes."

These seven baptisms are the representations of the changes that we will experience during the maturation process. Remember salvation is more than a single event that has happened to us. Salvation is the beginning of the transformation or sanctification process. It is a process that takes many of us a lifetime to complete; while some of us will never find its end until we see Jesus face to face. 1 Peter 1:9 reveals to us that faith has an end, and that the salvation of our soul is a progressive reality.

John's Baptism (The first two New Testament baptisms)

The New Testament is very clear on the subject of John's baptism. Matthew 3:11 shows us that John's baptism was with water unto repentance. The Greek phasing simply states, "John baptized with water to show repentance." This baptism was not the end of the baptisms; it was the beginning of the baptisms. This was not the final baptism it was the first baptism (i.e., the first recorded baptism in the New Testament). Jesus did not baptize with water, John did. Jesus never baptized with water, His baptism is declared to be the baptism of the Holy Spirit and with fire. The Scripture clearly states this.

> "And John bare record, saying, I saw the Spirit descending from heaven
> like a dove, and it abode upon him. And I knew him not: but he that
> sent me to baptize with water, the same said unto me,
> Upon whom you shall see the Spirit descending and remaining
> on him, the same is he which baptizes with the Holy Ghost.
> And I saw, and bare record that this is the Son of God."
> (John 1:32-34)

> "Though Jesus himself baptized not, but his disciples..."
> (John 4:2)

> "I indeed baptize you with water unto repentance:
> but he that comes after me is mightier than I...
> He shall baptize you with the Holy Ghost, and with fire."
> (Matthew 3:11)

Once we understand that there is a difference between John's baptism and Jesus' baptism it will be a simpler issue to look beyond water baptism and identify that there are other baptisms in the New Testament. John's baptism had a place and a purpose. As the first baptism, the baptism unto repentance is a beginning place for all Christians. As stated in the Scriptures, Jesus had a high regard for it. As stated previously, there are two kinds of repentance, true and false repentance. John clarified his purpose about this baptism when he prophesied,

> "Prepare ye the way of the Lord, make his paths straight.
> And they were baptized...confessing their sins.
> Bring forth therefore fruits meet for repentance."
> (Matthew 3:3, 6, 8)

There are four things John dealt with in his baptism. The first was "preparing the way of the Lord." The maturation process contains three things; the promise of God, the preparation that comes through discipleship, and then the performance of that promise of spiritual life in the believer as they unite with the Body of Christ. To prepare your heart is to be obedient to the Lord and His word. When I have an attitude of obedience, my journey of faith is much easier to live.

John's second purpose in his baptism was "make his paths straight," which means "make it easy on God to come in and make the changes in your life He wants to make." In other words, do not resist God, just do what is commanded. This is why Jesus said, "If you love me, keep my commandments." Do not cause the Holy Spirit to have to work around things in your life, make it easy for Him to open a path through the unbelief you are experiencing.

Thirdly, John stated, they "confessed their sins" (i.e., to agree with what God said about sin) and finally, they were to "bring forth therefore fruits meet for repentance." John wanted to see a change in them as the evidence of a real conversion. Jesus expects the same and this is why the woman who was caught in adultery was told to "go and sin no more." We can recognize the foundational truth that we must first repent in order for the water baptism to be real. What is water baptism a symbol of anyway? Was it joining a local church? Water baptism is not the mark of joining a local church, even though many denominations use it as such. In water baptisms origin there was no local church, it was reflective of the change true repentance had brought. In the Old Testament the golden laver was used to boil all the blood out of the meat. In essence, water baptism is a similitude of our repentance. Our life (i.e., the blood) has to be boiled out so Jesus' life can come in.

> "And this man was instructed in the way of the Lord;
> and being fervent in the spirit, he spake and taught diligently
> the things of the Lord, only knowing the baptism of John."
> (Acts 18:25)

"That word, I say, ye know, which was preached throughout all Judea,
and began from Galilee, after the baptism which John preached;
How God anointed Jesus of Nazareth with the Holy Ghost and with power."
(Acts 10:37-38a)

"The baptism of John, whence was it? from heaven, or of men?"
(Matthew 21:25)

"And all the people that heard him, and the publicans, justified God,
being baptized with the baptism of John."
(Luke 7:29)

"For John truly baptized with water;
but ye shall be baptized with the
Holy Ghost not many days hence."
(Acts 1:5)

These few Scriptures show that there is a distinction made between John's baptism and Jesus' baptism. The New Testament does not hold the two baptisms with the same regard because there was a difference in their purpose. What was John's purpose?

"And he (John) came into all the country about Jordan, preaching the
baptism of repentance for the remission of sin."
(Luke 3:3)

The baptism of repentance for the remission of sin was John's message to the people. This declaration was a message to the people to prepare themselves for the coming of the Lord. Some denominations use this statement as though it is the gospel. Let us be clear on this matter, this was John's purpose and not Jesus'. Jesus preached, "Repent, for the kingdom of heaven is at hand," and His baptism is with the Holy Spirit and with fire; not water. As we review the Scriptures on this topic we will see the truth of this clearly. As an example, when Peter preached and gave the invitation in the book of Acts 2:38, he was preaching from his experience, but he had forgotten something.

"Then Peter said unto them, repent, and be baptized every one
of you in the name of Jesus Christ for the remission of sins,
and you shall receive the gift of the Holy Ghost."
(Acts 2:38)

But later in the book of Acts Peter remembered something very important and said:

"Then I remembered the word of the Lord, how that he said, John indeed
baptized with water; but ye shall be baptized with the Holy Ghost."
(Acts 11:16)

Peter had realized the difference between John's baptism and Jesus' baptism. He remembered that Jesus had drawn a difference in the two baptisms and so he made a distinction as well. It was not the water baptism that mattered; it was the baptism of the Holy Spirit that signified the experience of salvation in Peter's mind. This is why Acts 13:24-25a states,

"When John had first preached before his coming the baptism of
repentance to all the people of Israel. And as John fulfilled his course..."

John is not the Messiah. His baptism therefore cannot have the power of salvation as some preach it to have. Even in Acts 19:3-4 Paul knew the difference between John's baptism and Jesus' baptism. These disciples had been water baptized, but Paul baptized them in the name of the Lord. Paul understood the place that John's baptism had, but he did not promote baptism as a means of salvation, nor did he promote baptism as the way to get our sins remitted. Paul said in 1 Corinthians 1:17:

"For Christ sent me not to baptize, but to preach the gospel..."

If water baptism is the only way to get our sins remitted, someone forgot to tell Paul! Paul's understanding of John's baptism is clearly understood to be an outward expression of true repentance in the New Testament, but Paul never elevated water baptism to where many have it today. We should not forget that it is the blood of Jesus that cleanses us from our sin and not baptism. When Paul wrote in Romans 6:3-4, he used the words "like as" and "even so" to show its similitude. John's baptism is truly necessary as an expression of one's faith, but not for salvation. Nothing should come between our Savior and us, not even water baptism. The doctrines that go along with the idea that our sins cannot be forgiven unless we are water baptized are used to shore up those false doctrinal positions. Those that believe water baptism is what washes away our sin cannot hold the entire New Testament in Canon because the Gospels perfectly declare their philosophy to be in error. Jesus is the only mediator between God and man and salvation is not of works, not even the work of baptism. Jesus honored water baptism as an expression of obedience, not that it had magical powers to wash away our sin. Jesus was water baptized in order to "fulfill all righteousness" and we should do the same. I do not want to dilute water baptism down as being unimportant; this is not my goal. Water baptism has great significance. After all, baptism is a matter of obedience. We can see through Jesus' example what the picture of water baptism is. To be baptized unto repentance and to be baptized unto water are experientially two different events.

"And Jesus, when he was baptized, went up straightway out
of the water: and, lo, the heavens were opened unto

> him, and he saw the Spirit of God descending like a dove,
> and lighting upon him: And a voice from heaven, saying
> This is my beloved son, in whom I am well pleased."
> (Matthew 3:16-17)

The water baptism was signified by the voice from heaven that said, "This is my beloved son." Water baptism is a similitude that represents the son-ship we enter into and that God has designed for us. This immersion in water symbolizes the new birth. I am no longer of the natural world; I am a child of the Father; Abba God is my new Dad. It is the presence of God, through the Spirit, that can change a man's mind, which has a reflection in his new life as one born-again and through his adoption into God's family. Once the adoption occurs, through repentance, the preparation into sonship can now come to pass. With the changes repentance brings to our profession of faith, we are then able to see God as our Abba (Daddy), Father. This baptism works within us to prepare the way for the next step. Jesus testified that John baptized with water; but you shall be baptized with the Holy Spirit (see Acts 1:5). Paul said in Acts 19:2,

> "Have you received the Holy Ghost since you believed?"

They had received John's baptism, but had not yet received the baptism that comes from Jesus.

Baptized with the Spirit and with Fire

The baptism with the Holy Spirit is one of the most misunderstood subjects in the Church today. There are extremes and abuses on every side, but the baptism, or the change that takes place when the Spirit of God fills us is seen in the life of Jesus.

> "Then was Jesus led up of the Spirit into the
> wilderness to be tempted of the devil."
> (Matthew 4:1)

When the Holy Spirit came upon Jesus, Jesus was led into the wilderness. Romans 8:14 explains,

> "For as many as are led by the Spirit of
> God, they are the sons of God."

Jesus who had the Spirit without measure gives us a practical example of this change. As he began his ministry the change was evident. The voice of God came to Him and said, "You are my beloved Son," and then Satan came to him to tempt Him away from that reality. When we receive the Word of God and the Holy Spirit empowers us to become witnesses unto Jesus, Satan will always attack.

The baptism with the Spirit must be recognized by its purpose, not its manifestations. The purpose of the baptism with the Spirit is to empower the believer in order for them to become witnesses.

> "But you shall receive power after the Holy Spirit is
> come upon you: And you shall be witnesses unto me."
> (Acts 1:8)

My ability to become a witness depends on the work of the Holy Spirit within me to change me into the image of God. There is more to being a witness than knocking on doors! In the original creation we were created in His image and in His likeness. When we are born again we are renewed into His image and likeness. God's Spirit regenerates us and renews us with His power and causes us to "become" His sons/daughters. To many times in our modern Church we think we are to "help" people change. My experience has taught me that it is the Holy Spirit's responsibility to change us; our part is to walk people through the process. Being a cynic or a critic does not help anyone in the process. As a Christian it is my obligation to love my brothers and sisters in the Lord, while leaving the rest to Holy Spirit. Romans 14:4 states,

> "Who art thou that judgest another man's servant?
> to his own master he standeth or falleth.
> Yea, he shall be holden up: for God is able to make him stand."

There is a dual attitude in the Church today: One is "don't judge me," while the other is the opposite, "Holy Ghost number two, always telling you what to do." Forgive my pun, but I find that many in the Church want to do whatever they want to; never mind what the Scripture says, while the other extreme has made everything sin. If you smoke cigarettes, that's a sin; if you have a drink of alcohol, that's a sin. If you wear the wrong clothes, that's a sin, or if you eat the wrong food, that's a sin. The last time I checked there are Ten Commandments that describe what "sin" actually is. Jesus did not add any more commandments; He told us what they actually meant. Love does not commit adultery, love doesn't backbite and gossip, love does not steal or murder, etc. Paul also expounded on them as well in 1 Corinthians 13. Love isn't boastful; love is kind and generous, etc. I am saddened to think that Christians have come to the place that we separate from other believers and break fellowship for the slightest reason. I know of churches that will "excommunicate" you if you smoke cigarettes, and they do it in the name of holiness. What a sad day when those who believe we are saved by grace cast people out of our fellowships for the sake of phony holiness. I am holy because Jesus made me holy. Not because of my works or lack there of. So many people today are weak in intimate fellowship. The true test of a church is its love, not its piety. We should reread James 5:17 in light of grace.

> "Elias was a man subject to like passions as we are,
> and he prayed earnestly that it might not rain:
> and it rained not on the earth by the
> space of three years and six months."

What does the Scripture mean when it says Elijah had "like passions?" It means he was subject to same temptations as we are and yet God honored his prayer. Why do we think that God holds us to a different standard than the Word of God says? If we believe that we are saved by grace, why do we preach that we are cursed when we make a mistake, or live differently than others? There are temptations everywhere. You cannot turn on a television and expect that immorality will not hit you right in the face. We live in a time that is almost exactly like the days of the Romans. They were a lustful people, and had great arrogance and hubris.

> "This day is a day of trouble, and of rebuke, and of blasphemy:
> for the children are come to the birth,
> and there is not strength to bring forth."
> (Isaiah 37:3)

> "Whom shall he teach knowledge?
> and whom shall he make to understand doctrine?
> them that are weaned from the milk,
> and drawn from the breasts."
> (Isaiah 28:9)

It is only the empowering of God's Spirit that enables us to become His sons and daughters. Without the change and the renewed mind, we will be unable to overcome anything. Satan came to Jesus in the wilderness to cause Him to fall. Jesus answered Satan's lie with the Word, because the Word of God is truth. Satan can be overcome by truth; Satan's only weapon is a lie. When the Spirit descended upon Jesus after His water baptism God made a declaration concerning his son-ship. We should accept our son-ship and bring honor to our Father through obedience to what Jesus says. When the Spirit led, Jesus went. The same applies to you and me. Where He leads me I will follow; what He feeds me I will swallow! The change that comes from the Spirit is an internal event that has external expressions. When we receive the Spirit, we receive Christ. Since the Spirit of the Christ now abides in me, I have His words in my mouth; I have His will in my heart; and I have His works in my walk. When the baptism with the Holy Ghost is real, it is confirmed by the change in a person's character. His character and the level of his integrity will grow and become fruitful. Why? Because to be filled with the Spirit is to be filled with the presence of God. You cannot fake the filling. People can learn to speak with other tongues and to prophesy, but they cannot change their disposition and the old man without the help of the Holy Spirit. When the presence of God baptizes you, you will be changed. No amount of tongue-talking can fool those that are truly filled. 1 Corinthians 13 explains that without love, tongues are nothing more than sounding brass and tinkling cymbals. To be filled with God's Spirit is to be filled with His nature. The manifestations of the Spirit are a present day reality, but they have no value without a changed heart. God is working through these internal manifestations so He can bring us to the next change.

"From where do wars and fighting's among you come?
Is it not from this, from your lusts which war in your members?"
(James 4:1)

"But I see another law in my members,
warring against the law of my mind,
and bringing me into captivity to the
law of sin which is in my members."
(Romans 7:23)

Winning the internal battle and the baptism with fire are necessary to bring about the purity of our faith. Without the change that occurs when we are baptized with the Spirit, the baptism with fire will not have the effect God desires it to have.

"For though thou wash thee with nitre (acid),
and take thee much soap,
yet thine iniquity is marked before me,
saith the Lord God."
(Jeremiah 2:22)

"But who may abide the day of his coming?
and who shall stand when he appeareth? for he is like a
refiner's fire, and like fullers' soap."
(Malachi 3:2)

If you cannot submit to the lordship of Jesus Christ and you resist His moving, you will never endure His internal purging. You cannot wash away sin, only the Spirit of God can do that work. The only way to be changed by the fire of God is to recognize His right of ownership and His desire for a pure bride. Malachi 3 says this fire is a purifier and is for purging. It cleanses us. Its purpose is to remove the nature of the old man. The old habits, the old ways, and the old desires are to be eradicated by this baptism. Many never overcome the old man because they have not been baptized by fire. They are not changed and their scent remains in them (see Jeremiah 48:11). They hold onto their old way of thinking, their old habits, and their old desires. I ask the people in my discipleship program if they have "fallen through the grate yet?" They know this means that our flesh must be burned away through this baptism. Does your flesh continue to control certain areas of your life? Unless a person is baptized with fire they will never be able to come to the purity of God's design. The fire has to burn your flesh to ashes before you can experience the next baptism in the series. Remember we are sinners saved by grace. This is the key. There is a false doctrine today that teaches that we will some how become sinless. It will never happen.

Baptism into the Body

"For by one Spirit are we all baptized into one body,
whether we be Jews or Greeks,
whether we be bond or free; we have been
all made to drink into one Spirit."
(1 Corinthians 12:13)

Baptism into the Body of Christ is simply having an inner change that has its external evidence in your relationships. One has a sense of being a part of the whole because their life is intertwined within a local church. The Body of Christ is not a dismembered body; it is a complete body with Jesus as its head. The name on the church should make no difference, because it is the name on the heart that matters. Are you Christ's or Satan's? Sons of God are anointed with the power of righteousness and should walk together in faith and hope. Satan's sons are the accusers of the brethren and stir up strife and contention. Let God be true and every man a liar (see Romans 3:4). The baptism into the Body will occur when God's Spirit fills us and when fire purges us. This allows us to experience a remarkable event. It cannot be taught. It must be experienced. When people gather in the name of the Lord, there is to be "communion" (2842-koinonia). Koinonia is not ritualistic; it is alive, just like the Word of God. We talk of fellowship as though it were a church dinner, when true communion (fellowship) happens as we experience a need for each other. Fellowship is the contribution one makes to his local church. It is his total contribution and not just how much money he gives! The tithe, alms, and "rightnesses" are just a part of the contributions one makes. Money is inconsequential when compared to what we bring to the Church as a co-laborer with Christ and as God's sons and daughters. When someone comes to the church, do they bring strife or communion? Are they involved in unity or contention? Are they argumentative and unteachable, or are they flexible and adaptable? Are they opinionated and full of bitternesses, or are they correctable and humble as the true servants of God are commanded to be? Have they had bad times in their life that manifest a lack of trust toward people, or are they able to overcome and control these feelings of rejection? We should comprehend that we contribute even when we are unaware of it. What spirit do you have, humble and lowly or haughty and uppity? Do you just go to a church or are you a part of the Church? Have you found your place in the Body or are you still struggling with detachment? If you seek a position in your local Body and there are none given, can you rest and wait on God's advancement? If the Spirit is not moving on your behalf can you sit still? If you cannot wait on God you are like a child on his way to grandma's house asking, "Are we there yet?" If the journey takes two and a half hours, frustration in thirty minutes will not help you get there any faster. My oldest son Joshua asked me a question some years ago; He said, "You are thirty eight?" "Yes", I said. "And I am eight?" "Yes, again!" "That means you are thirty years older than me." "Yes it does, Josh." "I want to be thirty", Josh said. "It'll take you twenty two more years to get there, son" is how the conversation ended. No matter how bad Josh wanted to be thirty. No matter how angry he could have become, it would still take twenty two years before it happened. He is twenty two now, but patience had to prevail so peace could reign. So it is in the

Body of Christ. Promotion comes from the Lord, not from the preacher, not from the deacons, and not from the elders; only God can give you a true promotion. You may get the title, but not the anointing if God has not promoted you into that office?

The change that comes to people when they are baptized into Christ's Body causes a union that is beyond comprehension. There is a deep sense of peace that comes to the house of God that is wonderful when the Body of Christ assembles itself together, rather than just a gathering on Sunday morning. Strife ceases and contention vanishes away, and there is always someone available and desiring to help in every area of need when the Church is assembled properly in Christ. The church building becomes a place of rest where the members are comfortable and excited, as the presence of God fills their life. Rest will come because the people of God are assembled, not just gathered together.

> "Not forsaking the assembling of ourselves
> together, as the manner of some is;
> but exhorting one another: and so much the more,
> as you see the day approaching."
> (Hebrews 10:25)

I have already used the example of the wagon that was gathered in the box, but have you ever bought a swing set or a model car? The pieces usually come in a box and are gathered together, and not assembled as well? Just because you come to church together does not mean you are assembled together. If there is contention and strife present, it is just an indication that the Body is not assembled together. Even if you can hide the problem, it still has a reflection in the disjointed Body. You cannot hide what you are not hiding! You cannot hide strife from God and others see it also. The Greek word "parakaleo" (3870) translated as "exhorting" means "to call along side of," with the purpose of helping, aiding, and or comforting one another. In order for the Church to be assembled together there has to be an underlying force binding the people of God together in one accord. This is what the true nature of spiritual communion is designed for; to bind us together under the banner of a common goal. That goal is the representation of the Kingdom of God in our local community.

> "And they, continuing daily with one accord
> in the temple, and breaking bread
> from house to house, did eat their meat
> with gladness and singleness of heart."
> (Acts 2:46)

The singleness of heart in a congregation manifests as their unity in the faith matures. We are built together to produce godly people. This is our purpose and only with the bond of peace will our churches be changed.

Baptism of His Death and in the Cloud

"Know ye not, that so many of us as were
baptized into Jesus Christ were baptized
into his death? Therefore we are buried with
him by batism (our change) into death:
that like as Christ was raised
up from the dead by the glory of the Father,
even so we also should walk in newness of life."
(Romans 6:3-4)

God has designed in His redemptive plan a transformation in the life of the believer. Jesus learned obedience through the things he suffered (see Hebrews 5:8), and we will learn obedience the same way. The Greek word translated as "suffered" means "to experience." We must have our hearts established in the faith before we will understand that suffering is a part of the Christian experience. Jesus taught it, His Word declares it, and you had better believe it. Life is full of troubles and trials. God did not send the trouble, but He will use it for His advantage. God did not send that divorce into your life, but He will use it for His benefit. He did not send disease, but He will use it. He did not cause poverty to catch you, but He will use it. We cannot allow the hurts and pains that come our way to destroy us or to affect the Body of Christ. We must be healed.

"Though he were a son, yet learned he obedience
by the things which he suffered."
(Hebrews 5:8)

When we make mistakes God is not caught off-guard. He loves us in spite of ourselves. Christ died for us "while we were yet sinners." We must overcome our own fear of failure so that we can succeed in life. We must overcome our own faithlessness and mature spiritually. Works do not save us, this is true, but we have a responsibility in our salvation. God is still working in us. It causes great pain in people of faith when they fail, but as people of faith we must continue to press on and not give up. The Church is a place where we help one another to grow and overcome. It is not a place where the sinless rest; it is a place where the saved walk.

At the mount of Transfiguration there was a change that took place. You will notice the natural transformation of Jesus' form in the passage, but did you perceive the change in the Father's testimony toward him? The Father added the "hear him" part. In 1 Corinthians 10 Paul stated,

"Moreover, brethren, I would not that you should be ignorant,
how that all our fathers were under the cloud, and all passed through the sea
And were all baptized unto Moses in the cloud and in the sea...
But with many of them God was not well pleased: for they were

overthrown in the wilderness. All things are lawful for me,
but all things are not expedient; all things are lawful
for me, but all things edify not."
(1 Corinthians 10: 1-2, 5, 23)

God led the children of Israel in the wilderness with a cloud by day and fire by night. The cloud of God is His glory. Today the cloud of God can be experienced as congregations are built together into a unified Kingdom force. This brings the glory of God down into that congregation. When the Body of Christ experiences the unity of faith the people assemble themselves as one. The word translated as "overthrown" could easily be translated as to "give up." They gave up their faith and where defeated.

"And the angel of God, which went before the
camp of Israel, removed and went behind
them; and the pillar of the cloud went from before
their face, and stood behind them:
And it came between the camp of the Egyptians and the camp of Israel;
and it was a cloud and darkness to them (i.e. the Egyptians),
but it gave light by night to these (i.e. Israel)..."
(Exodus 14:19-20)

The same water in the Red Sea that delivered the children of God destroyed their enemies. So it is with the baptism into the cloud. The cloud was light to the children of God and darkness to their enemies. It is challenging in these days seeing the prophecy fulfilled, "And the love of many shall wax cold." The hardening of people's hearts is the thing that hinders the work of God mostly. To be baptized into the cloud is to fulfill Exodus 14:31.

"And Israel saw that great work which the Lord did
upon the Egyptians: And the people feared the Lord,
and believed the Lord, and his servant Moses."

When we experience the fear of God in its perfect application, we will experience the fullness of the doctrine of baptisms. It takes wisdom to finish our faith. The high call of God presses us onward so that we can accomplish the work God has set before us. When a man has the Spirit of the Father within him, there is no denying the internal voice that calls him home, home to the presence of God. To be changed by the cloud is to understand that the Holy of Holies is the presence of God in the local fellowship and we should walk with God's leadership. It is simply being overshadowed by the power of God as we are led. This baptism is the consummation of the baptisms. To be baptized in the cloud is to have the ability to follow God's leading, whether He is leading me through the fire or leading me during a time of ease.

Chapter 11 — Laying on of Hands

"Therefore let us go on and get past the elementary
stage in the teachings and doctrine
of Christ (the Messiah), advancing steadily toward
completeness and perfection that belong to
spiritual maturity. Let us not again be laying the
foundation of...the laying on of hands."
(Hebrews 6:1-2 Amplified)

"Lay hands on no man suddenly..."
(1 Timothy 5:22)

"Neglect not the gift that is in thee, which was given
thee by prophecy, with the laying on of the hands of the presbytery."
(1 Timothy 4:14)

"Wherefore I put thee in remembrance that thou stir up the
gift of God, which is in thee by the putting on of my hands."
(2 Timothy 1:6)

Much of the traditional ideology in today's Church is quite different from the Church of old. The Hebrews had a sure foundation of faith, family, and heritage but could not move forward with God's revelation. The Church, on the other hand, has the revelation of Jesus Christ but tries to progress without first setting the foundation completely. This is one of the reasons why people who call themselves "Christians" fail spiritually and morally at times. Another purpose the foundation of laying on of hands can accomplish is to anchor the people of God with trust and acceptance. God's purpose is to secure a people who are obedient to him: those to whom He can entrust His ways. When people do not have hands laid on them, the closeness and intimacy that they should have in the Body of Christ is diminished. But the main reason we should lay hands on people is God commanded us to do so.

Obedience

Jesus is Lord and His way will prevail, even in the Church!
"Therefore let all the house of Israel know assuredly,
that God has made that same Jesus, whom you
have crucified, both Lord and Christ."
(Acts 2:36)

It is amazing how many Christians are unproven in God's Word. In the 1990's, Barna produced a survey in which the results showed that the majority of the Church was biblically illiterate. Two things I noted as I read the survey was that Pastors are seriously struggling in their ministries and the Body of Christ does not understand the basics of the Christian faith. I believe many people who profess to be Christian do not know what the "true" gospel is. We are the Body and He is the head. This is one of the basic tenants within biblical authority. Obedience to His will should be our priority. There are too many people in today's Church who do not believe what the Bible says, while others are simply apathetic about discipleship and the Lordship of Jesus. Many believers do not study or read God's Word as a discipline of faith. The Bible admonishes us to study (see 2 Timothy 2:15). People in the Church must be discipled and trained in the ways of God, not just led to salvation. Much of what is described as the salvation experience is actually a gospel of "walking the aisle." People are asked to "walk the aisle and pray a prayer", which is construed as salvation but there is no change in the person's heart. Christian strength is found in obedience, and obedience comes through pure and real faith.

"And being made perfect he became the author of
eternal salvation unto all them that obey him."
(Hebrews 5:9)

God does not, nor will He bless disobedience. There is a teaching in the Church today that the grace of God supersedes His commandments, and that grace is given to the unrepentant. It is true that God's grace covers our shortcomings, but one must take a hard look at individuals who sin willfully and crucify Christ anew (see Hebrews 6:6). The Scriptures declare that if we sin willfully there is no more sacrifice for our sin (see Hebrews 10:26). This simply means that if you continue to consciously sin and have no conviction, you may not be saved. When people have not been taught this, they have no fear of God, and Psalm 55:19 states:

"Because they have no changes,
therefore they fear not God."

Ministers who have not been trained properly will not have the ability to complete the process of discipling others. Just because one has been called does not mean he is ready to serve. The biblical model of acceptance and the impartation of power from the Holy Spirit and spiritual fathers to the spiritual sons and daughters must be adhered to if the people of God are to have a proper foundation of faith. Without acceptance, which is received by the laying on of hands, many individuals will carry a sense of insecurity in their ministries.

Believers will not mature properly if any of the elementary foundations have not been laid in their lives. All of the foundations must be laid in their proper place. I thank God that a year after I was licensed, several men of God took me aside and laid hands on me, stabilizing me and allowing me to go on with God now having a sure foundation in this area. One of the purposes in laying on of hands is to bring a sense of security to the people of God, to establish them in their calling through time-honored relationships, and to anchor their soul in the hard times that come their way. Every minister will go through rough times. It is during these times you can look back on your laying on of hands event and recall the event, which helps to stabilize you.

From Recognition to Separation

The Old Testament picture of spiritual release for the priests was to have oil poured on their heads as a symbol of God's anointing and authority. Even King David had oil poured on his head as a sign of God's ordination (see 1 Samuel 16:13), and despite the fact that David had the oil poured on his head, he was not the king for many years afterward. As a disciple, David had to mature first by experiencing the cave of Adullam. David had to prove himself. The same holds true today. God calls men and women into the ministry but expects them to be trained and matured before they receive their position. David was called but it took years to get him ready for his service and responsibility.

Today the oil is manifested through the Holy Spirit. One of the aspects of the Holy Spirit is that He comes to fill and to cover. Oil represents God's authority and His anointing. God is a Spirit and His authority is spiritually manifested in those whom He calls. We can recognize this authority in individuals who have been separated by the Holy Spirit and the power of spirit they walk in. When the Holy Spirit sets a person apart for ministry, He is the one who equips them with spiritual authority and power. If the person is slothful in their spiritual administration, they will never mature in the power of their anointing, even if they are called and set apart. Diligence reveals desire. God empowers and anoints those He calls before they are born (see Jeremiah 1). He then uses the orchestration of their life for His benefit. Those who are set apart have "stature" ('helikia' - 2244; i.e., maturity). *Helikia* is defined as "a suitable age for accomplishing a thing, or to have the mental comeliness to deal with adversity." This stature is relative to understanding authority and the laying on of hands. God's authority is progressively manifested in the life of the minister, practically speaking. We should be aware of the fact that obedience has to be discovered by the person who is called. What I mean by this statement is that we learn obedience by the things we suffer (experience) just as Jesus did. To whom much authority will be given, there will be much obedience required before it can be gained. As stated before, it is not a matter of whether the individual is called to be a priest or a prophet. Nor is it a question of whether a person is a prophet or a preacher, but the question is, "what kind of person is this prophet or preacher?" The number of people one has in his church does not determine his level of spiritual authority. Spiritual authority is determined by the amount of change you create in the lives of those you touch. In other words, is the minister a Daniel or is he a Balaam? This is the real issue.

> "Let the prophets speak two or three, and let the other
> judge (1252 – 'diakrino'; i.e., draw a distinction)
> If anything be revealed to another that sits by, let the first hold his peace...
> And the spirits of the prophets are subject to the prophets."
> (1 Corinthians 14:29-30, 32)

God expects a prophet to be temperate and to have his spirit in subjection (see 1 Corinthians 14:32). It is not who can prophesy, but who can be subject to God's Spirit when they prophesy. This question must be addressed in the Body of Christ today. One biblical principle states that ministers must first be "proved" (see 1 Timothy 3:10). In today's religious mindset, if you want to be a Pastor all you have to do is start a church somewhere. There are many who want to preach, but do they bear the marks of the Cross in their life? People who do not have the necessary experience to lead are called "novices" in the Bible. They must first be trained. The question for us to answer is: "What are the marks of a true minister who is called of God and ordained by the Holy Spirit?" They are the marks of the Cross that you receive and carry. A person receives these marks as they suffer for the truth and endure the hardships while their faith and character do not diminish. These are not the marks of going through the fire; they are the marks of coming through the fire and not smelling like smoke. When you endure sufferings you overcome and learn the value of faith. You learn that faith is the iron of your construction. Faith then becomes the only substructure *you* get to add to. When Jesus is your source and the foundation of your faith, any time of trouble can be endured. This is how we learn obedience in the things we suffer. Those who are babes in Christ are not ready to preach or lead. Those who do not bear the marks of Cross are not able to train or lead the Body of Christ.

The same holds true for ministers who do not have a peaceful home. Their discipleship is in theory, not in the reality of the Cross; they cannot truly impart rest and peace in the Church if they are not living in rest and peace. They set goals that cannot be attained, yet live as though they are the models of perfection. Preaching is not for those who serve a theoretical Jesus, who have a theoretical faith, and live a theoretical Christian experience. Leadership is for the mature and for those that have been proven over the process of time. How else will the people under these ministers mature in the faith? We must change our thinking and our ways. College or seminary alone cannot produce maturity. Galatians 4:1-2 teaches:

> "...the heir, as long as he is a child, does not
> differ from a servant, though he be lord of all;
> but is under tutors and governors until
> the time appointed of the father."

When were the priests allowed to be priests? And how did they come of age? The answer is: only after they were trained in the ways God. There was no oil poured on their head until they were ready. There was no such thing as a "young preacher-priest" back then! In our world today we are inundated with "young preachers." Praise God young people are surrendering into the ministry, but it is a detriment to the ministry when they are not fathered and still try to lead. They learn and grow as they fail, rather than growing through discipleship and then leading. Ministers must be disciplined and trained before they are released. Our problem in today's world is that we have multiple and different churches in the same town, and they are all vying for a Pastor when the position is vacant. I know I am being a bit sarcastic, but these issues must be addressed if we are to restore the Church to the glory it should walk in. Division and strife have diluted the anointing in the Church, and many people hear the call but are never trained. The Body of Christ is then full of division and false doctrine because of the immaturity of the leadership in it. Many churches have Pastors and Elders that run it like a business, never even realizing that the anointing is gone. They are oblivious to the lack of Spirit in their congregations, but they continue to sing their songs and preach, week in and week out. So now we have hundreds of different kinds of Baptists, Methodists, Full Gospel churches, and the division goes on and on. But true leadership is always manifested in the unity of the Body and its common voice. We will always have carnality in the ministry unless the standard is set at a high place for public ministry.

> "For Thou, O God, hast proved us:
> thou hast tried us, as silver is tried."
> (Psalm 66:10)

> "And let these first be proved; then let them use the
> office of a deacon, being found blameless."
> (1 Timothy 3:10)

> "And we have sent with them our brother,
> whom we have often times proved
> diligent in many things, but now much more diligent,
> upon the great confidence which I have in you."
> (2 Corinthians 8:22)

> "As it is written, He that had gathered much had nothing over;
> and he that had gathered little had no lack. But thanks be to
> God, which put the same earnest care into the heart of Titus

> for you. For indeed he accepted the exhortation; but being
> more forward, of his own accord he went unto you. And we
> have sent with him the brother, whose praise is in the gospel
> throughout all the churches; And not that only, but who was
> also chosen of the churches to travel with us with this grace,
> which is administered by us to the glory of the same Lord,
> and declaration of your ready mind."
> (2 Corinthians 8:15-19)

When men are unproved they cannot meet the challenges that people in the Body of Christ face in today's world. I am not saying "being proved" in the denominational sense, but "being approved" by God. Leaders should evidence spiritual authority in their lives before they are released to minister. Over the years I have had many young men and women in the churches I have pastored desire to enter the ministry. Some had God's call on their life while others did not. The right to challenge and confirm these people is a right that must not be waived. I've learned that just because someone feels the call on their life for full time ministry does not necessarily mean that they have the spiritual wherewithal to serve as a leader. We need people who know how to train sons and daughters in the faith. If those who feel they are called to a specific ministry have not been dealt with before they are released into the ministry, they will eventually manifest their sin and immaturity in the Church and the people of God suffer because of it.

In the ministry there are two individual things that become one: the Word of God and the ways of a man. If the person has not had their ways dealt with, they will mingle their weaknesses and corruption with the successes and the people of God will be misled or lorded over. Then how can people become ministers having a disciplined life that allows the Holy Spirit to use them? Only through the discipleship process can a disciplined life be fathered into our faith!

Church Government

In Numbers 27:15-23 we can see the beginning of the foundational doctrine of the laying on of hands. When we read about Joshua's experience in the wilderness, we will see how he was tried and how he was faithful for many years before he was set into his God-ordained position, and in the New Testament we find Paul admonishing us "to lay hands on no man suddenly." In Numbers 27:16-17 Moses said:

> "Let the Lord, the God of the spirits of all flesh, set a man over
> the congregation, Which may go out before them, and which may
> lead them out, and which may bring them in; that the
> congregation of the Lord be not as sheep which have no shepherd."

The Lord's instruction to Moses was to take Joshua and "to lay his hand upon him" and set him before everyone (i.e., in front of), and give him a 'charge' (6680). Verse 23 states:

> "And he (Moses) laid his hands upon him, and gave him a charge, as the
> Lord commanded by the hand of Moses."

This is the establishment of the "set man" principle. God sets a man over the congregation and he becomes responsible to lead. The Hebrew word translated as 'charge' means "to set in order as a position over". This Old Testament picture is God's original establishment of Church government. Even though this is established in the Old Testament, it has set the foundational order for Church leadership. This is an Old Testament passage, but Acts 7:37-39 states that the people of God were "the church in the wilderness." Stephen, who was chosen by the apostles, a man of good report, full of the Holy Spirit and wisdom, shows us that Jesus established and maintained this pattern in the Church. He stated that the prophet that God would bring in the last days was the same who gave Moses the instruction on Mt. Sinai (see Isaiah 63:8-9). Acts 7:46-47 teaches us that David desired to find a Tabernacle and was ordained to prepare for the building of it, but it was Solomon who built Him a house. David was a man out of his time. He saw something about God that fascinated him and he strived to walk with God in a new way. David saw that God wanted to fellowship with mankind so he broke the rules of his dispensation on several occasions. David planned for a different kind of Tabernacle than the one Moses had built. David's Tabernacle would be open to all people and there would be praise and worship twenty-four hours a day, seven days a week! The Ark of the Covenant was with David, and in David's Tabernacle, while Moses' Tabernacle was still offering the sacrifices, even though the Ark was not present with them during that time. It is much like a congregation that goes through the motions, but the Holy Spirit is not present. It was not God's plan to live in a house or a temple. God's desire has always been to live within us. This is why it is so necessary for ministers to be trained properly. When leadership is immature, they will teach that we go to church, rather than *be* the Church. Many people have been "churched," but have not been truly born again. Church government (i.e., Church leadership), as described in the New Testament, was implemented for the purpose of maintaining the truth of the Gospel, the Kingdom of God, and the maturity of the saints. The establishment of Church government was a necessary step that was implemented to assist the Body in its growth and maturity. Ephesians 4:11-16 declares this, as also does 1 Corinthians 12:28. The word translated as "governments" in 1 Corinthians 12:28 means directorship. In the books of first and second Timothy and Titus, the qualifications of Church leaders are given and these standards are to be followed.

Ordination

1 Timothy 4:14 commands the laying on of the hands of the presbytery. With this directive the Lord confirmed what we commonly call *ordination* by the laying on of hands. There is a fallacy

in the traditional idea of ordination in many denominational groups. In today's Church when we recognize that a person is gifted we have a tendency to promote that person above others. Every one in the Body of Christ is gifted, but God never commands us to lay hands on 'gifts'; we are commanded to lay hands on 'governments'. Again, everyone in the Body of Christ is gifted in some form or fashion. The Scripture teaches that God gives everyone gifts and manifestations of the spirit, so let me state again that it does not matter if you can preach or prophesy; what does matter is whether God has ordained you to lead or to follow. Again, why is this issue important? The mystery of God's ordination holds great value because if God did not give you the grace to lead, you will not lead from the spirit and will lead from the flesh. You may be a natural leader, but natural leaders lead by natural vision and insight, not spiritual vision and insight. God wants a man who will and can lead the people out of bondage, and who will and can lead the people into the Promised Land by the Spirit. When the ministry cannot lead by spiritual means, the people are like sheep without a shepherd.

"For it is written in the book of Psalms,
Let his habitation be desolate,
and let no man dwell therein: and his
bishopric (1984) let another take."
(Acts 1:20)

And when they had ordained them elders in every church..."
(Acts 14:23)

"And as they went through the cities,
they delivered them the decrees for to keep,
that were ordained of the apostles
and elders which were at Jerusalem.
And so were the churches established
in the faith, and increased in number daily."
(Acts 16:4-5)

"For this cause left I you in Crete, that you should set in order
the things that are left undone, and ordain elders in every city
as I have appointed you: If any be blameless, the
husband of one wife, having faithful children not
accused of riot or unruly, for the bishop must be
blameless (second time spoken of), as the steward of God; not
self-willed, not soon angry, not given to wine, no striker,
not given to the love of money; But a lover of hospitality,
a lover of good things, sober, just, holy, temperate; Holding fast

the faithful word in his teaching, that he may be able by
sound doctrine both to exhort and to convince the gainsayers.
For there are many unruly and vain talkers and deceivers (in the Church)."
(Titus 1:5-10)

What is the true purpose of biblical ordination? We are called and ordained to be with Him. It is from that relationship that we find the anointing. It is from our intimacy that the gold of biblical truth and revelation come our way. We are confirmed as a part of the Body of Christ by the laying on of hands. It is sad that so many congregations do not lay hands on one another. A loving touch brings security to any heart that experiences it. We are separated for His purpose by the laying on of hands. We are defined by our position by the laying on of hands. What we are is revealed by time, and there will be a full manifestation of the authority God has given us at the appointed hour. These are the various aspects of the laying on of hands.

As we read these Scriptures we should also consider the commandment to not lay hands on anyone suddenly. We must work to help smaller congregations in our communities find men who are called and qualified to lead.

"For I long to see you, that I may impart unto you
some spiritual gift, to the end you may be established."
(Romans 1:11)

Identification and Impartation

There are also two other facets in the laying on of hands: identification and impartation. The first, identification, is when someone joins the Body of Christ. The second phase, impartation, communicates what the Head has for that particular member. These two facets of the laying on of hands puts individuals into their proper place within the local church. The significance of the laying on of hands is that each member is identified and placed securely in the Body. They are identified by the leadership according to their place and then apprenticed and matured (discipled) to fulfill their role. The early Church took guessing out of the picture, because the apostles and elders followed the Holy Spirit's signification.

"And he (Jesus) went up into a mountain,
and called unto him whom he would:
and they came unto him. And he ordained
twelve, that they should be with him..."
(Mark 3:13-14)

Every called and anointed minister will tell you that being in the ministry is the ability to walk with Jesus. To be with Him every day, not in prayer only, but as a son who is walking out his life with his Father in heaven ("...on earth as it is in heaven...").

Stability and Acceptance

The establishment of the laying on of hands can also be seen as a safety valve in the local church. When we take the time to train faithful men, the Church will not be "lacking" (see 2 Timothy 2:1-7). This is the Church Jesus saw when He said, "Upon this rock I will build my church..." Because Pastors leave congregations on average every two years, there will never be an established foundation where mature ministry can be raised up unless the local Deacons or Elders are operating in a biblical way. When a congregation has a Pastor who moves on and they are not ill affected, it is because their deacons or elders are God-called. Godly deacons and elders who are biblically qualified, have the ability to teach and preach to the Body of Christ bringing edification and maintaining the bond of peace. If a Pastor leaves and the church finds itself in the midst of turmoil there is a major problem to be discovered there. As long as preachers travel from church to church, the Body will not mature. Just about the time a minister gets in a position to know the members' gifts, talents, and the depth of their character, they move to another church and start the process of discovery all over again.

The laying on of hands is a very practical part of the doctrine of the Kingdom of God. If the spiritual fathers do not give an opportunity to the sons and daughters to do the work they are being trained for, an opportunity for the son or daughter's gifts to flourish will be lost. When Paul told Timothy to "stir up the gift of God, which is in thee" (see 2 Timothy 1:6) he was reminding him that he had put his hands to the task of Timothy's growth. 2 Timothy 1:14 says:

> "That good thing which was committed unto thee keep
> by the Holy Ghost which dwelleth in us."

Paul had trained Timothy in the things of God over the years. In his travels, Paul had given Timothy the on-the-job training that was necessary for Timothy's maturation and service in the Kingdom. Spiritual fathers should recognize that the laying on of hands is more than just a charismatic concept. It is a necessity when establishing biblical men and women through the discipleship process. When elders and men of God lay hands on those that are younger in the faith, they give credence to them, help to remove feelings of rejection and insecurity which may be present, and give them confidence. Acceptance is a very important part of the emotional makeup of people. It is vitally important for the establishment of sons and daughters in the faith to have hands laid on them. Sons or daughters will not acquire the necessary virtue they will need in their service to the local church if spiritual fathers and mothers do not minister to their emotional need of acceptance.

One cannot edify a son or a daughter without first building acceptance into his/her life. This is what relationships are all about. We cannot expect relationships to have value if they do not have any depth, intimacy, or if they do not edify. Remember the Kingdom of God is not established in doctrinal credence, it is establish in relationships. Not a shallow "I'll see you at church" sociality, but impartation that only time and depth can disclose.

> "For the kingdom of God is not meat and drink; but righteousness,
> and peace, and joy in the Holy Ghost. For he that in these things serveth
> Christ is acceptable to God, and approved of men.
> Let us therefore follow after the things which make for
> peace, and things wherewith one may edify another."
> (Romans 14:17-19)

The Kingdom of God is not established by social gatherings (meat and drink), it is established by the righteousness, peace and joy that come from true Spiritual relationships. As we walk together with the ability to build each other up, righteousness is then seen in its ultimate form. Doctrinally, righteousness is our state of being and is the gift of God, but the righteousness that comes from spiritual relationships is a binding factor every God-fearing soul needs. When we pursue God's Kingdom, our place with the Lord, and relationships with our sons and daughters, we must have this firm foundation of righteousness established. One will never have the peace that passes understanding if the aspect of acceptance (righteousness) is not first founded. We know that righteousness is necessary in our relationship with our heavenly Father, so we should automatically carry a right standing over into our church relationships. Building a foundation of acceptance in the local church establishes emotional strength that is necessary for us to defeat a spirit of rejection and insecurity. Joy will be impossible to maintain if acceptance is disregarded in the discipleship process. None of us are sinless in any sense, but knowing you are received is a vital part of every believer's emotional health. Only with these parts of the Kingdom firmly in place will the true joy of Christianity be realized. Remember that we are to have life, and have life abundantly. Often folks who go to church live a closed and restricted lifestyle. Stress is killing people spiritually and physically as well. To say it bluntly, Christians are too uptight! They are stressed about everything. This is why the Church has tried to build itself on doctrines. God forbid if a believer drinks a glass of wine or a beer! Fear has so gripped the Church that everything, and I mean almost everything, has become a sin. Most all preachers know how to preach on sin, and many preach a salvation that is based on works. If you ask them many may deny it, but listen to their sermons and you will find them full of "thou shalt nots." Colossians 2:20-23 states it well:

> "Wherefore if ye be dead with Christ from the rudiments of the world,
> why, as though living in the world, are ye subject to ordinances,
> (touch not; taste not; handle not; Which all are to perish with the using;)
> after the commandments and doctrines of men?

Which things have indeed a shew of wisdom in
will worship, and humility, and neglecting of the body;
not in any honor to the satisfying of the flesh."

Ministers who do not walk in the spirit, and are not trained in the Word of God always preach from the flesh. I have heard sermons on the sin of drinking alcohol and I ask myself, "Who taught them that?" Take a look at Deuteronomy 14:22-26 and John 2. I bet you have rarely heard a preacher preach about tithing and drinking alcohol from these passages. One of the commandments concerning tithing is,

"And thou shalt bestow that money for whatsoever thy soul lusteth after,
for oxen, or for sheep, or for wine, or for strong drink,
or for whatsoever thy soul desireth:
and thou shalt eat there before the Lord thy God,
and thou shalt rejoice, thou, and thine household..."

The first thing a fleshly minister does when he sees this passage is to deny the Word of God and declare his tradition. Fleshly ministers can easily be identified by their inclination to fear the believer's liberty and freedom. Because some people have a limited self-control, they expect everyone else to have limited self- control, or none at all. It is true that some people have a limited self-control, but we should not blame everyone for this. The less of Christ there is inside, the more laws of control there has to be on behavior. When Christ is not the Lord the flesh will control you.

Healing and Gifts

There are several Scriptures that pertain to the laying on of hands when praying for someone. Rather than make comment on the laying on of hands for healing or establishing gifts, I will refer you to Mark 16:18, and ask you to review the following Scriptures to better understand the laying on of hands.

1 Corinthians 1:4-8
2 Corinthians 2:11
1 Timothy 4:11-14
2 Timothy 1:6-7
1 Peter 4:10-11
Romans 12:4-8
Proverbs 17:8
Proverbs 18:16
Proverbs 25:14

Chapter 12 — Resurrection of the Dead: Discovering the Power

"Let us leave behind the elementary
teaching about Christ and go forward
to adult understanding. Let us not lay over
and over again the foundation truths..."
(Hebrews 6:1-2 Phillips)

There is much debate among different Christian groups about the end times. Is there a rapture, when is the rapture, and what will happen to the Church during the time called the Tribulation? We should all understand the Scripture has the final word on this issue. When it comes to the doctrine of the end of days, the question that is important for the believer is not "Is there a resurrection?" The resurrection is clearly documented in the New Testament. The resurrection is a major factor in the doctrine of Christianity, and Paul said if there is no resurrection, we believe in vain. One question that must be addressed is "When does the resurrection occur?" Those who follow the Pre-Millennial Dispensationalist ideology believe that the resurrection will occur before the Tribulation begins. I find several flaws in this doctrine. First, Paul writes in 1 Corinthians 15:51-52:

"Behold, I shew you a mystery; We shall
not all sleep, but we shall all be changed,
In a moment, in the twinkling of an eye, at the last trump:
for the trumpet shall sound, and the dead shall be
raised incorruptible, and we shall be changed."

Notice the phase "at the last trump." On a simple reading of the book of Revelation you will find that the last trumpet does not sound until Revelation 11:15. Second, the first trumpet sounded in Revelation 8:7 after the Seven Seals have been opened. The sixth Trumpet does not sound until Revelation 9:13. Between Revelation 9:14 and Revelation 11:15 we find that the seven thunders have "uttered their voices" and the angels told John to "seal it up." John is told to "seal up" what is revealed by the seven thunders and to not write them down. God purposely did not reveal what was to take place during the seven thunders. One could speculate that whatever is to take place during that time will not be edifying. Immediately after the seventh trumpet John writes, "And the seventh angel sounded; and there were great voices in heaven, saying, "The kingdoms of this world are become the kingdoms of our Lord, and of his Christ; and he shall reign for ever and ever." The seventh Trumpet seems to be a victory cry because Revelation 11:18 says, "And the nations were angry, and thy wrath is come, and the time of the dead, that they should be judged, and that thou shouldest give reward unto thy servants the prophets, and to the saints, and them that fear thy name, small and great; and shouldest destroy them which destroy the earth." When these facts are coupled with Matthew 24:3 which states:

"And as he sat upon the mount of Olives,
the disciples came unto him privately,
saying, Tell us, when shall these things be?
and what shall be the sign of thy coming,
and of the end of the world?"

"What" and "when" are important identifiers in this passage. Jesus answered the "what" first, and then in verse 29-31 answered the "when."

"Immediately after the tribulation of those days shall
the sun be darkened, and the moon shall not give
her light, and the stars shall fall from heaven,
and the powers of the heavens shall be shaken:
And then shall appear the sign of the son of man
in heaven: and then shall all the tribes of the earth
mourn, and they shall see the Son of man coming
in the clouds of heaven with power and great glory.
And he shall send his angels with a great sound of a trumpet,
and they shall gather together his elect from the four winds,
from one end of heaven to the other."

To answer the question "when" will these things happen? It is…"Immediately after the tribulation…" God will send His angels to gather the elect. Many of the Scriptures used by those who hold the Pre-millennial view do not take into account the "when" of the rapture. They quote the "what," but fail to disclose the "when" of Jesus' declaration. Matthew and Revelation give us the explicit timing of the event, being after the tribulation. Thirdly, if one will study the parables of Jesus they will find that they always speak of the wicked that are taken out and not the righteous.

There are a couple of things about the resurrection that need to be mentioned. First, where are we going to be living after the resurrection? The Bible teaches us that we will not be in "heaven," but here on earth ruling with Jesus, not only during the thousand year reign, but afterwards as well. Revelation 21:2-3 speaks of this and declares that "New Jerusalem" comes down from heaven, and God will dwell with mankind forever and ever. Second, tradition has us going to "heaven" and staying there when the Bible states otherwise. That is the trouble with tradition! Disciples study the Word of God and know the truth; churchianity teaches many false doctrines and enslaves God's people to false theology, and endangers them through complacency. If you recognize that the Church will go through the tribulation, at the very least through Revelation 11, are you prepared for that time, or are you an unwise virgin (see Matthew 25)? Remember the unwise virgins were unprepared for the wait.

One of the lessons discovered by the story of the wise and unwise virgins is that is that they failed during the time of waiting. Many Christians believed the Y2K fiasco was going to be the beginning of the tribulation. After they saw that it wasn't they allowed their preparation to fall by the wayside. The lesson for us is to be prepared, and to stay prepared. We do not know when the Lord will return or when the time of trouble will begin, but preparation is the key and the pinnacle of wisdom in this matter. Since the last trumpet does not sound until Revelation 11, we should study Revelation chapter one through eleven to know what we are to prepare for. Just as Moses warned the children of Israel to prepare for the upcoming ten plagues (for God was judging Egypt, a pre-picture of the tribulation,) the Lord is maturing the spiritual sons of Issachar (see Genesis 49:14-15 and 1 Chronicles 12:32) in the Body of Christ who understand the times and know what the Church ought to do. The judgments are plainly stated so we should take heed and prepare. Food, water, and other essential supplies are a critical part of our preparation. Remember, God told Joseph to "take the fifth part" and store it up during the years of plenty, knowing the years of famine and drought were coming.

The resurrection of the saints is a sure guarantee given to us by God Himself. Now to the question, "What is the power of His resurrection?" Paul speaks of the power of Jesus' resurrection (see Philippians 3:10) and how it enables us to be overcomers. Overcoming is the real issue when studying the resurrection. The resurrection is the final blow to God's enemies. When the resurrection occurs the world will know that their judgment is set. John testifies of our need to be overcomers in Revelation Chapters 2 and 3 and is in agreement with Paul. Paul understood the reality of this power and wrote about it extensively throughout his writing in the New Testament. There are some interesting words found in 1 Corinthians 15:41-44, which demonstrate the relationship the resurrection has to various areas of our lives:

> "There is one glory of the sun, and another glory of the moon,
> and another glory of the stars: for one star differeth from another
> star in glory. So also is the resurrection of the dead.
> It is sown in corruption; it is raised in incorruption:
> It is sown in dishonor; it is raised in glory:
> it is sown in weakness; it is raised in power:
> It is sown a natural body; it is raised a spiritual body.
> There is a natural body, and there is a spiritual body."

In the resurrection of the dead we find all these truths listed above. All our troubles that the flesh produced are wiped away by the resurrection. How attentive and unwavering God is in preparing a Bride for his Son! The Scripture teaches that Christ will sit at the right hand of the Father until we make His enemies His footstool. We are called to defeat God's enemies and occupy till He comes again. Do most Christians believe that going to heaven is the only way glory will come to them? Are we so weak of heart that we fail to recognize the call and declaration of God that we are to go from "glory to glory?" In Matthew 25:26 the Greek word "slothful" comes from the root meaning "lazy," and in Hebrews 6:12 the word translated as "slothful" is defined as being stupid. Both translations illustrate the mind of Christ in the matter. Are we satisfied with our present state of being? Proverbs teaches, "The slothful says, a lion is in the streets!" They have an excuse for why they do not change. Their attitude is to not venture out into the deep things of God. They prefer to wait in fear for someone else to show them the way, and this same mentality was found in the children of Israel when they insisted that Moses go up to the mountain for them. Many people in the Church today want someone else to do for them what they refuse to do for themselves. They want someone else to pray for them. They want someone else to read the Bible for them and then tell them what it says. They want someone else to do the work of the ministry for them. This same spirit is in and is growing in America. People believe that they are entitled to something for nothing. They do not work, yet they have their hands out expecting the government to support them.

This same attitude is in the Church. This spirit causes people to expect others to pray for them rather than praying for themselves, to not tithe or support the local church, and to not be faithful in witnessing for Christ in their communities. It is amazing to read in the Bible that God will bless the faithful and I rarely see someone who tithes in a place of desperation, yet I often see people who do not tithe is a state of depravity and hardship. One would think after a while that people would get the hint! People believe that they cannot afford to tithe. (I have been tithing for years, and God has given me more than I could have ever imagined.) The doctrine of the resurrection of the dead unveils to us a power that is beyond the natural sight of man. The spiritual aspects of this doctrine enable us to see beyond the physical world into a place that holds the resources of heaven. The economy of the Kingdom is honor, respect, and charity. But before we will ever venture into this realm, we must have a faith that goes beyond the typical believer. By the way, in the Bible we are called believers, because we believe what the Bible says to us about God and the things of God!

There is a natural body and a spiritual body. There is the old man and the new man. The old man is carnal and his viewpoint is carnal and this is why he fails. The natural body desires natural things. The spiritual body seeks spiritual things. As we look further into 1 Corinthians 15, we find some interesting statements that also give insight into the doctrine of the resurrection of the dead. The first is:

> "And so it is written, the first man
> Adam was made a living soul:
> the last Adam was made a quickening spirit."
> (1 Corinthians 15:45)

The first Adam was "soulish" (i.e., he became a self-centered being). *Psuchikos* (5591) is the Greek word translated as soulish, carnal, and sensual in the New Testament; it relates the idea that one can be selfishly motivated and naturally inclined. We are born natural (soulish) people. We are 'naturally' inclined from birth and have to have a "change of nature." By this I mean we are inclined toward rebellion and selfishness, lust and desire, and are basically sinners before we are born again. How does this occur? Usually it is because we are raised by ungodly means and are stubborn. I am not saying that our parents were ungodly, but we were designed to live and grow in the Garden of Eden, not in the world. We were created to live with God and to not have the type of pressures we face in today's society. We were not created as weaklings, but our fallen environment shapes our emotional framework. I have seen two-year-old children who have learned how to embarrass their parents, throw a public fit in order to get their way. My family and I were at a wedding and I watched a little child tell her mother, "I want down." It was in the middle of the ceremony and the mother said "No!" The child then proceeded to go into a tantrum, forcing the mother to comply or be embarrassed by the child who would disrupt everything in order to get its own way. How is it that these things happen? The child, not being disciplined as the Bible teaches, grows up with a selfish concept that supersedes God's Word. The child did not ask to be this way; it is the nature found in unregenerate man.

When I was the Director of a day care in our church, I worked with children, parents, and caregivers on a daily basis. I recognized that many parents have not been trained how to discipline their children and many children have been raised expecting to receive whatever they want. All this is done in the name of, "I want my children to have more than I had." That is a philosophy that has at its inner core a worldly ideology that suffering is of the devil. As a father and a grandfather, I have learned that giving children everything they want causes them to not appreciate the things that they have. The power of God that was transferred to us through Jesus' resurrection helps us to recognize that suffering has a lesson attached to it. If children do not experience suffering they will not grow up tempered. Corporal punishment does not ruin a child's creativity; it enhances their discovery by training them in 'carefulness' (4710-see 2 Corinthians 7:11). Have you ever touched something that was hot and were burned? What was your first reaction? You jerked away from the thing! That is what corporal punishment does. It causes a jerk reaction in the mind of the child so they respond to the negative stimuli (lust, for example), and prevent it from happening again. The consequences of misbehavior are implanted into a child's psyche, which over the process of time motivates them to live within a standard of morality and personal integrity. The barrier of restraint has been shattered in America. 1 Samuel 15:23 teaches:

> "Rebellion is the sin of witchcraft, and stubbornness is iniquity
> and idolatry. Because you have rejected the Lord..."

Natural people who are not disciplined have a greater manifestation of selfishness and stubbornness than those that have been discipled. Even lost people raise children that are "good children," because they raise them to be honorable people. Their homes are free from strife and their homes have been established in a way that teaches basic morality. God reveals to us in 1 Samuel that stubbornness is actually a manifestation of idolatry. Idolatry is essentially self -worship. If I want certain behaviors to be acceptable, then I create a 'god' or a premise in the image that accepts that behavior. When those around these kinds of people do not accept their "lifestyle" or belief, then the selfish person becomes rebellious to the standard that has been established. They protest about their rights to be ungodly and if the society succumbs to that pressure, they will inevitably fall. It is the same in our society today. People want the freedom to do anything they choose to do. They march in the streets to gain their "rights," regardless of the self-centeredness of their lust.

God says that this rebellion is in reality witchcraft. The Hebrew word translated "witchcraft" can be better understood as "divination." Divination has at its root the notion of being divine. It is simply being a god unto yourself. This is what a worldly society and the propagation of evolution is designed to create; people who rebel against the biblical standard of morality to create a community of immorality. These people, when left to themselves without oversight, do what they want to do to fulfill their personal lust. 1 Corinthians 2:14 states that, "a natural man does not receive the things of God because they are spiritually discerned." When 'naturally' inclined people are allowed to lead, even by proxy, they can only lead others to the degree of their experience which is to the natural state of being. The same is true everywhere. Carnality produces carnality. God said in Genesis that everything produces after its own kind! Is it possible to raise people beyond their carnality and recreate them into a spiritual being? Of course it is, and Jesus showed us that it is possible. Saved people act saved! Jesus fathered his disciples; He rebuked them, corrected them, and even told some of them they had a devil on a couple of occasions! How do you react when you are corrected? The Bible says some "despise" (3643) it, some "faint" (1590), and some "endure" it (5278-see Hebrews 12:5-8). Hebrews 12:6 teaches us when you are received of the Lord, he "chastens" (3811) and "scourges" (3146) you. This is the evidence that you have been received by Him, and this is part of the Christian experience.

Consider what the Bible teaches. When does eternal life begin? Doctrinally, eternal life begins when we receive the Lord. The first Adam is the one who lives by his soulish nature and we are his heirs. We are naturally inclined toward sin because of it. We must battle our selfishness and must fight off temptations. Jesus, the last Adam, came as a quickening spirit. "Quickening" (2227-*zoopoieo*) means to 'revitalize' (i.e., to make us alive and to give us life). The Spirit of Christ makes us alive unto God. It is the Spirit of the resurrected Lord that inhabits us. The root words from where "quickening" is derived are *poieo* (4160) and *zoon* (2226). 'Zoon' means, "to be alive." 'Poieo' has been covered in Chapter 5 and means, "to build or make something". Again, the definition of 'poieo' means, "to make or do, in a wide application" (i.e., to...abide, bring forth, continue without any delay, exercise or execute, fulfill, gain, have, hold, to journey, to lighten the ship, to be one in which nothing moves you, ordain, perform, provide, to be purged, to secure, to shoot out, and to yield). Remember 'poieo' means, "to build a spiritual house". This is what the Spirit of God does to us. When the Holy Spirit quickens us, it comes through the power of the resurrection. This is why 1 Corinthians 15:51 states:

> "Behold, I show you a mystery; We shall not all sleep,
> but we shall all be changed..."

We shall be changed at the last trump. The Scripture teaches us so, but 1 Corinthians 15:58 admonishes us,

> "Therefore, my beloved brethren, be you steadfast, unmovable,
> always abounding in the work of the Lord,
> forasmuch as you know that your labor is not in vain in the Lord."

The ability the Holy Spirit gives us can be summed up in the statement, "the power of the resurrection." There is a form of godliness that lacks this power (i.e., denies the power - see 2 Timothy 3:5). The word translated as 'deny' in 2 Timothy 3:5 means to "contradict or disavow" the power. This form of godliness produces individuals who are ever learning, and never able to come to the 'knowledge' (1922) of the truth. The Bible teaches that these people shall "proceed no further" in their faith (see 2 Timothy 3:9). Without the power of the resurrection there can be no spiritual progression. Without the power of the resurrection there is no ability within a person to be an overcomer. Paul said:

> "That I may know him,
> and the power of his resurrection,
> and the fellowship of his sufferings,
> being made conformable
> unto his death.
> If by any means I might attain
> unto the resurrection of the dead."
> (Philippians 3:10-11)

When Paul stated, "being made 'conformable' (4833) unto his death" he used the Greek word *'summorphoo'*. This word means, "to be assimilated or morphed in to something else." To be 'conformed' is to have a predisposition toward the "becoming" process (the process of becoming something new). The Greek word translated as 'resurrection' in Philippians 3:10 is not the same word found in verse eleven. The Greek word *anastasis* (386) means, "to stand up" and is most widely known to be the 'translation' (resurrection) of the saints. When a dead man stands up, we know this as resurrection. But 'resurrection' in verse eleven is *exanastasis* (1815). This is the resurrection with the preposition *"ek"* attached to it, which denotes 'origin' (the point from where the motion or action proceeds)." There is an activity that stems from the power of resurrection. This activity stems from the Holy Spirit. This is the door of eternity that is within each of us who are born again. Jesus comes in and out of this "door" that is found in the heart of man. If the door is shut, Jesus stands outside and knocks (see Revelation 3:8, 20). If the door is open, Jesus comes in and "sups" (1172) with us. The word "sups" has a base meaning "to devour" (i.e., to consume). The word "sup" is a Jewish idiomatic expression for the evening meal, being the most exclusive meal of the day in their culture. Jesus makes an investment in us as overcomers. The power of His resurrection is the power of the Holy Spirit in you. The Spirit of God can only manifest in you what you allow him to manifest. You have the keys to the door of your life. You can open your life to the Lord or close it. This is what is meant by the statement "you have the keys of the kingdom (see Matthew 16:19)." This is true in salvation as well as beyond salvation. In John 10:3 Jesus says, "The porter (door keeper) opens the door." John 10:9 teaches that Jesus is the door. If we do not realize that we are the porters, we will fail to understand our part in the salvation process. Our part is not to work for our salvation, but to obey and open the door. When Paul stated in Philippians 2:12, "work out your own salvation with fear and trembling," this is what he was saying. We work on ourselves as we carry our cross daily, opening the door of our life to the Lord.

The resurrection of the dead has a dual manifestation. It is present and it is future.

> "But all things that are reproved are made manifest by the light:
> for whatsoever doth make manifest is light.
> Wherefore he saith, awake thou that sleepest,
> and arise from the dead, and Christ shall give thee light.
> See then that ye walk circumspectly, not as fools, but as wise,
> Redeeming the time, because the days are evil."
> (Ephesians 5:13-16)

We are called to awake from the dead to the things of God. This is what I call the present manifestation of the resurrection. The power of His resurrection is His power in me to discontinue a slothful existence! Simply stated, when I am spiritually awake it is the evidence that the Spirit of God dwells in me. When there are no changes in a person, there is no fear of God (see Psalm 55:19). To view this in light of the Old Testament, revelation is simple. 1 Corinthians 10:6 and 11 explain that the journey out of Egypt and onto the Promise Land is an 'example' (5179). The Greek word is *tupos* and means 'a die' (i.e., a stamp, a sampler, or type). *Tupos* is a type or a similitude of something in the natural realm that has its reality in the spiritual realm. In essence God gave us a spiritual picture of the maturity process. We begin our journey in Egypt, a type and shadow of the world. We are under Pharaoh (Satan), and in bondage to the system of sin. In our slavery we cry for a deliverer. Moses is a type of Jesus (see Deuteronomy 18:15, 18 and Acts 7:37-38); he was a deliverer of the people. Like Moses, Jesus took the people of God out from under the hand of Pharaoh (Satan). The process is simple. God commanded and demanded their freedom. Pharaoh would not release them. The Passover brought their deliverance, and Jesus is our Passover; remember the Lamb was crucified at the Passover. The Lord delivered them out of Egypt and they took the spoils of Egypt. In their journey they came to an obstacle, the Red Sea. With this barrier before them and Pharaoh behind them, they were between the proverbial rock and a hard place. God had to make a way for their deliverance. Without faith this journey will not be possible. We are like the Hebrews of old; though we are free from our bondage, obstacles lie in our path. The Lord led them out of Egypt in a specific way. He led them "by the way of the wilderness (see Exodus 13:18)." In the New Testament, Jesus followed this same pattern. He came out of Egypt (see Matthew 2:15) to fulfill the Word of the Lord. Upon Jesus' entrance into the ministry He first went into the wilderness to be tempted of the devil. After His wilderness experience Jesus came to the Jordan River just like the children of Israel. Gilgal is where Joshua circumcised all the men of Israel before they entered into the Promised Land. Joshua knew the men of Israel had to prepare themselves for the upcoming battles. Before they could possess the Promised Land there was something they had to do first. Israel could not face the Jericho and Ai experience until they were circumcised. They had to understand that the battle was the Lord's and remove idolatry and disobedience from within their midst. Without being circumcised they could not enter into their victory. Only after complete obedience could the children of Israel inhabit the land and live in the Kingdom of God. The Holy Spirit spiritually circumcises us (see Colossians 2:11). This pattern is paramount in the Scriptures and the process is simple. The foundational doctrines in Hebrews 6:1-2 are directly related to this journey:

- Egypt-------------Repentance from Dead Works
- The Red Sea--------------------Faith toward God
- The Wilderness----------------The Doctrine of Baptisms
- The Jordan River--------------The Laying on of Hands
- The Promised Land-----------Resurrection of the Dead
- The Kingdom-----------------------Eternal Judgment

Each of these stages in the maturity process has many sub-points and experiences; however, the power of His resurrection is His power to lead us through these stages and is the strength that brings about the victory.

Chapter 13 — Eternal Judgment

"Therefore leaving the principles of the doctrine of Christ,
let us go on unto perfection; not laying again
the foundation of...eternal judgment."
(Hebrews 6:1-2)

I have always thought of eternal judgment as either going to heaven or hell. And it is, in the ultimate sense of a religious perspective. But consider this: What gets you to heaven or what gets you to hell? The Greek words translated as "eternal judgment" in the Hebrews 6 passage is defined in the Greek language as "the age/time of eternal decision." Jesus said that Jerusalem had missed her time of visitation. There are several instances in the Bible where the notion of a 'visitation' (1984) from God is revealed. In Ephesians 5:16 is the statement:

"Redeeming the time, because the days are evil."

This kind of 'time' (2540) is defined as an occasion or a set time, the "*kairos* time". This kind of time is "an opportunity or a season of God's visitation." When the Lord comes to administer an occasion of His favor and grace, He wants us to know that an unwise heart does not understand His will and purpose; therefore an unwise heart may not be able to 'redeem' (1805) the opportunity and power the Lord brings. To 'redeem' (1805) one's time is "to buy up, rescue from loss, or improve one's opportunity" by definition. When we know God's will this can be accomplished more easily (see Ephesians 1:9 and John 17). One can fail God and miss His purpose simply by not paying attention. This is called *apeithia* (543) in the New Testament Greek and is defined as the word 'unbelief' in Hebrews 4:11. This is where the English word 'apathy' originated. In essence, one could miss their spiritual visitation simply by being apathetic. A decision that may seem small and insignificant could well be a life and/or eternity changing thing. This is the basic aspect of "eternal judgment" as a foundational principle.

When Paul preached the gospel to Felix in Acts 24, we get an interesting observation about eternal judgment:

> "And when Felix heard these things, having more perfect
> knowledge of that way...he reasoned of
> righteousness, temperance, and judgment to come..."
> (Acts 24:22 and 25)

Paul 'reasoned' (1256 - *dialegomai*) of these things. This Greek word comes from two root derivatives, *dia* (1223) and *lego* (3004). *Dia* is defined as "the channel of an act; that is, 'something' passes through 'something'". *Lego* means, "to lay forth" (i.e., to relate). What did Felix do? He 'related' to righteousness (1343), temperance (1466), and judgment (2917) to come! This is the message of the Kingdom gospel. Jesus Christ is our righteousness. He is our right standing with God the Father.

'Righteousness' is an easy word to understand yet one of the hardest to live by. Simply put, righteousness is our 'innocence' (i.e., our 'justification'). How do we get it? It is a gift from God. Romans 5:17 says that by this wonderful gift we can reign in this life. We are not to reign over one another, in the sense of worldly dominion and worldly forms of authority; rather we are to reign over our selfishness and the evil day. When we take an honest view of our motives, desires, and determinations we should quickly see our need for 'temperance'. Temperance is the continuance of faith. To continue in the faith is to have self-control.

'Self-control' is exercising self-restraint over one's passions. Whether these passions are food or drink, sexual or sensual cravings, attitudes or desires, we are commanded to be in control. If you do not control your self, something else will. Most likely Satan will control those things if we are not conscious of our lusts or are 'out of control.' The Greek root word translated as the English word 'temperance' means to be in the "dominion of God". In essence, self-control is the dominion of God or the Kingdom of God ruling over the soul of man. When Paul spoke of these things to Felix, Felix felt the weight of the truth (i.e., the impact of eternal judgment on his life,) and this weight is in the heart of every man. Only reprobates and those who are callused of heart do not feel it.

Everyone who walks with God knows the weight of His hand can be heavy at times. Our Father is a good daddy. He corrects His children. He does not allow His children to venture off the path without drawing them back quickly. Eternal judgment causes us as God's children to understand the consequences of sin. We remember Romans 3:23: "the wages of sin is death", yet sometimes we sin willfully anyway. We know that mankind has spiritually died (outside of Christ) because of Adam's transgression, and many believers fail to reach any spiritual high place.

It is only God's grace that has stayed our judgment at this time. Christians have already died in Christ and we must realize that the wages of sin brings spiritual apathy (i.e., no sensitivity to God).

Christians should know that the wages of sin brings mental, emotional and social death as well. When we fail to maintain our walk we suffer anguish of spirit. In Genesis the Lord God said, "in dying you shall die" (Genesis 2:17 – "thou shalt surely die"). This kind of death is not immediate, but progressive. We may not die physically for some time, yet the process of death has an immediate affect on us. The process of death affects the soul of man. For example, Cain was warned that selfishness could affect his behavior. One day in a field, Cain's degeneration and selfish conceit brought him to murder his brother. Hebrews 2:1 tells us:

"Therefore we ought to give the more earnest heed to the things
which we have heard, least at any time we should let them slip."

If we do not give an earnest heeding to love, our love will diminish and slip into apathy (see Matthew 24:12). Our understanding and our relationship to the foundational principle of eternal judgment is that we are constantly challenged to be aware of our thoughts and actions. We are to take heed and recognize that every idle thought will be judged. We should realize that our lives affect others, whether we know it or not. We make decisions without an understanding of their future impact in and upon our lives, our children, and/or others. *Laissez-faire* (complacent) spirituality is not spirituality at all. God comes to visit us and we do not even realize that He is present, so we miss our opportunity in the visitation. The writer of Hebrews warns us about apathy:

"Thou hast granted me life and favor,
and thy visitation hath preserved my spirit."
(Job 9:12)

"What is man that thou shouldest magnify him?
and that thou shouldest set thine heart upon him?
And that thou shouldest visit him every morning,
and try him every moment?"
(Job 7:17-18)

How is it that we are so preoccupied with the world that when the Lord comes to us we miss His visit? How have we become so insensitive? One thing about eternal judgment that we should fully apply to our lives is we should 'number our days' and then we would be able to 'apply our hearts unto wisdom' (see Psalm 90:10).

Before any of these foundations can come to fullness in the life of a believer, there must be a realization that spiritual insensitivity has to be defeated. Each and every day we have an opportunity to meet with God. He wants our deliverance, but if we miss our visitation, our lives will not receive the deposit He has purposed to give us during that time. If we are unaware of our *kairos* moment, His visitation will not accomplish its purpose. After a while, one becomes financially poor, physically sick, mentally weak, morally intemperate, and emotionally drained because they have missed their time of refreshing all too often.

> "Repent ye therefore, and be converted,
> that your sins may be blotted out,
> when the times of refreshing shall come
> from the presence of the Lord..."
> (Acts 3:19)

If you are experiencing any of these symptoms, maybe you have been making some wrong decisions lately? Or maybe, just maybe, you will consider your ways and seek a time of visitation with the Holy Spirit. He's waiting for you.

> "Beloved, I wish above all things that thou mayest
> prosper and be in health, even as thy soul prospereth."
> (3 John 2)

The Ways of God

Section 3

"And when he was demanded of the Pharisees,
when the kingdom of God should come, he answered them and
said,The kingdom of God cometh not with observation:
Neither shall they say, Lo here! or, lo there!
for, behold, the kingdom of God is within you."
(Luke 17:20b-21)

"Then I called a fast there at the river Ahava, so that we might humble ourselves before our God, in order to seek from Him a right way for us, and for our little ones, and for all our goods."
(Ezra 8:21)

Chapter 14 – The Kingdom of God

"From that time Jesus began to preach, and to say,
Repent: for the Kingdom of heaven is at hand."
(Matthew 4:17)

"And these signs shall follow them that believe;
In my name shall they cast out devils;
they shall speak with new tongues;
They shall take up serpents;
and if they drink any deadly thing,
it shall not hurt them;
they shall lay hands on the sick,
and they shall recover."
(Mark 16:17-18)

"And he (Jesus) said unto them,
I must preach the Kingdom of God
to other cities also: for therefore am I sent."
(Luke 4:43)

One of the major mysteries in the Scripture involves the Kingdom of God. The Kingdom of God is not a difficult thing to understand. Simply speaking, the Kingdom of God is the rule of God. It is Jesus' kingship and His ability to reign in the hearts and lives of His people. The only problem some believers face is that their tradition (see Mark 7:13) invalidates the Kingdom's power in their lives. They relegate the Scripture to where it has no value in their lives, or the lives of those they pray for.

What is the Kingdom's manifestation? In order for us to identify the Kingdom we have to have wisdom about it and we must understand its operation. The revelation of God's rule is not some new form of theology, nor does the Kingdom come by observation (i.e., it does not come noticeably), it manifests internally through obedience. We should know that the Kingdom does not come in word; it comes in power. What kind of power? It is the power to overcome the flesh and the world that allows the Church to become everything the Lord intended it to be. If there is no power in the Kingdom you preach or hear about, maybe it is the wrong kingdom being preached? Kingdom power is the Holy Spirit's ability to demonstrate His lordship in your life, but you are in control of that. You are the 'porter' (John 10). The Bible says that the Kingdom is not revealed by words, but that the Kingdom comes through the demonstration of power (see 1 Corinthians 2:4). Again, what kind of power? The Kingdom produces the power to overcome the world and the things that are in the world in the lives of Christians. When God's Kingdom permeates our lives it is not with words! The demonstration of His power is more than mere revelation. The Lord has hidden these things in a mystery (1 Corinthians 2:7). Within this mystery we find one single problem and it is sin.

I honestly believe that Christians do not understand sin. We have made sin so broad that we look at the affects of sin rather than the nature of sin. What has sin accomplished in our world? Since the days of Adam sin has affected mankind. We all think we understand sin, but in reality let us look at what sin has done to our world. Sin has produced such a lawless culture that we fear for our lives. We lock our doors to try to lock sin out; we get rid of our televisions because we do not want to have sin propagated in our households. We arm ourselves because we want to feel protected. Protected from what? Sin! We know Satan has corrupted the minds of people so we use burglar alarms to protect our property. We build fences because we know that sinful people will not respect our property. We pass thousands of laws because people will not live morally or are not sociably responsible. We have to protect children from wicked people who use and abuse them. We have to fight politicians who believe that God is dead! We have to fight sickness and fraud because of sin. We have to deal with emotional stress because our work environment is chaotic because of sin. We have to deal with adultery, fornication, and sexual immorality because of sin. You get the picture!

> "For this cause have I sent unto you Timothy,
> who is my beloved son,
> and faithful in the Lord, who shall bring
> you into remembrance of my ways
> which be in Christ, as I teach everywhere
> in every church....For the Kingdom of God
> is not in word, but in power."
> (1 Corinthians 4:17 and 20)

As stated, the Kingdom of God is the rule or reign of God. It is God's dominion in the life of a believer and the reality of His laws written on the hearts of people. The laws of God are misunderstood by most people today. The laws of God are not only unchangeable; they are eternal. His laws cover every area of the universe: both natural laws and spiritual laws. For example, take the law of gravity. It is a law established in the creation of the universe. Even if you do not believe in gravity, when you step off a ten-story building, you will suffer the consequences when this law is not respected. For the Christian, try praying in tongues while you step off that ten-story building and see if the manifestation of the Spirit will override the law of God.

The same holds true in God's spiritual laws. The biblical principle "you will reap what you sow" is given as a divine law for our understanding of this truth. You reproduce after your own kind. What you are, you give out. Even if you do not believe it, it still happens. If you do not live in peace and spiritual rest, then stress, depression, and the consequences of anxiety will eventually wear you down and destroy you. The results may be slower in their manifestation than stepping off a ten-story building but in the end it is just as deadly. Apples reproduce apples and oranges reproduce oranges. You do not have to tell an apple to be an apple; God's divine design has placed the ability to reproduce itself in everything. It is time for Christians to reproduce what God calls Christian, rather than some 'hybrid hyper-spiritual' individual who has no strength of being! The New Testament contains several laws that are spoken of as being spiritual laws (see Romans 7:14). The Church has failed God's laws the same way the Jews of old failed them. The Jews took the Ten Commandments and turned them into hundreds of religious laws. The Church has done basically the same thing. Even though Jesus turned the water into wine in John 2, many preach that it was "grape juice" to support their doctrinal focus. How absurd! It is not a sin to drink moderately. Drunkenness is a sin; social drinking is not. If someone has a problem with alcohol, the Bible gives guidelines in how we are to handle the situation. The Bible states that the laws of God are written on our hearts (see Romans 2:15). When a believer is not empowered to be in control by the Holy Spirit, they will fail and find themselves weak to the appetites of the flesh, drunkenness is just one of the weaknesses.

These laws are revealed through the manifestation of the Kingdom of God in the life of the believer. The Kingdom of God (God's ability to rule over us) is imprinted in our conscious mind. The Kingdom is the person of Jesus Christ, for the Bible inter changes them as the same. I am focusing on His leadership from within the lives of the believer in this chapter. His Kingdom is within you (see Luke 17:21).

> "But now the righteousness of God without the law is
> manifested, being witnessed by the law and the prophets...
> Where is the boasting then? It is excluded. By what law?
> of works? Nay: but by the law of faith.
> Therefore we conclude that a man is justified
> by faith without the deeds of the law."
> (Romans 3:21 and 27-28)

The above verse shows that the New Testament contains another basic law of God: the law of faith. This law of faith is seen as different from the Old Testament laws and the prophets (see Romans 3:21). The law and the prophets of the Old Testament bear witness to its truth. We are not justified by the law of works, nor can the law of works make one righteous. Paul declares that the law of faith has been implemented in Christ Jesus by God the Father as a means of salvation, through grace. Grace is the thing that allows us to learn about the Lord's Kingdom when we fall short at times.

Unless one is born again, they cannot even see the Kingdom of God (see John 3:3). Why? It is because God's Kingdom is a spiritual realm that has a particular manifestation in and through our lives. It is revealed over time in 'layers' of truth. Many individuals have made the Kingdom a doctrine, but their doctrine is a doctrine without application. Anything that God reveals has a manifestation of 'life' in its revelation. When God speaks a word it creates what was spoken and whatever His word creates is given 'existence' (see Genesis 1). One problem we face is that the knowledge of a something does not mean it is a part of our lives. When the Holy Spirit speaks a word to you, and your desire is to make it alive and active, you must submit it to the Kingdom of God (see Hebrews 4:12-16). You could be in the desert dying of thirst with the knowledge that water is what you need, and still die of thirst if you do not drink! One needs not only the doctrine of the Kingdom, but one needs the reality of the Kingdom. Drink the water! In other words, you have to do the stepping out in faith part. Belief in Jesus Christ opens our eyes to the reality of God's rulership, but in order for us to 'see' the Kingdom of God, we must be born again.

Many think being born again is what takes place at the salvation experience. The phrase "born again" is only found three times in the New Testament. In John 3:3 and 7 we find the most popular uses of the phrase and we find it again in 1 Peter 1:23. The words 'born' (1080) 'again' (509) mean, "to be born from above," "to be born from the beginning," or "to be born from the first." The words "being born again" (313) found in 1 Peter 1:23 are not the same Greek words that are found in John 3:3 and 7. Those in 1 Peter contain the idea of 'regeneration'. To be born again is to be "reconnected to the first Adam by the last Adam." It is our change of state (being) and a return to the manifestation of our original power and authority. We must change every aspect of our life, submitting it to the Kingdom, and renewing our mind is the first step in the process. Faith is the key. Faith is the ability to see into the spiritual realm. Faith is the 'substance' (i.e., the basis) of what we hope for. Faith gives me the confidence within my expectation. Faith is the 'evidence' (i.e., the proof or the conviction) of the Word God wishes to walk me through. My ability to see myself as being holy and righteous in Christ is necessary if I am going to have the ability to walk with God. When I do not have the ability to see what the Cross has done for me, I am unable to believe to the saving of my soul. This causes me to walk in carnality and fleshliness rules my life.

Back to the question, "What is the Kingdom of God's manifestation in the earth?" I have pondered this question for several years, reading the Bible and continuously asking God to show me what the reality of the Kingdom is, and how it is manifested in and through the Body of Christ. One night the Lord woke me and as I prayed and sought His guidance He gave me a vision of the Kingdom's manifestation. The vision began and I was looking for a set of pipe racks on which to store some water well drilling equipment. I was told that "Papa" had some, so I went to His shop to see if they were the right kind of pipe racks for me to use. When I arrived at the shop and looked at the pipe racks a young man came out and challenged me because he thought I was going to take them without asking for them. I assured him that I was an honest person and would not do such a thing. He directed me to a house across the driveway and as I pulled up to the porch, Papa and twelve men came out of the house and began to talk to me about my need. Papa said, "James, you are a member of my Church…" I answered, "Yes I am." Papa then inquired of my need and I told Him of the pipe racks and why I needed them. He said He would deliver them to me the next day. He then asked, "Would you like to receive the Blessing?" I told Him I would love to receive the Blessing. In my vision it became the next morning, and more than seventy-five trucks and cars pulled up to my house. I owned seventeen acres at that time and the vision unfolded swiftly. Papa came up to our porch and my family greeted Him. He had a five-gallon bucket that He sat down by the front door. He put some money into it and set a case of canned goods down beside it. Each and every person thereafter did the same as they came and greeted us. Following this, at a fast pace, the people built fences around my property, built a barn, painted our house, and gave me various and multiple kinds of live stock. By the end of the day all the projects were finished and the livestock had been placed in their own pens securely. Many of the ladies had made quilts and other necessary items, and as you can imagine, our "cup ran over!" As the Body left us, returning to their homes and Papa came into our living room and asked my wife, "How much money was provided?" She excitedly proclaimed the amount to be more than $78,000.00! The Lord then revealed Himself as Jesus Christ, gave us various instructions, and invited us to take part in the next person's Blessing. He then declared, "This is the way the real Church should function." Our needs and wants could not have been more wonderfully fulfilled. I understood what it meant to be a part of His Kingdom, and I could hardly wait for my chance to be a part of the Blessing to the next person.

Ever since that vision the Kingdom has been at the forefront of my ministry. I have helped my sons in the faith get their own houses and have given "handfuls of purpose" (see Ruth 2:16) as the Lord leads me. I have seen the reality of "all things common" in a new and meaningful way. Faithfulness has been the key to each of these blessings being "distributed" (one of the definitions of *koinonia* is 'communion'). I have been led to give the blessing of new tools to faithful carpenters in our church, food to the needy, time to the broken, money to various people, and I encourage the Body of Christ to have an active Kingdom mindset in distributing the Blessing, not waiting for someone to ask. The Lord has revealed to me that Kingdom living is the heartfelt purpose one finds in being more than a church attendee. He has also caused me to understand the absolute necessity of a Body who operates in these Kingdom principles. Churches will explode with growth when the Body functions as it has been intended to do. I am not trying to preach a "social gospel." The goal is to allow Christians to see the great benefit Kingdom living brings. I have seen the destitute and impoverished change their status in life. Changes in communities seem to be a slow and arduous task for most churches in today's society. I believe it is because the Church has forgotten about Jesus' Kingdom commandments and have focused on ministry to the mind and not to the spirit of Christians. The law of faith is holy, just, good, and spiritual, but we have become apathetic, carnal, and blind (see Romans 7:12-14). Faith opens our eyes to the reality of what God is saying. Satan comes with unbelief and a lie, pushing you away from what you know to be true. The Kingdom of God is a spiritual law that is written within each of us, written on our hearts. The battle rages in my mind. Sin is the cause of all of this. Sin keeps us from fulfilling the Great Commandment. Sin keeps us in fear and suspicion keeps us from loving. Paul says,

> "But I see another law in my members,
> warring against the law of my mind,
> and bringing me into captivity to the law
> of sin which is in my members.
> O wretched man that I am! who shall
> deliver me from this body of death?
> I thank God through Jesus Christ our Lord.
> So then with the mind
> I myself serve the law of God;
> but with the flesh the law of sin."
> (Romans 7:23-25)

Our flesh is with us every day, and every day, through faith, we have been given the ability to see the Kingdom of God, to recognize its enabling force, and to perceive and experience its power. Everyday, we can choose to look around ourselves for the needs of those we go to church with. Everyday, we can choose to live as we have been called to live, or ignore the things that God shows us. Grace covers each of us as we grow and learn of God's Fatherhood in us. Grace is God's way of empowering us, giving us the ability to do what God has asked us to do. God is growing us up, so to speak, in His Kingdom. With our mind we have been given the faculties to understand the laws of God. Paul teaches that this warfare is in our soul. "Shall I obey the laws of God and His Kingdom, or shall I surrender to the law of sin?" Paul also teaches us that the law of the Spirit of life in Christ Jesus has made me free from the law of sin and death if I believe and walk in the Spirit (see Romans 8:2-14). Walking in the Spirit is walking with my spiritual eyes wide open.

The carnal mind is not subject to the law of God because it does not submit to the Kingdom within. The carnal mind is at 'enmity' (2189) against God. Enmity against God is defined as "being hostile to God and the things of God." Enmity is to resist His Kingdom and grieve the Holy Spirit. Adam and Even decided to not submit to God's rulership and ate of the tree of the knowledge of good and evil. This was against the Lord's instruction. The same choice is present in us today, but those who are not born again cannot see it. They do not submit to it, but its power is still real and in them. They are willingly blind to the things God reveals to them. The law of sin and death gives power and weight to sin that will drag you down and take you out of God's rest and peace. Many people experience emotional depression because they are stressed out spiritually. They are being called and led to move in Kingdom things, yet they do not know how to "go out" or "come in" and give God their all. The age-old law of God still holds truth today…

"From that time Jesus began to preach, and to say,
Repent: for the kingdom of heaven is at hand."
(Matthew 4:17)

Jesus told the Pharisees in Luke 17:20-21 that "the kingdom is within you." The Kingdom's presence was right in front of them, but they were blinded to Him, and could not see the Kingdom's reality. They had decided to stand in what their understanding was about God even when God incarnate was trying to tell them they were wrong. Jesus is the master of Kingdom reality. He took the masses, (the 5,000 and the 4,000) and ministered to them the very thing they needed at the time...fishes and loaves! They didn't need more than that at the time, but because they were hungry, He feed them. How? Through the Kingdom! He took what few resources were available and multiplied them! Out of the masses Jesus chose seventy. What did Jesus give the seventy that He did not give the 5,000? He gave them authority. Out of the seventy He took twelve, and gave them something that the 5,000 or the seventy did not receive. The twelve asked Jesus, "Why do you speak to the people in parables but speak plainly to us?" Jesus said, "For unto you are given the keys to the kingdom (see Matthew 16:19)." Yet Jesus took three out of the twelve and gave them something that He did not give the other nine. They were allowed to go with Him to the mount of Transfiguration, and He told them to tell no one what they saw. That means Jesus commanded them to not tell the other nine disciples what they saw! Why? The Scripture teaches us, "To whom much is given, much is also required." The principle goes one step further. Out of the three, Jesus did something with John that He did not do with any other disciple. When Jesus was on the cross He asked John to take care of His mother. What kind of trust did Jesus give to John? The kind of trust He wishes each of us to walk in with Him. Can you trust God as much as He wants to trust you? The law of sin tells us our resources are inadequate. Jesus says, "Put it to the test" and trust Him.

Pharisees (pious religious leaders), then and now, resist the Kingdom and its power. The law of sin had convinced them to kill the Christ so they could continue in their own religious ways. The truth is that if you are not born from above (i.e., born again), you cannot even see the truth, even if it is right in front of you. Another thing to consider is even when someone follows after the law of righteousness, it does not mean that they are living by faith or that they are pursuing God's Kingdom (see Romans 9:31). The Scripture says Israel followed after righteousness but never attained it. Why? They did not seek it by faith (see Hebrews 4:1-2). Paul said in Romans 10:2, "they have a zeal of God, but not according to knowledge." They are blind to God's Kingdom and are trying to establish their own righteousness. The righteousness of God is found in His Kingdom (i.e., when one submits to Jesus as Lord, they are born again). Your life is renewed and is strengthened as though you were just born. A new life in a new family with a new purpose has begun with a new reality. Righteousness does not show up in the creation of one's own personal systematic theology. You can get the doctrines right and still not have on a heavenly wedding dress (See Matthew 22:1-14). This is why Romans 10:4 says that Christ is 'the end of the law'. Jesus is not a toy for us to play with; He is the King of kings and the Lord of lords. It does not matter whether you are king or a lord; He is your King. This is also why Romans 10:16-17 states:

> "But they have not all obeyed the gospel.
> For Isaiah saith, Lord who has believed our
> report? So then faith comes by hearing,
> and hearing by the word of God."

The Greek word translated as 'hearing' (189) in the above passage means "to hearken" (i.e., to perceive by hearing). How do we know we have truly seen God's Kingdom? Faith teaches us to recognize God's presence within. As we grow in the Lord we are to become more stable, more founded, and less susceptible to Stan's attacks. Our ability to stand against the attacks of the enemy should increase, not decrease. If salvation is our immediate goal when we evangelize, our ultimate goal for the believer is that they are able to walk in the power of God's Kingdom, manifesting His authority on this earth…as it is in heaven!

Romans 10:21 says, "God has stretched forth (His) hands unto a disobedient and gainsaying people" because they did not obey. If we would walk in Kingdom power nothing could stop our growth and purpose. The principle is clearly stated in Romans 11:22:

> "Behold therefore the goodness and severity of God:
> on them which fell, severity; but toward thee,
> goodness, if thou continue in his goodness:
> otherwise thou also shalt be cut off."

The principle is also stated in 1 Timothy 1:5-8:

> "Now the end of the commandment is love out
> of a pure heart, and of a good conscience,
> and of faith unfeigned; from which some
> having swerved have turned aside unto
> vain jangling; Desiring to be teachers of the law;
> understanding neither what they
> say, nor whereof they affirm. But we know that
> the law is good, if a man uses it lawfully."

The law of God is given for us to understand love; true agape love. Our service to God's Kingdom is to have our love originate out of a pure heart. In Creation God never intended for our conscience to be breached or consumed with feelings of guilt. Returning to our Genesis state is only possible when our faith is sincere and without hypocrisy. The Greek word translated as 'unfeigned' (505) means "without dissimulation". This is to be understood that our faith should be without pretension and without posturing. The Kingdom's power is not found in words, but in deeds. What kind of deeds? They are deeds that reveal our manifested communion, distributed to the saints (see Acts 4:35 and 2 Corinthians 9:13). They are found in the deeds of an overcomer. God is satisfied when we demonstrate the power of the Kingdom in our daily lives and through our faith. Of course He loves us and accepts us, but He as any good parent wants His kids to grow up and make it on their own. Remember, these signs shall follow "them which believe" (see Mark 16:17). No signs, no power. It is the power to see beyond the typical norm that one should seek and learn how to become more than just a church member; one who is part of the family in the Body of Christ.

Back to the Basics

The Greek word translated as 'kingdom(s)' in the New Testament is *basilea* (932). *Basilea* means the rule, the reign, or the realm of God's dominion. We must comprehend and assimilate this aspect of Christ into our lives. Submitting to the Word of God is paramount in the discipleship process, but the problem that many of us face is that we are blinded by our own traditional point of view. When Jesus taught the model prayer found in Matthew 6, He revealed that God's Kingdom was to be manifested "on earth as it is in heaven". God's rule does not automatically appear in the life of the believer; it does not happen by osmosis; it must be grown and nourished. Jesus said it was 'like a seed'. When planted in good ground it gives an increase thirty, sixty, or one hundred fold (see Matthew 13:23). When Jesus said, "The kingdom of heaven is at hand," He was stating the fact of its attainability. In John 3:3 Jesus said, "Except a man be born from above, he cannot even see the kingdom of God." Then again in John 3:5 Jesus stated, "Except a man be born of water and of the Spirit, he cannot enter into the kingdom of God." The Greek word translated as 'enter' (1525) means "to go in, through, or to come in unto". It carries the idea of a process of time. Therefore time is a factor in everyone's growth. Even despite the fact that the Kingdom is at hand, one must be born of the Spirit before access is granted. If you are not living by faith, you will never enter into Kingdom living. You will always be too small, too poor, or have too many needs to participate in Kingdom giving (from your perspective). When I say Kingdom giving, I'm not talking of giving to someone's ministry, I'm talking about seeing and doing your part in the Blessing. In my vision, some gave more, some less, but each gave according to their ability. So it is with the tithe. When everyone adds his part it is more than sufficient. We can catch sight of the progression of our Kingdom ability through the Kingdom passages of the New Testament. In Luke 10:9, the disciples were commanded to tell the people when they healed them, "The kingdom has come near to you". In Luke 11:20 Jesus told the people, when He cast the devils out, "no doubt the kingdom of God is come upon you." Devils are deceivers; no doubt you have met one!

Deceivers are cast out only through the power of the Kingdom. When we fully understand the authority of God's Kingdom and live in it, Satan cannot manipulate us. Jesus was always aware of Satan's presence and Satan's attempt to set a snare for Him. He did not give Satan an opportunity to take Him until He was ready to be taken, Jesus then He laid His own life down. The Scripture teaches that the Kingdom of God is first attainable, and then it comes nearer and is easier to comprehend. As the Kingdom manifests in the life of a believer its power has an effect upon them. This effect can be seen as the believer submits to God's authority and is obedient to His leading. Remember this: the Kingdom is not me, it is we! If you are under God's authority you are in the Kingdom to work together for the purpose of bringing the Kingdom to your church and community. Ephesians 1:9-10 tells us that the manifestation of God's will is to bring all things together: the things of God in heaven and the things of God on this earth. When God does not rule, He cannot heal (see Matthew 13:58). By healing the people, Jesus was saying the Kingdom of God is more powerful than the kingdom of sickness. When the beds of the sick were picked up, that was the evidence of the Kingdom's power. Jesus also declared that the Kingdom of God is more powerful than the kingdom of Satan and when the devils came out of the possessed, that was the evidence of the Kingdom's power.

The Pharisees questioned Jesus about the Kingdom of God. They were unaware of what or where the Kingdom of God was. This is true in today's Church as well. Many believers still see the Kingdom of God as though it was far off in heaven or that it will come at the end of time. Jesus contended with many people in the New Testament about the Kingdom. They were ignorant of its present reality so Jesus said, "it's my Father's good pleasure to give you the Kingdom," and He went about giving it away.

> "The kingdom of God does not come with an external
> show: Neither shall they say, Lo here! or lo there! for behold,
> The kingdom of God is within you."
> (Luke 17:20-21)

Please do not misunderstand where the Kingdom of God is; it is in you. If you do not operate out of love and soundness of judgment you are just doing *stuff*. The Holy Spirit desires to rule you from within. "They that are led by the Spirit, they are the sons of God" (see Romans 8:14). The Holy Spirit is not interested in writing His laws on tablets of stone anymore, but wishes to write them on your heart. He stated this in the Old and New Testaments. What each of us should ask is, "What is the Holy Spirit interested in?" The Kingdom is not a system of do's and do nots; it's a matter of one's desire and it is God's desire to give you the Kingdom. Are you submitted to the Lord? Does God rule your life? Many will say yes, but the evidence of their life may say no! The Kingdom is progressive. It does not, nor will it come all at once. Again it is thirty, sixty, and then a hundred fold in its manifestation. We must be focused and patient if we are to experience its manifestation. Please do not get discouraged if you are the only one operating in Kingdom things. God will always send you some help. Allow the Holy Spirit to lead you in to the area He is focusing on; become someone who is faithful, full of the Holy Spirit, and one who has been separated out of the mundane Christian life.

The Mystery of Iniquity

"Let no man deceive you by any means:
for that day shall not come, except there come
a falling away first, and that man of sin
be revealed, the son of perdition;
Who opposes and exalts himself
above all that is called God,
or that is worshipped; so that
he as God sits in the temple of God,
showing himself that he is God.
For the mystery of iniquity does already work:
only he who now lets will let,
until he be taken out of the way."
(2 Thessalonians 2:3-4 and 7)

"Know ye not that ye are the temple of God,
and that the Spirit of God dwelleth in you?"
(1 Corinthians 3:16)

"And what agreement hath the temple of God with idols?
for you are the temple of the living God;
as God has said, I will dwell in them."
(2 Corinthians 6:16)

"In whom you also are builded together for
a habitation of God through the Spirit."
(Ephesians 2:22)

Many of us have heard the theology about the antichrist in the Jewish temple from a dispensational point of view. That view is preached widely and accepted by many but is not biblically accurate in its concept of God's Kingdom and His temple. The above passages should prove to anyone that Christians are the New Testament temple and Paul states in the book of Romans that only those who receive Jesus are Abraham's seed. What is very interesting to me is how so many individuals can read these passages and still not understand where God's temple is! It is written that God is not a respecter of persons, yet most believe and teach that He respects an ethnic people who do not accept Jesus Christ as their Lord and Savior over other believers. As Christians we should support the nation of Israel, but this does not imply that we should affix our principles to doctrines that elevate them above the Church.

When you study the New Testament you find that the Church was grafted into Israel. The Bible says that Jesus is the only way to the Father. Jew or Gentile, bond or free, the only way to be saved is through the cross of Jesus Christ. How has such a double-minded theology crept into the Body of Christ? Why do some still believe God will revert back to an ideology of salvation that removes Christ from His plan by allowing the Jews to be saved outside of the cross? Not hardly! This theology is mainly due to people who have had the wrong understanding of the Kingdom of God. They see the Kingdom in the same light as the Sadducees and Pharisees of old. They look for an external manifestation of God's reign; when the Lord Jesus himself said, "The Kingdom comes not with outward observation." The Lord Jesus will rule and reign over all the earth, not by man's law, but by the Word of God. No doubt there are many antichrists in the last days as the spirit of antichrist is already at work and has been for the last 2,000 years (see 1 John 2:18). Jesus said in Matthew 24 that many would come in His name and deceive many. If we review 2 Thessalonians 2, we will see that it explains that this man of sin, this son of perdition, is internal and not external.

This internal battle is a battle within one's own heart. When someone loses the battle, the old man rules in the place of God. We can find the man of sin is within us by asking ourselves a question. "How is it that I love the Lord as much as I do, and yet still sin willfully at times?" Selah! If we could for a moment disregard theological concepts and return to God's Word, ask yourself when the man of sin, this son of perdition, raises his head in me, where does the power to overcome him come from? In other words, who wins when you are in the midst of a temptation: the Kingdom of God or the power of the flesh? Again I say, which internal voice and desire is stronger? That which draws on the fulfillment of the flesh or that which brings us to victory and gives God glory? Have you considered that these soulish (i.e. selfish) desires cause you to oppose the rule of God in your own life and cause you to exalt your own will above the will of God? When Jesus said, "If you look upon a woman to lust, you have already committed adultery in your heart". He was revealing that when the desire to do such a thing is present, all that is missing is the opportunity to do it. This is an example of 'opposing' and 'exalting'. When one has the mystery of iniquity operating within them they will oppose everything that is called God; such as the Word of God, Jesus, the Holy Spirit, the Father's Kingdom, and they will exalt their opinions above the Scriptures. They sit on the throne of their lives acting as if they are God! How many times have you heard someone in the Body of Christ tell someone they are "going to hell," as though they hold the power of hell in their hands? That is called *divination*. Divination is a part of the mystery of iniquity operating in the life of a person who gives out judgment or condemnation as though they are divine. They truly think within themselves that they are God; at least they are their 'god'. Notice in 2 Thessalonians 2:3 that this man of sin, this son of perdition, sits in the temple of God. Again, where is God's temple? Is it in Jerusalem or in your heart? The Lord prophesied that in these last days "God lives in a temple not made with hands" (see Acts 7:48). This type of argument is called an apology, but I do not apologize about the truth. As we grow in our Lord's grace we will come to know who our King really is. When we mature in our faith and become all that God commands us to be, we will recognize the Kingdom's power within us.

When Jesus explained the parable of the tares in the field (see Matthew 13:41) He revealed God's ultimate purpose:

> "The son of man shall send forth his angels, and they
> shall gather out of his kingdom all things
> that offend, and them which do iniquity."

God's Kingdom is on this earth as well as in heaven. Jesus will send his angels to gather offensive or scandalous things out of his Kingdom and also those who do 'iniquity' (lawlessness). Then shall the righteous shine forth (see Matthew 13:42). First, God has ordained the removal of the wicked, then the judgment, not the other way around. The Greek word translated as 'offend' is the Greek word *skandalon* (4625). This word was discussed in an earlier chapter and is where we get our English word 'scandal'. Remember that the word means, "to be seized" or "caught up in something". Jesus is sending his messengers out to gather the 'scandalous stuff' out of His Kingdom. What is scandalous? It is everything that separates people from God's rule and keeps the Body of Christ from becoming one. The Holy Spirit wants to rule our hearts without hindrance.

Matthew 13 is a synopsis of the Kingdom of God in lesson form. In the parable of the sower, Jesus' explanation makes some revealing statements. He uses the phrase, "anyone who hears the word of the Kingdom." He was not speaking of just any old word! He is teaching about the rule of God and its manifestation through the Body of Christ. He also revealed that there are four levels in receiving the Kingdom. The first, no reception of the Kingdom rule of God (by the wayside) and that is usually where you find these people, by the wayside. The second level is limited reception of the Kingdom rule of God. These individuals have no depth of rule in their life (this is the stony ground) and they usually have a root problem. They are unable to endure the experience of the Kingdom for very long and get offended often. These are the complainers commonly labeled as "high maintenance" people. The next level is chocked (as tight and as close as possible) reception. This level eliminates fruitfulness (thorns and thistles). Their focus is on the things of this world, and these things overshadow and hinder the fruitfulness of God's Kingdom. They are full of busy-ness instead of Kingdom business. They generally have worldly problems and carnal manifestations in abundance in their lives. The final level is good reception. It produces abundant fruit in their lives and can be recognized in those who overcome; they produce one hundred, sixty, or thirty fold because they are good ground. Good ground neither labors, nor toils. Good ground produces and you get results. You do not have to tell good ground to be good ground. Good ground produces "automatically"; translated as the word "herself" in Mark 4:28 (*automatos* - 844).

> "For the earth bringeth forth fruit of herself;
> first the blade, then the ear,
> after that the full corn in the ear."
> (Mark 4:28)

Mark 4:13 tells us that the interpretation of all the parables hinge on understanding this one parable. In essence this parable teaches about the heart of people. Without the revelation of this parable one cannot correctly interpret the many aspects about the Kingdom of God. Again, these are parables about God's internal rule and the manifestation of the power of His Kingdom.

The next series of parables in Matthew 13 reveal some additional aspects of the Kingdom of God. The mustard seed and leaven parables are pictures of the Kingdom's growth in the inner man. Notice how the mustard seed has been sown. It was sown "in his field," and remember, you are that field. These parables relate directly to the parable of the wheat and the tares. You can find both wheat and tares in every church. There are those who produce fruit and there are those who do not. The leaven represents the Kingdom's ability to permeate a believer until he/she is totally engulfed by God's rule and fully functional in the Lord's Kingdom work. This word of the Kingdom preached is good seed, but Satan corrupts the minds and hearts of people so they do not understand the internal rule of God or its external manifestation in the Church. Jesus sowed the seed of the Kingdom. Satan has come and sowed the seed of churchianity: the false seed. The Kingdom is full of unity and peace, whereas churchianity is full of division and carnality. These two types of people meet at the same time and in the same building, yet they have not originated from the same source. Jesus will not bring a separation to this phenomenon until the end; He alone can separate the sheep from the goats.

Remember the lesson found in the parable of the ten virgins. Matthew 25 teaches us that five were prepared and five were not prepared. The parable about the buried treasure reveals to us how God's children should view the Kingdom. It is so valuable that we should sell all we have to possess it. When we discover the value of God's Kingdom we will let nothing hinder our attainment of it. In relation to this, Luke 14:26-28 and 33 gives us some requirements of a disciple. Remember that disciples are grown and not birthed!

> "If any man come to me, and hate not his father,
> and mother, and wife, and children and brethren,
> and sisters, yea, and his own life (soul) also,
> He cannot be my disciple. And whosoever
> doth not bear his cross, and come after me,
> cannot be my disciple. For which of you,
> intending to build a tower sits not down first
> and counts the cost. So likewise,
> whosoever he be of you that
> forsakes not all that he has,
> he cannot be my disciple."

John 8:31 says that we must continue in His word, or you cannot be His disciple. John 13:35 demands that you must have love one for the other, or you cannot be His disciple. Moreover in John 15:8 it is stated that we must bear much fruit or you cannot be His disciple. These requirements of discipleship are Jesus' requirements. Churchianity has developed other requirements, but Jesus will not accept the tradition of men. (Some teach their tradition as though Jesus accepts it, but the Scriptures teach us otherwise). The Lord is not demanding sinlessness as a requirement of salvation as we are saved by grace, but He is expecting some effort toward obedience from those who are saved (see Hebrews 6:9 and 1 Peter 1:22). A disciple of the Lord, when he discovers the hidden treasure of God's Kingdom, will not allow anything to obstruct its growth and success in his/her life. The pearl of great price gives us the same representation as the buried treasure. The parable of the net, along with the parable of the wheat and tares, explains the separation that is coming to the Church at the hand of the Holy Spirit, as does the parable of the separation of the sheep and goats. Judgment begins in God's house first (see 1 Peter 4:17) and Matthew 13:52 finalizes the parables with an explanation of the parable of the soils. When you understand the value of God's Kingdom and implement its principles into your life, you will bring forth new and old treasures. These treasures are the application of our biblical instruction and the manifested power of His Kingdom, being the things we have learned as well as the things we will learn. The growth of virtue in the life of a believer is dependent upon the development of God's Kingdom within them. When there is no expansion of God's Kingdom within, there will be no external expansion of the virtue needed to mature. We must grow in stature with God and with man. On reflection, we must appreciate what the Word of God says about the Kingdom of God. Let us not mistakenly assume that our entrance into God's Kingdom will be a smooth one. Acts 14:22 states Paul and Barnabas were:

> "Confirming the souls of the disciples,
> and exhorting them to continue in
> the faith, and that we must through much
> tribulation enter into the kingdom of God."

Just because one may know about the Kingdom of God does not mean they are operating by Kingdom power. Again I say, the Kingdom of God is within you and has a definite power in any believer who lives by its principles. When we do not see a real manifestation of God's power it is generally because we are not allowing Him to rule us.

Recognizing the Practical Kingdom

> "But of the tree of knowledge of
> good and evil, thou shalt not eat of it."
> (Genesis 2:17)

I have discovered that one of the most difficult tasks in the Christian discipleship process is to remove old leaven from those who have been in churchianity. Most people still think the Kingdom of God is in heaven and will not come until the future. The practicality of the matter is simple. The Kingdom of God is righteousness, peace, and joy in the Holy Spirit. Consider this Scripture:

> "For the kingdom of God is not meat and drink; but righteousness, and peace, and joy in the
> Holy Ghost. For he that in these things serveth Christ is acceptable
> to God, and approved of men. Let us therefore follow after
> the things which make for peace, and things
> wherewith one may edify another."
> (Romans 14:17-19)

First of all, how are we made 'acceptable' (2101) to God? Common thought seeks acceptability to God through their basic religious philosophy without considering what the Bible states. Acceptance, biblically defined, is "full agreement with God" or "to be well pleasing to the Father." One must 'follow after' (1377) these things. This is more than mental assent knowledge. It is defined as to "pursue with vigor" (i.e. to press toward). This level of commitment is not generally understood in the Church. Most of the time people think as long as they go to church they are pursuing Christ. To pursue is a matter of lifestyle. Some individuals have never been trained to understand the tree of life; they only understand the tree of the knowledge of good and evil. Man's knowledge of what he considers to be good or evil is the very reason God cast him out of the garden in the first place. Sin caused man to try to make his own choices; he separated himself from the life God had designed for him.

How do we find 'life' in a Church? It is actually very easy. When the people of God gather as a Body does it produce righteousness? Righteousness is access to God and to one another. Does the Body of Christ where you attend produce an atmosphere of access to all those who name the name of Jesus? Are they restrictive and insensitive to the spiritually needy, the spiritually lame, and the spiritually sick? Are they sensitive to the moving of the Holy Spirit? I am not speaking of accepting sin into the camp, nor am I referring to doctrinal differentiation; I am referring to an atmosphere where the Kingdom is in operation and the peace and joy in the Holy Ghost prevails. If we would change our thinking as to what Church actually is, we would discover going to some building at a specific time for services is not the biblical definition of the church. This concept of church attendance is actually a Roman philosophy and originated in the paganistic society of the fifth century A.D. The Church is that which produces righteousness, peace, and joy in the spirit of the believers who attend there. Church is not ritual; it is relational. How many people do you know in the congregation where you are attending? I mean actually and intimately know? When people attend church and do not have any Christian relationships, this is not the Kingdom of God. That is religion. The first century Church had a relational basis where trust was the governing factor. If someone came into the first century Church and they were not a faithful believer, the entire local church could be martyred if they were discovered. They killed us back then, remember? When something disturbs the peace in a church, it is against the Kingdom. The Kingdom produces peace. When peace is not being produced it is the evidence that the Kingdom is not being manifest by that congregation. When peace is being produced the joy of the Lord will permeate the Body of Christ. 'Joy' (5479) is defined as "calm delight", and joy is a type of rest. It is a sense of well being that one finds with the presence of Christ. It is also satisfaction. When the Body is well satisfied it tends to follow after things that make for peace, and the things that edify or create a foundation in believers. This is the Kingdom of God, and it is surely time for believers to mature in their faith and especially in their understanding of Kingdom things. It's time for unity! It's time for power!

Chapter 15 — The Salvation of the Soul

"And the very God of peace sanctify you wholly;
your whole spirit and soul
and body be preserved blameless unto the
coming of our Lord Jesus Christ."
(1 Thessalonians 5:23)

Tradition has used the concept of being "soul winners" for many years. This is usually understood to be the effort of evangelism, but the Scripture makes a clear distinction between the 'soul' and the 'spirit' of man. Our 'soul' (i.e., our mind, will, and temperament) needs guidance when we are spiritual babes. Why? Basically, the soul of man is connected to the old and the new man. Without correction you will not know how to put your old man in his place, which should be under the control of the new man (your spirit). Having been born again we are a part of God's Family, but we are still babes in Christ until matured (see Galatians 4:1-2). This is the reason God calls us His children and this is exactly what we are. We should understand that there is a difference between the 'soul' of man and the 'spirit' of man.

The Old Testament makes reference to the soul of man approximately 539 times, while the New Testament references the soul only a mere fifty eight times. If we return to Genesis for a moment, a difference can be readily seen as to why this is so.

"And the Lord God formed man
of the dust of the ground (body),
and breathed into his nostrils the breath of
life (spirit); and man became a living soul."
Genesis 2:7

This 'becoming' is the development of our self-life: our 'person' or personality. The redemption of man is outlined in the Bible from cover to cover. One area of interest when dealing with salvation is to recognize that the Bible makes a distinction between the salvation of the body, the salvation of the soul, and the salvation of our spirit. Truly all of these have been accomplished by the work of the Cross, but the Scripture deals with them as equal, yet unique and separate events. The body of man was redeemed on the cross and in the grave of Christ, and we shall receive our celestial body when Jesus returns. In a moment and in the "twinkling of an eye," we will be changed and will put off corruption and put on incorruption (see 1 Corinthians 15). This is the power of the resurrection. Our spirit, on the other hand, will remain basically the same and it has already been reborn when we are quickened (bodily renewal). Our spirit was resurrected at the moment we were born again. Our old nature (the old man) was transformed into the image of Christ (the new man) and our future was secured.

> "For you are bought with a price:
> therefore glorify God in your body,
> and in your spirit, which are God's."
> (1 Corinthians 6:20)

What did Paul mean when he said your body and your spirit belonged to the Lord? Why was the soul not added to the equation? The answer is simple. When we review Genesis 2:7 and 1 Corinthians 6:20 we will see that God did two things for us: first, He is our Creator and our Redeemer. He created our body and therefore owns us and He also redeemed us by His blood, purchasing us again from our state of lostness. We are twice-paid for. The Lord could have said to Satan, "I own these people. Let my people go." But God said that we were all sold under sin; so He had to purchase us again. Remember Adam gave his dominion to Satan when he fell. God said, "In the day that you eat of that tree you shall surely die," and even after He warned us, our Creator decided to pay for His children's mistake. That is agape, that is love in the highest degree. That is the fullness of God's love.

Agape love is the degree of love that causes us to want only the best for everyone we commune with. Every parent who has experienced the growth of a son or daughter understands that sometimes we learn the hard way through the experience of life. Just as our Lord told Hosea to buy his wife back from the slavery of whoredoms, God bought us from death even when we were rightfully His anyway. Like Hosea's wife we put ourselves into a position where we fall into slavery by our actions. The second aspect of our creation is that God formed our body and breathed into us Spirit, but we became a living soul. We became self-aware and wanted to make choices for ourselves. Our Creator has given us free will knowing our potential; even the freedom to disobey and go astray, if that was your choice. But how else could God in His grand design ever have a people who loved Him for who He is, lest we had the ability to choose? We find that when we choose to love God and to see Him for who He is, our redemption has greater depth. Jesus redeemed us on His Cross, so now is the time that we bear our cross on a daily basis for Him (see Matthew 16:24). This cross-bearing is the "process" of the salvation of our soul and is our part as we walk in obedience. Faith alone is of no value. James said that faith without works is dead. Common sense should tell us that this is why He told us to bear our cross daily! We find that many discuss the various aspects of the salvation of the soul, yet do they bring the Body of Christ to an understanding of what this area of salvation actually is? This is not an area to try to develop in others if you have no experience in it yourself. People can talk about fasting but when they do not fast, they are speaking out of theory and not experience. In order to develop anything in another person you must first develop it within yourself; the husbandman must be first partaker of the fruits (see 2 Timothy 2:6). The salvation of the soul must be experienced and the salvation of the soul is experience.

We begin this study with an introduction to the subject of the soul; discover what the soul is, and what the soul's function is. We will learn that the process of salvation is dealt with on three different levels by the Scriptures: spiritual salvation which occurs instantaneously at the new birth, the salvation of the soul which occurs progressively throughout our lives, and the future salvation of our body transpiring at Jesus' second coming. This will be our resurrected body.

When we are born again our spirit is made alive unto God. The Bible says it has been 'quickened'. In the New Testament there are several different Greek words translated as the word 'quicken'. We were 'quickened' (4806 - *suzoopoieo*) together with him, in Colossians 2:8. This Greek word comes from the word *sun* (4862) and means, "to be in union with or to be together", and *zoopoieo* (2227) which is "to revitalize or to be built again". This word means that we are revitalized together with Him. I like that! When all was lost Jesus gives us a shot in the arm. He 'reenergizes' us (i.e., we are 'revivified' together with Him). Ephesians 2:5 explains the process. Even when we were dead in sins He has 'quickened' us (i.e., made us overcomers) through His strength.

The other noteworthy Greek word translated as 'quickened' is *zao* (2198) and this word means 'life'. It is used 123 times in the New Testament. Its definition is simply "to be alive and not dead". The Bible is telling us to be happy that we are no longer dead, so we do not have to have a self-pity party. In essence then, to be quickened is when I am born from above and have been spiritually resurrected. I am now a being that has met his Maker and has submitted to his Maker's will. Now, what about that guy we call the old man?

The word 'soul' is translated from the Greek word *psuche* (5590). *Psuche* is also translated in the King James Version of the Bible as the words: "heart, life, and mind". The soul has some basic attributes that include the mind, the will, and the temperament. Through these the determinations and the personality of an individual are established. The *nous* (i.e., the mind - 3563) is identified as the intellect, by implication the 'meaning' of the being. It is the conscious inner man who thinks, reasons, understands, and realizes. The mind is more than just the thinking process; think of it as the reason why we think the way we think. It is the thought as well as the intent of the thinking (i.e., the base or basic cause at the core depth of the person which leads them to think a certain way). The mind is the basis of intellect within the individual, and within the mind 'reasoning' produces the very foundation of thought. The mind is described as being 'in the heart' (i.e., the core or the center of a person's foundation).

Biblically speaking, the heart is the union of the spirit and the soul, and creates the very essence of who we are. As we grow we develop patterns of thought, due to our experiences: the trials and successes of life. This is how the *nous* (i.e., the mind) is developed over many years as a part of the soul. The *nous* is also the seat of reasoning and logic and sets the stage for our thought processes. The Lord has to remold the *nous* through the 'renewing of the mind' after we are saved. This is why we are commanded to be transformed by the "renewing of your mind" (*nous*) in Romans 12:2 and to be "renewed in the spirit of your mind" (*nous*) in Ephesians 4:23. The Lord, through our conscience mind, re-forms us when we release our will to Him.

> "And have put on the new man, which is renewed in
> knowledge after the image of him that created him."
> (Colossians 3:10)

The next aspect of the soul is the 'will' (*theleo* - 2309), which is defined as active volition and purpose (the ability to make a decision and act upon it). The very operation of initiating the will can be seen in an individual and is obvious to the trained eye. When one begins to maneuver toward a goal or in a specific direction we can observe how they enacted their will. This soul activity of initiating the will is overtly recognizable, whether the activity has been consciously or unconsciously performed. The best counselors and Pastors are trained to see these soulish maneuverings; the plotting and the schemes people strategize. The will also displays the options one will take in a set course or action. A person may say one thing, yet their will uncovers their true motives and purposes, by reflecting their inner man's intention. The will of an individual is always manifested. It is like gravity; the power and effect of the will draws the person in the direction of their intent and is always seen in their inclinations. The power of the will, when harnessed, can be a valuable ally. The will can be controlled by the old man or the new man. Knowing this, we are warned in Colossians 2:23 about the dangers related to the commandments and doctrines of men because when people 'will' something to be so, they will preach it as though it is. Religiosity produces 'will-worship' (1479). 'Will-worship' is the worship that one devises and prescribes that is contrary to the contents and nature of faith that ought to be directed to Christ. Many lexicons state that this is a "counterfeit worship". The Amplified Bible translates Colossians 2:23 thus:

> "Such [practices] have indeed the outward appearance
> [that popularly passes] for wisdom, in promoting self-imposed
> rigor of devotion and delight in self-humiliation and severity
> of discipline of the body, but they are of no value in checking
> the indulgence of the flesh (the lower nature).
> [Instead, they do not honor God but
> serve only to indulge the flesh]."

The idea of will-worship is simply that a person, by the choice of the will, creates a way to be saved or some other religious notion and then promotes his own religious interpretation of that idea. This is how so many different denominational doctrines have been created. It is also the religious practice of maintaining certain aspects of self-abasement in order to promote a sense of external holiness when the inner man of the heart is full of wickedness. Many denominational and religious mindsets such as dressing certain ways, or having one's hair fixed in a certain style is just a manifestation of false humility and the 'neglecting' (punishing) of the body as stated in Colossians 2:23.

The 'temperament' is the combination of one's feelings, emotions, tensions, anxieties, discernment, stress, senses, notions and ideas, and is described as the state of mind from where the mood is generated. We must recognize that our mood can be heavenly or demonically motivated. The soul is energized by the tree of life from God's Spirit or it will be energized from the tree of the knowledge of good and evil in the carnal mind. We must recognize that Satan understands this and can put us in a bad mood and thus hinder our worship. But our spirit can also motivate us to express genuine worship from the depths of our being.

These areas of our life set the stage for impartation. Remember what Peter said to Jesus in Matthew 16. When he rebuked the Lord, he told Jesus that he did not want Him to pursue God's plan. Jesus addressed the issue with Peter to show him how Satan had used him to try and hinder the purpose of God. Jesus said to him, "Get thee behind me Satan: thou art an offense unto me..." Peter's mind had been touched by the devil and his feelings were demonically controlled, even when he thought he was speaking the right thing. The Lord also rebuked James and John because they wanted to call fire down from heaven and destroy a city. This showed that they did not know "what spirit they were of" (see Luke 9:55). Jesus then revealed to them that the son of man came to save men's souls, not destroy them. Evil spirits had manipulated their temperamental state and had imparted error into them. They had not realized that their mood toward the Samaritans had been demonically influenced and they were manifesting a fleshly temperament (see Galatians 5:19-21).

Consider this: if our soul is not saved it has the power to affect the body negatively. If the soul is saved it has the power to affect the body positively. This is why many Christians with good intentions fail in their walk to be unified in their church or faith. The Bible speaks of a characteristic of the soul, and calls it the "carnal mind" (see Romans 8:7). The carnal mind is said to be 'enmity' (2189) against God. With this in mind, Matthew 13:24-30 and 39 describes an attack of the enemy. This 'enemy' (2190) of the Kingdom sows the seeds of enmity.

> "Behold, I give you power to tread on serpents and
> scorpions, and over all the power of the enemy:
> and nothing shall by any means hurt you.
> Notwithstanding in this rejoice not, that the spirits
> are subject unto you, but rather rejoice,
> because your names are written in heaven."
> (Luke 10:19-20)

When the above passage is viewed exegetically, we will see that the enemy and these of spirits are spoken of as being the same. The vital thing to discover is that they can 'hurt' (91) you. The idea of hurting you must be seen as the devil's ability to "afflict us in an unjust manner." We are redeemed but Satan attacks us anyway. The root word for the word 'hurt' in the Greek means "one who deals fraudulently with others or one who is deceitful." This is the way our enemy is toward us. He causes us to be angry or bitter, then uses the stress these produce in our bodies to harm or kill us. In other words, Satan gets us to agree with him in his accusations toward another person or toward ourselves; he then deploys his demonic forces against us and sets us up for the kill. Make a note of this quote,

> "There is no tissue in the human body wholly removed from
> the influence of the spirit...Recognizing that our bodies are
> subject to the disposition of the spirit and the habits of the soul."

Another author E.A. Strecker in his book "Mental Hygiene" states:

> "It is not an overstatement to say that fully fifty
> percent of problems of the acute stages of
> an illness and seventy-five percent of the difficulties
> of convalescence have their primary origin
> not in the body, but in the
> mind of the patient."

Many psychologists and physicians have stated that anger and resentment are the roots of ninety percent of all neuroses and nervous troubles. The great enemies of mankind's personality are resentment, fear, self-centeredness, and feelings of guilt, insecurity, and of rejection. The inner voice of enmity does more harm than any outward enemy's voice can ever do. We should see that there is a correlation between the state of a man's soul and the state of a man's body. In writing the first letter to the Church at Thessalonica Paul acknowledged his desire for the believers to be "wholly sanctified" (see 1 Thessalonians 5:23). This sanctification process should be understood as another aspect of the salvation of the soul. The word 'sanctify' is translated from the Greek word *hagiazo* (37), and means, "to be purified and consecrated". As for the soul, Paul teaches that its salvation is 'progressive' (i.e., it is saved over time - see Philippians 2:12). Through a renewal the *nous* (mind) is saved; through activated faith the emotions are saved and through patience the will can be changed. Luke 21:19 states:

> "In your patience possess ye your souls."

The word *hupomone* (5281) translated as 'patience' in the above passage is defined as "consistency, continuance, or hopeful endurance". It is the kind of patience one needs in dealing with circumstances. One thing to note is there are two different kinds of patience in the New Testament: *hupomone* and *makrothumia* (3115). We need both kinds of patience in order to have progress in the salvation of our soul. *Makrothumia* is the ability to endure or suffer for longer periods of time and is usually translated by the English word 'longsuffering'. It is the kind of patience one needs when dealing with people. In order for us to 'possess' (i.e., control) our soul we must learn to be 'consistent' (*hupomone*). For the Christian, separating the habits of the old man and walking in the newness of life should be a matter of abiding in Christ. This abiding is associated with hope and is reached when we do not give into circumstances or temptation. This is the active salvation we should walk in when dealing with the soul.

Another way to view the soul is that it is the self-life of an individual. This self-life is the internal mechanism that allows us to choose the things of the flesh or the things of the Spirit. The fruit that is produced in our life determines our choices. When the Spirit of God begins to turn us toward a given direction and we resist His move, this is the self-life deciding to go against the will of God. Hence we choose our will over God's will. We become the 'god' of our lives in this way. This is how the old man remains in control of our inner being and resists the changes that are necessary for our conversion.

The new man must be disciplined and trained to deal with the old ways and habits of the old nature (see Ephesians 4:22-32). When God speaks to us He reveals His will to us and He expects us to be obedient. The soul, when motivated by the old man, will influence your behavior so that you cannot accomplish the goal God has set for you; in essence, we talk ourselves out of it. This is called 'reasoning' (1260). The Greek word translated 'reasoning' is *dialogizomai*. Notice the word "dialog" found at the front of the word. *Dialogizomai* is the inner dialog of the mind. Notice it is dialog through the logic of our reasoning. God would not give us a goal that is unattainable. The very fact that God gives us a direction to proceed in is the evidence that He expects us to go there and He gives us the faith that is necessary for the completion of the process. The Lord leads us into the right way, but our soul acts up like a spoiled child and fusses when it has to be obedient. Isaiah 29:8 states that our soul has an "appetite" (8264). This primitive Hebrew word means to 'seek greedily' (i.e., to jostle one against another). This is one way Satan manipulates people. He causes you to fight with yourself! Our self-life has its own desire. When Satan touched Eve's soul in the Garden of Eden she was drawn into the temptation through her 'desire' (2530). The implication in the language of the Bible is that she sought her independence. Her desire to be wise was the product of the manipulation of her self-will. Satan touched the uniqueness of her being when he wooed her with the statement, "ye shall be like gods." Eve 'saw' (7200) something in her heart that she desired (see Genesis 3:6). The Hebrew word translated as "saw" means to advise self or to approve something for self, just like 'dialogizomai'. This is the flesh's nature. It wants its own way, it wants its own satisfaction, and it wants it now! The emotional high one's soul attains when it has its want fulfilled is a sense of gratification and fulfillment that acts as an emotional narcotic. The difference between getting my way and not getting my way can generate mood swings that push us into agony or ecstasy. Our emotions get out of whack because we do not get what we want. We murmur, complain, and justify our reasons for the want just like a little child.

1 Peter 2:25 tells us that Jesus is the Shepherd and the Bishop of our soul. We love Jesus the Shepherd, but what about Jesus the Bishop? The Greek word translated as 'bishop' (1985) means one who is a superintendent (i.e., one who has the office or is in charge of a church; we are the church).

To 'bishop' (to superintend) the soul is to oversee the soul through the process of correcting it. Acts 20:28-29 commands:

> "Take heed therefore unto yourselves, and to all the flock, over
> the which the Holy Ghost hath made you overseers,
> to feed the church of God, which he hath purchased with
> his blood. For I know this, that after my departing shall
> grievous wolves enter in among you, not sparing the flock."

Jesus is faithful to watch over our soul. He brings correction to us through those that are over us in the Lord and through the internal mechanism of our conscience. When our determinations become selfishly motivated, Jesus will bishop our soul, either by the power of the Holy Spirit or by the hand of one who is over you in the Lord. The Lord is determined to correct our selfish pursuits. This is what the office of Bishop is all about. It is to oversee and correct the manifestation of the fruits of the flesh in our lives. Carnality is so rampant in the modern church that when someone gets into open sin if a pastor rebukes him he puts his job in jeopardy at times.

Due to the fall, mankind pursues anything and everything that is self-indulging. Selfishness is 'carnality' and manifests through an individualistic ideology in the Body of Christ. These self-indulging individuals may be born-again, but they remain the same (i.e., 'fleshly'). The Lord wants to teach us how to deal with the root of our problem, which is selfishness. He is taking us past the rhetoric of carnal Christianity to the lifestyle of Christian reality. I'm not speaking about the traditional churchianity that views purity and holiness as being found in certain styles of hair and/or the type of clothes one wears, or whether make-up can or cannot be worn. This is external piety. True holiness is the manifestation of a lifestyle that results in unity and produces a fullness of faithfulness that lives a life of spiritual rest. True holiness is a fasted (firm, strong) lifestyle, an intimate and deep relationship with the Lord, and with the people of God. It is the inter-relationship of the Body of Christ and one's separation from the world that makes them holy, not a Victorian dress code. Even when people wear the right clothing the spirit of selfishness can rule them.

We should at this time consider why we have become a living soul. The idea articulated in Genesis 2:7 states that Adam "became a living soul;" Adam had a part in his 'becoming'. Our soul allows us the freewill expression of love and gratitude. The ability to independently choose (i.e., our self-will) was given to us by God for a distinct purpose. The problem is not 'individualism' (i.e., the uniqueness of one's being), but the independence of one's 'will' that can separate us from God through the self-exaltation of our personal choices.

Our soul was created so that we could express love toward God and toward others. Without the soul true expression is not possible and magnification of expression would not occur. The soul is a magnifier. Remember that Mary said in Luke 1:54:

"My soul doth magnify the Lord..."

As we dissect the structure of man we see how God has put us together. He made us spirit and body, and then we became self-existent (a 'living soul'). Through the spiritual birth we have access to God through Jesus Christ. God is a Spirit and we must commune with Him "in spirit and in truth" (see John 4:24). Since the Word of God is the only thing able to "divide asunder" (3311) the soul and spirit, we must realize that only God can separate man's entirety. Hebrews 4:12 states:

"For the word of God is quick, and powerful,
and sharper than any two-edged sword,
piercing even to the dividing asunder of
soul and spirit, and of joints and marrow,
and is a discerner of the thoughts
and the intents of the heart."

When the Bible uses the words heart or flesh these terms are of course, descriptive. The term 'heart of man' is defining the inseparable spirit and soul, while the flesh is the inseparable 'soul and body'. For a more basic description of the soul we could view it as being a processor and should appreciate that it is used to transfer information. The soul is like a light switch. The new man and the old man are the avenues of its expression. Who I am determines whether I relate to others through my spirit or through my flesh. The Holy Spirit can energize our spirit through the new man and that in turn manifests through our heart. If our new man is dominant then he will be reflected through our being. That is, the new man will direct us to overcome the world and the things of the world through our fellowship with God; the fruit of the Spirit will ripen and will be noticeable in our lives. When the new man is dominant he will use every aspect of the soul for victory and worship. He will serve God with his mind, his will, and his temperament, centralizing his determinations in Christ. If our new man is not dominant, then our flesh or demonic influences will motivate our soul through the familiarity of the old man and the fruit of the flesh will permeate our being. When the old man is dominating, the flesh will win the battle. The flesh or demonic influences will manipulate and work in you whatever purpose they desire by coercing the fleshly lust. Since sin is deeper than the soul, originating in the fallen nature, mankind is inclined toward sin.

Remember that Satan is a vagabond and has no place of his own. He therefore comes to us and seeks 'place' (*topos*). Satan schemed to produce the fall by tempting Eve so he would have entrance into our lives. Ephesians 4:27 says, "neither give place to the devil," because Satan can only have place if you give it to him. Satan can be given place consciously or unconsciously (he can gain entrance into areas of our life without being detected). Satan's fall came about because he exalted himself. This satanic manifestation continues to be promoted in mankind. He continuously tempts us to choose self over God. Satan is the motivator of selfishness using our flesh and the gravity of sin to motivate. We can see how Satan uses the lust of the eyes, the lust of the flesh, and the pride of life to cause us to work and live outside of God's ways. This is how he deceived Eve. Satan wants to drag us down to his level. He continuously tempts and manipulates us with the intent to recreate man into his image. Satan wants to be like the Most High (see Isaiah 14), therefore he directs man to become self-centered, self-conscious, self-indulgent, and self-righteous. When Satan gains entrance into someone's life he then has a platform of operation to launch his attack and to spread his control. The Bible says, "Satan comes to steal, to kill, and to destroy". What better platform is there for Satan to use than when a person does not realize they are being used? Satan maneuvered Eve and prompted her to eat the fruit from the tree of the knowledge of good and evil. In essence, the fruit of the flesh was tapped. It was the 'fruit' (2590) of her flesh that produced a 'place' (*topos*) for Satan's operation. How can this be? Satan can only affect us through temptation and disobedience. The fruit from the tree of life is the fruit of the Spirit and it sustains the new man. When Eve questioned the motive of God's commandment, "Thou shall not eat," she opened the door to doubt and unbelief. Satan cannot destroy God's plan; he can only hinder God's plan by attacking God's people. Satan, through the soul, manipulates our disobedience by causing us to doubt the truth. Eve gave in to doubt and unbelief in the garden. She was deceived (see 1 Timothy 2:14). Adam, on the other hand, was not deceived and he entered into sin. Adam enacted his will and made a choice to disobey. When he was offered the choice he disobeyed. 'Self' was thus accentuated and its manifestation was immediately seen in Adam's self-justification. Adam basically stated to God, "It's not my fault, God! You are the one who gave the woman to me." In Adam's mind it was clear. If God had not given him the woman this situation would have never occurred. His emotional state of embarrassment and self-justification led him into the ultimate snare: self-deceit. Matthew 6:23b says:

> "If therefore the light that is in thee be
> darkness, how great is that darkness."

That is what happened to Adam, he was deceived and did not know it, and that is the way Satan is manipulating us today. His goal is to offer the choices, but only provide the tree of the knowledge of good and evil for us to choose from. He has thereby set the outcome to always go his way. As the 'god' of this world Satan knows what the flesh wants and he makes provision for it. This is Satan's way.

Receiving the End of your Faith

> "Who are kept by the power of God through
> faith unto a salvation ready
> to be revealed in the last time...
> Receiving the end of your faith,

> even the salvation of the soul.
> Of which salvation the prophets
> have inquired and searched
> diligently, who prophesied of the
> grace that should come unto you.
> Searching what, or what manner
> of time the Spirit of Christ
> which was in them did signify,
> when it testified beforehand
> the sufferings of Christ, and
> the glory that should follow."
> (1 Peter 1:5 and 9-12)

> "But as He which has called you is holy,
> so you be holy in all manner of
> conversation (behavior); Because it is written,
> You be holy, for I am holy."
> (1 Peter 1:15-16)

Manifested holiness is accomplished as we mature in our faith. This maturing of our faith is the process of the salvation of the soul. This holiness, as stated before, is a separateness of life from the world. People in the world have a different point of view than Christians. "You are in the world, but not of the world" is the clarity Jesus gave His disciples. In other words, we should no longer live as the world lives. Passive churchianity should be seen for what it really is: being fleshly or carnal Christianity.

The Church has become so "new birth" conscious that it has forgotten how to mature the saints. Some denominations have created a total focus on winning others to Christ as though that was all God required us to do. I do not want to labor this point more than necessary, but the Church must change its focus. Jesus said in Matthew 28:19-20:

> "Go ye therefore, and teach all nations,
> baptizing them in the name of the Father,
> and of the Son, and of the Holy Ghost:
> teaching them to observe all things
> whatsoever I have commanded you."

The word translated as 'name' comes from the Greek word *onoma* (3686). It is defined as character and authority. When we see the word 'name' in the New Testament it means "in the character and the authority of the person whose name you are using". It is like the name 'Christian'. If you are not living as Christ taught and as the disciples did, then you have the name, but not the character or authority of the one in whom you call yourself. Remember the event in the book of Acts when the devils said, "Jesus, we know and Paul we know but who are you?" Those who were trying to use the 'name' did not have the character and authority of Jesus or Paul, thus they were beaten. *Onoma* also means likeness and representation. It comes from the Greek root word *ginosko* (1097) and is to know, to understand, and to be resolved. The word means much more than casual knowledge, *onoma* means knowledge that comes through experience. Since those who were using Jesus' name had none of these, they therefore had no power.

What traditional Christianity has done is to change the commandment from you shall "be" witnesses to you shall "do" witnessing. This has created a systematic theology that believes all you have to do is tell others about Jesus and you are doing the will of God, even if you are not becoming like Christ. Again, the word 'Christian' means to be like Christ and to be anointed. If all that a person does is to win the lost, they are not being obedient to God's commandment "to make disciples". In the earlier years of my ministry I was very evangelistic. When I started training people in the churches I pastored I was surprised at the level of resistance I received. (Training disciples is why Paul told Timothy to do the work of an evangelist. An evangelist's work will be discussed in chapter eighteen). The word 'teach' in Matthew 28:19 is defined "to make disciples." And again I say, Jesus did not say win converts, He said, "make disciples" and there is a difference between the two. 1 Corinthians 11:30,

> "For this cause many are weak and
> sickly among you, and many sleep."

Why are they weak, sick, and dying? They do not understand *koinonia* (2842 - communion). *Koinonia* had never been discipled into them. 'Koinonia' and its roots are translated by the following words in the King James Bible: partake, partaker, fellowship, communion, distribution, contribution, participation, society, and common. One of the aspects of communion ('koinonia') is when the congregation partakes and participates in Christian fellowship. 'Koinonia' is when they are a common society of believers who contribute to and distribute among themselves. Communion is more than just the ordinance of the Lord's Supper. Communion is the 'common union' of the believers in a specific community (any local church). Many Christians have become so ritualistic in the modern Church that they fail to recognize the true purpose of Jesus' statement: "This is my Body." Question: Was Jesus' body broken? Not according to John 19:36. So what is broken, Jesus or the Body of Christ (the Church). I believe it is *us*.

There are many ministers who do not focus on Christian maturity. Evangelism is an important part of ministry, but it is not the eternal formula for Christian success. When believers are not discipled they struggle with doubt and unbelief because of unresolved sin. Whole generations of believers are falling into the temptations of the world due to a lack of discipline (training), the only way to develop Christian maturity. We are commanded time and again by the biblical record to be doers of the word and not just hearers only. Many preach a pseudo-fantasy form of faith where the believer is all snug and warm in their sin. When someone hears but does not do what they hear, they deceive themselves. This is the way mystery Babylon comes into play in one's life. The word 'babylon' means 'confused'. The Babylonian church (the carnal church) does not understand the things of God. Babylonian churches use a different concept of ministry that has no real spiritual value. It is the feel good, self-pleasing church that is full of babies. We should call it "baby-lon" (baby land). Congregations led by babes are full of babes.

We are commanded to "train up a child in the way he should go," not just educate them in the things they should know. The soul must be weaned from the flesh and worldly desires. These desires are the inner habits we have formed and have grown accustomed to. Jesus said our first and foremost responsibility is "to love God with all our heart, mind, and soul, and to love His children (our spiritual neighbors) as ourselves". To be disciplined in the soul is to be someone who is sold out for God. It is a life (a soul) who recognizes God's great design. God wants us to be saved and actively become a partner in our local church. To be all that God has created you to be by living a healthy, emotionally sound, and spiritually vibrant life. We only have the life we are given and at its end we will stand before our Maker to have our first face-to-face meeting with Him. And guess what? As we say in Texas, the whole conversation will be about you! What will you say to Him when He asks about your salvation? Will we all feel confident that Jesus died and rose from the grave sacrificing Himself on the Cross? He is the Savior, but we are partakers of His Kingdom. If the individual church member is not trained, years of carnality will produce a soul that is religious. A religious soul is the most difficult soul to deal with.

In my spiritual training I have observed some of the most awesome men of God. They have taught me how to be wholesome and that I have a soul. When congregations are immature their Pastors are forced to spend most of their time changing spiritual diapers and feeding those who do not know how to feed themselves. Pastors oftentimes find themselves alone and feel isolated. They receive the blame when things are not going right but oftentimes not the credit when the church is doing well. Carnal believers (babes) cannot raise themselves. They will never mature in the faith without discipleship. Paul stated that the babes stir up strife in the house of God (see 1 Corinthians 3:1-3). Pastors find themselves overwhelmed as they minister to the wounded and fallen, which in turn requires Pastors to leave discipleship unattended. Unless a Pastor gets help he will become discouraged or burned-out.

Ministers must not rush to appoint leadership just for the sake of having leaders. Leadership must be mature. There is a far greater problem created when carnal leadership is appointed than when ministers have no help. The lone minister can at least train up others, while carnal leadership only brings division and strife into the congregation. Ministers must avoid the buddy system when searching for God's anointed. Mature leadership takes the burden off of the top and rests it on the shoulders of strong anointed people. Peace and rest come through discipleship. If a minister trains two people a year, so the trained can disciple another in their second year of training, there will be great increase after three or four years. One to three by the end of first year…three to nine by the end of second year…nine to twenty seven by the end of third year, and so it takes off exponentially after the end of the fourth year. It takes that long to disciple people in order to have a firm base of training in the local church. When two are discipled in the first year, even when the process of discipleship is incomplete, they should be trained to train others also under a spiritual father as part of the process (see 2 Timothy 2:2). These should be guided through the initial stages of spiritual growth. As the spiritual fathers continue to disciple leaders through the second year, they grow as they lead others as they were led. We learn by doing. When spiritual fathers recognize disciples that are growing, they should then release them into God's call. The first part of anyone's training should be his 'sonship'. They are God's children and He wants them to be complete (i.e., mature). I have learned that after the first year joint sessions are the best. The pastor can preside over the times of training, teaching and also allow sons and daughters to teach and operate in the office God has given them. It does not have to be a paid staff position; just let them take part of the total load. The prayer warriors, teaching pastors, and prophets will show themselves. Those trained earlier can then expand their boundaries, distributing the burden even further. When we are committed to long-term discipleship God's people will not suffer in ignorance for very long. The time will pass anyway; wisdom understands that training should be done patiently.

Another hindrance to discipleship, which in turn works against the salvation of the soul is when a Pastor leaves a church prematurely. Hopefully that local church already has a discipleship mechanism in place to bring balance to the congregation during these times.

The biblical church government model operates in a much different way than many of today's congregations are structured. Elder rule means to be governed by the *doma* men. God commanded elder rule as a means to protect the Church from carnal leadership, but if elders are carnal the whole congregation will suffer for it. When a leader or a member strays off the Scriptural foundation, he is to be chastened with the Word, not by a board. This is why these types of carnal situations reoccur in some congregations again and again. The governing unit, whatever it may be at the local church level, has the responsibility to disciple the members, oversee the Church, and strive to create an atmosphere of love, peace, rest, and joy throughout the congregation. I believe very strongly that the Body of Christ ought to bless individual church members and the less fortunate, helping them with any overload whether it is a spiritual, emotional (like making them feel blessed or noticed), or physical matter. Let wisdom prevail.

I believe this is part of communion (i.e., continually building up the Body of Christ from its foundation in every way). When you go to church take look around and notice the people. The Church is the people, not the building or the steeple. When discipleship takes the second seat the self-will of a people will take the first. They will not spend the time it takes to engraft the Word into a congregation and grow a congregation in quality and in quantity. When people's souls are not saved they are operating religiously, not according to God's Word. The daily ministry of any church will be organized through the personal desire of their soul, rather than the spiritual needs within the congregation. 2 Chronicles 15:3-4 states:

> "Now for a long season Israel had been without the true God,
> and without a teaching priest, and without law.
> But when they in their trouble did turn unto the Lord God of Israel,
> and sought him, he was found of them."

We are changed by the engrafted word as James 1:21 states:

> "Wherefore lay apart all filthiness and superfluity
> of naughtiness, and receive with meekness the
> engrafted word which is able to save your souls."

Engrafting the Word into the life of a believer is part of discipleship. The word 'engrafted' is the Greek word *emphutos* (1721) and means, "implanted or spliced". It comes from the idea that something has been germinated and has sprouted into life by being attached to something else. If the Word of God has to become flesh in us in order for our new man to be in control of our soul, we must allow the Word to take root and sprout. When we need patience, it is not enough to pray for patience and then wait on God in anxiety. We must allow the Word of God to sprout patience in us and then we will grow up into a consistent Christian lifestyle. This is how "patience will have her perfect work" (see James 1:4). Luke 21:19 says, "In your patience you possess your soul." When I am truly patient, then the "word of patience" has manifested in me. The Church has developed such a name-it-and-claim-it mentality we fail to allow the engrafted word to mature in our lives. Many justify their struggles with statements such as "it was not God's will for me" or the like. God has stated His will in His Word. The Word of God, the Bible, states that God's will is for us to be one in the faith (see John 17). The Lord has given us "all things that pertain to life and godliness" (see 2 Peter 1:3), and Isaiah 5:4 says; "What could have been done more to my vineyard that I have not already done in it?" The thing that must be imparted into the believer is the attitude and determination to succeed. We give up too easily these days. When Jesus said, "I am the way, the truth and the life," He meant it. He was not saying I am the way, but if the way is too hard for you sit back and wait for the rapture. He said in Revelation 3:21:

> "To him that overcometh will I grant
> to sit with me in my throne, even as I also overcame,
> and am set down with my Father in his throne."

It is not a question of human inability; it is the answer of simple obedience and effort. One thing is incontrovertible. You will never succeed if you do not try. You cannot win the race unless you compete and you cannot compete unless you enter and run. As believers we are commanded to run as though we expect to win. Paul wrote:

> "Not as though I had already attained,
> either were already perfect (mature):
> but I follow after, if that I may apprehend
> that for which also I am apprehended of
> Christ Jesus...I count not myself to have
> apprehended: but this one thing I do,
> forgetting those things which are behind,
> and reaching forth unto those things which
> are before, I press toward the mark for the
> prize of the high calling of God in Christ Jesus."
> (Philippians 3:12-14)

The Body of Christ must have this mindset: "What has Christ Jesus, the Creator, apprehended me for?" You have been apprehended as a child of God through adoption into the family of the Almighty God, but have you apprehended your soul yet? Are you growing and are you being fulfilled? Are you struggling with your call, place, and purpose? Mark 3:13-15 says you are called "to be with Him." Can you be satisfied with that? Our first obligation is to love God and to love God's people (see Revelation 2:4). Paul pressed out the pattern. We should do the same. Our struggle occurs because we have not been trained to keep our soul under control. If men of God bishop our souls in the traditional church (i.e., when they deal with our fleshly weaknesses,) you will see many that want to leave that church as quickly as possible. Not only will people leave if you correct them, but they will speak evil of you and create division in the process. When our Pastor bishops our soul as commanded by God, do you accuse that minister of being a dictator? The truth of the matter is that many Christians are immature and some are just spoiled little church brats! Ever hear of the term 'tare'? A 'tare' looks like a Christian, talks like a Christian, goes to church like a Christian, but manifests the "terrible twos" when they do not get their way, thereby causing division and strife in the Church of God.

> "Surely I have behaved and quieted myself, as a child that is
> weaned of his mother: my soul is as a weaned child."
> (Psalm 131:2)

David understood that his soul had to be dealt with. He did not hide the fact that his soul needed to be weaned from the flesh. We are raised by world's ideas and we have the notion that praying the sinner's prayer removes these concepts automatically from our lives. Just as children must be weaned from a bottle our soul must be weaned from the things it is accustomed to. Our soul looses its security without its spiritual bottle. Spiritual babes find themselves in a state of panic over the simplest of matters. David said, "I have behaved...my soul (see Psalm 131:2)." The Hebrew word translated 'behaved' (7737) means, "to equalize, to level, to adjust, or to counterbalance yourself". This is a picture of how we must train our soul. We must balance ourselves. When an offense comes we must 'balance' our fleshly desire that will call for revenge and will push us toward retaliation. We must get our soul under control so we can respond the way the Bible teaches. We expect our children to be obedient to us, but we excuse ourselves for our disobedience to the Lord.

Christ taught us how to live, act, and be. It is up to us to be obedient to all the Lord has commanded. If the old man is not weaned he thinks he still needs baby stuff.

> "When I was a child, I spake as a child,
> I understood as a child, I thought as a child:
> but when I became a man, I put away childish things."
> (1 Corinthians 13:11)

Every parent understands that the weaning process is not easy by any means, unless the child is ready to be weaned. For example, a youth pastor called me to discuss a certain teen in her church. She had been working with a young woman in her church that had recently been born again. In view of the fact that the teen had a worldly background, she was having some problems that stemmed from her prior sexual behavior. The teen had been promiscuous before she came to the Lord. These attitudes and desires were still strong in her life and her boyfriend had continued to expect sex. Neither was old enough to marry. This youth pastor was looking for answers because the teen was not mature enough to cope with the situation. We were sure the teen was sincere in her faith and discovered that the problem was twofold. First, the old man in the girl's life had not been dealt with. The teen was broken in spirit about the matter yet every so often she would give in to the temptation. The world had corrupted her mind through a philosophy of sexual expression. The American society teaches that sex is a natural part of the dating experience. Many teens have been inundated with these concepts through the public school system, television, and peer pressure, all of which had a strong influence over her. When our attitudes are coupled with self-will and self-pleasure the self-will is determined to fulfill its wants. This area of the teen's soul had to be weaned and renewed through the process of discipleship. Do not make a mistake by thinking this is easy to do. In order to accomplish God's purpose of deliverance we had to first teach the teen to deny her soul (old man) by training her to fast, and by developing her spirit (new man) in righteousness. It is foolish to demand obedience from a child when you do not teach them to obey. When dealing with any stronghold we must learn how to fast. Fasting (see Isaiah 58) is a training tool. Our Hedonistic, non-self denying society finds this difficult, plus it is just hard to fast a total fast. When this teen was trained to deny her belly the food it wanted, she learned how to deny her sexual desires at the same time. When this teen was trained to find her security in Jesus, she was able to deal with the boy who played on her insecurities for sex.

The second area that needed to be addressed with this young woman was her foundation of faith. When we are weaned, trained, and founded we become overcomers. In order for her to overcome (i.e., get the victory over her soul) she had to be disciplined. Only through the power of the Holy Spirit we can accomplish this goal.

"Whom shall I teach knowledge?
and whom shall he make to understand
doctrine? Them that are weaned from
the milk, and drawn from the breast."
(Isaiah 28:9)

The Bible teaches us how to walk in the Spirit. This walk comes with responsibility. If we have been weaned through the foundational principles (see Hebrews 6:1-2) and have progressed to a faithful lifestyle, then we can grow up in the admonition of the Lord. If our soul is not saved, we cannot mature in the faith. Remember soul salvation is not automatic! In order for Christians to have a unified faith, believers must mature beyond the petty backbiting and other childish behaviors that permeate some congregations and groups of believers. We are commanded to renew our minds and therefore we should focus on the discipleship of the Body of Christ as being the primary part of the Christian ministry. Churches should establish evangelistic ministries and couple them with discipleship training.

"To whom shall I speak and give warning, That they may hear?
Behold, their ear is uncircumcised, and they cannot hearken:
Behold, the Word of the Lord is unto them
a reproach; they have no delight in it."
(Jeremiah 6:10)

How can we learn to walk by God's statutes if we do not obey? The Lord says that their ear is uncircumcised. Many have not trained their ears to hear God. We still battle in our minds wondering if the Lord is speaking or not. The ability to hear God comes from the Word of God (see Romans 10:17). You can know God's voice when you know God's Word (see John 10). Study your Bible. In Jeremiah 6:16-19, we are commanded to ask for the 'old paths'. The old paths are the eternal paths. It is in these paths that we find the way of God: the right way. This is the place where we find rest unto our souls.

How do we enter into rest? Jeremiah 6:17 tells us how God will deal with us. The Lord will set watchmen over you that say, "hearken to the sound of the trumpet!" The Word of God is a trumpet in the right hands. According to Isaiah 58:1 the voice of the Lord is the trumpet we should hear. Biblical rest will occur when we discover our ability to allow God to work in us (through circumstances) and to acknowledge our need for Him. Once we realize He is our source for all things, and by Him are all things, then we can rest in His abilities instead of being frustrated with our inabilities. We do this through continuous prayer. If we are self-centered we will continue to focus on our inabilities rather than having an attitude of faith by trusting God in our abilities. This is how the teen was discipled. She was shown how to walk with God in the midst of her temptation and she was given the keys of the Kingdom and the desire to be pure. Through this she gained hope for a husband and was then able to save herself for him.

Many women never think that they have a part in the salvation message. When a sister can save herself for a man, she can surely teach a man to save himself for her. She/he can only teach what they are and cannot teach what they are not, lest it be by faith. But it takes a godly woman *or* man to understand the Spirit of this kind of wisdom.

God knows our need before we do. We can know the Lord is aware of our faults and failures without being afraid of Him: as long as we are repentant. He still loves us and accepts us when we sin, but repentance must be an active part of our walk. It is the goodness of God that brings us to repentance. Once we comprehend that He is our righteousness we will not have the need for self-justification. We can approach His throne and ask for mercy and grace in our times of failure. His righteousness is working in us and has an effect on us (even though we are sometimes unaware of it).

> "And the work of righteousness is peace; and the effect of
> righteousness is quietness and assurance forever."
> (Isaiah 32:17)

As we live in His righteousness it will work in us a sense of peace and the effect of this peace is a quietness of soul, with the assurance that God is causing us to rest in Him. Jeremiah 15:18-19 states:

> "Why is my pain perpetual, and my wound incurable,
> which refuseth to be healed? wilt thou be altogether unto me as a liar,
> and as waters that fail? Therefore thus saith the Lord,
> If thou return, then will I bring thee again, and thou shalt stand before me:
> and if thou take forth the precious from the vile, thou shalt be as my
> mouth: let them return unto thee; but return not thou unto them."

Carnality will never leave us until we take heed to Jeremiah's advice. Separate out the precious from the vile and not the vile from the precious. Focus on those things that are godly and God-centered in your life. Utilize your time and energy on the good vines. Work with believers in whose heart the passion of God burns; those that desire to manifest the fruit of the Spirit through practical living. Do not get frustrated as you serve, having to constantly change spiritual diapers. Sometimes you just have to say, "O.K. little one, it is time to get potty trained!"

Chapter 16 – The Path of the Root

"For everyone that uses milk is unskillful in the word of
righteousness: for he is a babe. But strong meat belongs to them
that are of full age, even those who by reason of use
have their senses exercised to discern both good and evil."
(Hebrews 5:13-14)

A friend of mine married into a family that owned an orange orchard in southern California. We were visiting one weekend when he discovered that he had an orange tree that had died. He pulled the old tree up by the roots, filled the hole that was left with a mixture of soil, and planted another orange tree in the same place as the other. I noticed that some of the roots from the first tree had remained in the hole. He called them "water roots." Not knowing what they were I asked him to explain. He showed me that by planting the new tree in the same spot the roots would have a natural path to the water source, and that the new roots would travel the same path that the former roots had taken. The Lord has used this revelation to teach me and to reveal to me that some emotional roots follow the same spiritual path in our lives. When believers struggle in areas of their lives and do not experience victory, the struggle is generally due to a lack of something within their foundation. One of the things that causes spiritual babes to struggle is they are inexperienced (unskilled) in righteousness. They do not know how to work out their own salvation (see Philippians 2:12-13).

Every believer has experienced some sort of an emotional pain and/or troublesome times in their lives. Many of these events create an emotional wound in us. When these emotional pains are not healed they produce a 'sore spot' in our soul. These sore spots, being emotional in nature, become a root of bitterness or hardness of heart. These roots of bitterness not only generate unresolved anger but they also cause frustration to manifest in an individual. Roots of bitterness also cause many to be defiled when they do not forgive or release others from their wrongs (see Hebrews 12:15). What does the Scripture mean when it uses the term defiled? It means, "to be tainted or contaminated" and articulates both moral and physical defilement. Deuteronomy 29 speaks of the covenant that God renewed with His people and the passage speaks of a poisonous root. The Lord dealt with the subject of bitterness in this passage and it carries a warning.

"Lest there should be among you man, or woman, or family, or tribe,
whose heart turneth away this day from the Lord our God, to go
and serve the gods of these nations; lest there should be among you
a root that bears gall and wormwood; And it come to pass, when he
hears the words of this curse, that he bless himself in his heart,
saying, I shall have peace, though I walk in the imagination of mine heart,
to add drunkenness to thirst: The Lord will not spare him..."
(Deuteronomy 29:18-20a)

The warning about the 'root' (8328) that causes gall or wormwood to be produced is direct and concise. The Hebrew word translated as 'root' is defined as "the bottom or depth" within something or someone. The primary meaning of the word means, "to pluck from." It is expressing that it is the soil that produces the root and then the root produces the fruit. The type of soil that the root is in will produce the strength or the weakness of the root (see Matthew 13). In other words, it is the strength of the soil that determines the strength or depth of the root. Specifically it is the depth of the good soil that determines the depth of the good root, because the root travels to its source of nourishment. Like the orange tree, when something is planted over the old roots, it will follow a similar path to its source. If one has a root of bitterness and tries to plant something else in its place, the new situation will follow an old course.

One such problem is serial monogamy. Old bitterness is replaced with new mates. The consequence of a series of relationships, when the root of the problem has not been dealt with, will be that divorce or a troubled marriage is the end result. Now we see why it is vitally important to know what path the root has taken within the life of a person. It will always take the path that the soil allows it to take. If there is good soil nurturing the root, the root will produce good fruit. If the soil is bad the root will produce bad fruit. Jesus declared that the soil is the heart within us (see Matthew 13:19). If the root has tapped into the old man the fruit will always be earthy, sensual, or devilish (see James 3:15). For example, if one's righteousness is not rooted in faith, then another root has produced his view of justification. "For other foundation can no man lay than that which was laid" (see 1 Corinthians 3:11). If our foundation was laid in Jesus the depth of the root goes to Jesus. If the depth of the root of our salvation was laid in doctrine, then the origin of our salvation is in doctrine. Some people have an undetected problem within their walk as a believer. The foundation laid in their life was not laid in Christ, but in their doctrine or theory of Him. Even though the name of Jesus is being used, their doctrine of Jesus (i.e., what they believe about Jesus) becomes their imparted truth rather than what is written in the Scriptures. Many religious groups follow this line of thinking.

"Many will come in my name, saying,
I am Christ; and shall deceive many."
(Matthew 24:5)

These groups say that Jesus is the Savior, but many are led astray by their doctrine and attitudes of how salvation is received. Salvation is received (to them) through their doctrinal belief system. When someone's faith is not based on God's redemptive plan and when one's salvation is anchored in believing in some doctrine, this is false conversion. For example, a minister had an issue about authority. He began to preach that if you did not submit to what he said it was because you were not a part of the Kingdom of God. This doctrinal belief system was formulated over a number of years and his congregation had submitted to this teaching. No one wanted to be disobedient to God and he had taught that when the church leaders spoke, God spoke through them. The Scripture is clear that God does speak through the prophets, but he had taken this premise in to Shepherding. This shored up his position and his control to the degree that this congregation viewed him as one who was never wrong in his judgment of another brother. He had maneuvered them into idolatry and the congregation not aware of it. When he said to someone "you are not saved," the people at that church took it as the gospel truth. They were so bound by idolatry that when someone would show them the Scriptures they would answer, "that is not what we believe." They had received a doctrine of devils and then they began to propagate that doctrine. If you did not believe their way, you were not a part of the Body of Christ. There are many cult groups in America who teach certain unbiblical concepts about Jesus. They deceive many by convincing them that salvation is attained through a belief in their doctrinal stance about Jesus, rather than faith in Jesus. This is becoming increasingly apparent in our nation. Many kinds of individuals have their faith rooted in something other than the risen Christ. They are sectarian and will not receive those who do not believe their doctrine. This is happening in many "main stream" denominational groups who will not accept another church's baptism, even when it is a Scriptural emersion. They only accept their denominational baptism as though they are the only true religious group.

Faith is more than mental assent or recognition of who the historical Jesus was. Faith is trust in the work of Christ, the belief that He is the Son of God, and the assurance that He is resurrected from the dead with the confidence of His return. Salvation is attained when we accept the Savior God has given. When we are aware of these false types of conversions, the question arises; what about those who are truly born again and yet fail in their walk? When we review Hebrews 5:13-14, we receive a simple explanation of this phenomenon. To briefly paraphrase the passage:

> "Babies are not experienced in the word of righteousness. They
> have forgotten how they were saved. The mature are able to overcome
> because they are experienced in separating the lies of their senses
> from the truth of their place in Christ."

The Greek word translated as 'senses' (145) is defined as "the organ of perception," and comes from the root meaning 'to apprehend' (by the 'senses'). The word simply means' "the organ of the soul." The senses "apprehend" something (i.e., the organ of the soul takes hold of something, like a thought, that has come into the mind). Because babes are inexperienced they misdirect their thoughts through the old man. The spiritually immature, when they have not been discipled, do not realize that their soul is without any mechanism to limit its 'will'; it has no 'governor'. Their spirit is quickened, but their mind, will, and the temperament have not been trained to redirect the path of the root through the new man. They cannot discern the proper response to the temptation they face. They are generally and usually captured by sin; the kind of sin that "so easily besets them" (see Hebrews 12:1). Even though they are compassed about with so great a cloud of witnesses, they do not know how to lay aside the weight or the sin that so easily snares them. The Greek word translated as the word 'weight' (3591) means 'an ache'. The weight of sin is the emotional ache or sore spot the root produces. When sin sprouts its roots they become frayed into multitudes of bitter or poison roots. In the untrained spiritual babe time has become the enemy. Spiritual babes are easily defiled because of these soul aches. Also, the Greek word translated as 'beset' (2139) in Hebrews 12:1 means "to well stand around". These things 'stand around' in the life of the believer just waiting to break through the surface. They are just hanging around like the sin at Cain's door (see Genesis 4:6-7) waiting for you to acknowledge them and, like Cain, spiritual babes fail because they listen to the lie. What was Cain's failure? What way did Cain follow (see Jude 11)? He did not deal with the thought that came to his mind. The thought of rejection manifested itself and since he did not take it captive, the thought matured into the murder of his brother because of the lie he believed.

Another way to view this is that spiritual babes do not know how to lay these things aside. They do not know how to distinguish between the reality of what they are experiencing, and the lie their soul is propagating. When one is a babe in Christ their thoughts lead them down a familiar path. When one is not experienced in taking the thought captive, the thought will take them captive. How does this transpire? The Scripture teaches us that the organ of the soul in the babe does not know how to separate and clarify the good and evil of their emotion. For example, if one was abused as a child the bitterness of the experience remains in them until they have been delivered from the root of that ache. Even when they have been set free in Jesus the path of the root will remain in their old man if it has not been dealt with. Even when the root is removed and the void is filled, over time the path of the root is still remembered in the soul. It is like a scar. The path of the root is the journey the root takes to its depth in one's soul (i.e., to its foundation or beginning). When someone experiences a 'familiar spirit' (i.e., a familiar disposition, thought, attitude or emotion) ten or fifteen years after an event has actually happened, the original force of the emotion is released into the present situation because they have channeled their senses through the old man.

The path of the root can be tapped into at any time. When the thought comes it taps into the path of the root, the senses apprehend the emotion and release it through fear or some other pertinent sensation. For the babe the wound is opened when these past feelings flood into the present and for all practical purposes the past experience is relived as though it just occurred in the emotional realm, or it rushes up and you have to get it under control. The warning of God in Deuteronomy 29 is for every man, woman, family, or people; if they discover an internal root that is poisonous or that produces a root of bitterness, they should not fall into the trap of self-deception. When we walk in the imagination of our heart, the Word says we add 'drunkenness to thirst'. The root definition of the word 'imagination' in Deuteronomy 29:19 means, 'obstinacy': "to be firmly opposite or hostile." A spiritual child will believe and imagine things that are opposite from the truth at times. They may live and react as though the emotions they feel from their past are a present reality. By example, if a man or a woman has been abused in a past relationship they will react to present situations through bitterness or fear. Their emotional level should be low to moderate when something similar occurs, but when the path of that root has been channeled through their old man, they have the potential to react to a situation violently and become out of control at the slightest offence. These things are common when the path of the root touches emotional bruises. Many of us have experienced this and can understand why people sometimes "freak out."

If you are reactionary, it is the evidence of immaturity. The immature are not able to rightly choose the proper course of action. The true deception manifests when these things are present in one's life and yet they are blind to it. This is how the behavior of a believer grows into hypocrisy. Jesus said, "If the light that is in you be darkness, how great is that darkness (see Matthew 6:23)." The mature believer has nothing to hide. Spiritual children play hide and seek. They try to hide their failures and past mistakes. They try to hide their "self" as though God is blind and they will deny that they have any emotional aches. Babes believe that if they can hide certain internal issues or if they ignore them they will go away. Babes forget their place of righteousness. The only thing that covers sin is the blood of Jesus and one must accept His forgiveness and sacrificial work. When I do not confess my sin, I lie against the truth. James 5:16 states, "confess your faults one to another, and pray for one another, that ye may be healed." The implication of this passage is that we are healed through the process of confessing our faults to one another and by praying together about them. Let wisdom prevail.

When you imagine that you can be emotionally healed without Christ, it is called delusion.

> "And for this cause God shall send them strong
> delusion, that they should believe a lie."
> (2 Thessalonians 2:11)

How does this delusion occur? It occurs because people do not receive the truth of love. They have believed something that was not godly. The mystery of iniquity is working in them, and they will oppose or exalt themselves above God or God's Word (see 2 Thessalonians 2:4). The sign and the wonder that Satan brought (see 2 Thessalonians 2:9) was a lie! Their 'delusion' (4106) has gripped them. The word 'delusion' means 'fraudulence.' The root of the word means "to be an impostor or to mislead." Their feelings were a fraud and misled them. A pseudo emotion has been attached to their present situation and they see it as reality. If we have not been founded in our Christian faith or edified in the truth of Christian doctrine and Satan lies to us, our stability in Christ is shaken. When we are not anchored in the truth we believe the lie of separation. Hope is "the anchor of the soul" (see Hebrews 6:19). Hope is the one thing that will help us to be secure in our emotions. Without hope, doubt can be introduced into the mind because a path of the root was portered into our soul (see John 10:3). Because Satan has deceived us he can now have his way with us.

Doubt is one of the doors Satan uses. There are several kinds of doubt in the New Testament. Their meanings range from "to take away the soul" (see John 10:24), "to separate thoroughly or withdraw from" (see Matthew 21:21, Romans 14:23, Acts 10:20), "to debate or to have internal discussion" (see Romans 14:1, 1 Timothy 2:8), "to be perplexed or confused" (see Acts 2:12, Acts 5:24), "to duplicate or waver" (see Matthew 14:21 and 28:17), and "to suspend or fluctuate" (see Luke 12:29). All of these have a common root. That root is in *pride*. Pride appears in one's life before they fail (see Proverbs 16:18). Proverbs 11:2 says that "when pride comes, then comes shame." The chart below expresses the way of sin and way of righteousness. The first evidence of sin is pride. Pride is the platform sin uses to work from. Sin then manifests into separation because separation is the first thing sin produces. Sin is a divider. Pride separates by making a distinction. Pride elevates itself as something it is not. This is why we are commanded to not think of ourselves more highly than we ought to think. When separation is established it then gives birth to rebellion. This rebellion results in spiritual death if it is left unchecked.

SIN		RIGHTEOUSNESS
Pride	The First Evidence	Peace
Separation	The First Work	Quietness
Rebellion	The Manifestation	Assurance
Error	The Result	Truth

Righteousness is opposite of sin as it brings us together. The first evidence of righteousness is the peace one has. This peace is an experience of rest (i.e., rest in our conscious mind - see Hebrews 9:14). When righteousness is present it affects the believer by producing a quietness of spirit through the salvation of one's soul. This manifests in assurance and stability of faith. The result of righteousness is a heart full of truth and confidence. The strategy of Satan is to use pride to unsettle our peace, he uses separation to affect our quietness, he uses rebellion to affect our assurance, and he uses error to affect our truth. Satan is skilled in manipulation and deception. He is the father of lies. He will use a one percent perversion of truth if that is all you give him. But Satan continues his efforts until he gets five percent, then ten percent, and so on. He never gives up. Mature Christians are experienced in the ways of righteousness and are not ignorant of his devices (see 2 Corinthians 2:11). Mature Christians are aware that Satan is relentless. Again, the word 'devices' (3540) means, "purpose, perception, and disposition" and is also translated as the word 'mind' (see 2 Corinthians 3:14, 4:4, 11:3, and Philippians 4:7), and as the word 'thought' (see 2 Corinthians 10:5) in the New Testament. Satan's thought planted within an individual is his device to produce spiritual death. He takes us on a journey of death rather than on a journey of life although he does not have the power of death anymore. Remember, Jesus took his keys. Satan therefore uses deception to get us to choose death. If the path of the root is not dealt with in one's soul, it will remain as a familiar path that directs the thought back to its carnal source. These familiar paths give place to familiar spirits. These paths do not leave unless one is discipled and set free through the deliverance process. Deliverance is not some mystical happening. Deliverance from these paths comes when true repentance is experienced. Repentance is the greatest and simplest form of deliverance. "It is the goodness of God that leads me to repentance." Repentance is a gift. The Bible states, "God peradventure will give them repentance (see 2 Timothy 2:25)." When we struggle through certain areas we should realize that we have a choice. We can pursue our own deliverance, which generally does not fully occur, or we can search for a true father or mother in the faith who will lead us through the healing process and personal restoration. One can experience deliverance individually, but the time can be shortened greatly when one is fathered (discipled) through the process. It must be said that not every minister is a spiritual father. Only people who are committed to the completion of the Christian's maturity and those who have been fathered can father others in the faith. You can only give and recreate what you are. All others will try to father out of their theory rather than by their experience of son-ship. True fathers and mothers in the faith raise their babies. "A child left unto its self will bring his mother shame" (see Proverbs 29:15).

The "path of the root" is a revelation that exposes the journey of emotional stress in the heart and soul. Every minister and counselor must recognize that these paths are a part of our lives. They are common and are widespread. Just the disclosure of these paths, many times, produces healing. Anointed preaching touches these areas in the congregation and healing occurs quietly, yet powerfully. At other times, the removal of a rotten root is a long and tedious process, but in the end, as we preach, we set the captive free. This is what we are called to do in ministry.

> "For this is the will of God, even your sanctification…
> That every one of you should know how to possess his vessel in
> sanctification and honor; Not in the lust of concupiscence,
> even as the Gentiles which know not God."
> (1 Thessalonians 4:3a-5)

The Greek word translated as 'lust' (3806) in the above passage is *pathos*. 'Pathos' is defined as "the soul's diseased condition out of which the various lusts spring." Pathos is also defined as 'an experience' (i.e., an emotion which is usually derived from a wound or a suffering). Pathos is the path of the root. 'Concupiscence' is defined as a 'longing', and its root word means "to set the heart upon." "Set your heart on things above" and keep your heart as you would "defend a city". Deliverance comes when we can control our soul. Then we can control the path any root may try to take. This is also known as being 'mature'.

Chapter 17 – Measuring Maturity

"But the natural man does not receive the
things of the Spirit of God...
because they are spiritually discerned.
But he that is spiritual judges all things...
And I, brethren, could not speak unto
you as unto spiritual, but as unto carnal,
even as unto babies in Christ."
(1 Corinthians 2:14-15 and 3:1)

There are several ideologies about spiritual maturity, many of which are based on "being filled with or baptized in the Spirit," as though this consummates the Christian experience. Some people believe that when you get filled with the Holy Spirit that equals maturity. Others have a concept that a college degree, being a Pastor, or some denominational hurdle must be climbed in order for you to gain spiritual maturity. But the real measure of spiritual maturity can be easily defined as the depth of our love for God, and coming out of a natural or carnal mindset.

The Bible gives us a clearer understanding of how God measures the maturity of believers. Paul in the opening passage is describing three different "vectors" that one may have emanating from their foundation. Paul teaches that every individual has a perspective, and that it is from this perspective that a common point of reference originates (i.e., the vectors). I use the example of 'vectors' from geometry because they give a better explanation of what I believe the Lord wishes to reveal to us. Consider this: geometry teaches that it takes two points to make a straight line. These points, the origin and the vector, give a line's starting point and an additional point that determines its direction. In other words, our spiritual origin should establish our foundational view of life; one's perspective establishes his direction and one's perspective is determined by his will. Some have natural tendencies, originating from a natural mindset. Others have carnal tendencies, which originate from a divisive heart and some have spiritual tendencies that originate from their spirit and the newness of their life in Christ. The Greek word translated, as our human 'will' is defined, "to make a decision and act upon it." Every perspective that an individual has is commonly called "a line of thinking." Every time we have a personal point of view about any subject we will without thought use our perspective to make an assessment of the subject. This is commonly called "our world and life view." With this understanding, we must ask the question: "Does our world and life view originate and point in a spiritual, carnal, or natural direction?" Many times we do not realize that we speak our opinions about matters and are not speaking from a spiritual origin. The attitudes that have a carnal or natural point of view cause many believers to build their theological concepts by biblically unsound measures. Our origin depends greatly on the wisdom we live by. This wisdom is either from God or it is a carnal or natural line of wisdom. Is our wisdom from above, or from below? Is it earthy, sensual, and devilish, or is it pure, peaceable, gentle, and easily entreated (see James 3:13-18)? How can we grow beyond the natural man's perspective, press through the carnality of our soul, and become the spiritual person God has called us to be? Only when we operate from a spiritual origin will we be successful in this matter. Can we accomplish the task of spiritual maturity through church attendance alone or must we rise above the norm of the modern Christian perspective to a height that supersedes even our own expectations? Can we answer the question honestly when asked: On which side of the fence are we standing? With this in mind let us continue.

The Natural Origin

The Scripture gives us a clear description of the natural man. "The natural man does not receive the things of God" (see 1 Corinthians 2:14). It is impossible for one who has a natural or worldly mindset to receive from the Spirit of God. The word 'receive' in the original language of the New Testament is the word *dechomai* (1209) and means, "to accept" or "to take something." The natural man will not accept the things of God. He will not take hold of the ways of God, or the principles God has commanded him to live by. This is why Proverbs 16:25 states;

> "There is a way that seems right to a man,
> but the end thereof are the ways of death."

These 'ends' are multiple. One with a natural perspective in life comes to many ends, which in turn lead to the very end of death or destruction. To the natural man his way seems to be right, but he sets himself on a course of action that, within his own logic and reasoning causes him to accept it as being right or godly, never knowing his journey will have a dead end. He will spend his time and energy pursuing a natural lifestyle he esteems to be wholesome, even when he has been instructed and given evidence that his ways are erroneous. He will continue to press in the direction his mindset has led him to follow.

Believers are responsible for their actions toward God and others. Some individuals focus on things such as dress codes or hairstyles, but leave the weightier matters of godliness and virtue unattended. If the clothes of an individual are 'naturally' inclined (i.e., if they wear sensuous attire), correction should come. Correction is part of the process when we want to oversee our soul. Those who focus on the outer appearance give little time to the inner being because their focus is on their "self." How they look, how they fit in, how they measure up to the standards the world has set for them is their focus.

Natural people focus on the natural concepts of life without knowing that they are doing it. The spiritual man separates the precious from the vile (see Jeremiah 15:19). If the vile raises its head in your life, put it back into submission. Some people think it is a sin to wear make-up. That is generally because they are trying to mandate some form of holiness. Holiness is not determined by the outward adorning, but it is by our 'ways' that we will be judged. The inward origin and perspective may manifest in one's outward appearance, but it is the way we become Christ-like that determines our maturity. Some may look on the outward appearance, but God looks on the heart. I bless my wife because of her heart, not because she wears her hair a certain way. Others will recognize how blessed I am through my wife's faithfulness, not by the clothes she wears. (Modesty is the key. We should not dress as though we are trying to attract another people's attention. That is not profitable for any marriage or relationship.) The husband or the wife seeking attention outside the marriage is an indication that a problem exists within that household. You know there is a problem in a home when the husband, wife, or children are out of order. You may not be able to identify it, but you discern that a problem exists.

1 Corinthians 2:14 reveals that a person with a natural origin and vector will believe that the things of God (anything spiritual) are foolishness to them. He considers them silly and absurd and that is what the word 'foolishness' means. The Greek word translated as 'foolishness' in this passage is the Greek word *moros* (3474). We get the English word 'moron' from it. The naturally minded person considers the things of God to be morbid, dull, stupid, and without real purpose. Naturally inclined people are bored with spiritual matters. These are individuals who will not give spiritual matters any consideration. Pride gets in the way and hinders them from fulfilling their call and purpose in God. They cannot know the ways of God, nor are they able to turn toward faith in a full and lasting way. A new mindset must be pursued (i.e., a new way of thinking) which is the only thing that will change the old man into the new man. This is why the Scripture says we must be renewed in the "spirit of your mind" (see Ephesians 4:23 & Philippians 1:27).

The Carnal Origin

The 'carnal' or self-idolized person also has a number of distinct characteristics. The carnal man's view of himself is shaded with self-worth. His relationship to others, as well as his relationship to the Lord, is a reflection of his own selfishness. He sees himself as being the center of his world and everything revolves around him. His carnal worldview will always be at the center of his framework, whether he is relating to people or to circumstances. The carnal man is self-conscious and self-absorbed. He wants everything his way or you must take the highway. The word 'carnal' comes from the Greek word *sarkikos* (4559) and means, 'fleshly'. In other words, when one is 'carnal' they have fleshly pursuits. The word 'carnal' also carries the idea of a person's vanity. They are mainly concerned with the outer man rather than the inner person, especially how they are seen or viewed by others. If you tell a carnal person that they are immature, get ready for the fit. At its worst, carnality is like the 'terrible twos.' A synonym in the Greek language to *sarkikos* is the Greek word *psuchikos* or 'soulishness'. These words are used widely in the New Testament. Paul tells us to "work out the salvation of our souls" and in Luke 21:19 he says, "in your patience posses ye your soul."

The carnal man can be seen in the life of King Saul. Before he became a king he viewed himself as an insignificant individual (i.e., he was humble). After he became a king something changed in his mind. No longer did he need to wait on God's man, Samuel, to lead or direct him. He thought he was able to sacrifice in Samuel's place. No longer did he have to do what God commanded, for after all he was the king! Being the king in Saul's eyes caused him to believe that he was not subject to anyone's terms or commands except his own. When Saul found himself in disobedience, he would blame others for his failures. Saul's attitude when he disobeyed was that "the people made me do it." He felt justified in his own mind that what he had done was right. He always had another way to accomplish his task rather than the way God had commanded. When David came into the picture, Saul hated him because the people gave David honor. The carnal man wants glory and does not want anyone else to have prestige in his presence. He has a tendency to talk down to you. If you share a word, he has a better word. If the Lord has spoken to you, he is quick to define it as being less significant than what he has heard from God. If you share an experience, he has had it too, though his is better! It is Satan's way to be full of pride and to not submit to authority; Satan imparted that into man at the fall. Carnality will cause people to strive for place, power, honor, and control. Carnality demands control, either by subtle or open means. It is easy for someone to see the carnality in others, yet virtually impossible for them to see it in themselves without the Lord's help.

Carnality is the very thing that causes strife and division in the home, as well as in the Church. Paul says you are a babe and carnal when strife and division are present with you. A carnal person will stir up envy, strife, and division everywhere they go. When one has carnality as the origin of their direction in life, according to 1 Corinthians 3:2 they cannot maintain the lifestyle of the mature believer. They are not able to. Carnal individuals must be fed with milk. (The term "milk" in this passage is idiomatic in the language of the New Testament. An idiom is a word that is used to reflect a meaning other than the one normally intended. When we say, "That guy is a nut!" We mean he is crazy or out of control, and use the word idiomatically.) The word 'milk' represents teaching or basic instruction. The use of idiomatic language also applies to the word "meat"; it means 'lifestyle' and 'ability'. Paul stated, "I have fed you with milk, and not with meat: for hither to you are not able to bear it." Carnal individuals must be taught and re-taught. They have a form of godliness, but never come to the knowledge of the truth. They are given spiritual direction, but cannot effectively live out the Christian experience. The overriding factor in the Christian must be love. Love is the key, but natural and carnal people find it difficult to love others.

Maturity can be directly measured by the way one enters into communion in the Body of Christ. Our personal communion should be multi-faceted in our interaction and fellowship, not just in the ordinance of partaking the bread and wine. Carnal people struggle through life trying to love their brethren, but are unable to manifest the love the Lord has commanded us to live by in a full and meaningful way. They will have a reason why they do not love unconditionally and without a judgmental attitude toward others. It is the other brother who is in sin, or they will have some personal grievance that will manifest against another. To the carnal person there is a logical reason why they have the offense against another. Jesus taught us that offense must come, but "woe to that man by whom the offense" comes. We will all be offended occasionally, but the person who takes hold of the offense and maintains the offense shows that he is carnal.

Prejudice often is a factor in the carnal man. When we, with or without a reason, are offended, our heavenly Father does not accept that offence in any form. He straightforwardly commands us to leave our gift at the altar and to go and get the situation resolved before we return. And again, the Scripture teaches us that God looks on the heart and not the outer man. Carnality will look on the outer and never consider the heart of the one they are judging. The tragedy in carnality is that carnal people judge themselves by their intentions and others by their actions. If you correct a carnal person with the Word, they will rebel because they cannot see the error in their ways or they feel that you are a subordinate to them and have no authority to correct them. Even if they have repetitious failures they are blinded to the truth of it. Paul shows us that when envy, strife, and division are in a congregation they are "walking as mere men," and not as men of God. The carnal person, the babe, and tares are all labels the Bible uses to describe people who have not come to an understanding of God's ways. We are commanded to grow in love, and yes, it is a process. The Scripture teaches us that our works and service for the Lord will be burned up if we do not love one another and are carnal.

The Spiritual Origin

The Spiritual man walks according to God's grace. He is an active participant in the ways of God. The spiritual man compares spiritual things with spiritual (see 1 Corinthians 2:13). He is able to judge according to the Spirit in any situation. This enables him to combine various aspects of any issue into a cohesive understanding of what is actually taking place within the life of any person. The spiritual man knows the deep things of God. He is not void in understanding the mystery of God's will (see Ephesians 1:9-10). He is continuously learning the truth and is full of life (see Proverbs 16:21-24).

Spiritual people are relational people. Their personal walk with the Lord reflects in their personal walk within their church and its members. Intimacy is not foreign to them. As a person of wisdom they pursue unions of peace (i.e., lasting friendships). In their personal life they do not accept the excuses their old man tries to manifest. They are a challenged people. Wisdom teaches them to discern all things that pertain and relate to them. They do not feel threatened by exposure. When you have a spiritual origin you have nothing to hide and will not allow sin to reign over you. The spiritual person has a 'fasted' lifestyle (a life of moderation). Not just a person who fasts, but one who lives temperately in all things. One with a spiritual origin will not try to cover over their personal sin. They seek God's Presence to overcome anything that has become a hindrance to their spiritual being. They strive for Christian maturity, will not accept second best in their relationship with the Father, and this is evident in the relationships they have with their Christian brothers and sisters. There is a longing and a desire for the greatest of fellowship with the Lord. The only offence they hold is with Satan and not the family of God. The spiritual man lives within the baptism of repentance. They continuously monitor their walk by a 'carefulness' (4710) of lifestyle (see 2 Corinthians 7:11). They are focused and are set on 'clearing themselves' (627) of any attempted attack of the enemy or wrongdoing they find in their life. They have 'indignation' (24) toward the devil and his attacks. (Indignation is our annoyance with the problems our flesh creates within us. The Greek word means, "to be greatly moved.") Spiritual people are vexed in spirit when areas of their lives cause them to fall, especially in matters pertaining to their walk with God (being vexed is an internal 'grieving of the spirit'). This indignation produces a 'fear' (5401) or spiritual reverence for God as we recognize the consequences of sin in our lives. Spiritual people recognize the truth of God's Word. They fight to take their thoughts captive, but they recognize how tempted they actually are. The spiritual person has a 'vehement desire' (1972) to overcome the flesh. This desire becomes compulsive in those who press into God's plan. It becomes a driving force within the believer to represent their Father in every area of their life.

One pitfall to watch out for is the old man's ability to push us into unrighteous thinking, which causes us to get into a 'law' mentality. A law mentality is where we began to feel as though the Lord doesn't love us when we fail or do not do some particular religious thing. It is a trick of the soul that makes us feel as though we must do something to make up for our failures. A righteous desire pushes us into a longing for the Lord. The spiritual person's need for complete fellowship with the Father cannot be countered. The spiritual person will not accept a second-best attitude and they have a desire to change. They develop 'zeal' (2205) toward obedience. Their heart is fixed on serving God within the direction and purpose of the Lord's Word. They will not compromise with the carnal confinements placed upon them. There is no room for compromise within the heart of the spiritual person. They quickly retaliate against Satan to 'revenge' (1557) the hindrances demonic activity creates within their soul and life. The spiritual person will take custody of Satan when he attacks! They know their place in Christ and they stand on their convictions. The spiritual men and women of God meet Satan at the gate of their life and are determined to be 'clear' (53) in every aspect of repentance. The spiritual person has recognizable strength; they operate in the power of the Holy Spirit, and have risen above the carnality of the age. They are aware that in these last days many are being influenced by demonic forces, so they keep themselves guarded against the enemy's power. They will press toward the mark of the high calling of God, and not fear the fellowship of His suffering (see Philippians 3:10).

This is the way we measure our spiritual life. We are not measured by our wealth, place, power, or name. There is one name under heaven and in earth to whom we will be compared. You and I will meet Him face to face soon enough!

Chapter 18 – Unfolding Christ's Ministry

"A Study of the Pastor/Teacher, the Evangelist, the Prophet, and the Apostle"

Many of the issues that will be addressed in this chapter will not be the typical traditional line of thinking that so many believers are familiar with. I will also repeat some of the information I have already covered in earlier chapters, due to my desire to show how relational many aspects of Scripture are. I will also show how they associate in the various aspects of our ministry. I apologize for the redundancy, but I believe it is necessary in the overall study of the ascension order of God's government gifts.

For many years I have studied the Bible in relation to ministers and ministry, but I do not find a correlation between what I have seen in the modern Church and what the Bible has to say about Apostles, Prophets, Evangelists, and Teaching Pastors. I have found that many ministers are frustrated with their Pastoral role, duties, and the box they have been put into. Pastoring has a God ordained purpose, but our limited understanding of the Kingdom's operation causes Pastors to minister in a constrained anointing that limits their true unction and function. The Church has held on to many of the old traditional concepts of ministry formulated at the beginning of the Reformation. We must put aside many of these old concepts of ministry and administration, and search the Scriptures for the true manifestation of the four-fold ministry.

The Shepherd/Teacher

"And he gave some, apostles; and some, prophets; and some,
evangelists; and some, pastors and teachers..."
(Ephesians 4:11)

We have all heard the term "five-fold ministry," but when you take an exegetical look at Ephesians 4:11 you will find that it is a "four-fold ministry." As you read Ephesians 4:11 take notice of the word "some" which identifies each of the four *doma* gifts. Traditionally these are seen as five gifts, but the word 'some' is an identifier of only four. The word 'some' is an affirmation of each of the individual gifts. The Greek definite article simply means "the, this, that, one, he, she, it," etc., but it identifies each gift specifically. Also the Greek phrase translated as "pastors and teachers" is ποιμενας και διδασκαλους (in the Greek) that would be better translated as "pastor teachers" or "teaching pastors." The Greek word και (2532) translated as 'and' in the phrase, is "a primitive particle having a copulative and sometimes also a cumulative force; and, also, even, so, then, too, etc." In other words και joins the words "pastor and teacher" together making them a "pastor teacher" or "teaching pastor." This runs contrary to the common thought in today's Church, but a study of the Scripture will prove my exegesis to be true that every minister must be a teacher. Let us begin by looking at a well-known passage in John 21:15-17:

> "So when they had dined, Jesus saith to Simon Peter,
> Simon, son of Jonas, lovest thou me more than these?
> He saith unto him, Yea, Lord; thou knowest that I love thee.
> He saith unto him, feed (1) my lambs. He saith to him
> again the second time, Simon, son of Jonas, lovest thou
> me? He saith unto him, Yea, Lord; thou knowest that
> I love thee. He saith unto him, feed (2) my sheep.
> He saith unto him the third time, Simon, son of Jonas,
> lovest thou me? Peter was grieved because he said unto
> him the third time, Lovest thou me? And he said unto
> him, Lord, thou knowest all things; thou knowest
> that I love thee. Jesus saith unto him, feed (3) my sheep."

Most of the times I have heard this passage preached, the preacher focuses on the word 'love' and its different meanings. Let us, for this subject, focus on the word 'feed' and we will get another view of Jesus' intent in the passage.

The first time Jesus tells Peter to 'feed' the lambs, the Greek word *bosko* (1006) is used. *Bosko* is defined in the Strong's Concordance as "to pasture" or to "tend" the sheep, while Thayer states the definition this way; "to feed: portraying the duty of a Christian teacher to promote in every way the spiritual welfare of the members of the church." When speaking of 'lambs' (i.e., babes in Christ), Jesus is making a point about the necessity to pasture or tend to them differently than the other sheep. Lambs are vulnerable and need to be tended with oversight to keep the wolves from stealing them (see 1 Samuel 17:34; Isaiah 5:17 and 40:11) and the older sheep from harming them. Yet the second time Jesus uses the word to 'feed' the sheep, the Greek word *poimaino* (4165) is used, which is defined as "to tend as a shepherd" (or figuratively a supervisor) is used. When shepherding the sheep the teaching pastor has a different role of 'supervising' versus 'protecting.' Yet the third time Jesus uses the word to 'feed' the sheep, He returns to the word *bosko*. When we put it all together we find that Jesus is saying, "If you love Me, pasture the lambs" with their status in mind. Babes in

Christ should be cared for differently than older believers. One of the common practices in our local churches is to 'pasture' the babes and the older sheep together. We herd them all into the sanctuary and feed them all the same food. It is common knowledge that babes need milk and not meat (see Hebrews 5:12), yet we shovel meat to them and hope they do not choke. If they start 'choking', the general answer is: "they need more faith". It is not more faith that is necessary; it is milk that is they need. Babes cannot digest meat until their spiritual digestive systems have matured. Jesus used the word *bosko* to relate this issue to Peter. Jesus was in essence teaching Peter how to be a loving shepherd by using the two words in the context of the passage.

Let us learn a lesson about the shepherd/teacher from the book of Proverbs.

> "The desire of the righteous is only good: but the expectation of the wicked is wrath. There is that scattereth, and yet increaseth; and there is that withholdeth more than is meet, but it tendeth to poverty. The liberal soul shall be made fat: and he that watereth shall be watered also himself. He that withholdeth corn, the people shall curse him: but blessing shall be upon the head of him that selleth it. He that diligently seeketh good procureth favour: but he that seeketh mischief, it shall come unto him. He that trusteth in his riches shall fall: but the righteous shall flourish as a branch. He that troubleth his own house shall inherit the wind: and the fool shall be servant to the wise of heart. The fruit of the righteous is a tree of life; and he that winneth souls is wise."
> (Proverbs 11:23-30)

We find rich and marvelous advice to the shepherd/teacher in this passage. If the shepherd has expectation and the sheep do not meet his expectation, it will cause him to "make an outburst at times," as the Bible puts it. This is the definition of the word 'wrath' (5678) in verse twenty-three. When the shepherd scatters the seed of God's word, it increases, but when he withholds the necessary word from the Body, it leads to spiritual poverty. The words 'increase' (3254) and 'poverty' (4270) are at odds with each other in this passage.

Bringing increase is the result of the distribution that comes from the 'overflow' in one's heart. When the Holy Spirit is leading and you do not follow His unction because of the "fear of man," the Body of Christ is not getting the necessary and proper food the Lord intends for them to have; this leads to spiritual poverty and the result will be a malnourished church. This idea is carried over into verse twenty-five which tells us that the 'blessings' that the shepherd ministers will result in his personal blessedness. If the teaching shepherd withholds "the corn, the wine, or the oil," the people will curse, that is, speak evil of him. The teaching shepherd must freely scatter the word of God by diligent prayer and study, he must move in the power of the Spirit, and he must distribute his anointing in an open and free way (without reservation).

Verse twenty-seven is conveying that backbiting and speaking "evil" of God's people will bring it right back to you again. You will reap what you sow. The godly shepherd will avoid the temptation to criticize church members, knowing it only produces division and strife in the church (a description of 'carnal' people). Another temptation to avoid is the money trap. Satan uses this weapon against many godly men to turn them with a spirit of 'whoredoms' (see Ezekiel 16). If the shepherd finds that he distressed financially, he will find that prayer goes much further than manipulation or whining. Much complaining about your needs and asking for more may get you a bit more money, but it will also get you a bad reputation quickly. The 'fruit of righteousness' (see Hebrews 12:11 and James 3:18) will carry the shepherd/teacher through tough times, and a clear focus on winning souls through discipleship will cause the Body of Christ to bless you more readily than will complaining. This is some sound advice from the Old Testament. Paul gives similar advice:

> "For I determined not to know any thing among you,
> save Jesus Christ, and him crucified. And I was
> with you in weakness, and in fear, and in much trembling.
> And my speech and my preaching was not with enticing words of man's
> wisdom, but in demonstration of the Spirit and of power:
> That your faith should not stand in the wisdom of men,
> but in the power of God."
> (1 Corinthians 2:2-5)

Humility and an understanding heart (see 1 Kings 3:9) will carry the shepherd/teacher into the depths of God's wisdom. An 'understanding heart' is a hearing heart. A heart in tune with God is one in which God can put His trust. The greatest lesson I have learned in all my years of service to the Lord is the message Jesus gave Mary and John when He was on the cross:

> "When Jesus therefore saw his mother, and the
> disciple standing by, whom he loved, he saith unto
> his mother, Woman, behold thy son! Then saith he
> to the disciple, Behold thy mother! And from that
> hour that disciple took her unto his own home."
> (John 19:26-27)

Does the Lord trust you enough to put His mother into your care? Of all the groups to whom Jesus ministered: the 5,000, the 70, the 12, and the 3, He was looking for the 1; the one He could trust.

Being a shepherd is an awesome responsibility. Your first and primary goal should be a virtuous ministry; to minister with integrity, being a person with godly character; one who has great depth in his constitution and one who seeks the Lord's glory over his own with a ministry that demonstrates the Kingdom of God. There are two ways to demonstrate the Spirit and power of the Kingdom. Acts 2:22 says that God shows His approval of us by manifesting miracles, wonders, and signs. These are the evidences of a godly Kingdom ministry. Changed lives are miracles, and wonders, and signs, but the status quo and church as usual are evidences of a backslidden ministry. Another demonstration of the Spirit and power is the effectiveness one's ministry in his community. Does your ministry stop at the church doors or are you ministering outside the church walls?

Before we can look at the ministry of the shepherd/teacher, every man and woman called of the Lord into His service must ponder these questions:

"And Moses' father in law said unto him,
The thing that thou doest is not good.
Thou wilt surely wear away, both thou, and this
people that is with thee: for this thing is too
heavy for thee; thou art not able to perform it
thyself alone. Hearken now unto my voice,
I will give thee counsel, and God shall be with thee:
Be thou for the people to God-ward, that
thou mayest bring the causes unto God:
And thou shalt teach them ordinances and laws, and
shalt shew them the way wherein they must
walk, and the work that they must do.
Moreover thou shalt provide out of all the people able men,
such as fear God, men of truth, hating covetousness;
and place such over them, to be rulers of thousands,
and rulers of hundreds, rulers of fifties, and rulers of tens:
And let them judge the people at all seasons:
and it shall be, that every great matter they shall
bring unto thee, but every small matter they
shall judge: so shall it be easier for thyself,
and they shall bear the burden with thee.
If thou shalt do this thing, and God command
thee so, then thou shalt be able to endure,
and all this people shall also go to their place in peace."
(Exodus 18:17-23)

One thing we find as we unfold the ministry and aspects of the shepherd/teacher is that the position is more of a title in the New Testament and a function in the modern Church. The word 'pastors' (*poimen*) is used only in Ephesians 4:11, but is translated as "shepherd(s)" and used only eighteen times in the New Testament. One can glean that the faithful shepherds watch diligently over their flocks, that the true shepherds enter by the door, that shepherds and hirelings are not the same, and that Jesus is the Shepherd and the Bishop of our souls. One would be hard pressed to find a Pastor of a church anywhere in the New Testament. Even the book of Acts never uses the terms "pastor" or "shepherd" when mentioning various aspects of church government, so we have to glean from the Old Testament many of the duties and functions of the shepherd/teacher. Apostles and Elders governed all the churches in the New Testament, and one thing to note is that no church in the New Testament had only one pastor; you always find more than one in the leadership positions.

Notice in Exodus 18 Jethro spells out the basic duties of the shepherd/teacher:

1. to teach ordinances and laws
2. teach the way wherein they must walk and
3. the work that they must do
4. they are to be rulers
5. they are to judge the people
6. and they are to help bear the burden of leadership

In the New Testament there are two passages that relate to the shepherd/teacher in similar fashion:

"Take heed therefore unto yourselves,
and to all the flock, over the which the
Holy Ghost hath made you overseers,
to feed the church of God, which he
hath purchased with his own blood."
(Acts 20:28)

"The elders which are among you I exhort,
who am also an elder, and a witness of the
sufferings of Christ, and also a partaker of the
glory that shall be revealed: Feed the flock of
God which is among you, taking the oversight
thereof, not by constraint, but willingly; not for filthy
lucre, but of a ready mind; Neither as being lords
over God's heritage, but being ensamples to the flock.
And when the chief Shepherd shall appear,
ye shall receive a crown of glory that fadeth not away."
(1 Peter 5:1-4)

Both passages use the Greek word *poimaino* when pertaining to feeding the flock of God and they both also bear witness that the shepherd/teachers are elders (overseers - Have you ever wondered who the "elders" were and how did they originate in the book of Acts? These are the elders Paul ordained as he traveled from town to town). Peter digs a bit deeper into the duties and includes some qualifications of the shepherds, reminding them that when the Chief Shepherd comes, He will give a reward to the faithful shepherds. In addition to these duties, the New Testament also says that the shepherd:

1. will lay down his life for the sheep
2. will be attacked
3. is a bishop
4. divides the sheep from the goats
5. has compassion for the sheep
6. will offend the sheep
7. must enter by the "door"
8. will fight off the wolves
9. understands the uniqueness of each of the sheep

There are also the five laws of God that we are to follow in the New Testament:

1. The law of the Spirit of Life – Romans 8:2
2. The law of Love – Romans 13:10; Matthew 22:37
3. The law of Christ – Galatians 6:2; Mark 12:30
4. The perfect law of Liberty – James 1:25; 2:12; Romans 14
5. The Royal law – James 2:8; Luke 10:27

Going beyond the duties of the shepherd we find that they can have different degrees of responsibility. Jethro said to set them over "tens, fifties, hundreds and thousands" showing that they vary in their personal responsibility and accountability. This shows that the shepherd, depending on his faithfulness, commitment, trustworthiness, and ability in administration can obtain a greater degree of honor. Jeremiah 33:12 writes about the "habitation of shepherds," which when operating properly, will cause rest to come to the local church.

In conclusion, the teaching shepherd functions in the local church and has a responsibility to rule over ten heads of families, fifty heads of families (five groups of ten), 100 heads of families (ten groups of ten), or a thousand heads of families (100 groups of ten). The lesson here is that when the local church grows, families can be divided into home churches (I like to call them *boskos*) and the sons in the faith can began shepherding these groups. As the sons in the faith mature, gain spiritual stature, and the signification of the Holy Spirit, they can gain greater administrative experience as an 'under-shepherd' and mature in their anointing and spiritual abilities. The *boskos* provide growing space and a training field for the sons in the faith and allow the Church leaders to oversee the younger ministers in their progressing discipleship training process. One of the things I have found in the modern Church is that most Pastors are not "pastors," they are usually Evangelists, Prophets, and Apostles, without the title.

The tradition of the modern Church has put obligations and formal duties on Pastors that are not connected to their anointing. I have met 'pastors' who are anointed Prophets and the sheep get frustrated with them because they are "so demanding," as one congregation said. Many Prophets are accused of not loving the sheep or of being too harsh. Many Pastors, who are actually Apostles, are often times accused of being too hard due to their high sense of Church order (we will review the Apostles ministry later). Finally, every elder
or bishop (one who oversees) in the local church has the responsibility to rule and function as a shepherd/teacher. If you study the qualifications of an elder or a bishop in the New Testament you will discover why one of the qualifications is for them to be "apt to teach" (see 1 Timothy 3:2) and to hold "fast the faithful word as he hath been taught, that he may be able by sound doctrine both to exhort and to convince the gainsayers" (see Titus 1:9).

The Evangelist

Evangelist - *euaggelistes* (2099) - a preacher of the Gospel.
> From 2095 and 32 in the Strong's Concordance:
> (2095) good or well and *aggelos* (32) a messenger, an
> angel, by implication a pastor; to bring tidings;
> messenger: Derivative of *ago* - to lead; by implication, to drive,
> (fig.) induce. *agele* (71) - a herd

The writers of the New Testament, under the inspiration of the Holy Spirit, had a particular concept of ministry in mind when they used the Greek word *euaggelistes* in describing the evangelistic ministry. An evangelist in the first century Church had a greater purpose than just traveling and preaching. In fact, the apostles accomplished this type of ministry we commonly associate with evangelism and Paul gave Timothy a charge to "make full proof of your ministry" by doing the work of an evangelist. (It was the Apostles, not the evangelists, who started churches then.) I heard this statement more than fifteen years ago:

> "We are not called to start churches today;
> we are called to get involved in the
> Church that was started 2,000 years ago."

This statement is probably offensive to some folk because tradition has clouded this church issue greatly. I am not implying that churches should not be "started," I am stating that there is a way the Bible lays out the function of ministry and when we stray from it we weaken the purpose and power of it.

When identifying the ministry of the evangelist, we know Philip guided the Ethiopian eunuch to the Lord, but this lone event does not constitute a doctrinal manifestation of the evangelistic ministry. It does, however, show some simple truths about the work of an evangelist. One thing is for sure, the eunuch knew God, but wanted to discover whom the prophet Isaiah was speaking about (see Acts 8:27-38). This is very similar to when Jesus was talking to Nicodemus. Nicodemus knew God but did not understand how the Kingdom of God was going to manifest, or what the Messiah's role was in the salvation of mankind. Even the disciples did not understand the Christ's purpose. Philip revealed Christ to the eunuch. The same holds true in the Apostle Paul's conversion experience. Paul knew the Lord God, but did not understand the work of Christ. He had believed the traditional interpretation about the Messiah, but had to be led into an understanding of what had taken place. When the revelation hit him, the scales fell off of his eyes and he understood. Acts 18:25 speaks of Apollos in the same way. It says:

> "This man was instructed in the way
> of the Lord; and being fervent in the
> spirit, he spake and taught diligently
> the things of the Lord, knowing
> only the baptism of John."

Aquila and Priscilla took him and expounded unto him the way of God more perfectly. Ephesians 4:11 explains that evangelists are a part of the ministry of the Church, so they should not be seen as a ministry outside of the Church. Evangelists are not a ministry in the world, but a ministry to the Church. What is commonly understood to be the evangelist's ministry is described in the Bible as the responsibility of the congregation. We all understand that the Apostles went about and 'evangelized,' but we should all be ready to be a witness when we are asked about the hope others see in us.

The evangelist is a *doma* man (i.e., gifted man). The Greek word *doma* (1390) is translated as the English word 'gift' in Ephesians 4:8. The 'doma' gift is like an umbrella (dome) of strength that covers every congregation. These are the covering gifts: gifts of authority and gifts of power in the Church. These gifts came to the Body of Christ on the fortieth day after Jesus' resurrection (see Mark 16:19-20) and are called 'ascension' gifts, distinguishing them from the manifestations and grace gifts that were given by the Holy Spirit. Jesus gave these gifts and so their spiritual order is different from the "gifts of the Spirit." This was just one of many beginnings of blessings bestowed on God's people during the first part of the Church's birth. Paul told the Ephesians that when Jesus ascended, he gave gifts (*doma*) to the Church. These gifts were not given to every individual; this is why Paul said that He gave them to 'some'.

There are several different functions within these spiritual giftings. When one studies the Greek language they will discover three different kinds or levels of gifts. One kind of gifting is found in Ephesians 4:11. These are the 'operations' (1755) of God (see 1 Corinthians 12:6). The Greek Lexicon defines these 'operations' as "those which accomplish something in the life of the believer". The Lord gives the 'workings' (*energema* - 1754) for an effective edifying (building up) of the Body of Christ.

The 'administrations' of the Lord (see 1 Corinthians 12:5) are the *diakonia* (1248), (i.e., the service gifts) which are 'supporter' gifts in the ministry. These gifts are manifested in the people who are assistants to ministries and are known as 'helps' (see 1 Corinthians 12:28). They help the 'doma' operations or governments in the Church to distribute ministry effectively.

The gifts of the Holy Spirit are found in Romans 12:6-8, and not in 1 Corinthians 12:7-10. The Greek word translated as 'gifts' (5486) in Romans 12:6 is defined as "a spiritual endowment." These gifts are given to individuals in relation to their proportion of faith (see Romans 12:6). These gifts flow through the believers in a local Body. The word 'anointing' would better describe the common idea here. These 'anointings' are given to the congregation for their ministry responsibilities.

The more common group of spirituals is found in 1 Corinthians 12:7-11. These are not gifts at all, as they are commonly called; they are 'manifestations' of the Spirit (5321). Many Christians call these "the gifts of the Spirit", but they are 'exhibitions' or 'expressions' of the Spirit, and not gifts. Calling them 'gifts' is just a part of the modern tradition. The root meaning of 'manifestations' is found in the Greek word *phaneroo* (5319) and means, "to render apparent" (i.e., to show oneself). The manifestations of the Holy Spirit reveal His presence to the believer. These manifestations are given to individual believers to 'profit' (4851) withal (on account of this). Their design is to aid in the unity of the faith. The word 'profit' is defined as "the ability to bring together for a better purpose." We should all realize that these different manifestations were given for specific functions in the Body of Christ. Paul instructs us about manifestations in 1 Corinthians 14. The difference between the 'manifestations' found in 1 Corinthians 12 and the 'gifts' found in Romans 12 are that manifestations are to be used primarily for private use, while the gifts are primarily used for public use. There are instances for the public use of manifestations, but Paul gives very clear directions about their operation (see 1 Corinthians 14). They are designed to bring us together for the better, not for the worse, and the Corinthians were not using the manifestations properly. This is why Paul preceded chapter twelve with this verse in chapter eleven.

> "Now in this that I declare unto you I praise you not,
> that you come together not for the better, but for the worse."
> (1 Corinthians 11:17)

The gifts of the Spirit that are found in Romans 12 can more readily be understood as 'functions' of Christians in the Church. These gifts signify the differences in the spiritual order of certain believers. Paul draws a clear distinction between believers as he instructs them in this matter (see Romans 12:3).

> "For as we have many members in one body,
> and all members have not the same office."
> (Romans 12:4)

In Ephesians 4:12, Paul's instruction concerning the 'doma' gifts and ministry continues as Paul uses the word 'for' (4314). The Greek word *pros* translated as 'for' in verse eleven means, "forward to" or "toward." These 'doma' gifts are designed for the progression of spiritual growth and the maturity of the saints. Paul is teaching us that these special operations of ministry cause the "perfecting of the saints." These perfected saints can now do the work of the ministry, and the edifying of the body of Christ. This is shown by the use of the Greek word *eis* (1519 - for) in verse twelve. This is a different 'for' and this Greek word has a different meaning. These four operations of God are 'for' (*pros*) the perfecting, so that the saints can do both the work and the edifying.

> "For (*pros*) the perfecting of the saints,
> for (*eis*) the work of the ministry,
> for (*eis*) the edifying of the body of Christ."
> (Ephesians 4:12)

It is the work of the Church to perform the ministry (service) to the Body and they are to edify (build up) the saints as well. It was never intended by the Lord that the Apostles and Prophets do this (see Acts 6:2). Ephesians 4:13-16 gives us the expectation God has for the 'doma' ministry and office. These chosen and anointed people are expected to unify the Body, establish the Body in the knowledge of Jesus, and mature the Body unto the measure of the stature of the fullness of Christ. Why? God the Father does not want us to remain beaten, defeated, and immature. Verse fourteen states:

> "So then, we may no longer be children, tossed [like ships] to and fro
> between chance gusts of teaching and wavering with
> every changing wind of doctrine, [the prey of] the cunning
> and cleverness of unscrupulous men, [gamblers engaged] in
> every shifting form of trickery in inventing errors to mislead."
> (Amplified)

Jesus established the pattern, that is to say, the 'norm' in Christian ministry. His pattern of disciplining spiritual sheep was simple and practical. He walked with the disciples as a spiritual

Father to train them in His doctrines and in His ways (see Hebrews 6:1-2). Jesus often told the disciples that their faith was small (immature). He evangelized the disciples to bring them to a fullness of spiritual life. Jesus' message was the good news about God's Kingdom. Jesus always led people to the Kingdom of His Father. Jesus evangelized the twelve disciples and other individuals during His Ministry. How? He raised them in faith by leading them through various trials and by sending them out on practice runs (see Luke 10:1-12, Mark 6:7-13 and Matthew 10:1-15). Paul understood evangelism and told Timothy to do the 'work' of an evangelist. That work is simply the disciplining (training) of the baby sons and daughters of God. Paul traveled with many sons in the faith and instructed them practically through a hands-on form of ministry. This occurred at the "University of Experience" and was the only seminary the Apostles used in the first century.

Scripture References to the Evangelist

The word 'evangelist' is found only three times in the New Testament:
1st -- Acts 21:8 (Philip the evangelist at whose house Paul and his company stayed)
2nd -- Ephesians 4:11 (Evangelist gift given to the Body of Christ)
3rd -- 2 Timothy 4:5 (Do the work of an Evangelist)

The word 'evangelism' is not used in the New Testament and is a modern traditional concept. There are two Greek words translated as gospel or good news that are commonly thought of as evangelism:

Euaggelizo (2097)-used twenty five times in the New Testament: to speak of glad tidings
Euaggelion (2098)-used seventy five times in the New Testament: to announce good news about God's Kingdom

The 'Work' of the Evangelist

We have to study the Scriptures to better understand the basics of the evangelist's ministry. After we study what the Bible actually says about the evangelist, we will be able to discover a more complete idea of the evangelist's calling and anointing.

The recognition of one's purpose is the stabilizer of one's ministry. When we know our place and purpose we are free to operate in our calling and function without wavering. Many fail to realize that their place is with God the Father. Only from our place with Him or in Him, are we able to serve. We are called to be the sons and daughters of God before we are called to do any work for God. The Lord is interested in our character more than our ministry. If our character is lacking, then our ministry will be lacking as well. When we first come to Christ we come by the message of the Gospel. This Gospel, with the drawing on our hearts by the Holy Spirit, has the power to change lives and set men free. The message of the Gospel is clear: "Repent, for the Kingdom of God is at hand!"

To proclaim the Gospel in one's community is commonly thought of as evangelism. This is only a type of evangelism. This type of evangelism leans heavily to one side of the scale. This is not complete evangelism. It is just easy or simple evangelism. The easiest thing a Christian can do is to share his faith for we are not ashamed of the Gospel of Jesus Christ (see Romans 1:6 and 2 Timothy 1:8). The Lord expects us to share our hope and faith with others, but a question arises and must be answered. What are we going to do with all the spiritual babies we bring into the Church? The Church may be reaching out, but are we reaching in as well? Are we reaching into the ministry God has given to the Saints which draws out things old and new?

> "Wherefore when he ascended up on high, he
> led captivity captive, and gave gifts (doma) unto men."
> (Ephesians 4:8)

As stated previously, there are several separate occasions when gifts and manifestations were given to the Body of Christ. The gifts that were given are generally associated with the coming of the Holy Spirit, but when you study the various types of gifts and manifestations you will find two different orders: dissention order and ascension order. The Holy Spirit gave gifts when He descended, and Jesus gave gifts when He ascended. When Jesus ascended He gave 'government' anointing to the disciples. When the Holy Spirit came, He came on three separate occasions to the disciples; on resurrection day (see John 20:22 and Luke 24:49), on the day of Pentecost (see Acts 2:1-6), and when persecution arose (see Acts 4:31). These three 'comings' of the Holy Spirit were designed to empower the believers so that they can endure the trying times and have the resources to do what was necessary. We believe in a living God, not a stagnant or distant God. Our Father is totally aware of what is necessary in the Body of Christ and He wants us to see our need for Him as well. This is why God gave these 'fillings' to the Church. Luke 24:49 states the first coming of the Spirit this way,

> "And, behold, I send (present tense) the
> promise of my Father upon you: but
> tarry ye in the city of Jerusalem, until ye
> be endued with power from on high."

The Spirit sealed the disciples on resurrection day. Luke associates the first coming of the Holy Spirit with the gift He came to give them; an understanding of the Scriptures (see Luke 24:45, John 2:22 & John 20:9). The disciples were not empowered until the fulfillment of the day of Pentecost (the second filling). This empowerment is directly related to the evangelistic work (see Acts 1:8). One hundred and twenty disciples were empowered in Jerusalem. Acts 2:42 tells us about the evangelistic work they performed. The apostles continued steadfastly in training the new converts (second work of the evangelist) in the doctrines of Jesus (called the Apostles' doctrine), fellowship, the breaking of bread, and in prayer. Every babe in Christ should be trained in these four areas. When preaching the gospel we are sharing a word about God; it is the Word of salvation. When people come to Christ the evangelistic ministry has an opportunity to display its effectiveness. Since evangelists are given to the Church they have a work in the Church. The foundational principles (i.e., the apostles' doctrine) should be taught to the new converts. By the way, we find no commandment in the Scriptures that directs the evangelistic ministry to the world. Just the opposite is true; the purpose is for the believers (see Ephesians 4:11-16). The present day concept of evangelism has been handed down to us from the Reformation. We use the same meaning for evangelism as they did. In the middle ages the Church was just beginning to come out of the perversion of indulgences and many other common heresies. The Reformers did not have a complete revelation of the Gospel of the Kingdom at that time. They were warring against the Catholic traditions and distortions of the Gospel, trying to bring the word of God to the common people. The early Reformers were discovering the simplicity of salvation by grace, water baptism, profession of faith, etc. Over a period of hundreds of years various Reformers were given different revelations concerning the New Testament faith. Luther, Zwingli, Calvin, and others moved the Body of Christ progressively on in the Reformation. The movement continued as the Puritans fled the European persecution and came to America. In the late 1800's the Welsh Revival revitalized the Church in Europe and spread to America. It was during this time that the missionary movement expanded with a worldwide vision. The goal was to "reach the ends of the earth with the Gospel." The Church picked up the common notion of evangelistic ministry during this time and the tradition of it is now established.

The most dangerous thing a believer can do is to stand against common tradition. When they do they usually get crucified for it. Paul was an apostle yet he evangelized the churches he started. We are now in the midst of a new Reformation. It is not the same as the earlier Reformation. Today's Reformation is a reformation within the Church, a reformation of ideas. It is a return to the purity of God's design; just as much as the first Reformation changed the face of Christianity, so will this one. Again, the first Reformation centered on salvation, the priesthood of the believer, and on distributing the Word of God to the common man. Our Reformation focuses on the Kingdom of God and on how Christians are reacting to the Church's impact in our modern social, educational, technological, economic, and our political sphere of influence in the world. As you read the book of Acts you will discover Paul's journey of faith and ministerial focus. The evangelistic ministry has a word to the lost and a work in the Church. You cannot separate the two. Paul was led by the Spirit and traveled to different places sharing his faith and raising what he had birthed. There are many examples of this (see Acts 14:3, 7, 21-23). Luke wrote in the book of Acts that believers were 'commended' (3908 - Acts 14:23) to the Lord. This Greek word means to "place alongside, to deposit, or to present." The apostles Paul and Barnabas (see Acts 14:14) were sent out from Antioch to continue the pattern of discipleship established in the Church. With this in mind let us consider the work of an evangelist.

"But watch thou all things, endure afflictions, do the
work of an evangelist, make full proof of thy ministry."
(2 Timothy 4:5)

"And the things that thou hast learned of me
among many witnesses,
the same commit thou to faithful men,
who shall be able to teach others also."
(2 Timothy 2:2)

Paul was apprenticing Timothy in basic ministry and he instructed him to "recognize everything that is going on in the lives of the members, endure the hardships of ministry, train disciples, and fully 'prove' (4135) your ministry (i.e., carry it out fully or entirely in order to accomplish your ministry goals). Do not stop short of what you have been taught. Train the faithful to train the faithful! To Paul, displaying proof of your ministry was to exhibit the ability to reach the lost and to disciple people from the cradle to the grave. In essence, the evangelist must have the ability to minister at every level. Paul was a wise master builder (753 - see 1 Corinthians 3:10). He knew Timothy needed to focus his ministry on the spiritually immature. Paul understood that the Church needed to grow stronger. That is why Paul told Timothy to do the work of an evangelist. As stated above, the word 'evangelist(s)' is only used three times in the New Testament. When we take an honest look at these passages we discover some simple truths.

First, the Bible tells us emphatically what an evangelist's purpose is. Second, the Bible tells us that evangelists are given to the Body of Christ, not to the world. And third, the evangelist has a work in the Church.

The work of an evangelist can be more clearly understood when we expand our study to learning about spiritual babes. There are two kinds of spiritual babes listed in the Bible. The Greek words are *nepios* (3516), an infant in the faith, and *paidion* (3813), young child (one who is in the spiritual potty training stage, sometimes successful, sometimes has an accident and makes a mess). The babe in the Spirit is much like the baby in the natural. The spiritual babe needs to be carried, fed, changed, and nurtured. Simply speaking, the babes (*nepios*) are helpless. One tendency in many congregations is to bring in the lost, get them saved and then put them directly in with those who have a greater degree of spiritual maturity, and expect these babies to get with it! Spiritual babes cannot get with it. According to the Scripture spiritual babes are still naturally and carnally minded and are not experienced in the word of righteousness (see 1 Corinthians 3:1-2 and Hebrews 5:13). They are still 'naturally minded' (i.e., they have a tendency to revert back to that which is natural for them to do and live from the old man, rather than from their newness of life). If a spiritual babe had a problem with anger before he was born again, you can bet Satan will use circumstances to bring that familiar spirit back as often as he is able. If someone has been raised in the world by worldly standards they will have an inclination to revert back to worldly thinking; especially when temptation or persecution comes their way. It is part of human nature to do those things that are habitual. Just because I attend church now does not mean that I am immune to temptation or the desires of my soul. The Greek word *paidion* is defined as "one who is a young child in the Lord." A *paidion* is comparable to the natural age of two to twelve years old. This is a believer who is in the earliest stages of childhood; when one is barely able to spiritually walk and not able to control themselves.

The paidion must be trained. The task of training disciples is not complete when the babe can walk, it has just begun. I have noticed in some churches that the discipleship process is viewed as complete with the ending of a six or eight week new Christians' class. Natural babies at six to eight weeks are just learning to respond to the parent. Spiritual babes are just learning to respond to God. New Christian classes are useful, but they do not satisfy the will of God for discipleship. We must recognize our obligation as a spiritual parent, knowing that maturity is not complete until the child is grown. As you grow, the progression of the maturing process brings one from potty training, through puberty, and on to adulthood.

> "An instructor of the foolish, a teacher of babes, which have
> the form of knowledge and of the truth in the law."
> (Romans 2:20)

In Romans 2:20 there are two things that need to be understood in light of evangelistic ministry. The phrases "teacher of babes" and "instructor of fools" express an idea that should be seen as the basics of evangelistic ministry. The word 'instructor' is one of the keys. These teachers and instructors are in place because these 'foolish' (878) and babes (*nepios*) have only the form of knowledge and of the truth. They have not fully developed in their walk and so there are just a few external traces of Christianity in their lives. Notice that believers were first called Christians at Antioch, which by the way was full of prophets and teachers (see Acts 11:26). We should also notice that they spent a year training the disciples. These disciples were Jews and therefore had an understanding of God already. Once they came to Christ they were then discipled in the doctrines of Jesus. The word 'foolish' in the above passage means, "to be mindless" (about the things of God; i.e., by implication, to be ignorant about the things of God). Specifically, it means, "to be egotistical (soulish), rash, and not full of faith". We can recognize these traits and tendencies as those that describe what the spiritual babe and the spiritually immature are like. It is not sin to be young in the Lord; it is sin to remain ignorant when the opportunity is available for growth. The word 'instructor' (3810) is the Greek word *paideutes* (i.e., an instructor of spiritual children). This instructor is a shepherd, a trainer, a teacher, and a discipliner. He is a *doma* father whose purpose is to deal with the fleshly tendencies that are present within spiritual children. The word *paideutes* is also found in Hebrews 12:9 but is translated by the English word 'corrected'. These fathers of the flesh need to correct our flesh. Once the child of God becomes an adult in God, they will then submit to the Father of spirits and live.

A word related to *paideutes* is *paidagogos* (3807) and is defined as a 'tutor' (i.e., a servant who takes children to school). It is also translated as 'schoolmaster' in Galatians 3:23-24. The word 'instructor' can also be found in 1 Corinthians 4:15 and shows the need in the early Church for instructors of babes. Paul said, "for though you have 10,000 instructors in Christ, you have not many fathers."

The growth of a congregation determines the size of the evangelistic ministry within that local church. The evangelist is a spiritual father or mother whose ministerial responsibility covers the new converts. The child of God must be instructed in the Word in order to overcome the flesh that rules him. Newly born-again believers will not automatically overcome the old man. If you do not train the spiritual children they will bring their mother to shame whether it is their mother in the natural or their mother the Church.

Going back to Hebrews 12, we can discover more about the evangelist's work. In verses five, seven, eight, and eleven, the word *paideia* (3809) is found. The translation of the words 'chastening' and 'chastisement' also show the purpose of the evangelist's work. The definition of *paideia* is education or training (i.e., disciplinary correction). *Paideia* is also translated as 'nurture' in Ephesians 6:4. Spiritual children are to be 'nurtured' (i.e., admonished). God nurtures His children and commands ministers to nurture them as well. Nurturing (i.e., chastening) does not taking mean dominion over or exercising authority on another. Chastening is disciplining (correction). When ministers believe that the disciplining process is completed through a pulpit ministry only, the door is opened for immorality to creep into houses and lay waste the people of God. This is a common practice because some ministers were never discipled so they do not know how to disciple others. They will either be too hard or too soft in their correction of a church member. No chastening at present is joyous for the believer, but the result will be a man or woman of God in control of their flesh. Pulpit ministry alone will not produce the correction or the nurturing necessary for the changes God has commanded us to be a part of. This chastening (again, 'correction') must not be misunderstood; it is through chastening that virtue is added to our faith. There are many false prophets in the world who try to exercise dominion over and authority upon the young in the faith. 1 Corinthians 11:32-33 states:

> "But when we are judged, we are chastened of the Lord, that we
> should not be condemned with the world. Wherefore, my brethren,
> when you come together to eat, tarry one for another."

When we judge ourselves, the chastening of the Lord bears witness to us that we are maturing. We will not be able to overcome without each other. 2 Timothy 2:25 speaks of those who "oppose themselves" and we are to help each other in the overcoming process. This process is said to be complete when we are able to "edify" one another in love. Discipleship is to be carried out in humility. Those who are spiritual extend the hand of help to those in need of strength (see Galatians 6:1). They are to be 'instructed' (3811 - 2 Timothy 2:25) for repentance sake. God grants repentance to those who receive and apply correction to their Christian walk. Disciples must learn to be flexible, adaptable, and correctable. Without this they will never come to maturity. Hebrews 5:13 gives us another clue about spiritual babes. The word 'unskillful' (552) means to be inexperienced. This is a main point in discipleship. It is to walk the spiritually immature through the growth process and bring them to experience the completeness God's grace brings to us. Neither you nor I can speed up the process of maturity. Every person will mature at their own pace, which is determined by their effort. When we train and discipline the young in the faith we will strengthen and stabilize them.

When I attended boot camp in the military, the training was not for punishment, it was for preservation. We were pressed hard every day in the tasks set before us, but it was for our benefit and not our destruction. My drill sergeant made me do things that I thought would kill me at times. He had seen the attitudes of men for years and it was not strange to him when I murmured and groaned. He just continued in the training process.

Immovable and steadfast is what we are commanded to become. This is what edifying the Body is about! Take the time to read 1 Corinthians 2:10 thru 1 Corinthians 3:3. The definition of the word 'instruct' in that passage is defined as "to drive together" (i.e., to unite; in association or affection), to infer, to show, or to teach. This is the evangelistic work. God did not implement evangelist ministry to preach to the lost and then leave the spiritual babes with the local church Pastor to tend to. This is the wrong spirit; it is the spirit of the world. It is worldly to produce children and leave them for someone else to rear. Men of God should raise their children in the natural and their children in the faith; those produced through their ministry. The spirit of the world should not be manifested in the Church. We must rear what we birth. When we do not feel responsible for our natural or spiritual children, this is the spirit of a gigolo. That is wisdom that is from below. It is earthy, sensual, and devilish (see James 3:13-18). That type of ministry is disobedient to biblical truth. It is written, the Word and the Spirit must agree. Any vision we have should fit into God's plan. The Bible teaches us that carnal people separate themselves. Carnal people divide, but spiritual people search out the deep things of God (see 1 Corinthians 3:1-3). Spiritual people understand the *poieo* of the Lord. When you walk with God He unveils His heart to you. Evangelists are designed to bring you into Christ, training you up in His ways. The evangelistic ministry is to be a nursing ministry (see Isaiah 49:22-23). The evangelist's purpose is to lift up the standard of faith and edify the young in that standard. I can honestly say no ministry will benefit you if you do not read your Bible and apply its truths to your life! Complete evangelistic ministry is needed in the Church today. Without it the Body will be weak and incomplete. Remember when one of us suffers, we all suffer. When one believer is not mature it impacts us all. Evangelistic ministry is not a sideline ministry. It is an active part of the fathering process where the anointing to raise and edify the Church is found. The evangelistic ministry was created to be the first ministry that would impact the believer when they were born again. After this process they are passed under the hand to the shepherd's who then maintain a steady flow of life-giving Word in their weekly diet. Have you noticed a need for the true evangelistic ministry in your congregation? You most likely do.

The Prophet

"Before I formed thee in the belly I knew thee;
and before thou camest forth out of the womb I
sanctified thee, and I ordained thee a prophet unto the nations.
Then said I, Ah, Lord God! behold, I cannot speak:
for I am a child. But the Lord said unto me,
Say not, I am a child: for thou shalt go to all that
I shall send thee, and whatsoever I command thee
thou shalt speak. Be not afraid of their faces: for I
am with thee to deliver thee, saith the Lord.
Then the Lord put forth his hand, and touched
my mouth. And the Lord said unto me, Behold,
I have put my words in thy mouth. See, I have
this day set thee over the nations and over the kingdoms,
to root out, and to pull down, and to destroy,
and to throw down, to build, and to plant."
(Jeremiah 1:5-10)

"Let the prophets speak two or three, and let the
other judge. If any thing be revealed to another
that sitteth by, let the first hold his peace. For ye
may all prophesy one by one, that all may learn,
and all may be comforted. And the spirits of the
prophets are subject to the prophets. For God is
not the author of confusion, but of peace,
as in all churches of the saints."
(1 Corinthians 14:29-33)

"And he gave some, apostles; and some, prophets;
and some, evangelists; and some, pastors and teachers;
For the perfecting of the saints, for the work
of the ministry, for the edifying of the body of Christ:
Till we all come in the unity of the faith, and of the
knowledge of the Son of God, unto a perfect man,
unto the measure of the stature of the fullness of Christ."
(Ephesians 4:11-13)

I believe one of the major problems found in the modern Church is that we rarely see a true manifestation of a God-called Old Testament style Prophet. One may say that we are in the New Testament era and that is why prophets are somewhat different in today's Church. Most of the

Prophets with whom I have had experience (which is limited to my encounters), I would term as superficial. When I read the Bible I discover prophets giving "the Word of the Lord," but these are not superficial words, they are life and death words. I honestly believe that most of the individuals who call themselves 'prophets' today are called of God, but are so underdeveloped and untrained that they operate in only about ten percent of their anointing. I suspect that all they have been taught or more likely seen has been a shallow form of the ministry of the prophet. While they have only seen the superficial, which is the example they follow. This does not hold true for every prophet I have encountered. I have met the real deal on several occasions and trust them and their words of direction. I am mainly dealing with the difference between the seasoned prophets and the 'charisma' prophets that move among members of the Body of Christ.

When dealing with this question I must consider the four levels of prophecy dealt with by the Scriptures. The first level of prophecy is found in Revelation 19:10 and is called "the spirit of prophecy."

> "And I fell at his feet to worship him.
> And he said unto me, See thou do it not:
> I am thy fellowservant, and of thy brethren that
> have the testimony of Jesus: worship God:
> for the testimony of Jesus is the spirit of prophecy."

Each of us in whom Christ dwells has within our heart the "spirit of prophecy." Each time we bear witness to the life of Christ within us or bear witness to the power of the Holy Spirit in our life; we are exhibiting the spirit of prophecy. The second form of prophecy is found in 1 Corinthians 12:7-11:

> "But the manifestation of the Spirit is given to every
> man to profit withal. For to one is given by the
> Spirit the word of wisdom; to another the word
> of knowledge by the same Spirit; To another faith
> by the same Spirit; to another the gifts of healing
> by the same Spirit; To another the working of miracles;
> to another prophecy; to another discerning of spirits;
> to another divers kinds of tongues; to another the
> interpretation of tongues: But all these worketh that
> one and the selfsame Spirit, dividing to
> every man severally as he will."

This type of prophecy is called "a manifestation of the spirit" (see verse seven). The manifestation of spirit is an 'expression' or 'exhibition' of the spirit. The root of the original Greek word translated as 'manifestation' (*phanerosis* - 5321) means, "to render apparent" (i.e., to appear or show itself). It can be seen when the Spirit of God moves on a certain person and reveals something to them. They then, by course, prophesy.

The third form of prophecy is found in Romans 12:6:

> "Having then gifts differing according to the grace
> that is given to us, whether prophecy, let us
> prophesy according to the proportion of faith."

This is the gift (charisma - 5486) of prophecy. A charisma is defined as "a (divine) gratuity, that is, deliverance (from danger or passion); (specifically) a (spiritual) endowment, that is, (subjectively) religious qualification, or (objectively) miraculous faculty" by Strong's Concordance. Its root means you have been "granted favor" by God. When one has the gift of prophecy they can only prophesy according to the "proportion of their faith." The less faith one has, the less one sees. The more faith one has, the more one sees. You could say that each of us has the capacity to prophesy to the depth of our spiritual strength. Anything beyond our capacity is mere assumption if it is not ministered by faith.

> "The prophet that hath a dream, let him tell a dream;
> and he that hath my word, let him speak my word
> faithfully. What is the chaff to the wheat? saith the
> Lord. Is not my word like as a fire? saith the Lord;
> and like a hammer that breaketh the rock in pieces?
> Therefore, behold, I am against the prophets, saith
> the Lord, that steal my words every one from his
> neighbor. Behold, I am against the prophets, saith the
> Lord, that use their tongues, and say, He saith.
> Behold, I am against them that prophesy false dreams,
> saith the Lord, and do tell them, and cause my people
> to err by their lies, and by their lightness; yet I sent
> them not, nor commanded them: therefore they
> shall not profit this people at all, saith the Lord."
> (Jeremiah 23:28-32)

Some prophets in today's Church do not speak for the Lord. They speak their doctrine, their ideas, or their beliefs, but they do not profit the people of God (pun intended). When Jeremiah says, "and by their lightness" (6350), he is speaking of their 'frivolity'. The Hebrew root of this word means, "to be unimportant" (i.e., to be reckless). God says one thing is obvious when these prophets minister to the local church. Nothing changes and a few weeks after they are gone you are hard pressed to find any residual effects in the church of their presence. When a seasoned prophet (i.e., the forth type of prophet) comes to your congregation there is a definite mark left on the Body of Christ.

The fourth level of prophet is called the *doma* or a prophet that has been given a 'governmental' anointing by God (1390). Ephesians 4:8 and 11 describe the *doma* gifts to be apostles, prophets, evangelists, and pastor/teachers. It is necessary to understand the difference between the 'descending' order of the manifestation of the spirit from the 1 Corinthians 12:1-3 and the Romans 12 perspective and the 'ascension' gifts God gave the Church. Each "level" of gift has a specific clarification as being a service, an administration, or an operation. The charisma gift has been explained. The administration (*diakonia* - 1248) is a 'service' presentation. Individuals who function in this capacity administrate their spiritual office as a service to the Body of Christ. The *doma* prophet however, has an 'operation' (1755 - i.e., an 'effect' and an 'efficiency') that they are specifically called to perform in the Church. One thing of note: a *doma* prophet has a God-called authority in the Church; they set individuals in order. Prophets speak to the nations, but their ministry is to the individuals in that nation. When a prophet speaks to the masses it is a call for individuals to hearken to the word of the Lord. Change in a church does not and will not take place unless each individual takes heed to what is being said.

> "Now ye are the body of Christ,
> and members in particular.
> And God hath set some in the church,
> first apostles, secondarily prophets, thirdly teachers,
> after that miracles, then gifts of healings, helps,
> governments, diversities of tongues."
> (1 Corinthians 12:27-28)

> "Now therefore ye are no more strangers and
> foreigners, but fellow-citizens with the saints,
> and of the household of God; And are built
> upon the foundation of the apostles and prophets,
> Jesus Christ himself being the chief corner stone;
> In whom all the building fitly framed together
> groweth unto an holy temple in the Lord: In whom
> ye also are builded together for an
> habitation of God through the Spirit."
> (Ephesians 2:19-22)

Our focus in this section of this chapter is the doma prophet: his gifts and function in the Body of Christ. When the Scripture uses the word "secondarily" it is not saying the ministry of the prophet is less than the apostolic ministry, it is stating that the prophet's ministry comes after the initial apostolic encounter. Apostolic and prophetic ministries are foundation- building ministries. If the local church is to have success in its duties and ministry to their local communities they must have a spiritual foundation laid, which only comes through these two ministries. Pastor/teachers and evangelists are 'maintenance ministries'. They serve the Church in their individual capacities to shepherd the flock of God and to train the lambs. The Church cannot be fitly framed together or built without Apostolic and Prophetic ministry. As I have stated before, the Old Testament is the New Testament concealed and the New Testament is the Old Testament revealed. In order for us to comprehend the ministry of the prophet we must look at his origins and his development in the Old and New Testaments.

> "(Beforetime in Israel, when a man went to enquire
> of God, thus he spake, Come, and let us go to the
> seer: for he that is now called a prophet
> was beforetime called a Seer.)"
> (1 Samuel 9:9)

One aspect of the prophet's ministry is that he is a 'seer' (7200). There is nothing complicated about this aspect of the prophet. He 'sees' things in the future that relate to the past, because the prophet has an ability to "put things together" so they can be understood. He sees things, events, moods, dispositions, attitudes, tendencies, and yes, things to come. God's purpose in making him a 'Seer' is for him to 'advise' the Church to move and prepare for a specific event, to change their direction and focus, and to know what is coming and how we are to prepare for it. He is a 'protector' of the Church. He not only sees the future; he also sees the present and the past. One area every prophet has strength in is discernment (not suspicion or assumption). The prophet has the ability to see into someone's life and to discern "life patterns." prophets make good bishops and counselors (see 1 Peter 2:25) due to their insight and spiritual make-up. Prophets have the God-given ability to see beyond the superficial aspects of someone's rhetoric and know motive and hidden agenda. God gives clarity to prophets, but one pitfall many prophets fall into is presumption. Conjecture is a snare to anyone, but prophets must be on guard against this tool of the devil at all times.

Prophets are spiritual fathers. But one of the main aspects of the prophet is the development of virtue within the lives of believers. In the Old Testament God was displeased at the priests in Aaron's linage and established Zadok as an example of the godly prophet.

> "The king said also unto Zadok the priest, Art not thou a seer?
> return into the city in peace, and your two sons with you,
> Ahimaaz thy son, and Jonathan the son of Abiathar…
> Zadok therefore and Abiathar carried the ark of
> God again to Jerusalem: and they tarried there."
> (2 Samuel 15:27, 29)

Zadok and his sons were a class of priests that differed from the other Levites. In Ezekiel 44 God acknowledged the Zadok line and called the Seers to a different operation and service. Take the time to read the entire chapter to get an idea of what God expected from the ministry of the Seer.

"And they shall teach my people the difference
between the holy and profane,
and cause them to discern between
the unclean and the clean.
And in controversy they shall stand in
judgment; and they shall judge it
according to my judgments: and
they shall keep my laws and my
statutes in all mine assemblies;
and they shall hallow my sabbaths."
(Ezekiel 44:23-24)

Notice the "teaching ministry" of the prophet. They are to teach the difference between the "holy and profane" and "cause them (the people of God) to discern between the unclean and the clean." The prophet was required to "stand in judgment" even when it was controversial. The prophet's judgment was to be "according to my (the Lord's) judgments" and was to make sure the laws and statutes of God were kept in all of the assemblies. Along with this, God had given them authority to keep the Sabbaths holy. The prophet is God's sergeant at arms. When God commanded them to teach the people the difference between the "holy and the profane and the clean and the unclean" He was speaking of virtue.

Many Christians are not trained in areas of purity of life or virtuous living. There are too many Christians who do not keep their word, who do not have integrity or character, or who borrow their neighbor's tools (or something else) and do not return them or return them broken. The prophet's ministry is very necessary in the Church if there is to be a return to a spirit of excellence in the Body of Christ. Discipleship will not reach its fullest potential if the ministry of the prophet is not a part of the discipleship team.

"And he said, Hear now my words: If there be a
prophet among you, I the Lord will make myself known
unto him in a vision, and will speak unto him in a dream."
(Numbers 12:6)

All seers have the ability 'to see' and two aspects of the prophet's ability are found in visions and dreams. The Hebrew word for 'vision' (4759) means, "a mirror." It carries the idea that a prophet has the capacity to look into the Spirit and behold spiritual 'shapes' or 'forms'. He has the capability to understand the things God shows him and the temperament to search out their meaning. God uses signs, wonders, visions, dreams, and similitudes to speak to the prophets.

"With him will I speak mouth to mouth,
even apparently, and not in dark speeches;
and the similitude of the Lord shall
he behold: wherefore then were ye
not afraid to speak against my servant Moses?"
(Numbers 12:8)

"I have also spoken by the prophets, and I have multiplied visions,
and used similitudes, by the ministry of the prophets."
(Hosea 12:10)

God takes each prophet individually and teaches him using every means at His disposal. There are four different Hebrew, and three different Greek words that are translated as 'similitude(s)'. They range in meaning from "to compare; by implication to resemble, liken, or consider," "resemblance; concretely model, or shape," and "something portioned (that is, fashioned) out, as a shape, that is, (indefinitely) phantom, or (specifically) embodiment, or (figuratively) manifestation (of favor) in the Hebrew, and "a form," "resemblance," and "assimilation" in the Greek. The similitude covers a wide range of areas that God uses to show the prophet what He wants the prophet to see.

"If any man think himself to be a prophet,
or spiritual, let him acknowledge
that the things that I write unto you are
the commandments of the Lord.
But if any man be ignorant, let him be ignorant."
(1 Corinthians 14:37-38)

One thing is certain; if an individual claims to be a Prophet and does not teach or believe that the Word of God is infallible and inerrant, he is a false prophet.

"But there were false prophets also among the people,
even as there shall be false teachers among you, who
privily shall bring in damnable heresies, even denying
the Lord that bought them, and bring upon
themselves swift destruction."
(2 Peter 2:1)

"Beloved, believe not every spirit, but try the spirits
whether they are of God: because many false
prophets are gone out into the world."
(1 John 4:1)

We seem to have a problem in the Church today. We are afraid to challenge people who hold ungodly views or who do not have a biblical worldview. We have been duped into believing everyone has a right to believe whatever he wishes to believe. In one aspect they have the right to believe anything, but in another, if it does not agree with the Scripture, they are "anti-Christ." They are against Christ and the things of God. They are misleaders or whatever term you wish to use. In any case they are not to have a position in the Church or the ability to spread their deception. But as the Scripture says, if you can't change their mind, let them be ignorant. This brings up my last point about the prophets' ministry.

> "Take, my brethren, the prophets, who
> have spoken in the name of the Lord,
> for an example of suffering affliction, and of patience."
> (James 5:10)

Prophets who stand up for God and His Word will suffer persecution. Those in who are the marks of the cross can and should be an example to the Church.

The Apostle

> "Am I not an apostle? am I not free? have
> I not seen Jesus Christ our Lord?
> are not ye my work in the Lord?
> If I be not an apostle unto others,
> yet doubtless I am to you: for the seal
> of mine apostleship are ye in the Lord."
> (1 Corinthians 9:1-2)

One of the things I most often try to explain to the various congregations that I minister to is the "seal of apostleship." When understanding the apostolic ministry, its seal is the most profound declaration of maturity I know of. The seal of apostleship is the signet of maturity. It is the completeness of a renewed mind and the fullness of God in the believer: spirit, soul, and body.

> "He that hath received his testimony
> hath set to his seal that God is true."
> (John 3:33)

> "Nevertheless the foundation of God
> standeth sure, having this seal,
> The Lord knoweth them that are his.

> And, Let every one that nameth the
> name of Christ depart from iniquity."
> (2 Timothy 2:19)

Jesus had ordained twelve apostles to work with him, but the Scripture reveals that after his resurrection other apostles were ordained to serve the Body of Christ; of which at least eight others are named. The apostle is the most misunderstood *doma* gift in the modern Church. Too many people in the Church do not believe that there are any apostles in the modern era, or they believe that there were only twelve apostles in the New Testament. If we would study the Bible we would discover that there are twenty apostles specifically identified in the New Testament. They are:

1-12 --The Twelve identified in Matthew 10:2-4 (Simon Peter, and
Andrew his brother; James the son of Zebedee, and John his
Brother; Philip, and Bartholomew; Thomas, and Matthew the
Publican, James the son of Alphaeus, and Lebbaeus, those
Surname was Thaddeus; Simon the Canaanite, and Judas
Iscariot." We also find:
13-14--Andronicus and Junia – Romans 16:7
15--Matthias – Acts 1:26
16-17--Paul and Barnabus – Acts 14:14
18--Titus – 2 Corinthians 8:23 (called a "messenger" which is the word *apostolos* {652})
19--James, the Lord's brother – Galatians 1:19
20--Epaphroditus – Philippians 2:25 (also called a "messenger"-*apostolos*)

All these are specifically identified as apostles. Now back to the question, "What is the seal of apostleship?" We can glean a few things from 1 Corinthians 9. First, we see in verse one that Paul declares the people to be his work. Many individuals who call themselves apostles in our modern times are busy building networks and buildings, while Paul and the apostles of old built people. This is why Paul calls himself a "wise master-builder" in 1 Corinthians 3:10. As a wise master-builder Paul tells us he builds 'foundations' for others to build upon, and the first thing we discover about the seal of apostleship is a firm foundation of Jesus Christ. Paul says:

> "...I have laid the foundation, and another buildeth
> thereon. But let every man take heed how he buildeth
> thereupon. For other foundation can no man lay than
> that is laid, which is Jesus Christ. Now if any man
> build upon this foundation gold, silver, precious stones,
> wood, hay, stubble; Every man's work shall be made
> manifest: for the day shall declare it, because it shall
> be revealed by fire; and the fire shall try every man's
> work of what sort it is. If any man's work abide

which he hath built thereupon, he shall receive a
reward. If any man's work shall be burned, he shall
suffer loss: but he himself shall be saved; yet so as
by fire. Know ye not that ye are the temple of God,
and that the Spirit of God dwelleth in you? If
any man defile the temple of God, him shall God
destroy; for the temple of God is holy, which temple
ye are. Let no man deceive himself. If any man among
you seemeth to be wise in this world, let
him become a fool, that he may be wise."
(1 Corinthians 3:10b-18)

"And are built upon the foundation of the apostles and prophets,
Jesus Christ himself being the chief corner stone;
In whom all the building fitly framed together groweth unto an holy temple
in the Lord: In whom ye also are builded together for an
habitation of God through the Spirit."
(Ephesians 2:20-22)

When unfolding the Lord's ministry it must be said again that there are two types of ministry in the Church: foundational ministry (the Apostle and the Prophet) and the maintenance ministry: (the Evangelist and the Teaching Shepherd). The question must be asked, "What is the difference between foundational ministries and maintenance ministries?" The answer is simple; maintenance ministries maintain the sheep in their duties, anointing and administration, building onto the preexisting spiritual structure that has been laid by the Apostles and the Prophets; while the foundational ministries of the Apostles and the Prophets form the basic spiritual substructure each Christian is established onto; Jesus Christ being the "chief corner stone" of the process. Notice the statement found in Ephesians 2:21, "the building fitly framed together groweth." One of the aspects of the foundational ministry is to not only frame, but to fitly frame 'together' the building. The Greek word translated here is *sunarmologeo* and is defined in its original sense of "laying" something down, to render something that is closely jointed together, that is, organized compactly. In other words, the apostolic seal is a foundational structure that is level, plumb, and well anchored to the Lord in which the Body is not only organized, but also organized in a way where the Church is a complete unit. Foundational ministry in one sense pours the foundation and frames the structure, while maintenance ministries finish the building and maintain its functionality.

To better understand each of the unique ministry functions it is necessary for us to know that each ministry has a specific operation. The Shepherd/Teacher sets the Word in order for the Body, the Evangelist sets the Gospel in order, the Prophet sets the individual believer in order and the Apostle sets the Church in order. When they work in unison they create by God's design, a congregation that is mature and functioning in all the manifestations, gifts, administrations, and operations necessary for the completeness of the whole. One reason there are so many issues in today's Church is that the full ministry is not functioning as God designed it, so the Body of Christ is not fully and fitly framed together. This is evidenced by noticing how the different churches in any given community are generally at odds with each other; not working together to win their communities to Christ. This will have a negative impact on the Church in the coming tribulation if it is not rectified.

The apostolic ministry is the key to a church that is fitly framed together. Why? Because the apostolic ministry sets three things in order: that which is "lacking", that which is "wanting", and that which "comes behind", strange terms which are the second aspect of the apostolic seal.

"Night and day praying exceedingly
that we might see your face,
and might perfect that which
is lacking in your faith?"
(1 Thessalonians 3:10)

"For this cause left I thee in Crete,
that thou shouldest set in order the things
that are wanting, and ordain elders
in every city, as I had appointed thee."
(Titus 1:5)

"So that ye come behind in no gift; waiting
for the coming of our Lord Jesus Christ."
(1 Corinthians 1:7)

The idea of things that are 'lacking' (5303) in one's faith shows that a deficiency has been realized and must be corrected. The root word from which 'lacking' is derived means, "to be later, that is, (by implication) to be inferior; to fall short (be deficient)". Apostolic ministry has the power to affect the Church's faith and reverse any deficiency the Body is experiencing. The apostolic anointing demonstrates the Kingdom's power by finishing the foundation in the unfinished believer. Only the Prophet has a similar spiritual operation, because they are both foundational in their operation and have a specific anointing to deal with these issues. The word 'wanting' (3007) is defined as "a primary verb; to leave, that is, (intransitive or passive) to fail or be absent." The fact is: Apostles are the ones ordained by God to set Elders (or Deacons) in the Church, as stated in Titus 1:5. When Elders are set in by maintenance ministries (i.e., Pastors), they have a tendency to become "maintenance men," and they will feel an inward necessity to maintain the status quo, but when they are set in by Apostolic ministry they receive an anointing to focus on foundational issues (these are matters of the spirit and not of the flesh) and will lead the local church, taking great concern in foundational matters. Having worked with many different denominational churches I find this to be the one issue that hinders congregations the most. I know a large number of Elders who love the Lord and want their church to blossom, but struggle with the process of leadership roles and duties. I recall one particular man (Elmo Marrs), who was a deacon in a Baptist church and he found himself in so many circumstances where he did his best to keep the other Deacons from moving in their flesh. I talked to him so many times, listening to his heart hurt for righteousness to prevail in their meetings. He was a godly man and full of faith and wanted his church to experience a move from God, but found all too often that when God started to move his move was misunderstood and fleshly attitudes squelched His purpose.

Each ministry gift has its own particular anointing (see 1 Corinthians 12:27 and Romans 12:4-6) and their operation is unique to that particular office.

> "Now ye are the body of Christ,
> and members in particular."
> (1 Corinthians 12:27)

The word 'particular' is the Greek word *meros* (3313) and one of the ways it is translated is as the word 'craft', or 'course'. One of the notable definitions of the word 'craft' is the word 'technique'. In essence, each ministry gift has a different method and modus operandi; each with sustaining value, yet each in their own function.

> "For as we have many members in one body,
> and all members have not the same office:
> So we, being many, are one body in Christ,
> and every one members one of another.
> Having then gifts differing according
> to the grace that is given to us…"
> (Romans 12:4-6)

Each, not having the same 'office' (4234) has 'gifts' (*charismas*) that are different because they do not have the same grace. The word 'office' is the Greek word *praxis* and is defined as "practice, that is, (concretely) an act; by extension a function," and comes from the Greek root that is "a primary verb; to "practice", that is, perform repeatedly or habitually; by implication to execute or accomplish." Foundational fathering brings maturity to sons in the faith in a shortened time, whereas maintenance ministry does not build foundation; their operation differs but is nonetheless vital in the function of ministry. Expeditious maturation is accomplished due to the anointing and office that the foundational ministry holds and because of the apostolic commission.

> "And he called unto him the twelve,
> and began to send
> them forth by two and two;
> and gave them power over unclean spirits."
> (Mark 6:7)

> "Then he called his twelve disciples together,
> and gave them power and authority over all
> devils, and to cure diseases. And he sent them to
> preach the kingdom of God, and to heal the sick."
> (Luke 9:1-2)

The word translated as 'power' in Mark 6:7 is the Greek word *exousia* (1849) and means "authority; (in the sense of ability); privilege, that is, (subjectively) force, capacity, competency, freedom, or (objectively) mastery (concretely magistrate, superhuman, potentate, token of control), delegated influence;" while the word 'power' in Luke 9:1 is *dunamis* (1411) and is usually, by implication, a miracle in itself. The apostolic commission given by the Lord bestows all these things to the apostolic ministry. Spiritual force, capacity, mastery, and ability are but a few of the strengths found in the apostolic anointing. They have power over unclean spirits and clean them up quickly! This is why Paul said that they would 'come behind' (5302) in no gift (5486), i.e., no *charisma*. They would have no 'inferiority' in any gift due to the power of the apostolic anointing. Apostolic ministry is very effective due to its 'warfare' nature and function.

> "For though we walk in the flesh,
> we do not war after the flesh:
> (For the weapons of our warfare
> are not carnal, but mighty through God to the
> pulling down of strong holds;)
> Casting down imaginations, and every
> high thing that exalteth itself against
> the knowledge of God, and bringing
> into captivity every thought to the
> obedience of Christ; And having in a
> readiness to revenge all disobedience,
> when your obedience is fulfilled."
> (2 Corinthians 10:3-6)

The Greek word translated as 'warfare', is *strateia* (4752) and is defined as "military service, that is, (figuratively) the apostolic career (as one of hardship and danger)." It comes from the Greek word *strateuomai* (4754) that is defined as "to serve in a military campaign; figuratively to execute the apostolate (with its arduous duties and functions), to contend with carnal inclinations." What makes apostolic ministry so difficult and why do most Christians fear apostolic ministry? The Apostle's spiritual job is to "deal with carnal inclinations" that manifest in the Body of Christ. Remember, he has authority, ability, and force over unclean spirits and carnality has an unclean spirit at its core.

There are three terms every church leader needs to know and understand: the first is the "Apostolic Campaign," the second is the "Apostolic Company," and the third is the "Apostolic Career." The Apostolic career is a dangerous ministry, as stated before. When you deal with carnality you are dealing with carnal people, and carnal people have no conscience when they try to destroy you. Carnal people usually maneuver themselves into a position of control in the local church and some churches have two or three of them working in agreement. One thing about Apostles, even men who do not understand their anointing in this area, is that they have the ability to stir up a hornet's nest everywhere they go. I know a Pastor who did not know he had an apostolic anointing and he struggled for years trying to be a "Pastor;" but with much heartache. Every church he was called to loved his teaching ministry, but hated his anointing. He stirred up the spirit of Jezebel and every carnal devil within a mile of the church. He had people he had never met speaking evil of him and he found himself battling depression for years. One day God set him free when the Holy Spirit sent a Prophet to the local church he pastored. The Prophet prophesied the truth over him and touched the depth of his spirit; iron sharpens iron. His ministerial career made a drastic change. God gave him clarity and delivered him from a confused state of operation and anointing. Let every man of God take heed to this example.

The Apostolic Commission has at its core what I call the "duo duo" principle. It is the principle of "two and two," for Jesus never sent a minister out by himself. That is a modern tradition that has been the spiritual death of many a Pastor and ministry. First of all, every minister needs someone to work with him in the ministry. Study the New Testament concerning this subject and you will discover two things: first God never sent a man to a church; He always sent him to a city and second, He never sent anyone out alone. The attitude of independence is just pride, ego, and generally the inability to work well with others. The independent spirit has its origin in insecurity and rejection, and also comes from being stabbed in the spiritual heart too many times. It is time for the principles of God's Word to be adhered to in our "modern" Church. When you are weak you will find your brother in the faith to be strong. And when he is weak you will be strong. The "duo duo" principle is a check and balance to help ministers to be empowered by the Holy Spirit, to overcome temptation, and to defeat arrogance. Plus, if one can put a thousand to flight and two can put ten thousand to flight and then you add the Holy Spirit to the mix it is a cord of victory that is not easily broken. Open your hearts, men of God, and bring another man of God into your ministry; he'll be strength and rest to you in troublesome times. When all else fails, you will never lack a friend. This is called an "Apostolic Company" (two or more functioning ministers operating in the same local church). It does not mean that the two of you have the same authority, but it does mean that the two should have the same stature, and the increase of power and anointing will bring smoother transition and change, more depth and balance in spiritual matters, and will give you a greater capacity to reach others in your local community. The apostolic company can form and grow from the room you give your sons in the faith. Acts 13 speaks of all the "prophets and teachers" they had at Antioch, and remember Antioch was the strongest of the churches during this time of the Church Age.

We must take heed to the Scriptures where the operation of the Apostle is involved. Today many of the people who call themselves 'apostles' try to put churches under their supervision, because many of them are looking for the tithe of the tithe. Do not be fooled. If their anointing is apostolic they will be humble in their spiritual power and you can be sure that they are not looking for the check and the microphone! This does not mean that you "muzzle the mouth of the ox that treads out the corn" (see 1 Corinthians 9). The Apostle is worthy of the blessing you give him and should be greatly blessed.

I am dealing with the attitude of superiority found in false apostles. Everyone is on the same playing field in the Church. False apostles usually always set themselves up as though there are none higher. Every 'set man' in every local church is in authority over that Body of Christ. Apostolic ministry that is genuine comes into that field with this in mind. They never 'usurp' (831) authority over the 'set' man (the Pastor) and they never usurp authority upon a 'set' man (see Matthew 20:24-28). This does not mean they do not have authority, it just means their authority is in the spirit. 'Set' men can 'submit' to apostolic ministry in the form of sonship, but I caution you to 'try' them, as it is stated in Revelation 2:2 to verify their heart and status.

> "Issachar is a strong ass couching down
> between two burdens: And he saw that
> rest was good, and the land that it was pleasant;
> and bowed his shoulder to bear, and became a servant unto tribute."
> (Genesis 49:14-15)

> "And of the children of Issachar, which were
> men that had understanding of the times,
> to know what Israel ought to do; the heads of them were two hundred;
> and all their brethren were at their commandment."
> (1 Chronicles 12:32)

Another aspect of the Apostle (and the Prophet) is the manifestation of the "spirit of Issachar" in their anointing. The "spirit of Issachar" is the anointing to carry a double burden and it produces a double portion. The Apostle has dual vision. He has an understanding of the times and the seasons of God, knowing what God desires to produce in each of the spiritual periods, and he knows when it is time to rest. The Apostle knows how to lead, direct, and turn a congregation in order to catch the wind of the Spirit, but he also knows how to yield, giving place and honor to others as he serves the Lord.

To the Apostle every administration is about the Lord's Kingdom and its preeminence in the local church. His focus is on the growth and maturity of the Church and is someone who understands relational ministry. Apostolic ministry is about relationships. Not needing superficial titles, Apostles love and cherish the Pastors they serve. They know what is necessary and needful and what the church "ought to do."

> "Now ye are the body of Christ, and members in
> particular. And God hath set
> some in the church, first apostles,
> secondarily, thirdly teachers,
> after that miracles, then gifts of healings, helps,
> governments, diversities of tongues."
> (1 Corinthians 12:27-28)

Apostolic ministry is the primary ministry every church should experience and the "Apostolic Campaign" is a process in the maturation of the Church. God set them in 'first' (4412 *proton*, 'firstly'; in time, place, order, or importance). When a church does not experience apostolic ministry it falls short of God's foundational order and does not attain the spiritual growth that only comes from the foundational ministry. This is why too many churches are full of babes in Christ.

When speaking of the Prophet, the word 'secondarily' (1208 - *deuteros*; second, in time, place or rank) is used in relation to the Apostle. One gift is primary and the other secondary; this means they work in a sequential order. These two combine and give iron and concrete to the foundation of every believer, leveling and plumbing every Christian under their operation and administration. Following these are the teachers, maintaining the building and administrating daily upkeep that is necessary for spiritual maturity to flourish. After these are set in place, miracles, healings, and the rest will follow. Consider this: could it be that many churches do not experience miracles and healings because their foundation has not been properly set and they are not in spiritual unison? This gives us something else to ponder!

Chapter 19 – The Principles of Fathering

> "Behold, I will send you Elijah the prophet
> before the coming of the great and dreadful day
> of the Lord: And He shall turn the heart of
> the fathers to the children, and the heart of
> the children to their fathers, lest I come
> and smite the earth with a curse."
> (Malachi 4:4-6)

Once we recognize the relevance of the four-fold ministry we can move more easily into the principles that spiritual fathers should operate in. The "Principles of Fathering" are some of the most relative, if not vital aspects of discipleship. I use the term fathering in a generic way and for the sake of brevity; it is interchangeable with the concept of nursing mothers (see Isaiah 49:23) as well. What criterion determines who can be or who is a spiritual father or nursing mother? We are commanded to make disciples and if we are to become wise master builders we must learn to deliver the child of God from their spiritual womb (see 1 Corinthians 3:10) and raise them to maturity so that they may become a friend to God, rather than just a church member.

One thing is true, only those who are mature in their own personal faith can father others to maturity. Spiritual fathers and nursing mothers must be called and anointed of God. They must be patient, full of the fruit of the Spirit, and have a sound call on their life. Malachi prophesied about the spirit of fathering and its purpose, which is to turn the heart of the fathers to the children, and the heart of the children to the fathers. Fathering, one should know, is a three-fold work in a triune person. We are spirit, soul, and body and as such we are to be wholly saved (see 1 Thessalonians 5:23); which means we are to lead God's children into a completeness or spiritual wholeness. Being born-again is the beginning, not the end of the salvation experience. In fact, the Scripture reveals that we are "being" born again, which is representative of the idea that the salvation of our soul is progressive (review Chapter 14 - The Salvation of the Soul). God commands spiritual fathers to turn their hearts to their spiritual children. As Christian leaders we are given discernment concerning those under our hand. This revelation is for the disciple's benefit and God does not intend for us to use the word of knowledge, the word of wisdom, or the discerning of spirits toward another's demise. We have a ministry of reconciliation and not a ministry of destruction (see Luke 6:36-49). Fathering is more than a call; it must be a desire. The spirit of fathering is the fire of God burning within (i.e., the anointing to build) a believer so that he is a useful tool in the Master's hand. It is not cloning! It is fathering!

Fathers in the faith should not try to reproduce themselves, but as Paul said we are to be examples for people to follow (see 1 Corinthians 4:16). Fathers are stewards of God's children and should be reproducing Christ in the life of a believer. It is being one who is older in the faith with the purpose of bringing maturity to the child of God, where the process in the end produces a man or a woman of God. As stated before, it is not a sin to be young in the Lord, but we must use our past experiences to strengthen others rather than allow our past mistakes or troubles to dictate our fears. Our wounds and mistakes do not hinder God's plan. He foreknows us and so He made His plans concerning us according to His knowledge and understanding of us. He does not feel threatened by our assumed inabilities; He works through us in spite of our shortcomings. He is certainly aware of our weaknesses and when our hearts and purposes are turned to the spiritual children in our congregations, this is the evidence that we have faith enough for fathering. Our work in them is our inheritance for them. Though some spiritual children may be carnal, we look forward to the day of their release through spiritual insight (i.e., we see the day of perfection in them). We want to mark those under our hand and stamp a seal upon these tablets of flesh.

The Seal of Fathering

> "Nevertheless the foundation of God
> stands sure, having this seal,
> The Lord knows them that are his. And,
> Let everyone that names the
> name of Christ depart from iniquity."
> (2 Timothy 2:19)

When a foundation is laid in the life of a new believer it is called the "seal of fathering (or the apostolic seal)." You can always recognize a person who has been founded in the faith by their ability to stand firm in any situation. One thing to mention is that many Christians have a firm foundation even when they have not been fathered, but you will find that the process took a much longer time to develop in them. The process that produces maturity in Christians is known as the "edification of the saints." Jesus, who is our example, fathered twelve sons and taught them how to father others in the faith.

When the Holy Spirit came down on Pentecost in Acts 2 there were 120 disciples in the upper room. When the disciples left the room and went into the streets (see Acts 2), 3,000 souls were added to them. What did they do with all of those spiritual babies? They did not complain about the task, because they understood the work. Acts 2:42-43 says:

"And they continued steadfastly in the apostles doctrine and
fellowship and in breaking of bread, and in prayers.
And fear came upon every soul: and many
wonders and signs were done by the apostles."

As we continue this lesson let us consider the differences in the two invitations Peter gave in the book of Acts. In Acts 2:38 Peter said, "Repent and be baptized...for the remission of sins," but in Acts 3:19 he said, "Repent and be converted...that your sins may be blotted out." Peter did not change his message; His newly found experience in working with the 3,000 spiritual babies mandated the difference in his perception. His knowledge of the 3,000 that were saved caused him to recognize the dynamics of the discipleship process. Fathering supports the conversion experience, because developing the new man is what discipleship is all about. Spiritual development does not happen by osmosis. Even Jesus told Peter in Luke 22:31-32 to strengthen his brethren when he was converted and conversion is the by-product of discipleship. Conversion in the traditional sense is thought of in terms like "coming to Christ," but conversion in the biblical sense is the development of the new man. Peter understood the things that the Lord taught him, but it was not until after Jesus' resurrection that they had the faith and insight to reproduce what he knew.

Acts 2:42 lays out a plan of action in the discipleship process. The 3,000 continued in these four things. The Apostles utilized their doctrine, fellowship, breaking of bread, and prayer as a four-part program. The main doctrinal influence the Apostles taught to the disciples was the foundational doctrines of Christ (i.e., the Apostles' doctrine found in Hebrews 6:1-2). The Apostles' doctrine will take you through the changes that occur in the five stages of spiritual growth. These five steps are the baby stage, the childhood stage, the young adult stage, the stage of maturity, and the fathering stage of development.

This is the process of adding to the believer's faith according to 2 Peter 1:5. Peter said that you should add to your faith virtue, and then add knowledge to virtue, and so on. The book of Hebrews states there are things that accompany salvation (see Hebrews 6:9) and Paul said you need to know how to behave in the house of God (see 1 Timothy 3:15). These are all similar and contemporary statements about discipleship. Peter said in Acts 11:16 "then I remembered the word of the Lord," because he had forgotten a clear principle in the spiritual growth process. Peter had been acting out of what he understood truth to be. He was not able to differentiate between the truths of the Holy Spirit's purpose in baptism until the Lord brought this awareness to his mind. Peter had been operating by his own insight and in this realm he only recognized John's baptism in his ministry (see Luke 3:3). He had not fully understood the doctrines of Christ, even though his training had been by the Lord Himself. It is through the doctrines of Christ that truth is seen, understood, and implemented into the disciple's lives. (In Galatians 2:11, Peter had to be rebuked by Paul because of his separation from the Gentile believers when the Jews came around).

There will never be a sound manifestation of truth if there is no revelation of it first. When the reality of discipleship is understood and utilized we will have greater success and a lasting result.

Many see fellowship as an "eattin' meetin'". This was not so in the first century. The breaking of bread was the sitting down to a meal of some sort. "Eattin' meetin's" are part of the Christian experience, but they are not the completion of fellowship that needs to be expressed in the Church. The word 'fellowship' is the translation from the Greek word *koinonia* (2842 – also translated as 'communion' in Acts 2:42). *Koinonia* is defined as a partnership (i.e., participation, or (social) interaction, or (pecuniary) benefaction: contribution, distribution, fellowship).

Notice two words rarely mentioned in relation to *koinonia*. The first, 'social interaction', is an intimacy in relationships where intense trust is developed. Spiritual fathers and nursing mothers work with people to develop a greater level of confidence in every area of their life and they work people through their failures toward success. This is the inner dealing of God whose end result is designed to complete personal restoration of the individual. When one desires to walk with God and they have areas of immaturity in their life, it takes love in abundance to walk them through the process of recovery and restoration.

Some disciples may not walk in the forgiveness and grace of God. Fathers in the faith must walk Christians through their past sins and must also walk them through repentance from dead works. They may know they are saved, but not walk in the fullness of their repentance or in the grace of God. As in all things, God separates areas of His work in the inner man to clarify His purposes in these dealings. Many fall back from discipleship at this point (see John 6:66) and many spiritual fathers fail to work sons in the faith through these areas so they can be completed in Christ. Some spiritual fathers may have a difficult time when training people beyond this point, so every spiritual father should count the cost of leaving things undone.

Fathering is perfected through the experience of sonship. It is difficult to father beyond your personal experience of sonship. This means that if you have never been fathered in the faith it may be difficult for you to father others. Every one of us has weaknesses. If the relationship you have with a disciple is weak the end result will be weak! If you cannot "eat their flesh and drink their blood" in every area of fathering, your final product will not be complete. To "eat someone's flesh and drink their blood" means to be able to put up with their personal weaknesses and fleshly nature. God gives us grace through the process and through much prayer successes will come. To eat someone's flesh or drink someone's blood simply means you must recognize the frailty of the disciple's humanity and have the strength to work through his personal peculiarities.

You have to learn to put up with some things because everyone makes mistakes. No one is perfect and spiritual fathers must know that. Spiritual fathers have faults and flesh as well and disciples must realize this, so everyone must walk in grace toward each other. One person's flesh has the same weaknesses as another's. The pain they feel is no different than the pain you feel. The emotions they have are normal for the human condition. Remember that Jesus was left alone on Gethsemane and was emotionally troubled. What is the difference between Jesus and us? Jesus was rejected, but not affected. His faith and God's love covered him. He was obedient to His Father and was able to accomplish His task, because His Father told Him to do it that way. Jesus was contrary toward Satan and the religiously minded Jews, but not with God's people. He was focused on the work God had given Him, not on the obstacles the enemy placed in His way. He disciplined Peter in the discipleship process even when Peter was influenced by demonic activities. When Peter denied the Lord, Jesus did not cast him off because of it; He walked him through it. This is the kind of love fathers should relate to people as they develop their spiritual maturity. This is the right kind of fathering. It is making disciples and not just preaching to people. It is more than telling them what is wrong, but preaching Christian living without strife or contention as you are blessing them.

> "I write not these things to shame you,
> but as my beloved sons I warn you.
> For though you have ten thousand instructors
> in Christ, yet you have not many fathers:
> for in Christ Jesus I have begotten you through the Gospel.
> Wherefore I beseech you, be ye followers of me."
> (1 Corinthians 4:14-16)

Paul teaches us that fathering is different from pastoral or evangelistic instruction in several ways. First, fathering is unique in that there is more cultivation necessary as saints grow older in the Lord. This is the Abba factor. It is being a spiritual daddy to people who may have never had a dad. It is a great privilege when God the Father allows us to raise His children. We are commanded to be spiritual daddies, not just preachers.

We are told in the Bible that darkness flees from light. Sometimes we have hidden sins and are embarrassed because we are unable to overcome them. The "sins that so easily beset us" become an obstacle and a hindrance to our spiritual growth. Fathering is the *koinonia* (the fellowship) that weans our soul from these fleshly desires. Always remember that not everyone desires to be fathered. Jesus fathered only those who the Father gave Him. Every Christian should desire to be fathered, because we are to follow Jesus' example, but that is not always the case. The Scripture commands us to be discipled, though not everyone is obedient to that commandment. In America most everyone says that they believe in God, but not everyone obeys the commandments of God. Independence within the heart of people is rampant in our society. Many want to go their own way. Serving God is a matter of the fear of hell in their minds, rather than the love of the brethren in their hearts. These false notions should be purged out of the Body of Christ through the fathering process.

Example of Fathering

2 Kings 2 gives us an example of the fathering process. Elijah took Elisha through the various stages of son-ship. The first stage in the fathering process is described in the Old Testament as the 'Gilgal' stage. 'Gilgal' (1537) represents the cycle of life (i.e., individuals are successful for a while and then they experience a spiritual failure of some kind). These failures repeat themselves in a cycle (like a wheel), which is the meaning of the Hebrew word 'Gilgal'. Around and around we go. We walk with God, go through a spiritual decrease, experience some sort of a defeat, work through the process, and then repent and return to God. Through the course of time we return to God, serve Him, and then eventually through some means, fail again in some other area of our life. This is a natural course. These failures are generally the habits of our past that creep in and repeatedly seduce us. Elijah asked Elisha a question, "you going to stay here in Gilgal?" The implication is that we can stay in this kind of cycle if we do not do something about it. Elisha said, "as thy soul liveth, I will not tarry." Elisha was saying, "No! I will not linger in this Gilgal area." They then went to Bethel, the second stage in the process of sonship. 'Bethel' (1008) means the house of God. It is an interesting place. The sons of the prophets were there. 1 Samuel 19:20 speaks of Samuel and states that he was standing "as appointed" over these sons of the prophets. There is order and respect at Bethel. The house of God is the place where a son recognizes that he is the temple of God and he witnesses the changes the Holy Spirit is making in his life.

Sons are to be fathered in their commitment to the local Church and in all levels of 'koinonia'. The purpose of this stage is to train the disciple to accept and understand his son-ship, his place in Christ and his responsibility to Christ and that he is accountable for his spiritual failures. I remember the transition I went through at my Bethel. My father in the faith asked me, "Why did you come here?" My original plan was to be fathered in the faith. I remember saying, "I thought God sent me here to be fathered, now I realize that God sent me here to be a son." I had discovered God's plan for me in my journey of faith.

Sons in the faith are to be given place in ministry, room to grow, and space to be released. It is God's way to give His sons place and to make room for them. Most of the time God will open a door for that son or daughter in a specific area in the local church, the fathers will not have to do anything except recognize the need that the disciple can fill. It is in the DNA of God's children to have dominion; God put it there. It is not rebellion for a son to want place. We all want to fulfill our call. Rebellion is found when the son in the faith follows his own desires through an independent disposition (when he refuses correction, rises up as though he is not subject to the correction of God's Word, or brings division into the local church). Referral is a key in this stage of growth. Sons in the faith are to be fathered in the principle of "Recognize, Refer, and Respect" at the Bethel stage of fathering. Recognize those that are over the sons in the Lord, refer to the fathers out of admiration and honor, and respect the decisions they make concerning you. The Bible is the highest authority. Elijah again asked, "Are you going to stay here at Bethel?" Elisha knew he could not stay in that place forever. Elijah did not intend for Elisha to remain under his hand forever, any more than Jesus could remain physically on the earth. It was Jesus Himself who said that it was expedient for Him to go. It is Jesus who has the authority to send sons into the Church. No father in the faith can tell a son to remain at a certain place of his own accord. Neither can a spiritual father try to force sons to stay in his local church. Elisha understood the way of God and again said "No! I'm not staying here." Elisha knew his journey of faith was not complete, so he continued in the process.

The third place to take a son in the stages of growth is to Jericho. 'Jericho' (3405) means "to be flavored or to be seasoned" and is the time where disciplined growth and maturity are more fully developed in the fathering process. The root word that 'Jericho' comes from means, "to perceive or anticipate." Jericho is the place where learning responsibility and accountability must flourish. It is the place to learn how to submit to your call and to the operation of your call. Remember, we are called to be with Jesus (see Mark 3:13-15). This Jericho experience is the grooming and the sanding of our relationship with our Lord and is a place of anticipation. It is the place of preparation for the release of the spiritual son. The final fashioning process of a disciple is to be molded at Jericho.

We must bring the walls down in the life of the disciple, which helps in the development of worship, perception, and discernment. Personal discussions and intimate dealings concerning the son's successes and failures is a must for the fathering process at this stage. The son ought to recognize the areas of his life that are manifestly fleshly and that have the potential for his demise. Spiritual fathers have the responsibility to minister to the sons and meet their restorative needs at this point. Time spent with the sons is extremely important. The more one-on-one time spent with a son in the faith is proportional to the increase of strength released into the son's life by the fathers. There is no substitution for time!

Jericho is also the place of the Lord's work. The fathers must guide the sons in spiritual matters, but allow the Holy Spirit the right of separating them for the work of the ministry. The sons should develop their anointing in a fuller way at this stage of discipleship. Sons are to add to their faith, walk in the fullness of their abilities, minister openly, and be guided by the fathers into the ways of God, not just in His acts. The Word must become flesh in the sons at Jericho. Again, the ministry of the son comes from the Master, not the spiritual father. The work of release comes from God the Father. Spiritual fathers are guides and not the releasers; that's the Holy Spirit's job. Spiritual fathers cannot decide who gets this or that; it is the Holy Spirit that signifies the individual and separates them for His purpose and plan. For years I have understood that God puts something into His sons and daughters. It is a driving force that moves them in very specific directions. Mark 16:20:

> "And they went forth, and preached
> everywhere, the Lord working
> with them, and confirming the
> word with signs following. Amen."

This passage declares that the disciples went out preaching and the Father worked "with them", not doing it for them, but working "with them" in their endeavors.

1 Samuel 10:7 also reveals this aspect of God's design when Samuel told Saul, "And let it be, when these signs are come unto thee, that thou do as occasion serve thee; for God is with thee." The principle is clear. Do what you see is the right thing to do and God will bless it, if it is a godly thing. King Saul had many troubles in his life because he would not do the things God commanded. Why? Because he substituted and trespassed, not fulfilling God's purpose, which was to destroy Israel's enemies. In the beginning of Saul's anointing he became righteously angry when he saw the Philistines on "God's hill" with a garrison. (The people's enemy had set up a military fort in the place where they worshipped.) This would be like having Satan's worshipers set up a booth in Church. This is why Jesus turned over the moneychangers in the Temple and Paul understood this principle (see Acts 14:10-15).

Can you imagine the elders at Antioch telling Paul and Barnabas that they did not believe they were ready to be sent? Spiritual fathers should guard their hearts from idolatry; the self-idolatry of thinking more highly of yourself than you should. Satan loves to deceive men of God into shepherding. Shepherding is when a spiritual father in the faith starts thinking he has the right to control God's sons or daughters. True spiritual fathers will not exercise authority over, nor will they usurp dominion upon a son or daughter in the faith. We must learn that we are God's children and do not belong to the preacher. The fathers are to be honored, but not worshipped. Without the release of the Holy Spirit there will be no journey to Jordan. Elijah, a third time, asked Elisha "Are you going to stay here?" Elisha said again "I'll never leave you." True sons in the faith will automatically stay until they are released.

The next phase, Jordan, is the experience that represents the total release, the crossing over, and Elisha knew he had to cross over from son-ship into fatherhood himself. The fathers can give the signified sons their own mantle. They can pour into the son's spirit by the laying on of hands, giving an impartation of strength by giving the son in the faith respect. Respect and honor are two keys needed to function in a successful ministry. Being anointed is the first key. Insecurity hampers too many men of God. If a spiritual father does not comply when the Holy Spirit has released a son, he has begun to shepherd, a form of control. But know this as well; no spiritual father can be forced to agree with a spiritual son's release. This is not a paradox. Fathers must have confirmation in their heart about the son being released. If a father in the faith has not heard from the Holy Spirit where a son in the faith is concerned, he should seek confirmation with the other elders. When a son's anointing is recognized, the spiritual fathers have the obligation to send the sons back to Jericho once they have crossed over in this stage of development. These trained sons can then develop and train the other disciples in the faith. Through this the disciples become spiritual fathers and nursing mothers.

This is the pattern of training and release in the Body of Christ. From Jerusalem disciples were trained and released. Some of these sons found themselves in Antioch. As this local church grew God added prophets and teachers to the apostles, such as Paul and Barnabas. The Scripture says,

"Now there were in the church that was at
Antioch certain prophets and teachers."

So at this church were these sons in the faith Barnabas, Simeon, Lucius, Manaen, and Saul. As the sons ministered to the Lord (i.e., in His Body) the Holy Ghost said, "separate" them. To separate means, "to release." How did the Holy Spirit separate? "As they ministered to the Lord" their maturity became obvious to everyone. A good lesson to learn is to not be overbearing, and give the son in the faith some room to grow. Do not cast the son out if he fails, on the contrary, train him, encourage him, and secure him as you walk him through the process.

The Church is quick to throw stones nowadays. Grace is not an excuse to sin, grace strengthens believers in weakness and grace gives us the ability to overcome in any situation. The spiritual fathers should train disciples and release them into the local church that others may grow and that other disciples may be sent out.

One lesson to learn is that the Holy Spirit does not send everyone at the same time. He signified Paul and Barnabus for a specific purpose. The others stayed at Antioch, for a while at least.

"And the things that thou hast heard of me
among many witnesses, the same commit thou to
faithful men, who shall be able to teach others also."
(2 Timothy 2:2)

When sons are fathered correctly, they will father correctly. When a disciple is not fathered correctly, that is when they are not trained through the Word and Spirit, they will not father by the Word and Spirit. Disciples will only reproduce what has been put into them. This is why it is so important to father sons and daughters by the spirit of fathering having the purpose to turn their hearts toward the fathers as you turn your heart to them. If they are raised under the law they will reproduce the same atmosphere everywhere they go. As an example, my eldest son Joshua wanted to make some kool-aid when he was a young boy. He forgot to add the sugar. The end result was pretty, but the flavor was not right.

This lesson teaches that even when something looks right it does not mean it is right. The same is true in fathering. All of the ingredients must be added to a disciple for maturity to be complete. Remember this note of caution; no disciple in the faith is sinless. Do not expect sinlessness. You will never get it! Spiritual fathers must be men of mercy and grace; this is the true reflection of the

Father. People are imperfect and so spiritual fathers and disciples will be imperfect. We all struggle with our imperfections. I cannot repeat this enough. If spiritual fathers do not recognize this they will have unjust expectations of disciples. Unjust expectations cannot be fulfilled and the end result will be failure. If a spiritual father succumbs to this trap of the enemy, I repeat that it is usually because the spiritual father has not himself been completed. In closing this section of fathering, a note of grace must be spoken. If you make a mistake, repent and start anew. God loves spiritual fathers and nursing mothers and you will find yourself in the center of God's will when you try.

Fathers and Teachers

1 Timothy and Titus give the qualifications for elders. These qualifications are God's qualifications and cannot be supplanted by any Church or denominational dogma. God originated this pattern in Samuel and Elijah followed his example. Samuel was the first prophet (see 1 Samuel 9:9) and Samuel had a pattern of fathering as well. 1 Samuel 7:16-17 confirms this pattern. Samuel went from Gilgal to Bethel, from Bethel to Mizpeh, and from Mizpeh to Ramah. We have already looked at Gilgal and Bethel, but 'Mizpeh' (4708) means to observe or to be a high place. This represents the spiritual father as the observer or overseer and gives a different perspective of the same fathering process. The spiritual father is the helper or 'Ebenezer' (see 1 Samuel 7:12) of the disciple. The spiritual father has the *topos,* or the high ground. He has the best point of view in the process. Mizpeh is the place for disciples to be observed, corrected, and helped. Spiritual fathers walk sons through by integrity. It is akin to Jericho. Watch the son, guide him, and teach him by example. In other words, give him pointers and room to grow. Samuel lived at Ramah. 'Ramah' (7414) means 'uprightness'. Ramah is where the spiritual father is to dwell (i.e., he is to be a righteous man). It is the position where a spiritual father is to establish the highest of ethics. Jesus said, "Come and see" when the disciples asked, "Where do you dwell?" If you desire to be a spiritual father you have to live in Ramah. All the elders of Israel came to Ramah (see 1 Samuel 8:4). The pattern established by Samuel is also a similitude of the fathering process. 1 Samuel 11:14 states:

> "Then said Samuel to the people, come, let us
> go to Gilgal, and renew the kingdom there."

What kingdom? It is the rule of God in the lives of God's sons and daughters (see 1 Samuel 12:7, 14, 20-24). In Genesis 18:19 God reveals His attitude toward the spiritual fathers and their purpose:

> "For I know him, that he will
> command his children and his
> household after him, and they shall keep
> the way of the Lord, to do justice and judgment; that the
> Lord may bring upon Abraham that which he hath spoken of him.

We are commanded to father faithful men. Make a big note of faithful men (see 2 Timothy 2:2). The training is not for just anyone, it is for faithful men and by faithful men. Proverbs 23:10 says, "Remove not the old landmark; and enter not into the fields of the fatherless." When we do not father faithful people, maturity will decline in our churches over the long haul and God's people will suffer in the end. The Lord will not tolerate this. He is jealous over His people. Moses asked the Lord in Numbers 11:12, "Should I carry them in my bosom, as a nursing father beareth the sucking child (paraphrased)?" The Lord answered in Numbers 11:17 that He would put the spirit of fathering on the elders and they will bear the burden of the people with you. Isaiah 49:20-23 also states this principle to us and says a standard is to be lifted up so the Body of Christ can see it. "And kings shall be your nursing fathers and their queens your nursing mothers" and when you serve God as a spiritual father or mother He will cause you to become a king or a queen; God will esteem you highly!

Elders are to serve the local church with this purpose in mind and in this capacity. Galatians 4:1-7 gives some important details about fathers and sons. Even if the son is signified to be an Apostle or a Prophet he is a "be not" (see Romans 4:17) until released by the Holy Spirit. These sons and daughters are to be under tutors and governors until the appointed time of the father (Galatians 4:2). The fathering process is also the manifestation of the Spirit of adoption in the hearts of the sons or daughters. Spiritual fathers and mothers produce a spirit of service from the foundation of sonship. We serve people because we are sons of God, not because we are God's slaves.

Maturing the Sons into Fathers

> "And the things that thou have heard of me
> among many witnesses, the same commit thou
> to faithful men, who are able to teach others also."
> (2 Timothy 2:2)

One of the keys to fathering is to recognize that the job of fathering is incomplete unless the sons have been trained to be fathers. If one has never been fathered the number one sign of it is that they do not know how to release sons. The field of the fatherless (i.e., the church of one who has never been fathered) has some distinct characteristics. The fellowship is usually tainted with idolatry, legalism, and has been touched by the spirit of slumber. The blame game comes into play and the rudiments of accusation permeate the Body.

We commit things to faithful men so that they will also commit these same principles to others. This is where the principle of the father's father takes effect. I call this is the principle of the Spiritual Grandfather and should be understood as the Patriarchal aspect of fathering. God said I am the God of Abraham, Isaac, and Jacob signifying that He sees Himself as a generational God. The spiritual grandfather is a father in the faith who has fathered sons in the faith and is now assisting the sons in fathering their sons. That which is natural is first, and afterward that which is spiritual (see 1 Corinthians 15:46). Spiritual grandparents support and assist their sons and daughters in the faith. Grandparents assist by wisdom and experience. They give the spiritual parents a time of rest and provide a confirming factor in the discipleship process. I remember my grandfather in my youth. He seemed to always know what to say to me. He built strength into me that no one can take away. The same holds true for the spiritual grandfather. The word 'premium' describes the par (equal) value of a person and a spiritual grandparent can impart great prime value into the heart of the disciples. This is how you add virtue to someone's faith and his self-worth can be greatly increased.

> "It shall seem hard to thee, when thou sendest
> him away free from thee; for he hath been worth
> a double hired servant to thee, in serving thee..."
> (Deuteronomy 15:18)

Value added to a disciple develops a double portion of blessing in him.

The matter of trusting ones sons must be addressed. When spiritual fathers do not trust their sons in Christ, a sense of rejection is then imparted into the son and he is diminished. If the spiritual father is insecure, he will ultimately reproduce insecurity. You must learn that "impartation comes by association." You will impart what you are, not what you want to be. This is why it is so important in the fathering process to utilize multiple fathers and spiritual grandfathers in the training of sons. This is why God created dimensionalized ministry. God never intended for disciples to have a one-sided or lop-sided influence, but you have to start somewhere. Our communion is the loaf that the fathers and the sons are to partake of. It is that one bread which is our communion. It is the Body of Christ.

> "The cup of blessing which we bless, is it not
> the communion of the blood of Christ? The bread which
> we break, is it not the communion of the body of Christ?
> For we being many are one bread, and one body:
> for we are all partakers of that one bread."
> (1 Corinthians 10:16-17)

The cup of fathering is a part of the cup in the communion of the Body of Christ. Each of us has a "common union" that we partake of. As the fathers in the house break the bread of sonship and as the members receive the Word of sonship, there should be an increase of sonship by the spirit throughout the entire church. This is why the statement is made: for we are all partakers of that one bread. This is simple enough for most to understand, but it is God bringing us to the place where we comprehend that we are part of the Body. The word "blessing" (2129) found in 1 Corinthians 10:16 is defined as a consecration, an enlargement, or a bounty. Communion is the cup of increase!

The Body of Christ will never mature until we see the need for multiple fathers in the same church, who must be people of communion and increase; men who understand their need for one another. One father in the faith can cover another father's shortcomings and vice-versa. When multiple spiritual fathers operate in the local church a greater the level of maturity can be gained in that fellowship. When we train faithful men to train others also, we are completing the commission of God. Anything less creates a hindrance to the goal of founding the Body of Christ in maturity. God never intended for the Church to reduce itself to a hodge podge of buildings. God intended for the called-out ones to increase in every corner of the earth. This will only happen when we train the faithful to train the faithful.

Fathering Disciples: A Practical Approach

"He that has no rule over his own spirit is like
a city that is broken down, and without walls."
(Proverbs 25:28)

"And why do you call me your only Lord, and yet
do not do what I say? Whosoever comes to me and
hears my sayings, and does them, I will show you
to whom he is like: He is like a man which built a
house, and digged deep, and laid the foundation on
a rock: and when the flood arose, the stream thrust
through and burst upon that house, and could not
shake it: because its foundation was set on rock..."
(Luke 6:46-48)

"Son of man, show the house to the house of Israel,
that they my be ashamed of their iniquity:
and let them measure the pattern."
(Ezekiel 43:10)

"Howbeit for this cause I obtained mercy, that in me
first Jesus Christ might show forth all longsuffering,
for a pattern to them which should hereafter
believe on him to life everlasting."
(1 Timothy 1:16)

"The aged women likewise, that they be in
behavior as becometh holiness, not false
accusers, not given to much wine, teachers
of good things; That they may teach the young
women to be sober, to love their husbands,
to love their children, To be discreet, chaste,
keepers at home, good, obedient to their own
husbands, that the word of God be not blasphemed."
(Titus 2:3-5)

"Young men likewise exhort to be self-controlled.
In all things showing a pattern of good works:
in all your teaching showing a
strict regard for truth, and show that you appreciate
the seriousness of the matters you are dealing with.
Truth filled speech cannot be contradicted, and
will cause those who are contrary to be ashamed, because
they can find no evil thing to say of you."
(Titus 2:6-8)

"He that has ears to hear, let him hear
what the spirit says unto the Church."
(Revelation 3:22)

"When any one heareth the word of the kingdom,
and understandeth it not, then cometh the wicked one,
and catcheth away that which was sown in his heart.
This is he which received seed by the way side."
(Matthew 13:9)

Paul taught in 1 Corinthians 3:10-11 that he was a wise master builder and said; "I have laid the foundation" and "another will build on it". Paul had laid the foundation of the Church in Corinth and had set the pattern for the future as he had received it from the Lord. Where was the foundation laid? It was laid in the people of God. Remember the new commandment Jesus gave? In simple terms: love God and love the people of God. The King James Bible states it this way,

"Thou shalt love the Lord thy God with
all thy heart, and with all thy soul,
and with all thy strength, and with all
thy mind; and thy neighbor as thyself. And he said

> unto him, Thou hast answered right: this do, and thou shalt live.
> But he, willing to justify himself, said unto
> Jesus, And who is my neighbour?"
> (Luke 10:27-29)

Luke shows the necessity of a pure and stable foundation in the parable of the rich man. Luke 10:29 uncovers the rich man's heart (i.e., his hidden agenda), "But he, willing to justify himself" asked the question that would seemingly prove his worthiness and acceptance by God. The question he asked is not the issue here, but the nature of his heart will be our focus. This is the first place we must begin. The Amplified Bible states a bit of wisdom from Proverbs 24:27 "Do first things, first." If a minister's hidden agenda is to have a large church, then his ministry should be seen as it really is; self-seeking. If we focus on how many we bring to Church rather than on the maturity that is being produced in those who are in our congregations, our churches over time will become full, but without discipleship, carnal and immature.

What was Paul's focus? Paul understood that it takes time to build a foundation in a disciple. He also knew others would build on the foundation that he had laid in their life. What was Paul's advice? "Take heed how you build." We must look to the patterned son, Jesus, for the answers. It is important to realize that Jesus taught us the right way to father disciples. As I have stated before, it is almost impossible to father disciples if you have not been fathered yourself. If you find yourself in this place much prayer and help will be necessary. Find some men of God to help you with the process. Experience has taught me that the spiritual father must keep his soul in check as well as the disciple's. Jesus discipled men, these men discipled the Timothy's, Titus', and the Luke's; then these sons in the faith became fathers and discipled faithful men, and the faithful men became fathers and discipled others also (see 2 Timothy 2:1-6). This pattern was established to maintain maturity in the Body of Christ. When this pattern ceases, the church declines in power, purpose, and maturity. When the pattern is broken, the next generation of believers will decay spiritually, morally, and carnality will take root in the lives of some believers. (This occurred during the Middle Ages and produced a great failure in the Church that caused heresy to flourish).

> "I write not these things to shame you,
> but as my beloved sons I warn you.
> For though you have ten thousand
> instructors in Christ, yet have
> ye not many fathers:
> for in Christ Jesus I have begotten (fathered)
> you through the gospel."
> (1 Corinthians 4:14-15)

The Corinthians focused on the multitude of instructors. That is why they had so many problems.

Many churches do the same thing. When churches focus on the instructor model for church growth, they have given in to the wrong pattern unless they have trained sons and daughters functioning in the classrooms. The problem with a Sunday school full of "un-fathered" instructors is that it is the wrong pattern and does not generally produce virtue. We are commanded to disciple the people of God. The emphasis in discipleship should be the application of the biblical principles, not just giving information about the Bible to the class. The Lord brings growth to congregations and sometimes He brings drastic growth. The evangelistic ministry model (training the babes) must be utilized, but God's way is to train beyond the beginning stages.

Discipleship is truly a lifelong process with various stages of growth along the way. Each of us should grow daily in the Lord. One of the greatest desires for many people of God is to have the answer to the question; "how can I build a Body of Christ that is spiritually strong, mentally healthy, and active in their faith?" The question is answered throughout the Old and New Testament. The struggle is not in finding the answers, but in implementing them. When one's goal is to start a church and the Bible teaches us to build a people, there is a struggle in the attempt to produce Kingdom things because one's foundation is wrong. Jesus said you make the Word of God of none effect by your traditions and this is the struggle. In essence, the rule of God is greatly diminished in the lives of those who are in these types of congregations, unless they are founded through discipleship. These believers may want to mature but their growth is hindered by tradition if they are not fathered (discipled).

Jesus also said "new wine goes into new wineskins." If you do not put the new wine into a new wineskin, the new wine will be lost because it will cause a breach in the old skin. If you try to have a new wineskin without the new wine, all you have is an outward sepulcher that is void of life (see Matthew 23:27). When you try to implement Kingdom principles into a traditional church, all that will be produced is schism. This is why so many churches have split in recent years. God is speaking about the Kingdom; people are hearing His Word but do not know how to implement its reality.

Paul says these things should be done and that there should be no schism in the body (see 1 Corinthians 12:25). Schism is always the evidence that discipleship is not being accomplished. There is a tendency in our society to think division is a natural part of the Christian experience. Division is not godly by any means. Division is the by-product of carnality. The denomination that I came out of prided itself on the fact that they grow out of division. What good are three new churches if division produced them? When the biblical pattern of the Church is not followed or when denominations have a better idea than the Scriptural pattern, schism enters in. It is rather difficult, if not impossible, to father sons in the faith without making some changes in the church structure as well as in the training schedule.

Fathering sons in the faith is as old as Abraham, was instituted by the Lord through Samuel and the prophets, was practiced by Elijah, was perfected in Jesus, and is taught in the New Testament.

It is the spirit of Elijah that Jesus spoke of and is the part of the 'doma' ministry. Many do not fully understand the Prophet's role. This is why so many Prophets in today's churches only prophesy. They are unaware of their God-called purpose! Samuel, the first Prophet (see 1 Samuel 9:9) trained sons. Elijah trained spiritual sons of whom Elisha was the most well known. When Elijah and Elisha went through Bethel and Jericho the sons of the prophets were there. God made Abraham a father of many nations and promised him a son, why? Because fathering was and is God's purpose.

"And he (Abraham) believed in the Lord;
and he counted it to him for righteousness."
(Genesis 15:6)

By definition the word translated as 'believed' in the Hebrew text means, "to build up or support; to foster as a parent or nurse; figuratively to be firm or faithful, to trust or believe, to be permanent or quiet". In other words the statement means to look to and to rely on one as a parent, a teacher, and a healer. As a parent you are to train up your children in the way they should go. As a teacher you challenge and impact your children with wisdom and knowledge, and as a healer you protect your children from anything that is detrimental to their well-being; this includes pride and sin. Abraham looked to God as a Father and the Lord our God took on the task of being a Father to him. Again, Genesis 18:19 shows why God trusted Abraham:

"For I know him, that he will command his children and his
household after him, and they shall keep the way of the Lord,
to do justice and judgment; that the Lord may bring upon Abraham
that which he hath spoken of him."

Abraham was faithful concerning the things of God. He produced fruit in his family and in his substance. Deuteronomy 6:4-7 relays the commandment of the Lord and the responsibility of God's people:

"You will teach these commandments to
your children and live them yourself..."
(Paraphrased)

God says; "I trained you, now you train your children and your children's children." We are commanded to not only father those under us in the Lord, but we are to also father our children's children.

When Solomon spoke of the fields of the fatherless he was warning us not to go into them. Fathering is an old landmark and cannot be removed. Elijah fathered Elisha and their relationship is clearly seen in 2 Kings 2:1-12. When Elijah was taken, Elisha did not cry out for a Prophet or a Pastor, but for his father. (That is a 'father' with a little "f".) Galatians 4:1-7 also speaks of fathering and discipleship. The spiritual sons are under tutors and governors until the appointed time of the father. That's 'father' with a little "f" again. When I first surrendered into the ministry one Pastor told me, "You'd better be ready when the spotlight hits you!" One needs to be ready, but how is one new to the faith, that is, a novice supposed to know the ways of God unless he is discipled into them? The Scripture teaches us to not put a newly converted one in the service because by doing so we push them into a conflict they are not prepared to meet. Anyone who has walked with the Lord for any time at all will tell you that some things can only be learned by experience.

Spiritual things cannot be learned through the receiving of information in a classroom; they must be experienced in your life. For example, eat a piece of chocolate and try to describe it to someone who has never eaten chocolate before. It is an impossible thing to do. You have to eat a piece of chocolate before you can understand how it tastes. The same holds true when trying to understand spiritual matters. Explanations are necessary, but the reality will not be known until someone experiences it. Again, we are to train them in the way they should go, not educate them in the things they should know. Faithfulness in one's life, marriage, and church can only be understood by an individual who has endured the hard times, and came through the fire not smelling like smoke. We learn spiritual things by resisting the devil and overcoming sin. It is not how many times you have been through the fire, but how many times you overcame the fire that counts. It was not, nor is it, how many times you journey around the mountain, but when did you decide to leave the wilderness and enter the Promised Land? Discipleship is also like an individual who has watched 1,000 baseball games and someone who has played in fifty games. The one who has watched does not have the experience of the one who has played. He may know much about the game, but he will not understand many of the dynamics of the game until he gets onto the field. When you put him in to play he finds himself in unfamiliar circumstances. So it is in fathering disciples.

> "For it became him, for whom are all things,
> and by whom are all things, in bringing many
> sons unto glory, to make the captain of their salvation
> perfect (mature) through suffering."
> (Hebrews 2:10)

Jesus died and rose from the dead to establish salvation in the earth, but it was in bringing many sons unto glory that caused him to not be ashamed and to call them brethren (see Hebrews 2:11). One must understand the ways of God before they can understand maturity. The respect of a father comes from the process of sonship and the anointing, not from his position or title. Many people seek out churches where they can see signs and wonders. Signs and wonders are an evidence of God's presence, but we are not to be seekers of signs. Jesus said an adulterous generation seeks signs. God manifests himself for his people and does that in spite of their sin at times. Just because a congregation claims to display signs and wonders is not reason enough to move your membership there. What is a biblical sign and wonder anyway? Is it the replacing a white tooth with a gold one? No. It is an event where God is glorified, not the church, not the person, nor anyone's ministry.

"Bind up the testimony, seal the law among my disciples...
Behold, I and the children (the disciples) whom the
Lord hath given me are for signs and for wonders."
(Isaiah 8:16 and 18)

God is looking for people who can transform lives. It is a sign for all when drug addicts change their lives or when prostitutes are changed and become wonderful wives and mothers. This is a sign for all to wonder after when they see sinful people being changed. Are you a sign and a wonder? I knew a man who was a drunkard, on drugs, an adulterer, and an all-around pervert. He gave his life to the Lord, was discipled and is now a faithful husband, responsible father, and a Pastor. His family is still wondering what happened to him. He is a wonder and a sign of God's ability to transform people.

The basis of discipleship is discipline (training, not punishment). Again, fathering is simply not a short-term process. Disciples are made, not birthed. This is why Jesus commanded us to make disciples. Paul spent fourteen years of his life in discipleship before the Holy Spirit signified him and the elders confirmed him. He was an active minister in Antioch before that time, but the Holy Spirit did not send him until he was ready. We all know the impact Paul has had on Christianity. He was effective because he had been fathered in the faith and disciplined for many years. Today we have the attitude to just send our young preachers off to the seminary. We do this because it is easier to let someone else do the work for us. Many of these seminaries are just learning centers and do not train people in the ways of God. They teach you things about the Bible and about the Lord, but they do not father anyone in virtue. Most people only learn "stuff" about the Bible and do not get changed in the process. Most of the professors that I know want to disciple those that attend their classes, but are hindered by the constraints of their tradition. The Bible states, "Knowledge puffs up." When will we believe that? Knowledge is necessary, but knowledge without application and discipline has no value. It is just information without application. Recognize this; Jesus called Paul and Barnabas years before they were sent out. The Church at Antioch with its Prophets and Teachers trained its members and through discipleship, Paul and Barnabas were developed, matured, and sent out. The church at Antioch was committed to the Kingdom of God and its principles and became one of the strongest congregations in their day.

The principles of fathering should be followed with prayer and fasting. It is the establishment of foundational relationships (i.e., nursing fathers with spiritual sons, and nursing mothers with spiritual daughters). It is when men and women of God are developed to be nursing fathers and nursing mothers rather than just ministering teachers. It is when men of God invest time and resources into the lives of specific faithful individuals who will be trained to train others also. When we do not follow the pattern of the Lord, then we will fall under the curse prophesied in Malachi 4:6.

Ephesians 2:19-20 gives us another basis to adhere to. We are built upon the foundation of apostolic and prophetic ministry where Jesus Christ is the primary and chief corner. The work of Jesus is the first stone laid in every new believer. Who He is, what He did for us, His gift of righteousness, and His grace are the primary stones in any strong foundation. Without these stones Christians will be spiritually insecure in their faith. The whole body must be fitted together, not as individuals doing their own thing, but as a unit, an army of God. Jesus is the leader of this army and the Bible is the manual for its organization.

> "For the weapons of our warfare are
> carnal, but mighty through
> God to the pulling down of strongholds.
> Casting down imaginations, and every
> high thing that exalteth itself against not
> God, and the knowledge of God,
> and bringing into captivity every
> thought to the obedience of Christ;
> And having in a readiness to revenge all
> disobedience when your obedience is fulfilled."
> (2 Corinthians 10:4-6)

The definition of the word 'warfare' (*strateia* - 4752) is military service, i.e., (fig.) the apostolic career (as one of hardship and danger). It is derived from *strateuomai* (4754) which is defined as "to serve in a military campaign"; fig. "to execute the apostolate (with its arduous duties and functions), to contend with carnal inclinations". Notice the statement, "arduous duties and functions". These are dangerous duties and functions. They always stone the Prophets! Often people will say, "You are judging me." Apostolic ministry is not carnal; it is mighty through God in that it pulls down carnal strongholds. Apostolic ministry functions as it breaks strongholds. When Christians have strongholds that have been a part of their lives for years, it is dangerous territory to venture into. Apostolic ministry stands opposed to carnality in the Church.

What is a major stronghold? Carnal thinking. Carnal thinking is revealed in 2 Corinthians 10:7,

> "If you think you are Christ's, even as you
> are Christ's and are still fleshly
> in some areas of your life,
> remember we are Christ's also."
> (Paraphrased)

Is it any wonder Satan fights so hard to remove apostolic ministry from the Body of Christ? His deception has occurred and many do not even believe that there are any apostles today (review chapter 18). Religion has created its own criteria for the apostolic ministry and mission. If there were only twelve original Apostles then why did Paul charge Timothy to war a good warfare (see 1 Timothy 1:18) when this is the same word "warfare" that is defined above? In 2 Timothy 2:1-5 Paul commanded him as a "soldier" (4757 and 4758) and used the word 'warreth' (4754); these are the same words and roots. In Acts 14:14 the Scriptures say, "and when the apostles (plural) Barnabas and Paul," signifying that Barnabas is an apostle as well as Paul. Barnabas was called with Paul and was sent out as an Apostle at the same time from Antioch. Romans 16:7 lists Andronicus and Junia as being "noteworthy apostles", who were Apostles before Paul was called according to the Scripture. Philippians 2:25 states that Epaphroditus is their 'messenger' (652- i.e., their apostle). If we look at all the times the word *apostello* is used (i.e., one sent from God to do apostolic work) in connection with individuals in the New Testament, we will discover twenty apostles listed in the New Testament. This includes Matthias who was chosen to replace Judas. We have reviewed all this in an earlier chapter, but it must be seen again.

Many of these false theological concepts continue to be propagated throughout the Body of Christ because people do not read their Bibles. The situation warrants a change in our thinking. We must assemble (build or construct) the church and not just gather for services. If we just gather together on Sundays to do some singing, Sunday school, and a sermon, how have we fulfilled the Great Commission? Or are we 'assembling together' (1997) to advance the lives of those who meet with us?

The Bible is our manual to assemble the Body of Christ. The Body of Christ is to be formed and fashioned in the same way as it was originated. I recognize that there are different dynamics in our modern world, but they are not outside of God's pattern. You may have all the parts of your church gathered in the building, but if they are not assembled (joined in unity) they will not function according to their purpose. When there is no expression of Ephesians 4:12-16, the congregation is not assembled. It is as simple as that. Remember that a congregation is never stronger than its weakest member. We are commanded to strengthen the novice, train the faithful, build up the Body, and win the lost. Most congregations spend their resources on buildings or various ministries, rather than on the needs of the people of God. Religious programs will never mature the people of God; neither can Sunday school books build a foundation in the congregation. The modern church has substituted programs for Christ. Many times people want things to do because they are works-oriented. Before men can turn toward fathering they will have to rethink their focus and repent from program-mindedness. When people are program minded and someone has a need, they send them to the church program rather than to Christ. When a marriage is struggling, the couple is sent to a program, when they should be led to Christ. The Church cannot replace Christ Jesus with programs.

> "Nevertheless the foundation of God stands sure,
> having this seal, The Lord knows them that are his.
> And, Let everyone that names the name of Christ
> depart from iniquity. But in a great house there are
> not only vessels of gold and of silver, but also of
> wood and of earth; and some to honor, and some
> to dishonor. If a man therefore purge himself from
> these, he shall be a vessel unto honor, sanctified,
> and meet for the master's use, and
> prepared unto every good work."
> (2 Timothy 2:19-21)

Fathering is also the establishment of 2 Timothy 2:19-21 within our congregations. It is the beginning of a sure foundation of God, which empowers the Body of Christ to overcome iniquity and realizing that the process of discipleship must cover various levels of Christian maturity. It is in doing these things that we become sanctified, meet (suitable) for the Master's use, and prepared unto every good work. Fathering must also include the sending sons out. You must let the children go sometimes. Jesus did.

Another principle to consider is that there is always a promise from God and a time of preparation before there can be a performance of ministry. I experienced this reality from my spiritual fathers. I am pleased that my spiritual fathers were grace-full. They endured much from many and I know from me as well. We have experienced what happens to men when they do not have character and integrity and they move into ministry. Their foundation was not established so they fall. When men of God fall publicly it affects the entire Christian population.

To the degree sons put forth effort is the degree that they receive. Some receive more, some less. It all depends on the person. The same holds true in the Church. If there is pressure on the fathers to complete a disciple, they must be diligent to train disciples, make time for them, and deal with them. We must make room for young men and women to be trained, publicly and privately. We must give them place in the local church to grow, to allow them to make mistakes, and to fail with dignity. Remember, there is only one perfect man, the son of man, Jesus Christ. Even though Peter had been with the Lord for three and one half years, he still failed and denied the Lord. But even when he denied the Lord he was recovered and accepted. Jesus warned us not to be as the hypocrites who do two things; set a standard that is too high for anyone to reach and then act as though they had attained perfection. If we judge without mercy then we are truly deceived. Grace and love cover a multitude of sin. It is better to forgive sin than to be a judge over others. John 20:23 says,

> "Whosesoever sins you remit, they are remitted unto them;
> and whosesoever sins you retain, they are retained."

God is calling spiritual fathers to a standard of excellence. This standard is Jesus. He established the pattern set by the Almighty God and no one can change it. He is the only way, He is the only truth, and His life is the only life. When one lives differently than the Bible commands this is to live in lost-ness. Salvation is recognizing the truth that God has sent His Son to be an example and a pattern of living, as well as a giver of life. We now bear witness to this truth (see Acts 1:8).

Fathering should not be administered as a teaching. It is the process of experiencing God. It occurs when we, through the fruit of the Spirit, and by the fruit of the Spirit, reproduce the fruit of the Spirit within the lives of those who God has called to be sons in the faith. By the way, this is the purpose of ministry, is it not?

Chapter 20 - Church Structure

Now that we have come to the final chapter in this book, we can try to put all of this together for you. Over the years I have been studying the Scriptures and relating them to our modern day Church Structure. Having been connected to many different denominational Pastors and churches, and having had the opportunity to minister in those churches, I have witnessed various forms of church governments and policy structures; some functional in Christ and others that are completely religious formations. There are a few things that have become very obvious to me when dealing with those who are ordained as church leaders or are Deacons, Elders, or hold positions of authority in the Church. First, whom should we ordain, and when should they be ordained? The second is that churches are not practically ordered or structured. And third, how should we train the Body in common sense things such as preparation for Christian living and in preparation for the tribulation?

These are some of the questions I will address in this chapter. The first question can be answered in the following statement: we should not ordain people who are gifted, but only lay hands on (i.e., ordain) people who are anointed in governments. Every Christian is gifted. One of the problems we face in the modern Church is that many leaders do not know how to see into the Spirit to know whether a gifted person in the congregation has been separated by the Holy Spirit in a 'government' capacity and is anointed to lead others in the Spirit. We find many people in the Church who are out of order, do not follow, or do not know how to follow a 'set man' that God has given authority to. A 'set man' is a term used in Numbers 27:16. It is representative of the person God has set over a congregation to be the spiritual leader. Many times people are given leadership positions due to popularity or some other issue that usually arises in the local church. This issue has caused the Church some difficulty and I have lost some friends because of my conviction in this matter. The main reason I have followed this path is that I have seen many Pastors and congregations go through hell when gifted people were ordained into a position of leadership and God had not anointed them in governments. I have witnessed godly men and women who held a position in a church and governed by their soul because they did not have a clue about the spiritual dynamics of leadership. To them, though they were godly people, the Church was to be governed like a business. Their focus was on the bottom line of the checkbook or they see themselves as a 'watchdog' over the

Church. Elders are commanded to rule over the congregation, but we must establish what Elders are by the Scriptural canon.

> "Now faith is the substance of things
> hoped for, the evidence of
> things not seen. For by it the elders
> obtained a good report."
> (Hebrews 11:1-2)

It is absolutely important that an Elder must be a person of faith. That is simple enough for us to recognize, but that is not the only quality Elders should have. The Bible shows us exactly what kind of person God had in mind when He commanded Elders to be ordained. It is not the richest people that should be considered, just because they have wealth, nor was it the most pious. The Lord did not tell us to ordain the most popular, nor did He tell us to ordain the next person in the supposed line of progression. Many churches ordain these types of people, mostly because the Pastor was put on the spot or in several instances that I have witnessed, the congregation nominated them to the office. I honestly believe (being the cynic that I am) that the reason many churches have contention and strife is because they did not follow the mandates of the Lord when installing church leadership. I have pastored congregations where the Deacons of that church would "run the Pastors off" after two or three years. In their mind, it was better for the church to have a new Pastor ever so often. The truth is they had power and control issues, which has since destroyed that 100+-year-old congregation.

Moses had the right idea and understanding of what leadership was supposed to be when he set the course and asked the Lord for some help in Numbers 27:15-17:

> "And Moses spake unto the Lord, saying, Let the Lord,
> the God of the spirits of all flesh, set a man over the
> congregation, Which may go out before them, and
> which may go in before them, and which may lead
> them out, and which may bring them in; that the
> congregation of the Lord be not as sheep
> which have no shepherd."

When Moses asked the Lord to 'set' (6485) a man 'over' (5921) the congregation he asked for some specific details in the person's ability. Notice the statements: "Which may go out before them, and which may go in before them, and which may lead them out, and which may bring them in..." Something was vitally important in a leader; they must have already 'gone out' and 'come in', so they could lead (not teach) the people how to 'go out' and 'come in'.

'Going out' and 'coming in' are statements that reflect the idea that we move in and out of spiritual times and seasons. Leaders that are full of the Holy Spirit and have the spirit of Issachar understand these seasons and the spiritual movement the Body of Christ should move through. No one should have a title or position of any kind when they are unable or unwilling to go out or come in to these spiritual seasons. Any form of ministry or church leadership position, no matter the title or designation you want to put on it (Deacon, Elder, Prophet, Teacher, etc.) must have the experience and the ability to lead people out of bondage and into deliverance and freedom, as well as recognize the spiritual motion and direction of the Holy Spirit. When speaking about Elders Paul says in 1 Timothy 3:6, "Not a novice, lest being lifted up with pride they fall into the condemnation of the devil." A 'novice' (3504) is a new convert by definition, and carries the idea of someone who is inexperienced.

There are several aspects that must be understood about God's spiritual seasons. What are these 'seasons', what are they for, and what does the Bible say about them? To answer the first question, let us establish some basic groundwork. Genesis 1:14 states:

> "And God said, Let there be lights in
> the firmament of the heaven to divide
> the day from the night; and let them be
> for signs, and for seasons,
> and for days, and years."

God said that He created the stars in the sky to be "for signs (226), and for seasons (4150), and for days, and for years." God designed the heavens to show us the natural seasons (spring, summer, fall, and winter), but to also show us His spiritual seasons. God established the three major feasts: Passover, Pentecost, and Tabernacles. These are God's feasts that He has invited us to be partakers of. They are not Jewish feasts and are never stated as such in the Bible, other than as a declaration of them being expressed in the Jewish culture. These feasts are specific spiritual times that God has ordained for us to go into and come out of so that we can receive from God His purpose during these times. (These feasts were outlawed in the middle Ages by the Catholic Church, as was anything that was Jewish. They substituted Easter for Passover and Christmas as Christ's birthday when He was actually born in Tabernacles. The pagans' feasts were 'Christianized' and brought into the Church, while God's feasts were put on the back burner). This is why most Christians have never heard of God's appointed times. These appointed times are 'signs,' that is they represent God's awe-inspiring seasons for deliverance, empowerment, and movement.

Passover was not only the time that God delivered the nation of Israel out of Egypt, but it was also the eschatology of Christ delivering us out of the bondage of Satan. Pentecost was not only the season of the harvest, but it was also the eschatology of the coming of the Holy Spirit. Tabernacles is not only the season of the "latter rain," but it is also the eschatology for the End of Days. Passover saw its fulfillment in the sacrifice of Jesus Christ. Pentecost saw its fulfillment in the coming of the Holy Spirit, but Tabernacles has not yet been eschatologically fulfilled.

The ultimate purpose of Passover is deliverance. Each spring God brings His season of deliverance to the Church. If leadership is not aware of this spiritual dynamic they will miss their time of visitation. 'Set men' who understand God's seasons and know how to go into the season and come out of it in strength can lead the local church into its power and purpose, and come out of it stronger than before. The same holds true with Pentecost. If the 'set man' knows how to go into God's time of empowerment, he can lead the local church into this season and facilitate the Body of Christ's appointed time for God's visitation. He can lead them in and lead them out so that the Church can not only experience these seasons, but also receive the anointing God has ordained for them. The season of Tabernacles is the "season of the latter rain," while Pentecost is the season of the first rain. If the Holy Spirit came down at the first with such enabling power, what do you think His Presence will bring at the 'latter rain'?

It is exciting to think about these spiritual seasons and God's design for the Church in the Last Days. One aspect of spiritual seasons is found in understanding the spiritual significance of the feasts of the Lord. Leviticus 23:2 states as a fact:

> "Speak unto the children of Israel, and say unto them,
> concerning the feasts of the Lord, which ye shall
> proclaim to be holy convocations, even these are my feasts."

These feasts were ordered in their due season. As an example, Jesus was crucified at Passover and rose from the dead during the feast of unleavened bread (not on Easter Sunday). The Holy Spirit fell on the feast of Pentecost, which occurs fifty days after Passover. The Lord utilized these two feasts in His plan for the Church's salvation and empowerment.

The same holds true in the spiritual manifestation of the feast of Tabernacles (the only feast the church has not spiritually experienced). The spiritual fulfillment of tabernacles will occur during the End of Days.

> "Three times thou shalt keep a feast unto me in the year.
> Thou shalt keep the feast of unleavened bread: (thou
> shalt eat unleavened bread seven days, as I
> commanded thee, in the time appointed of the month
> Abib; for in it thou camest out from Egypt:
> and none shall appear before me empty:)
> And the feast of harvest, the firstfruits of thy labours,
> which thou hast sown in the field: and the feast of ingathering,

which is in the end of the year, when thou hast gathered in
thy labours out of the field. Three times in the year all thy
males shall appear before the Lord God."
(Exodus 23:14-17)

Three times in a year there are cycles of God that peak with specific spiritual purposes and spiritual power. The first cycle is the Passover season. It is during this time that the Spirit of God focuses on deliverance, redemption, and cleansing. I learned many years ago to focus on what God was interested in. As a Pastor, I knew God was interested in salvation during this season so I held a revival, focusing in on the spirit of redemption. In one small congregation I pastured, we had about eighty members. I had only been leading this congregation for about six months and during our revival more than fifty people were saved in that church. Discipleship was easy for the most part and an evangelistic team was put together to train the new converts and to reach out into our community. We geared up our discipleship program and by the time Pentecost (the season for spiritual empowerment) came around, we set our focus on the Holy Spirit and most of those folks were walking in a greater level of manifestations (see 1 Corinthians 12) and their spiritual gifts (see Romans 12) began to blossom. The commandment of the Lord during this time is that no one is to come "empty handed." I also utilized this season as the time of 'blessing'.

Pentecost is the time of provision and empowerment. It is an opportunity to move the local church into spiritual issues at a greater level and start the process of building faithful members in all three areas of their lives: spirit, soul, and body. Discipleship ministers to their spirit; love gifts and focusing on their physical need ministers to their soul and body. All the church members who raised gardens brought their extra fruits and vegetables to the church to share them with other members. People started bringing all sorts of things to give away at the church. Food, clothes, tools, and some started helping others work on their homes and such the like. It was so awesome to experience these types of blessings! The new mothers were given diapers and all the necessary items for their babies, the widows were blessed and visited, and even the church building was worked on and repaired. I had a Prophet come to the church during Pentecost of that year and we had an explosion of growth, both spiritually and in numbers.

The Feast of Tabernacles, on the other hand, occurs at the end of the year. This is a spiritual picture of the End of Days. The Feast of Tabernacles is also known as the 'Ingathering' and is a time of entrance into Kingdom things. These feasts were important in the early Church and Paul scheduled his apostolic trips around them (see Acts 20:6-16 and 1 Corinthians 5:7-8). Jesus celebrated and acknowledged the feasts (see Matthew 26:2-5 and 17; Luke 2:41-42 and 20:46; John 2:23, 4:45, 5:1, 6:4, 7:2-14, and 37, 10:22, 12:12 and 20, 13:1; Acts 18:21; and Jude 12).

God wants us to recognize the times we live in. The feasts lost their relevance due to the tradition of the Church. These seasons are not only *kairos* times (opportune times or times of opportunity), but they fit into the chronology of the last days. When we know how these spiritual seasons work we will be able to invest our time rightly, rather than waste it. Daniel is an example (see Daniel 9). He understood the times and seasons of the Lord and was able to prepare the way for the return of the Jews to the Promised Land. He focused on the Children of Israel's deliverance from Babylonia and his knowledge caused him to intercede for the people, motivating the king of Babylon and God's heart to move on their behalf.

God's seasons follow a general pattern: conception, birth, and age of accountability, rebirth, receiving hope, maturation, demonstration, manifestation, and completion.

- Conception - God begins His purpose.
- Birth - The new life God gives comes forth.
- Age of Accountability - God makes us aware of His plan and we tap into His resources.
- Rebirth - We are quickened and develop the framework of God's design.
- Receiving Hope - God meets our expectations.
- Maturation - Three stage process:
  - Illumination for Revelation
  - Separation for Clarification
  - Transformation for Manifestation
- Demonstration - God demonstrates His power and wisdom.
- Manifestation - God manifests His glory through the Kingdom.
- Completion - The dynamics of the Kingdom are operating in the local Church.

God's biblical calendar is the key to understanding His appointed times and seasons of spiritual and natural growth, and the development of times of increase and prosperity. Understanding these times allows us to prepare for the spiritual momentum of the Holy Spirit. The Jewish calendar contains two beginnings and two ends in every year. Passover starts God's ceremonial year, while Tabernacles begins God's civil year. These feasts are relevant to Church structure due to the anointing the Holy Spirit brings to the Body of Christ in these seasons.

> "Blessed shalt thou be when thou comest in,
> and blessed shalt thou be when thou goest out.
> The Lord shall cause thine enemies that rise up
> against thee to be smitten before thy face:
> they shall come out against thee one way,
> and flee before thee seven ways."
> (Deuteronomy 28:6-7)

God has promised us that He will smite all of our enemies. "Issachar" leaders have the experience to recognize when the congregation is under attack because they have already been through the fire themselves. They know how to go out against the enemy and they also know how to lead people back to their "peaceable habitation." When the feasts are incorporated in the structural calendar in the local church, ministry becomes much more effective. Victory is more than an end of the circumstance, victory comes to the Christian when he is led through the fiery trails and does not smell like smoke. Jesus taught this principle in John 10: 3-4:

> "To him the porter openeth; and the sheep
> hear his voice: and he calleth his own
> sheep by name, and leadeth them out.
> And when he putteth forth his own
> sheep, he goeth before them, and the sheep
> follow him: for they know his voice."

We know that Jesus is the door, but who are the 'porters'? We are the porters of our lives and the set man and the Elders are the porters of the Church. If the porters do not know how to open the door, the congregation will miss their appointed time. In essence, God has set a yearly cycle to bring increase to the Body of Christ. This principle is also stated in Revelation 3:12, "Him that overcometh will I make a pillar in the temple of my God, and he shall go no more out." When we get to the place God wants the Church to be, all of God's people will be whole and complete, and will experience the deliverance God has ordained during His appointed seasons and will never go out of that deliverance. The season of Tabernacles is when the Church becomes unified and one in Christ Jesus (see John 17).

'Going out' and 'coming in' also reflects leaders who are both goal-oriented and people-oriented. They are leaders with a vision and a standard that is set high. Their character will not allow them to lower the standard of God, nor diminish the vision of God, but they are willing to lead the people into the victory and success of the Church.

People in God's government are God's ambassadors, delivering the dictates of the King to His subjects, not wavering in their dedication or commitment to His cause. In the beginning of Solomon's reign, Solomon knew he lacked something that was very necessary. (If you ask anyone what Solomon asked for and they will most likely answer "wisdom." That is the wrong answer. I know many of you were taught that in Sunday school, but you were taught wrongly.) The following verses tell us what he asked for:

> "And now, O Lord my God, thou hast made thy
> servant king instead of David my father: and I am
> but a little child: I know not how to go out or come in.
> And thy servant is in the midst of thy people which
> thou hast chosen, a great people, that cannot be

numbered nor counted for multitude. Give therefore
thy servant an understanding heart to judge thy people,
that I may discern between good and bad: for who
is able to judge this thy so great a people?"
(1 Kings 3:7-9)

Solomon asked for an "understanding heart" (8085/3820) so he could have wisdom. Notice that he said, "I know not how to go out or come in." Without an understanding heart no one will be able to lead properly in these seasons. The Hebrew words could have been translated as "a hearing heart." Solomon wanted what so many church leaders pray for; the ability to hear God clearly so they can answer any situation wisely; this is Issachar ministry.

When God answered Moses call for leadership, He added character to the mix.

"And the Lord said unto Moses, Take thee Joshua
the son of Nun, a man in whom is the spirit, and lay
thine hand upon him; And set him before Eleazar the
priest, and before all the congregation; and give him
a charge in their sight. And thou shalt put some of
thine honour upon him, that all the congregation
of the children of Israel may be obedient."
(Numbers 27:18-20)

David was commanded by God to "build the Temple" according to the pattern he had received by the Spirit of God (see 1 Chronicles 28:11-12). The Old Testament gives us practical truths which we may use as examples of the spiritual reality according to 1 Corinthians 10:6 and 11. The Greek word translated as 'example' (5179) is used eighteen times in the New Testament and is translated into the English words: example(s) (2 times-1 Corinthians 10:6; 1 Tim 4:12), ensample(s) (5 times-1 Corinthians 10:11, Philippians 3:7, 1 Thessalonians 1:7, 2 Thessalonians 3:9, 1 Peter 5:3), pattern (2 times-Titus 2:7, Hebrews 8:5), print (2 times-John 20:25), remembrance (2- times-2 Peter 2:12, Jude 1:5), fashion (Acts 7:22), figure(s) (2- times-Acts 7:43, Romans 5:14), form (Romans 6:7), and manner (Acts 23:25). The Greek word means, "a type or a figure," and carries the idea of a pattern. Thayer defines an 'example' in the technical sense as the "pattern in conformity to which a thing must be made." The Lord has given us an example or a pattern of leadership. The Old Testament gives us the practical application of things and the natural representation of those things that have great spiritual truth in the New Testament. David had a practical pattern for the Temple and he gave it to Solomon to build. The Bible says that God would not allow David to build the Temple because he was "a man of blood," not a man of peace. This is a good example for us to learn by. If you are a "man of blood" you will not be able to build the Kingdom in your church. Church leaders should be people who are full of peace. We are the Temple of God and the realistic manifestation of His pattern is manifested in us, through the Holy Spirit. Church leaders must be built like the Temple of old without changing the details. If we change the details we are not qualified to lead. This is a hard saying, but worthy of note because God added character to the mix when He told Moses to anoint Joshua. The Lord also commanded Moses to put "some of thine honor upon him." Affirmation is a must when ordaining leadership.

> "For this cause left I thee in Crete, that thou shouldest
> set in order the things that are wanting, and ordain elders
> in every city, as I had appointed thee: If any be blameless,
> the husband of one wife, having faithful children not
> accused of riot or unruly. For a bishop must be blameless,
> as the steward of God; not selfwilled, not soon angry,
> not given to wine, no striker, not given to filthy lucre;
> But a lover of hospitality, a lover of good men, sober,
> just, holy, temperate; Holding fast the faithful word
> as he hath been taught, that he may be able by sound
> doctrine both to exhort and to convince the gainsayers.
> For there are many unruly and vain talkers and deceivers,
> specially they of the circumcision: Whose mouths
> must be stopped, who subvert whole houses, teaching
> things which they ought not, for filthy lucre's sake."
> (Titus 1:5)

The New Testament gives us the qualifications that Elders must be. One does not ordain a person and then expect them to become an Elder; you must ordain that which already is. In essence, the Holy Spirit will separate those whom He chooses for you to work with. To 'separate' means to make a distinction. Leadership, who are called by God are recognized by their ability to set in 'order' (1930) the things that are 'wanting' (3007) in the local church with the same connotation as Apostles. They will be able to fill the void that the Holy Spirit wants to fill. When the Lord sees something that the church needs He calls and separates a person to fulfill that task. Pastors should not have to minister to a congregation by themselves. God will add people to their ministry who will be able to complete some things that are necessary for the Church's spiritual growth. If someone is put into a position who is not the person God has ordained, two things will happen. First, the person God has ordained will be frustrated, not being able to accomplish their purpose in life. Secondly, the need in the Church will not be completed because the person who is over that area cannot accomplish the task. The lack produced in the Church may get a good whitewashing, but the underlying deficiency will remain and the congregation will 'want' fulfillment in that area and not obtain it. The Bible uses the word 'wanting' to represent the underlying hunger the emptiness creates. By example, when a local church needs someone to minister to their youth or children's ministry, and someone who is not qualified fills the spot, the position may be filled, but the unmet need will cause the youth or children to not grow as is expected. I set a couple into the position of youth pastor several years ago, because I knew the youth wanted a cohesive program. This couple had zeal to serve and I had a need so I allowed them to serve because they had been 'Youth Pastors' in another Church. Instead of the youth program growing and being built up, I noticed a great amount of division and strife among them. As I dug deeper it was obvious that the couple had a hidden agenda. They were more interested in building their ministry than ministering to the youth. They had their own goals and philosophies of holiness and caused great damage to some vulnerable kids. I had not followed God's pattern for church leadership, and the congregation suffered the loss.

It is always easier to be patient and wait for God's person to come to the forefront than to have to remove the wrong person from their position. People who desire to minister in the Church desire a good work, but if they are not what the Lord ordered they will do more harm than good. Even when there is no strife or contention in the area of need, unqualified people will not edify their area of responsibility. That means it will become stagnant. If we will make a note of this principle and take an honest overview of the Church it is easy to see the results of failing God's pattern. Research has stated that ninety percent of our Christian youth do not attend church after they graduate from High School. That is a tragedy. The irresponsibility of this failure is destroying the next generation of believers and leaders. Consider this: where will that leave us in twenty years?

> "The elders which are among you I exhort, who
> am also an elder, and a witness of the sufferings
> of Christ, and also a partaker of the glory that
> shall be revealed: Feed the flock of God which
> is among you, taking the oversight thereof, not by
> constraint, but willingly; not for filthy lucre, but
> of a ready mind; Neither as being lords over God's
> heritage, but being ensamples to the flock."
> (1 Peter 5:1-3)

Elders and church leadership should be able to feed the flock of God. I realize that a majority of church Elders does not teach in their local church. If you cannot teach the Body of Christ you are not qualified to be an Elder. Elders that do not teach may be godly men, but because they do not teach they are not able to lead. One must be able to tend the flock, but Paul says they must teach as well.

> "Let the elders that rule well be counted worthy
> of double honour, especially they who labour
> in the word and doctrine. For the scripture
> saith, Thou shalt not muzzle the ox that
> treadeth out the corn. And, The labourer is worthy

of his reward. Against an elder receive not an
accusation, but before two or three witnesses.
Them that sin rebuke before all, that others also
may fear. I charge thee before God, and the Lord Jesus
Christ, and the elect angels, that thou observe these
things without preferring one before another, doing
nothing by partiality. Lay hands suddenly on no man,
neither be partaker of other men's sins: keep thyself pure."
(1Timothy 5:17-22)

The word 'honour' (5092) in the above passage should have been translated as money, because that is what it means. Elders in the practical sense should be four-fold ministers and not just church members. One of the reasons churches find themselves in disarray is because their Elders are not four-fold ministers and therefore are unable to lead properly.

The book of Acts always uses the terms "the apostles and elders" when describing church leadership. Elders in the New Testament were four-fold men and one thing to note is that you always find there are more than one in each Church mentioned. Jesus sent them out two by two because He was following God's design. This is why it is necessary to have more than one Pastor serving in each local church. Also, Paul never traveled alone. The multiplicity of Church administration should be a common form of government in the Church, but you rarely find it. Jethro told Moses that being alone was not good for him or the congregation. God established the practical pattern of leadership in Exodus 18:14-23:

"And thou shalt teach them ordinances and laws,
and shalt shew them the way wherein
they must walk, and the work that they
must do. Moreover thou shalt provide out
of all the people able men, such as fear
God, men of truth, hating covetousness;
and place such over them, to be rulers
of thousands, and rulers of hundreds,
rulers of fifties, and rulers of tens: And let
them judge the people at all seasons..."
(Exodus 18:20-22a)

The pattern is simple. How many Elders and under-shepherds do you need? The Bible teaches us that we should have an under-shepherd over the heads of every ten families. 'Under-shepherds' are given the responsibility to minister to their flock and to bring any needs they are not able to fulfill to the next tier of leadership. Elders are then over the ten under-shepherds (the 100) but they bring the weightier matters to the tier above them, whether that would be another layer of Elders for larger congregations or the apostolic leadership (the Pastor or 'set man') of that congregation. Jeremiah 33:12 states this principle this way:

> "Thus saith the Lord of hosts; Again in
> this place, which is desolate without
> man and without beast, and in
> all the cities thereof, shall be an
> habitation of shepherds causing
> their flocks to lie down."

God's form of government in His Kingdom utilizes discipled and trained people to oversee the congregation. God's Kingdom government causes the flock of God (the local church) to lie down (i.e., to be in a state of rest and peace). This creates an environment of stability, edification, unity, and growth, which allows Church leadership to pursue the things of God and focus on the blessing of the Body, rather than the curse of disunity and divisiveness.

Elders who have the responsibility of preaching the word and administering doctrine to the Body should have double honor (pay). It is weighty and necessary to bless God's leaders. When Church leadership is blessed according to the Word their abilities and administrations flow much easier. I have pastored some churches and did not accept a salary. God has taught me that I robbed that Church and did more harm than good (see 2 Corinthians 11:7-9). Paul did not say we are to pay every Elder, but he makes it clear that those who labor in the Word and doctrine should receive double honor, because they perform a double duty. Not only do they tend the flock, but they also teach the Body as well. It takes an exceptional amount of time to prepare a good feast of the Word when training the trainers and the Church.

Doctrinal training should always start at the top and filter through the "habitation of shepherds" to the congregation. The practical side of this principle is for every Pastor to take a few faithful people and train them for a year. After the first year, allow the Holy Spirit to separate them into units of under-shepherds as their anointing dictates. Utilize the under-shepherds in home groups under the direct supervision of the Pastor and/or associate Pastor. Schedule the teaching times and administer the lessons that have already been taught to the under-shepherds allowing them to teach the same lessons to each group. At the beginning of each week meet with the under-shepherds and give them overview of the upcoming week. In their first year of release, distribute the teaching material. Then as the Holy Spirit separates and signifies the individual teams (see Acts 13), release them to do their calling and work. The Scripture teaches us to "show them the work that they must do and the way that they must go." Trust God, He will raise them up or set them down. The difference between the two will be very obvious.

Make a note: Do not create a 'position' in the church's government for under-shepherds; home group leader is a fine place for them to start and establish a precedence to rotate home group leaders each year. This will diversify the training base and impart various applications of 'spiritual giftings' in the local church. If you have a problem, this makes it easier to fix. Do not be afraid to admit mistakes if you put the wrong person in the wrong place. This is more easily corrected in the under-shepherds class than in the public forum. You will find that those who are signified as leaders by the Lord will rise to the top of the arrangement. They are usually always the faithful, obedient, and trustworthy ones. They may not agree with everything you are trying to do with them, but will always be people of peace as long as they are secure. (Be careful with tender lambs, they bruise easily!)

Women should be incorporated into the under-shepherds to minister to the single women, divorcees, and younger widows. They will be an invaluable asset and will help church leaders avoid many a pitfall. Never allow under-shepherds to counsel in their first year of training. Patience is a virtue. If patience does not prevail, satanic snares will be set and will cause reproach (see 1 Timothy 3:1-7).

> "Is any among you afflicted? let him pray.
> Is any merry? let him sing psalms.
> Is any sick among you? let him call for the
> elders of the church; and let them pray
> over him, anointing him with oil in the
> name of the Lord: And the prayer of faith
> shall save the sick, and the Lord shall raise him up;
> and if he have committed sins, they shall be forgiven
> him. Confess your faults one to another,
> and pray one for another, that ye
> may be healed. The effectual fervent prayer
> of a righteous man availeth much."
> (James 5:13-16)

When it comes to ministering to the sick, Elders are commanded to minister as a group whenever possible. Ministering to the sick is not only focusing on their physical situation, but also to any root underlying the root cause (review "The Path of the Root," chapter 16). Sometimes people are sick because of sin in their life. Again, a private ministry time is much better than a public display in these situations.

With this in mind let us move on to the bishop's ministry.

> "This is a true saying, If a man desire the
> office of a bishop, he desireth a good work.
> A bishop then must be blameless, the husband of
> one wife, vigilant, sober, of good behaviour, given

> to hospitality, apt to teach; Not given to wine, no
> striker, not greedy of filthy lucre; but patient, not a
> brawler, not covetous; One that ruleth well his own
> house, having his children in subjection with all gravity;
> (For if a man know not how to rule his own house,
> how shall he take care of the church of God?) Not a
> novice, lest being lifted up with pride he fall into
> the condemnation of the devil. Moreover he must
> have a good report of them which are without; lest
> he fall into reproach and the snare of the devil."
> (1 Timothy 3:1-7)

I have already addressed the office of the bishop in the Church, but will cover it again in this chapter in order try to bring a defining clarity to the subject. Church history has not been kind to the office of the bishop. The New Testament bishop is not someone who wears a red hat and a white robe. A 'bishop' (*episcope* - 1984) is defined as an investigator who, according to Thayer, is "installed by an act of God by whom God looks into and searches out the ways, deeds, character of men, in order to adjudge them their lot accordingly, whether joyous or sad." I have only witnessed one Church in my twenty-eight years of ministry that had this office in the church government. They properly utilized this office as a church counselor. In this fellowship, they mainly ministered and counseled the under-shepherds as well as performing all of the marriage counseling. They were utilized so as to give relief to the Pastor and Elders in these matters. They were given the administration and were trained to minister to the less fortunate in the Church. They also helped people acquire work or aid, depending on the need and ability of the people. An under-shepherd, preferably one who has a prophetic anointing and who has been in training for more than two years, should occupy the office of the bishop. A developed discernment is a must for the bishop, coupled with the intuitive ability to separate fact from fiction. The bishop's ministry is also the functional administration to relay information to the Body through the habitation of shepherds. Whatever the leadership wishes to disseminate throughout the Body should be administrated in the under-shepherds class and dispersed by the under-shepherds to those they are over.

Another aspect of Church Structure is the arrangement of church services. Traditionally church services are held on Sunday morning, Sunday night, and a mid-week service. The times and days of these services is not as important as their content.

> And they continued steadfastly in the apostles' doctrine and fellowship, and in breaking of
> bread, and in prayers. And fear came upon every
> soul: and many wonders and signs were done
> by the apostles. And all that believed were
> together, and had all things common;

281

"And they continued steadfastly in the apostles'
doctrine and fellowship, and in breaking of bread,
and in prayers. And fear came upon every
And sold their possessions and goods, and parted
them to all men, as every man had need.
And they, continuing daily with one accord in the
temple, and breaking bread from house to
house, did eat their meat with gladness and
singleness of heart, Praising God, and having
favour with all the people. And the Lord added
to the church daily such as should be saved."
(Acts 2:42-47)

There are four types of services the book of Acts affirms which occurred in the first century Church. These services have a specific focus: the apostles' doctrine, fellowship, breaking bread, and prayer meetings. Each of these types of meetings had a particular purpose in mind.

As stated before, the Apostles' doctrine is the foundational teaching and doctrines of the Christian faith, which should be used to train the spiritual babes. The basic tenants of the faith should be taught and imparted throughout the Church at this type of meeting. It is akin to our basic Sunday morning service with a doctrinal emphasis that focuses on the spiritual wellbeing of the individual. The fellowship (*koinonia* - 2842) meeting is actually the 'fathering' process of discipleship. Outside the apostles' doctrine, this meeting should be a more private affair where personal one-on-one dealings can take place in a smaller group. In Acts 2:44-45, the Bible brings about the aspect of communion where the Church gives attention to helping people have all things in common. The fellowship meeting is for the fathers in the faith and should be a time that the spiritual fathers minister to the sons in the faith as Jesus did in John chapters 13-17. Jesus taught them, washed their feet, and served them as an example.

The nursing mothers and the spiritual grandmothers in the local church can have a lasting impact on the younger women in this type of meeting. Titus 2:1-5 gives some guidelines for the older women in what they are to teach the younger women. My wife has given me great insight into the needs of the younger women. The older spiritual women can help the younger women with their children to understand the growth process of children and can teach them from experience rather than theory. The Scripture says to teach them how to love their husbands and how to be keepers of the home. Some young mothers need the social intimacy these relationships can bring. The older mothers can bring clarity and wisdom to the younger women, teaching them how to minister to their husbands, keep the home, and juggle home life with being a carrier.

The next type of meeting is the breaking of bread. Every Church needs to have a well-established meal for the local church members to participate in. This is also social intimacy and a time for the members to get to know one another better. The social life of a local church is a vital aspect in its development and growth. Social intimacy is an opportunity to develop spiritual intimacy and will have a manifestation of joy and happiness. The feasts of the Old Testament were a time of great joy and focused on the blessings of God. They thought of all that God had done for them and rejoiced with one another.

The prayer meeting is one of the most vital times necessary for the local church. A Church that prays together empowers their congregation to overcome in difficult times, as well as to seek guidance and direction from the Lord. There is a real necessity for a local church to set apart a time to seek God and to discover what He is interested in. When a local church gets interested in the things that God is interested in, they will find that God will supply all their needs in their endeavors. Every local church needs a relational intimacy with each other and with the Lord. By scheduling these types of meetings the Pastor and Elders will save themselves from the common mishaps many churches face. Developing a lasting and productive Body of believers is the goal and heart of any discipleship program. Having a sound biblical Church structure is conducive in the process. Gird yourself, and prepare for the times ahead!

> "And he shall go before him in the spirit and power
> of Elias, to turn the hearts of the fathers to the children,
> and the disobedient to the wisdom of the just; to
> make ready a people prepared for the Lord."
> (Luke 1:17)

The final area I wish to cover in this chapter is how the Body should be trained in areas of common sense, especially in relation to the last days. I know of only a few churches that are training the Bride of Christ to be prepared for the coming times of trouble, known as the tribulation. Most churches live in a dream world as though they will somehow be miraculously translated out of the times of trouble when the Bible clearly states otherwise (see 1 Corinthians 15:51-52). If the Bible is true and the Bride will not be taken until the last trumpet, which by the way is found in Revelation 11:15, then the Church will experience all that is found in Revelation 1-11:15 and most likely beyond. Are you, as a Church leader, prepared and have you taught your congregation to be prepared? Each of us will answer to God for what we have done or have not done. The rapture theology has only caused the Body of Christ to become slothful. Very few Christians are prepared for the end of days.

> "Then shall the kingdom of heaven be likened
> unto ten virgins, which took their lamps, and went
> forth to meet the bridegroom. And five of them
> were wise, and five were foolish. They that were
> foolish took their lamps, and took no oil with them:
> But the wise took oil in their vessels with their lamps.
> While the bridegroom tarried, they all slumbered and slept.
> And at midnight there was a cry made, Behold, the

bridegroom cometh; go ye out to meet him. Then
all those virgins arose, and trimmed their lamps.
And the foolish said unto the wise, Give
us of your oil; for our lamps are gone out.
But the wise answered, saying, Not so; lest there
be not enough for us and you: but go ye rather
to them that sell, and buy for yourselves."
(Matthew 25:1-9)

One of the things that many congregations do not consider is what they should do collectively and what they should do individually in preparation for the tribulation. What would you do if a natural disaster caused the normal transportation of food, water, or electricity to stop for an extended period of time? I have researched this topic and spoken to many experts who state that in a time of major crisis the one thing they are certain of is that people will loose all sense of rightness during an event like this. The book of Revelation describes a series of events that will happen over a period of forty-two months. Couple this with governments who will use the "mark of the beast" to control their populations and you have a disaster in the making for Christians. Do you have the strength to watch your family and friends starve or will you accept the mark of the beast because of hunger? It is written, "no man can buy or sell" without the mark. The Bible also states that a loaf of bread will cost you a day's wages. The Lord has told us about these events before they will happen so we can prepare in advance for these days of trouble. Some will say, "The Church will not go through the tribulation." I tell you it will and if you are not prepared you will suffer the consequences as unwise virgins. The Kingdom of God is our Ark of protection in the time of tribulation. As the Lord told Joseph to prepare in the goodly years for the time of the lean, so should we prepare in the same way. Joseph took the "fifth-part" (twenty percent) and saved it up so that when the bad times came he was prepared. Pharaoh became very wealthy because Joseph prepared. So wealthy that he gave the Land of Goshen (the best land) to Joseph's family.

The unwise virgins had not thought about the waiting process. They trimmed their wicks had lamps, but did not prepare for the wait. The parable of the 'talents' (see Matthew 25:14-30) has the same basic meaning. Matthew 25:19 states, "After a long time…" the Lord returned and found those who buried their talents in the earth. Matthew 25:13 also says, "Watch therefore, for ye know neither the day nor the hour wherein the Son of man cometh." The point is: true faith remains strong, while false faith has no patience and does not endure.

Pastors and church leaders should take the initiative in these matters. Preparations should be made quietly and discretely. Congregations should be trained in areas of food canning and storage, small area gardening (square foot gardening), greenhouse gardening, food rotation, as well as in doctrine. During the days when the Church was persecuted in the first century, the Church had "all things common." Why? Because it was necessary for their very survival. The modern Church had better take a good lesson from these events and move with practical common sense to prepare in the matters. It is a matter of life or death.